IDENTITY OF THE LITERARY TEXT

Literary criticism today is dominated by the debate about whether texts have a fixed identity with established meaning or a variable identity with changing meaning. The very nature of what the critic does and what he can provide for his readers is being questioned; the challenge to the traditional view comes especially from the various theoretical formulations which, agreeing on the need to go beyond formal analysis, have been called post-structuralism. At the core is the fundamental question of what a literary text is. *Identity of the Literary Text* addresses this question.

In five sections – textuality and intertextuality, textual deconstruction, hermeneutics, analytical construction, and ideological perspective – fifteen scholars, many with world-wide reputations, consider such key aspects of literary criticism as the structure of texts, the relationship between text, author, and reader, the psychological and sociological implications of literary texts, and whether or not a general theory of literary criticism is possible.

This book brings together, in the spirit of dialogue, the arguments on both sides of the most important issue in literary criticism today. It will be of interest to all concerned with textual theory, regardless of which literatures are considered.

MARIO J. VALDÉS is Professor of Comparative Literature and Spanish at the University of Toronto.
OWEN MILLER is Associate Professor of Comparative Literature and French at the University of Toronto.

EDITED BY MARIO J. VALDÉS
AND OWEN MILLER

Identity of the Literary Text

UNIVERSITY OF TORONTO PRESS
Toronto Buffalo London

© University of Toronto Press 1985
Toronto Buffalo London
Printed in Canada

ISBN 0-8020-5662-8 (cloth)
ISBN 0-8020-6564-3 (paper)

For Wolfgang Iser, friend and colleague,
whose idea of critical dialogue on texts was the genesis
of this book.

Canadian Cataloguing in Publication Data

Main entry under title:
Identity of the literary text
  Includes bibliographical references and index.
  ISBN 0-8020-5662-8 (bound). – ISBN 0-8020-6564-3 (pbk.).
  1. Criticism – Addresses, essays, lectures.
  2. Literature – History and criticism – Addresses,
  essays, lectures. 3. Reader-response criticism –
  Addresses, essays, lectures. I. Valdés, Mario J.,
  1934–   II. Miller, Owen J., 1936–
  PN85.132 1985   801'.95   c84-099649-7

This book has been published with the help of a grant from the Canadian Federation
for the Humanities, using funds provided by the Social Sciences and Humanities
Research Council of Canada, and a grant from the Publications Fund of the
University of Toronto Press.

Contents

OWEN MILLER

Preface

There are no more remote and easy perspectives, either artistic or national. Everything is present in the foreground.
Marshall McLuhan, *The Mechanical Bride*

One of the features of titles is the absence of verbal forms. Heavily weighted with nouns and adjectives, they offer the reassuring presence of a stable world, a static moment in the rush of time which the succession of words, pages, chapters, processed in linear fashion, emulates. Here, within the limited and isolated space of the title, we have access to the metalinguistic ground in terms of which we will be able to conceive the whole text. The reasonable assumption, we think, is that the title is a heuristic encapsulement, a point of departure as well as a point of arrival, a delimited and enclosed object. It is this very assumption not only about titles but about any discourse claiming to have ultimate explanatory power that many of the essays brought together in *Identity of the Literary Text* seek to question.

As Jonathan Culler points out in his introductory essay, a reader of thirty years ago, confronted with this title, could safely have assumed that he was being presented with a selection of papers dedicated to the problem of how 'authorized' versions of texts are to be established: he would have reasonably anticipated that he was to be instructed in the theoretical, methodological, and practical problems associated with the preparation of the critical editions of texts – a rich field, even today, as the variety of recent writings in English, French, and German testifies. At the same time, a reader of thirty years ago might also have concluded that the operative term in the title was 'literary' with the expectation that the terms 'text' and 'identity' were, by common consensus, relatively unproblematic. He would thus have inferred, with some justification, that *Identity of the Literary Text* was concerned with such perennial questions as what identifies a text as literary or what constitutive features allow us to distinguish literary from non-literary texts.

This collection of essays neglects the first question entirely, and if it addresses the second, it does so indirectly either by submerging it, or, in some cases, by validating it within a complex network of problems where more radical issues are at stake. If there exists a unifying factor bringing together the divergent views expressed here, it is the realization that we may no longer relegate such terms as 'identity' and 'text' to the background of our concerns and rely on their unproblematic meaning and usage. Everything, as McLuhan would say, is present in the title, which is also to say that nothing is present and easily identifiable.

For Robert Weimann, the title itself is open to interpretation, and, if we are to identify the specific issues it raises in the eighties, we must situate it in relation to a historically determined 'subtext' which makes the question of textual identity a problem both as an object of communication and as a vehicle of cultural and critical endeavour. In his essay, Weimann provides a very lucid overview of the specific historical situation in which traditional notions and usages of the literary text have been subjected to a radical reassessment in recent years.

1 The demise of Romantic sources of poetic thought have undermined the prevailing idea in New Criticism of the text's identity as a self-referential verbal structure or as a self-contained organic whole.

2 The formalist criterion of poeticity or literariness has been challenged by speech-act theory and post-Saussurian linguistics with the result that the notion of literature as linguistically autonomous or functionally distinct from other forms of verbal utterance has eroded and, with it, the whole liberal conception of poetic language as a cultural mode of knowledge and value.

3 The radical disintegration of genre, tradition, and the literary canon has weakened the ground in which the literary text might be secured in terms of its identity. Here a variety of forces – the repudiation of standards of high culture, the broadly cultural bases of *Rezeptionsästhetik*, the anti-humanist bias of post-structuralism, the new interest in *Trivialliteratur* and the mass-media, the post-modernist exhaustion or parody of traditional literary forms, and finally the rise of a new powerful prose, documentary and autobiographical in nature – has upset the literary traditions and the social contracts between writers and their public.

4 The demise of the notion of individual literary authorship has led to the collapse of the author as an authenticating agent of identity in the text itself and its replacement by notions either that readers experience texts in terms of their own identity or, in Derrida's words, that 'writing is an orphan.'

5 These trends have also eroded the critic's role as mediator between the literary text and audience expectation with the result that the critic's credibility as a sensitive vehicle of common literary opinion has been undermined. At the same time the whole project of interpretation and its epistemological status has been challenged from various quarters, among them certain phenomenological theorists and dominant representatives of post-structuralism from Althusser to Barthes. The critic therefore is in danger of losing his authority as a cultural mediator of the text's identity.

6 Finally the attack of the Nouvelle Critique on the Critique Universitaire in France and the triumph of Reception theory in Germany have created a crisis of social and educational ideology, thus weakening traditional notions of education in the humanities. Radical theories of textuality (especially those proposed by deconstructive criticism) have raised the question whether identity is indeed a meaningful category at all.

From this radical reassessment of the literary text, a reassessment whose international scope Weimann so clearly sketches, two central questions emerge. In his introductory essay, Jonathan Culler has summarized them as follows: (a) What remains the same in the literary text under conditions such as different readings? (b) What is the text's distinctive unifying force? The issues at stake in the first question involve only to a very limited extent challenging the validity of different interpretations by the same reader, by different contemporary readers, or by historically distanced readers. Nor is there much support in this volume for reaffirming interpretation as a form of uncovering or retrieving some determinate, authorially intended meaning for the text. On these issues there seems to be some relative consensus. What *is* of concern to the contributors to this collection is whether a reader's interpretation is more the result of pre-established interpretive strategies than the consequence of some identifiable constraints or regulating features which can be attributed to the text. Specifically challenged is the radical tendency of reader-response theory to move entirely away from the notion of textual constraints and to attribute all acts of interpretation to certain strategic predispositions towards the text on the part of the reader.

The second question raises a different set of issues, though on several points they tend to merge with the first set. What is of concern here is whether or not the notion of identity itself can any longer be held to be a meaningful category applied to the literary text. In other words what is being assessed is whether it is feasible any longer to conceive of the text as a distinct entity, marked by constituent features and viewed in terms of some sort of analogy with personal identity, which itself, to many, appears to be a dubious concept. This does not imply, necessarily, abandoning the term 'identity,' but clears the ground for redefining it in a non-essentialist way, in terms of dynamic process rather than of static product or object. Finally there is the issue whether the term 'literary text' itself does not promote an internal contradiction in so far as a broad spectrum of views, sustained mainly by post-structuralist characterizations of 'text' and 'textuality,' has as its goal the replacement or displacement of both the terms 'work' and 'literary'; the latter especially is felt to have little validity.

In her excellent introduction to an anthology of some of the most important theoretical statements on readers and the reading process, Jane Tompkins has traced the gradual progression of reader-response theory from its beginnings in New Criticism (Walker Gibson), through its appearance in structuralism (Gerald Prince, Jonathan Culler), stylistics (Michael Riffaterre), phenomenology (Georges Poulet, Wolfgang Iser, Stanley Fish), psychoanalytic criticism (Norman Holland, David Bleich) and post-structuralist theory (Fish, Walter Benn Michaels). What characterizes the evolution that Tompkins traces is the replacement of the literary text as the centre of critical attention by the reader's cognitive activity. 'If meaning is no longer a property of the text but a product of the reader's activity the question to answer is not "what do poems mean?" or even "what do poems do?" but "how do readers make meaning?"'[1] Tompkins attributes this crucial move in reader-oriented theory to Stanley Fish in his essay 'Literature and the Reader.' She notes, however, that this shift of emphasis from text to reader was merely a preliminary step to a more radical assertion in a subsequent essay ('Interpreting the Variorum: part 2'), namely that a reader's interpretation of a literary text is the result of the interpretative strategies that he possesses.

The problem with Tompkins's account is that, by organizing her selection of statements in a chronological fashion, she tends to present them with an evolutionist slant, presumably on the basis of a scientific model, as if each successive statement represented an advancement of knowledge. Rather than seeing each position as a different and competing way of conceiving of the text-reader relationship, she implies that the later and more radical assertions have in some sense moved beyond the earlier positions and rendered them obsolescent. Thus many of the essays in *Identity of the Literary Text* involve a questioning of the assumptions and directions which the radical tendencies of reader-response theory have taken over the past five years. Such a reassessment may be viewed in some quarters as regressive, as a turning back to the heyday of New Criticism and Formalism. In response, one might argue that an objection of this sort fails to recognize the speculative nature of much literary theory today and its own implicit ideological commitment to an evolutionist model as a strategy to assert dogmatically its own radical premises.

In the first part of his essay, Jonathan Culler takes issue with the tendency of reader-response theory to resolve the text-reader dualism in favour of some sort of radical monism, whether it be that of textual meaning or reader meaning. Wolfgang Iser's phenomenology of reading illustrates the former sort of monism while Stanley Fish represents the latter. To interpret a text is to interpret something; one cannot so easily get rid of the something. Thus in Culler's view one is forced, in the end, out of monism and back into dualism since it seems impossible to distinguish what the text signifies and the reader symbolizes in an act of interpretation. Peter Nesselroth cautions us also to weigh more carefully the shift of reader-response theory from conceiving of a text's literariness in terms of identifying immanent features to seeing the activity of the reader of a piece of discourse in terms of a priori literary conventions which have been intersubjectively negotiated by a particular 'interpretative community.' Whether one claims that certain immanent features incite a particular strategy or whether one asserts that the particular features are discovered by a pre-existent strategy, the fact remains that the constituent features are there, either explicit or implicit. Nesselroth's argument leads him to ask what we are to do with a text which, while making claims to literary identity (e.g. it occurs in a collection of poems), does not possess any immanent literary features and cannot be forced to reveal any by any interpretative strategy we might call literary. What do we do, he asks, with such 'poems' as Apollinaire's *Lundi, rue Christine*, which reproduces discursive elements that are immediately identifiable as non-literary and meaningful only at their surface level? Nesselroth's assertion is that such a text takes on the identity of a poem because of its intertextual relationship within a volume of poems and, in this way, acquires a citational status which establishes its literariness.

Michael Riffaterre's essay also sets itself against the radicalizing tendency of reader-response theory to shift all meaning production to the reader and to neglect certain constraints imposed on interpretation by constituent features of the text. Riffaterre's assertion is that there is one specific textual feature which controls reading and guides the reader to the significance of the text. To illustrate his position, he examines two 'identical' poems by Rimbaud, both entitled *O Saisons, ô châteaux*. One single and seemingly insignificant variation, the shift from the definite article 'le' to the possessive adjective 'son,' leads to two entirely different and incompatible readings, the first mystical, the second erotic. The separate identity of each text is attributable to the significant lexical item which determines the two incompatible interpretations and is perceptible only through an intertextual reading which brings into focus the important function it performs in the poem. The effect of Riffaterre's essay is to bridge the distinction between the two sets of issues I outlined earlier. On one hand, the text's identity is assured by its power to constrain the shape of various readings; on the other, the same significant features confer on the text its unique identity by distinguishing it from other texts.

Félix Martínez Bonati's essay also represents an attempt to redress the balance by countering the relativist tendency of reader-response theory to insist on the text's unstable identity and thereby challenge the premises of literary and humanistic education. What works against the traditional view of the text's stable identity and its enduring power within a continuous cultural tradition is a belief in the historicity and cultural variety of human life and the mutability and plurality of languages. To overcome these objections, one must try to show that readers can adopt transitorily other life-worlds and other semantic systems. Martínez Bonati argues that language survives because there are some permanent features of man's experience and that these form the basis for transhistorical concepts. He insists equally that, to a certain degree, the semantic aspects of language and the codes of past historical periods may be retrieved through scholarship, though he concedes that, even if the referential core of language is recoverable, the stylistic aura is less easily accessible. His contention, however, is that literature, as an institutional form of writing, demands some sort of subjection to institutional will and that it would not have survived if principles of universality and objectivity were illusory. Thus part of literary identity involves precisely the search for transcircumstantial significance and for the universal possibility of meaning. Martínez Bonati's stance is essentially polemical. He is not arguing for a return to an exlusively text-oriented approach to meaning; rather, like Culler, he sees that total emphasis on the reader's individual activity leads to a radical monism which overstates its case and needs some sort of corrective to redress the balance.

Lubomír Doležel's essay also takes issue with the tendency of the radical side of reader-response theory to emphasize the role of the reader and thus end up in a teleological type of criticism where everything is recuperated in terms of individual or collective ego-identity. Though he does not mention them by name, it is fairly clear that he has in mind the psychoanalytic theories of critics such as Norman Holland and David Bleich, though it is with Stanley Fish that he takes up the question of whether or not interpretive procedures are independently specifiable or not. Doležel's contention is that, if meaning is the product of the reader's interpretive procedures rather than a product of the text, it is not necessary to conclude that such procedures cannot be rationalized and clearly designated by models which text semantics has constructed or is in the process of constructing. His argument is that reading is a practical activity based on semantic competence and that the interpretive strategies of the reader need themselves to be explained by semantic and pragmatic theories.

Doležel considers also that the ultimate goal of literary semantics is to give to the text its individual identity, which he conceives as being analogous to personal identity to the extent that they are both constituted by a set of permanent and recognizable features differentiating one entity from another. He does qualify this position, however, by suggesting that the analogy with personal identity does not commit one to the search for singularity or uniqueness as part of textual identity. On this point, he parts company with Riffaterre. For Doležel, the two aspects that define the text from the perspective of literary semantics are its capacity to construct its own circumscribed fictional world and to display its own idiosyncratic literary style.

Doležel's conception of textual identity on an analogy with personal identity brings us not only to the second set of issues raised earlier but also into sharp conflict with the position espoused by other contributors to this volume. There can be no doubt that a powerful link exists between theories of the self and theories of the text. In fact such a link seems a crucial aspect of the contemporary insistence on notions of textuality and the metamorphosis of the 'literary work' into the 'Text.' The rejection of the text as an autonomous entity, as a self-regulating organic whole, seems logically consistent with the demise in belief in the Romantic notion of a discrete, independent, enduring self. It is therefore no coincidence that a strong correlation exists within the framework of post-structuralist thought between Derrida's concept (or anti-concept) of the text and Lacan's concept of the self. As Susan Suleiman points out: 'If Derrida sees the internal difference and the continual deferring of presence as constitutive of the literary text, that is precisely how Lacan sees the human subject.'[2] But it seems paradoxical, to say the least, to dismiss on one hand all concept of the text as a self-sufficient entity and to claim on the other that a deconstuctive strategy, at work in all texts subverting identity, is 'constitutive' of the new sense of textuality.

The essays of Patricia Parker and Hillis Miller offer readings of specific texts in what might broadly be called a deconstructive mode. Barbara Johnson has very lucidly explained the notion of 'textual difference' which underlies the process of deconstructive criticism and which runs counter to the conception of reading as the search for some uniquely different quality in each text:

a text's difference is not its uniqueness, its special identity. It is the text's way of differing from itself. And this difference is perceived only in the act of re-reading. It is the way in which the text's signifying energy becomes unbound, to use Freud's term, through the process of repetition, which is the return not of the same but of difference. Difference is not what distinguishes one identity from another. It is not a difference between (or at least not a difference between independent units). It is a difference within. Far from constituting the text's unique identity, it is that which subverts the very idea of identity, infinitely deferring the possibility of adding up the sum of the text's parts of meanings and reaching a totalised, integrated whole.[3]

It is clear that much of the difficulty we encounter in speaking of the text in deconstuctive terms derives from our having recourse to a nominal form which reifies it into a concept or an object. Thinking of it in terms of an activity, a process, a strategy, or even a methodological field (i.e. as textualization or textuality) is merely to shift from one level of conceptualization to another. If 'textual difference' is a marker of all texts, it must be 'conceived' of as a constitutive feature that confers on all texts a distinguishing identity. If texts and works are to be distinguished (and Barthes is ambiguous on this point), then 'textual difference' acts as a marker (of degree or kind) of difference between some verbal artefacts and others; in short it acts as a marker of a group identity.

Patricia Parker's reading of Emily Brontë's *Wuthering Heights* illustrates how the novel seeks to establish its own unified identity as an Enlightenment narrative where its sequentiality, order, and closure is secured by its generic patterning and by the 'narratorial voice' of Lockwood. At the same time those very features in the novel which ensure identity – proper names, property, and propriety – are subverted by the 'narrative voice,' which Parker, drawing on a Derridean distinction, calls 'a neutral voice that utters the work from the placeless place where the work is silent.' Thus the text, through its exclusions, calls into question its own epistemological claims; it illustrates the notion of identity and simultaneously transgresses it.

What is left open in Parker's paper is whether *Wuthering Heights* is to be considered as a general paradigm of textual functioning or whether its paradoxical claim to, yet transgression of, identity derives from its specific historical situation, i.e. its challenge to the classical episteme which it both embraces yet distances itself from. If the latter is the case (and it would seem to be so) then it could well be argued that the novel's location within a historical framework where the problem of identity itself is being questioned *distinguishes* it from other texts situated at a different historical moment; in short *Wuthering Heights* may have an identity after all, marked out by its historical situation and its very questioning of identity. Hillis Miller's deconstructive reading of Thomas Hardy's *In Front of the Landscape* raises a similar problem. In Miller's view, 'the identity of the literary text for Hardy is the proliferating act of translation.' What is left unclear by this statement is whether a deconstructive reading of the poem has ramifications beyond it. Is the 'proliferating act of translation' a marker of *In Front of the Landscape*, of Hardy's view of textuality, or of textuality in general?

Miller's starting point is the experiential effect of the formal rhythms of the poem: the organization of stanzas and rhymes creates the pattern which the figure of the poem, 'a tide of visions,' names. This pattern repeats itself from stanza to stanza as if engendering through repetition its own form and language while at the same time laying the ground for the reader's experience of the poem. Certain words embedded in the text, such as 'misprision,' capture the process that is being played out in *In Front of the Landscape*. In Miller's view, the poem communicates the sense of writing as translation, as tropology where the linguistic moment is seen as a triple act of translation of the phantoms of the poet's mind: into words, into metaphor, into the formal order of the poem. The tropological or translative act, far from putting the phantoms to rest, reveals itself as a misreading, a distortion, giving them life again and leading inevitably to a new poem which will proliferate the same problem. The reader's experience of the poem parallels the act of writing. In searching for a whole that will put the poem to rest, the reader lives the experience of writing. The images do not hold together either individually or collectively; they respond to the reader's search for a comprehensive logic that will shape the poem's identity, but in doing so they undo his attempts to translate them into an order satisfying to the mind. Thus the reader is caught in the proliferating act of translation or interpretation which defers any way of delimiting the text's identity.

It would be difficult to argue that, whatever other effects it may achieve, Miller's deconstructive reading of *In Front of the Landscape*, through its attention to the formal and thematic aspects of the poem, does not confer on it some very specific qualities which distinguish it from other poems and secure for it some sort of identity. Yet Hardy's poem enacts at the same time that rejection of boundaries or closure which defines the older notion of text. As Vincent Leitch has cogently expressed it: '[The new notion of textuality] touches and tampers – it changes and spoils – all the old boundaries, frames, divisions, and limits. The identity of " text" alters. The overrun of all old borders forces us to rethink the "text" ... The new *text* consists of differential traces that refer to other differential traces: it is a differential network. Its excesses complicate all borders, multiplying and dividing them in a process of luxurious enrichment.'[4] It is small wonder then that 'translation,' 'transgression,' and 'tropology' are favoured words in the deconstructive lexicon, undermining not only the identity of the text but the very notion of identity itself.

It would be misleading, however, to conclude that the attack on textual identity is restricted to critics of deconstructive persuasion. Cyrus Hamlin's essay takes issue with the burgeoning senses that the term 'text' has been made to assume in recent theory and suggests that we should restrict the term to the verbal artefact, which in no way prejudices a hermeneutic or semiotic approach. Having taken aim at deconstructive criticism, Hamlin nevertherless concludes that the 'very notion of identity, as it applies to the interpretation of art, is anti-hermeneutical.' What works against conceiving any traditional notion of identity for the text is its mobility, by which he means its mediating function within two axes of communication: the presentational, between speaker and audience and the representational, between verbal code and world. In Hamlin's view, our concern for the identity of the text is, in a sense, misplaced, since it rests on the presupposition that we are to conceive of the text as a static entity. We should, he argues, view the text, dynamically, as an *event*, in a mobile process of reflectivity. Identity is thus not something to be found in the text but is constituted by the experience of reading. His conclusion is that the measure of identity for the reader of poetry is a reflective knowledge to be achieved paradoxically in the radical breakdown and destruction of identity itself.

The effect of Hamlin's essay is not to reject identity as a meaningless category applied to literary texts. What he *does* assert is that psychological identity is an inappropriate model in so far as it treats the text as a static unity to support Romantic mystifications of poetic individuality and organic whole. Identity only becomes a meaningful concept if we conceive of it as dynamic process and the text as event. What it left unclear in Hamlin's account is whether he envisages that, in the final analysis, the reader constitutes some identity for the text, provisional though is may be, or whether interpretation should rather be conceived as an unending process of identification, never to achieve even provisionary consummation. If his position is the latter, then it would seem that we are faced with a situation not unlike that of deconstructive 'textual difference.' In short, Hamlin's notion of 'dynamic identity' seems very much to emphasize the reader's activity and thereby to join the radical trend of reader-response theory.

Paul Ricoeur's essay also introduces the notion of 'dynamic identity,' but he gives the term a very different slant. His point of departure is a search for a middle path between logical identity, the assertion of minimal criteria of identification, and the radical notion of identity (or difference) advocated by deconstructive criticism. His field of investigation is narrative, both historical and fictional. The operative concept which he explores, at various levels, is that of emplotment, which he conceives as a dynamic and integrative process of structuring. Though the emphasis is on narrative, Ricoeur's essay envisages a broader vista which sees the act of poetic composition in general as having features which support procedures of identification, yet are compatible with various modes of historicity.

The structuring process of emplotment is at work in the text mediating between the scattered events and the whole story. It also involves the process of 'narrative intelligibility,' which generates rules to be systematized at the level of philosophical discourse. It draws on the notions of sedimentation and innovation to illustrate how the text becomes integrated with, yet at the same time diverges from, other texts that constitute historical tradition. Finally it brings into play the reading act's own dynamism, which is grafted on to the configurational act of emplotment. Ricoeur's notion of dynamic identity opts for a dialectical tension within the text, between a text and other texts, and finally between text and reader. It carefully steers a middle course between text-oriented and reader-oriented theories. At the same time it avoids the lack of concern for criteriology reflected by deconstructive criticism without falling back into the affirmation of identity as a non-contradictory, tautological acknowledgment of an a-temporal entity.

Both Hamlin's and to a lesser degree Ricoeur's essays emphasize the presentational axis of communication, the mobile situation of the text between writer and audience. Wolfgang Iser's paper explores the representational axis where the text mediates between verbal code and world. He accepts fictionality as a marker of literary identity but challenges the real/fictional dichotomy which constitutes the basis for the traditional boundary between the fictional and the non-fictional text. Iser argues specifically for a triadic system: the real/the fictional/the imaginary. A text's identity cannot, from this perspective, be confined to real or fictional elements, but derives from their interaction, which brings into play the imaginary. In an argument reminiscent of Ricoeur, Iser speaks of fictionalizing as a process rather than of fiction or the fictional as an independent, autonomous entity. At work in the act of fictionalization are processes of selection of systems outside the text and of combination which produces relationships within the text. Thus the text's identity, created by simultaneous processes of selection and combination, involves the boundary crossing of literary and socio-cultural systems on one hand the intratextual field of reference on the other. The final feature of the act of fictionalizing is the process of self-referentiality, or, as Iser calls it, the principle of disclosure, the *as-if* construction, whereby the text reveals itself, or is to be unmasked, as fiction. Though insisting on fictionalizing as a process of mediation between text and world, Iser leaves open the role of the reader to produce the meaning of the text and thereby its identity, which may differ from reader to reader and in different historical situations. In this, his essay finds common ground with those of both Hamlin and Ricoeur.

Both Ricoeur's emphasis on emplotment as process of structuring and Iser's concern with the process of fictionalizing redefine the notion of identity in what I have called, in my own paper, relational rather than constitutive terms. For

Iser, textual identity is not a question of isolating entities (the real and the fictional) but involves a relational process in which both entities are apprehended only in an interactive process that dissolves boundaries. Similarly, Ricoeur's notion of dynamic identity explores relational tensions between continuity and discontinuity at various levels: within the text, between the specific text and textual models, between texts themselves, and finally between text and reader. My own essay in this volume explores identity in terms of the relationship between texts, in terms of what it has become fashionable to call intertextuality. Intertextual concerns are implicit in both Nesselroth's and Riffaterre's essays, but my own perspective differs in several aspects from theirs. The demise of source-influence studies corresponds to the need to replace the author as the 'authenticating source of identity' (to use Weimann's expression) by the reader as the agent who confers identity on the text by locating it within the co-ordinates of his own literary repertoire of texts. In my perspective, the text does not have a fixed stable identity but is protean in nature, taking its shape in terms of other texts to which the reader chooses to relate it.

Such a perspective does not undermine the notion of identity itself but rather enhances it while insisting that the text is capable of revealing many differing identities, realized in a variety of intertextual relationships. Consistent with a reader-oriented theory of intertextual identity is the necessity to abandon, with certain reservations, the constraints of both causality and temporality. On the other hand, to avoid being counted among the more radical advocates of reader-response theory, I have advanced the notion of 'plausible intertextuality,' by drawing, paradoxically, on Derrida's notion of the supplement, and suggesting that there are some constraints imposed on the text in the reading process and thereby on the differing identities that the text may assume.

For Hans-Robert Jauss, intertextuality is only one aspect of a far broader context for a discussion of identity. At the centre of his concerns is the notion of 'horizon' to which he has so splendidly contributed. For Jauss the notion of 'horizon' in its broadest sense 'constitutes all meaning in human behaviour and in our primary understanding of the world.' It accounts for all historical understanding as well as all understanding of culturally different worlds. It is the problem of aesthetic experience when one reconstructs the horizon of expectations deriving from contemporary experience of reading texts. The notion of 'horizon' is the problem of intertextuality when other texts constitute a special horizon. It becomes the problem of the social function of literature when the text mediates between the horizons of aesthetic and everyday experience. It involves the problem of historical understanding when the diachronic dimension of texts is brought into play. And finally it is the problem of ideological criticism when the text is seen against the latent horizon of concealed interests and repressed needs. From this it follows that the only identity a text may possess is a relational one, established between it and the various horizons which bring it into focus and shape its varying identities. For Jauss, literary communication is dialogical and, in this, he concurs with the general hermeneutic position espoused by other contributors such as Hamlin, Ricoeur, and Iser. His contribution to the problem of identity is to trace historically how contemporary notions of the dialogical nature of literary communication have evolved over the past fifty years and to survey how his own work has progressed in developing and refining the notion of horizon.

It will be clear from the foregoing discussion that the most serious challenge to literary identity or textual identity derives from the deconstructive camp. Most of the contributors to this volume recognize in varying degrees that, if the text is conceived of as a self-sufficient and autonomous artefact with determinate meaning which it is the task of interpretation to recover, then indeed the notion of identity can no longer hold much sway as a valid concept in literary theory and criticism. What emerges from this consensus is not the abandonment of identity per se, but a reformulation of it as a relational rather than a constitutive notion. The belief that textual identity is not an a priori given but a process worked out in the act of reading would seem to be a position likely to command fairly widespread acceptance in today's intellectual and cultural climate. Deconstructive criticism, however, seems unrecoverable within any consensus. Impervious to assimilation or accommodation (to use Piaget's terms), it represents a frame of reference which speaks its own language and establishes its own epistemological claims. In one sense it is unchallengeable, for it is founded on the negation of any meta-discourse capable of transcending it and thereby mounting a critique from the outside. Like all the great Western ideologies – Christian dogma, existentialism, Marxism, and Freudianism – it retains, within its frame of reference, strategic mechanisms to ensure that its opponents will reveal themselves as dependent on assumptions which are the very object of its specific critique. Unless one is to dismiss it entirely, one's only recourse is to mount a critique of deconstructive criticism from within. Such a strategy, while on one hand granting it some sort of credence, seems also capable of exposing its limits and establishing its historical relevance.

Geoffrey Waite concurs with the consensus view that textual identity, in the sense of the recovery of determinate meaning, has been shattered. He expresses some reservations, however, about the way this has been accomplished within the framework of deconstructive criticism. Waite sees Nietzsche and his analysis of style as a forerunner of current trends to shatter the notion of textual identity; but his critique takes issue with Nietzsche and the recent reception of Nietzsche, specifically Derrida's reading of the Nietzschean text. His conclusion is that such ways (both that of Nietzsche and that of those who 'misread' Nietzsche) must be rejected to the extent that both obscure the ideological and political impact of their formulations. The necessary corrective, in Waite's view, is to distinguish between Nietzsche's own mode of posing the question of style and the criminal insanity of his proposed solutions. We must face the ideological dimension of Nietzsche's work and its reception rather than attempt to elevate objective, historically determined conditions to general conditions of human existence. 'Deconstruction and post-structuralism always pull up short and by their symptomatic silences seem to collaborate with that ideology, its sources, its influences, its reception. ... They end up only by celebrating the break-up of the identity of Nietzsche's text as open and undecipherable ... To read Nietzsche from an essentialistic point of view, to take him literally in terms of his style, whether displacing political ideology with misogyny or repressing the persuasive aspect of rhetoric, is to risk again and again the dangerous consequences of irrationalism.'

Robert Weimann's essay, which concludes this volume, insists on the speculative nature of much contemporary theory and on the necessity to be aware of the historical circumstances that have given birth to this mode of questioning and speculation. What is needed is less a dogmatic and exclusory adherence to one specific conception of textual identity than an awareness of the differing and competing formulations of the notion of the text. In this way we will be more conscious of the critical assumptions upon which each is founded and the historical conditions pertinent to the cultural and pedagogical institutions of Western culture that make the identity of the text a problematic issue. With this in mind, Weimann proceeds to bring out the incompleteness of post-structuralist differentiations between 'text' and 'work.' Having explored some of the dubious aspects of Roland Barthes's use of these terms, Weimann seizes on one crucial passage where Barthes speaks of the work as an object of consumption while the text 'decants the work from consumption, gathering it up as play, task, production and activity.' Weimann turns this argument against itself, pointing out that the self-isolating tendence of this view of the text could well be seen, in many cases, to inhibit the very values of 'play, task, production and activity' that it seeks to promote. The process of purification, implied in the metaphor of decanting, needs a complementary reverse process, a movement from text back to work, a reabsorption of the text into the 'impurity' of historical situations and communicative relationships. 'If the methodological trajectory from work to text involves the textualization of all discursive practices, the trajectory from text to work involves the actualization of the inscribed discourse and its subtext.' Thus, for Weimann, the identity of the literary text is to be engaged at the intersection of these two different operations. The intersection will be revealed at the point in history where the process of textualization and that of actualization establish a reciprocal relationship.

Weimann's essay brings us to the central paradox of this volume. If deconstructive criticism, supported by many other positions of different persuasion, has sought to dismantle textual identity in terms of determinate, authorial-intended meaning or of a self-sufficient, autonomous, unique whole, it has done so by revealing that such notions have no universal claims to validity but arise out of specific critical endeavours (Romanticism, New Criticism, Structuralism, Formalism), located at particular moments of cultural history. But by raising the historical question, they insert themselves into history, which becomes the marker of their own identity. More important, however, is the challenge of historicity to all attempts to dispense with the identity of the text as a meaningful category. For if we confer on the reader the source of all meaningfulness of the text, we cannot escape from the historical dimension of reader-strategies themselves, which in a circular movement confers identity on the text. Moreover, textual difference, which, we are told, undermines identity, must postulate itself as a trans-historical, constituent feature of texts or work its way out through specific texts in terms which are comprehensible with their historical circumstances. In either case the text will be seen to have some form of identity.

NOTES

1 Jane Tompkins, ed., *Reader-Response Criticism from Formalism to Post-Structuralism*, Baltimore 1980, p. xvii.
2 Susan R. Suleiman and Inge Crosman, eds., *The Reader in the Text: Essays on Audience and Interpretation*, Princeton 1980, p. 41.
3 Barbara Johnson, *The Critical Difference*, Baltimore 1981, p. 4.
4 Vincent Leitch, *Deconstructive Criticism: An Advanced Introduction*, New York 1983, pp. 118–19.

INTRODUCTION

JONATHAN CULLER

Introduction: The Identity of the Literary Text

The topic of this collection of essays is especially intriguing because one is not certain precisely what is at issue. Only a short time ago one might have expected a collection of essays on the 'Identity of the Literary Text' to focus on problems of textual editing and textual scholarship: what is the true text that an editor attempts to reconstruct? what is the importance and the authority of a copy-text? what is the rationale for regularizing and emending accidentals? That these are not the questions to address here can be inferred from the names of the contributors to this volume. For though their meditations on these matters might be quite interesting – indeed, might be very interesting curiosities – they all speak with greater ease and authority about other questions.

When puzzled about the meaning of a phrase, we tell our students, use the dictionary; and indeed, this strategic recourse to empiricism, as Derrida calls it, proves effective in generating thought. *Identity*, says Webster's, is 'the state or fact of remaining the same one or ones, as under various aspects or conditions.' In these terms, the problem of the identity of the literary text would be a problem that has recently come to occupy theorists and critics: the question of what in the literary work or literary text remains the same under different conditions, such as different readings. The emphasis on reading and reception in a whole range of critical and theoretical writings has made it more imperative to reflect upon what might constitute the identity of a literary work whose meaning varies from reading to reading. We used to be satisfied with the notion that a literary masterpiece was inexhaustible in that new readings – including one's own rereadings of a text – could always uncover new beauties that belonged to the work's identity but had not thitherto been revealed. Recent emphasis on conflicting interpretations has made this notion of an all-inclusive identity seem inappropriate, and theorists have attempted to work out what is 'in' the text – part of its unchanging identity – and what is contributed by the reader. Is the text, for example, a determinate structure with certain gaps that the reader must fill in, or is it a set of indeterminate marks on which readers confer structure and meaning?

This problem proves surprisingly refractory. The recent career of Stanley Fish, as recorded in the twists and turns of his recent book, *Is There a Text in This Class?*, might serve as a cautionary tale for anyone hoping to solve the problem of the identity of the literary text. In trying to answer the question of what is 'in' the text, stable and unchanging, and what is contributed by the reader, Fish has run through a series of positions. Each change of position attributes to the activity of the reader something that had previously been located in the text. At first Fish argued that the meaning of the work was not a property of the text but the experience of the reader, but he still regarded the work as a determinate structure whose words (and their meaning), whose syntactic organization, and whose formal patterns remained the same from one reading to another: as a rich, determinate, identical text that readers experience. But when he turned to examine stylistics, which purports to describe the objective and persistent linguistic features of texts, Fish concluded that it was the reader's interpretive hypotheses that determined which of the many formal features and patterns count as facts of the text. In the third moment or third stage, Fish claimed that formal patterns are not *in* the text at all. Commenting on the lines from *Lycidas*,

> He must not float upon his wat'ry bier
> Unwept ...

where he notes that the line ending after 'bier' leads the reader to experience *He must not float upon his wat'ry bier* as a resolution bordering on a promise, only to have that anticipation destroyed by the subsequent 'Unwept,' Fish goes on to argue as follows:

I appropriate the notion of 'line ending' and treat it as a fact of nature; one might conclude that as a fact it is responsible for the reading experience I describe. The truth I think is exactly the reverse: line endings exist by virtue of perceptual strategies rather than the other way around. Historically the strategy that we know as 'reading (or hearing) poetry' has included paying attention to the line as a unit, but it is precisely that attention which has made the line as a unit (either of print or of aural duration) available ... In short, what is noticed is what has been made noticeable, not by a clear and undistorting glass, but by an interpretive strategy.[1]

This formal feature is not in the text but is created by a historical perceptual strategy. The same argument can be repeated for the most basic phenomena: any repetition of the same sound or letter is a function of phonological or orthographic conventions and thus may be regarded as the result of the interpretive strategies of particular communities. There is no rigorous way to distinguish fact from interpretation, so nothing can be deemed to be definitively *in* the text prior to interpretive conventions.

Fish takes one further step: like the text and its meanings, the reader too is a product of the strategies of an interpretive community, constituted as reader by the mental operations it makes available. 'At a stroke,' Fish writes, 'the dilemma that gave rise to the debate between the champions of the text and the champions of the reader (of whom I had certainly been one) is dissolved because the competing entities are no longer perceived as independent. To put it another way, the claims of objectivity can no longer be debated because the authorizing agency, the center of interpretive authority, is at once both and neither.'[2] 'Many things look rather different,' he claims, 'once the subject-object dichotomy is eliminated.'[3]

This radical monism, by which everything is the product of interpretive strategies, is a logical result of analysis that shows each entity to be a conventional construct; but the distinction between subject and object is more resilient than Fish thinks and will not be eliminated 'at a stroke.' It reappears as soon as one attempts to talk about interpretation. To discuss an experience of reading one must adduce a reader and a text. For every story of reading there must be something for the reader to encounter, to be surprised by, to learn from. Interpretation is always interpretation of something, and that something functions as the object in a subject-object relation, even though it can be regarded as the product of prior interpretations.

What we see in Fish's turnings are the moments of a general struggle between the monism of theory and the dualism of narrative. Theories of reading demonstrate the impossibility of establishing well-grounded distinctions between fact and interpretation, between what can be read in the text and what is read into it, or between text and reader, and thus lead to a monism. Everything is constituted by interpretation – so much so that Fish admits he cannot answer the question: 'What are interpretive acts interpretations *of*?'[4] Stories of reading, however, will not let this question go unanswered. There must always be dualisms: an interpreter and something to interpret, a subject and an object, an actor and something he acts upon or that acts on him.

The relation between monism and dualism is particularly striking in the work of Wolfgang Iser. His account of reading is eminently sensible, designed to do justice to the creative, participatory activity of readers, while preserving determinate texts which require and induce a certain response. He attempts, that is, a dualistic theory, but his critics show that his dualism cannot be sustained: the distinction between text and reader, fact and interpretation, or determined and undetermined breaks down and his theory becomes monistic. What kind of monism it becomes depends on which of his arguments and premises one takes most seriously. Samuel Weber argues in 'The Struggle for Control' that in Iser's theory everything ultimately depends on the authority of the author, who has made the text what it is: the author guarantees the unity of the work, requires the reader's creative participation, and through his text, as Iser puts it, 'prestructures the shape of the aesthetic object to be produced by the reader,' so that reading is an actualization of the author's intention.[5] But one can also argue convincingly, as Stanley Fish does in 'Why No One's Afraid of Wolfgang Iser,' that his theory is a monism of the other sort: the objective structures which Iser claims guide or determine the reader's response are structures only for a certain practice of reading. 'Gaps are not built into the text but appear (or do not appear) as a consequence of particular interpretive strategies,' and thus 'there is no distinction between what the text gives and what the reader supplies; he supplies *everything*' the stars in a literary text are not fixed; they are just as variable as the lines that join them.'[6] Iser's mistake is to take the dualism necessary to stories of reading as theoretically sound, not realizing that the variable distinction between fact and interpretation or text's contribution and reader's contribution will break down under theoretical scrutiny.

The possibility of demonstrating that Iser's theory leads to a monism in which reader or author supplies everything helps to show what is wrong with his eminently sensible notion that something is provided by the text and something else provided by the reader, or that there are some determinate structures and other places of indeterminacy. Jean-Paul Sartre proves one of the best correctives when discussing, in *Qu'est-ce que la littérature?*, the way in which readers 'create and disclose at the same time, disclose by creating and create by disclosing.' 'Ainsi pour le lecteur,' Sartre writes, 'tout est à faire et tout est déjà fait' (Thus for the reader everything is to be done and everything is already done).[7] For the reader the work is not partially created but, on the one hand, already complete and inexhaustible – one can read and reread without ever grasping completely what has already been made – and, on the other hand, still to be created in the process of reading, without which it is only black marks on paper. The attempt to produce compromise formulations fails to capture this essential, divided quality of reading.

Stories of reading, however, require that something be taken as given so that the reader can respond to it. E.D. Hirsch's arguments about meaning and significance are relevant here. 'Meaning,' which Hirsch identifies with the author's intended meaning, 'refers to the whole verbal meaning of a text, and "significance" to textual meaning in relation to a larger context, i.e. another mind, another era, a wider subject matter.'[8] Hirsch's opponents reject the distinction, arguing that there is no meaning in the text except in a context of interpretation; but Hirsch claims that the activity of interpretation depends on a distinction between a meaning that is in the text (because the author put it there) and a significance that is supplied. 'If an interpreter did not conceive a text's meaning to be *there* as an occasion for contemplation or application, he would have nothing to think or talk about. Its thereness, its self-identity from one moment to the next allows it to be contemplated. Thus, while meaning is a principle of stability in an interpretation, significance embraces a principle of change.'[9] The indispensability of this distinction is confirmed, for Hirsch, by his opponent's willingness to claim that he has misinterpreted them (and thus that their works do have stable meanings different from the significance an interpreter might give them). But what Hirsch's arguments show is the need for dualisms of this kind in our dealings with texts and the world, not the epistemological authority of a distinction between the meaning of a text and the significance interpreters give it, or even the possibility of determining in a principled way what belongs to the meaning and what to the significance. We employ such distinctions all the time because our stories require them, but they are variable, and ungrounded concepts.

This point is well made by the philosopher Richard Rorty in a discussion of the problems raised by Thomas Kuhn's treatment of science as a series of interpretive paradigms. Are there properties *in* nature which scientists discover, or do their conceptual frameworks *produce* such entities as subatomic particles, light waves, etc.? Does science *make* or does it *find*? 'In the view I want to recommend,' writes Rorty,

nothing deep turns on the choice between these two phrases – between the imagery of making and of finding. ... It is less paradoxical, however, to stick to the classic notion of 'better describing what was already there' for physics. This is not because of deep epistemological or metaphysical considerations, but simply because, when we tell our Whiggish stories about how our ancestors gradually crawled up the mountain on whose (possibly false) summit we stand, we need to keep some things constant throughout the story. The forces of nature and the small bits of matter, as conceived by current physical theory, are good choices for this role. Physics is the paradigm of 'finding' simply because it is hard (at least in the West) to tell a story of changing physical universes against the background of an unchanging Moral Law or poetic canon, but very easy to tell the reverse sort of story. Our tough-minded 'naturalistic' sense that spirit is, if not reducible to nature, at least parasitic upon it, is no more than the insight that physics gives us a good background against which to tell our stories of historical change. It is not as if we had some deep insight into the nature of reality which told us that everything save atoms and the void was 'by convention' (or 'spiritual,' or 'made up). Democritus's insight was that a story about the smallest bits of things forms a background for stories about changes among things made of these bits. The acceptance of this genre of world-story (fleshed out successively by Lucretius, Newton, and Bohr) may be definatory of the West, but it is not a choice which could obtain, or which requires, epistemological or metaphysical guarantees.[10]

In much the same way, the notion of a given text, with an unchanging identity and determinate, discoverable properties, provides an excellent background for arguments about interpretation and accounts of changing interpretations. Reader-oriented critics have themselves found that it makes a better story to talk of texts *inviting* or *provoking* responses than to describe readers' *creating* texts, even when their theories should incline them towards the latter sort of tale. But the advantages of the notion of unchanging, identical texts do not make the text's identity a given – a solid foundation on which one could depend. The more an account appeals to an unchanging identity of the text, the more it makes itself vulnerable to criticism by theories that make the text a reader's construct and show the dependency of any supposedly permanent textual feature on historical conventions of reading.

But my dictionary, that indispensable empirical instrument, gives a second sense of *identity* that is also relevant to our problem: *identity*, 'the condition or fact of being some specific person or thing; individuality.' Our notions of the identity of persons do not refer unchanging physical properties but to central distinguishing characteristics that develop in time and are seen as both unifying and individuating a person. The identity of the literary text, in this sense, would be what makes it a unified whole while distinguishing it from other texts. Literary interpretation has frequently been conceived as an attempt to identify the distinctive unifying force of each work: to describe how the various parts contribute to an organic whole different from other such wholes. Such a notion of the identity of the literary work has been challenged in contemporary criticism. For example, on the opening page of *S/Z*, variously regarded as a monument of structuralist or post-structuralist criticism, Roland Barthes speaks not of the text's identity but of its difference.

This difference is not, obviously, some positive, irreducible quality (according to a mythical view of literary creation); it is not what designates the individuality of each text, what names, signs it, initials it, concludes it. It is an unarrestable difference that is articulated upon the infinity of texts, of languages, of systems: a difference of which each text is the return.[11]

Barbara Johnson, commenting on this passage in her superb collection of deconstructive readings, *The Critical Difference*, writes,

In other words, a text's difference is not its uniqueness, its special identity. It is the text's way of differing from itself. And this difference is perceived only in the act of rereading. It is the way in which the text's signifying energy becomes unbounded, to use Freud's term, through the process of repetition, which is the return not of sameness but of difference. Difference, in other words, is not what distinguishes one identity from another. It is not a difference between (or at least not between independent units), but a difference within. Far from constituting the text's unique identity, it is that which subverts the very idea of identity, infinitely deferring the possibility of adding up the sum of a text's parts or meanings and reaching a totalized, integrated whole.[12]

This is a difficult passage, especially in its linking of repetition, reading, internal difference, and the deferral of totalization to the subversion of the idea of identity. The example Johnson immediately cites shows how a supposedly unique identity – Rousseau's – might prove to be an internal difference that forestalls totalization. Rousseau opens his *Confessions* with the claim that 'I am unlike anyone I have ever met; I will even venture to say that I am like no one in the whole world'; but we soon discover that this unique self is distinguishable by its difference from itself: 'There are times when I am so unlike myself that I might be taken for someone else of an entirely opposite character.'[13] This example bears only indirectly on the problem of the identity of a literary text, but to illustrate the pertinence of Johnson's comments one must make a different approach.

The psychoanalytic notions of the unconscious and of transference and counter-transference may be of some help here. The discovery of the unconscious is in some ways a threat to notions of a person's identity: the self can no longer be identified with consciousness, and the subject, as they say, is not master in its own house. However, some analytic schools, such as the American ego psychologists, were soon able to reappropriate the unconscious for theories of personal identity, claiming that each individual is defined by his or her distinctive repressions, which become special 'hang-ups' and contribute to a personal identity. The workings of transference and counter-transference, however, suggest that the unconscious is more subversive of identity and cannot be divided so easily into mine and thine. The unconscious is not to be thought of simply as something belonging to the patient that is disclosed and interpreted by the psychoanalyst's metalanguage; it emerges in the dramas that analyst and analysand find themselves playing out. 'Le transfert,' say Lacan several times, 'est la mise-en-acte de la realite de l'inconscient.'[14] Transference is the putting into action of the reality of the unconscious. A common conception of psychoanalysis puts the analyst in a position of mastery and exteriority: like the critic standing outside a text, the analyst is said to interpret the patient's discourse, revealing his unconscious and his true identity. But transference, which Freud called a 'factor of undreamt-of importance,' complicates the picture considerably, by disrupting the relation of mastery and problematizing the notion of identity. Analyst and patient get caught up in stories or scenarios – displaced repetitions in which the unconscious emerges. It is no longer quite clear whose stories these are, yet it is in this playing of roles that cures seem to be effected.

Like the analyst, the literary critic is generally thought to be in a position of mastery and exteriority: outside the discourse he explains, interprets, and judges. But we discover transferential relationships here too. In a formidable discussion of literature and psychoanalysis which gives pride of place to transference, Shoshana Felman studies the relationship between Henry James's *The Turn of the Screw* and its critics, and she discovers that when critics claim to be interpreting the story, standing outside of it and telling us its true meaning, they are in fact caught up in it, playing interpretive roles already dramatized in the story. The quarrels between critics *about* the story are an uncanny repetition *of* the drama of the story, so that the structures of the work emerge most powerfully in the dramas played out by critics who are implicated in the work. In general, she remarks,

the reader of *The Turn of the Screw* can choose either to believe the governess and thus to behave like Mrs. Grose, or not to believe the governess, and thus to behave precisely like the governess. Since it is the governess who, within the text, plays the role of the suspicious reader, occupies the place of the interpreter, to suspect that place and that position is, thereby, to take it. To demystify the governess is only possible on one condition: the condition of repeating the governess's very gesture.[15]

Thus, Felman writes, 'it is precisely by proclaiming that the governess is mad that Edmund Wilson inadvertently imitates the very madness he denounces, unwittingly participates in it.'[16] This transferential repetition emerges when a later critic – here Felman – transferentially anticipating a transferential relation between critic and text, reads the text as dramatizing the activity of earlier critics.

A more complicated example of this sort of transference, which there is not enough space to go into here, is presented by Barbara Johnson in an article called 'Melville's Fist: The Execution of Billy Budd' in *The Critical Difference*. As one collects these and other examples one comes to posit a compulsion to repeat, independent of the psychology of critics but based on a complicity of reading and writing, a repetition that makes it unclear whose stories these are. But more important for our purposes, one notes that in identifying structures of transference one repeatedly focuses on what seems to be moments of self-referentiality or self-reflexivity in literary works, when statements in the text ostensibly about something else prove to apply to the text itself and the problems of interpreting it. Felman, for example, focuses on modes of interpretation dramatized in the text of *The Turn of the Screw* and which prefigure, in a complex reversal, models employed in critical interpretations of the text.

Now moments of self-referentiality are often regarded as key moments in establishing the identity of a literary text, just as self-knowledge and self-consciousness have been central to conceptions of personal identity. I want to suggest that these moments of self-consciousness or self-referentiality do not, as we generally think, establish the identity of the literary work, in the sense of making it a distinctive, unified whole, autonomous and self-conscious. Towards this end I want to examine a poem that has been authoritatively interpreted as a supreme example of the self-conscious, self-enclosed self, autonomous artefact, and show how the transferential relations at work attach to these moments of supposed self-consciousness and how, through repetition, displacement of differences, and deferral of totalization, they raise some questions about 'identity.'

We associate the notion of the good poem as self-conscious, self-descriptive artefact with the New Criticism; and the book which most authoritatively established this conception of the poem is *The Well-Wrought Urn* – a title which is also the name of the sort of poem the book describes. The poem with which Cleanth Brooks begins his argument is Donne's *The Canonization*, which he celebrates as a major achievement of the poetic imagination that also describes the sort of imaginative achievement that it is. For Brooks it is a model of self-conscious self-referentiality, which accounts for itself and becomes a self-contained fusion of being and doing. 'The poem is an instance of the doctrine which it asserts,' he writes; 'It is both the assertion and the realization of the assertion. The poet has actually before our eyes built within the song the "pretty room" with which he says the lovers can be content. The poem itself is the well-wrought urn which can hold the lovers' ashes and which will not suffer in comparison with the prince's "halfe-acre tomb".'[17]

What the poem says about urns and rooms is taken as self-reference, and this self-reflexivity is seen as consciousness of self, self-description. The question is, what is the relationship between this self-consciousness and the transferential process that problematizes textual boundaries by revealing something like a literary unconscious? I want to show that in interpreting the poem as self-referential and self-conscious Brooks comes to occupy or enact a role in the text – the role of a prior interpreter. *The Canonization* begins its self-referential conclusion thus:

> Wee can dye by it, if not live by love,
>> And if unfit for tombes and hearse
> Our legend bee, it will be fit for verse;
>> And if no peece of Chronicle wee prove,
>>> We'll build in sonnets pretty roomes;
>>> As well a well wrought urne becomes
> The greatest ashes, as halfe-acre tombes,
>> And by these hymnes, all shall approve
> Us *Canoniz'd* for Love:

The narrator posits that the legend of his love will be fit for verse, sonnets if not chronicles, which will function as hymns for those who hear them. Moreover, listeners will be moved to speech upon hearing these verses:

> And by these hymnes, all shall approve
> Us *Canoniz'd* for Love:

> And thus invoke us: You whom reverend love
>> Made one anothers hermitage;
> You, to whom love was peace, that now is rage;
>> Who did the whole worlds soule contract, and drove
>>> Into the glasses of your eyes
>>> (So made such mirrors, and such spies,
> That they did all to you epitomize,)
>> Countries, Townes, Courts: Beg from above
> A patterne of your love!

The speaker thus imagines that those who have heard the verse legend of his love will invoke the lovers in idealizing descriptions which, more powerfully than anything in his own account, portray the lovers as triumphantly gaining the whole world's soul by seeking love alone. The response to the legend which the speaker imagines and represents is an invocation and further representation of the lovers which asks them to invoke God and to ask him for a further representation of their love which could serve as pattern. We have, therefore, not so much a self-contained urn as a chain of discourses and representations: the legend describing the lovers, the verse representation of this legend, the celebratory portrayal of the lovers in the response of those who have heard the legend, the request which the lovers are asked to formulate, and the pattern from above which will generate further versions of their love.

The chain of representations complicates the situation Brooks describes, especially when one focuses on the question of self-reference and asks what is the 'pretty room,' the 'well wrought urn,' or the 'hymn' to which the poem refers. Brooks answers, the poem itself, 'the poem itself is the well-wrought urn which can hold the lovers' ashes.' 'The poet has actually before our eyes built ... the pretty room with which he says the lovers can be content.' If this is so, if the poem itself is the well-wrought urn, then one of the principal features of this urn is that it portrays people responding to the urn. If the urn or hymn is the poem itself, then the predicted response to the hymn is a response to the representation of a response to the hymn. The most hymn-like element of the poem is the last stanza, the invocation addressed to the lovers by those who have heard the hymn or verse legend of their love. The earlier stanzas of the poem can scarcely qualify as a hymn, so if the poem refers to itself as a hymn it is including within itself its depiction of this response – a response to the hymn it claims to be.

This may seem a perverse description of what is happening in the poem, an excessive exploitation of the skewed tightening that self-reference brings; but this account gives us a surprisingly apt description of what has happened. Brooks, after reading the verse legend of these lovers, invokes them, celebrates them as saints of love: 'The lovers in rejecting life actually win to the most intense life. ... The lovers, in becoming hermits, find that they have not lost the world but have gained the world in each other. ... The tone with which the poem closes is one of triumphant achievement.'[18] He responds much as the poem predicts, taking the role the poem's drama provides, praising their exemplary love, and asking for a pattern of their love, which he interprets as 'the union which the creative imagination itself effects.'[19] His book invokes *The Canonization* as canonical example, as pattern: his project, as he describes it, is an attempt to see what happens when one reads other poems 'as one has learned to read Donne and the moderns.'[20] The saintly yet worldly union celebrated in the poem – the union effected by the creative imagination – is taken as the pattern to be reproduced elsewhere. The phrase 'well-wrought urn,' which this exemplary example, *The Canonization*, applies to poems and to itself, is taken up and applied by the book to other poems, and also to itself. Brooks's own book is called *The Well-Wrought Urn*: the combination in his pages of Donne's urn and Brooks's response to it becomes itself an urn.

This self-referential element in Donne's poem does not produce or induce a self-possession in which the poem harmoniously is the thing it describes. In celebrating itself as urn the poem incorporates a celebration of the urn and thus becomes something other than the urn; and if the urn is taken to include the response to the urn, then the responses it anticipates, such as Brooks's, become a part of it, a replaying or uncanny continuation of its drama. Self-reference does not close it in upon itself but leads to a proliferation of representations, a series of invocations and urns, including Brooks's *The Well-Wrought Urn*. There is a certain neatness to this situation – but it is the neatness of transference in which the analyst finds himself caught up in a structure of repetition when he thought he was analysing the object before him – and this surprising proliferation disrupts the aesthetic unity the critic seeks. The structure of self-reference works in effect to divide the poem against itself, creating an urn to which one responds and an urn which includes a response to the urn. If the urn is also the combination of urn and response to the urn, then this structure of self-reference created a situation in which responses such as Brooks's are part of the urn in question. This series of representations, invocations, and readings which, like moments of self-reference, are at once within the poem and outside it, can always be continued. Analysis is endless and unending because it involves transference. We say that critics can always find new things to say about a poem; this may be because the uncanny repetitions of transference continue with the analytic situation.

To sum up: I am arguing that what critics identify as moments of self-reference or self-consciousness in literary works may be the marks of a situation of transference. The critic who claims to stand outside the text and analyse it seems hopelessly entangled with it, caught up in a repetition that can be described as discovering structures in the text that (unbeknownst to him) repeat his own relation to the text, or as repeating in his interpretation a relation already figured in the text. It is not clear, as I say, at these moments, whose story this is: the text's story, the critic's story, or reading's story. And this uncertainty may carry further. If the issue in *The Canonization* is one of power – the power of discourse to reproduce and to canonize – and if the issue in *The Well-Wrought Urn* is also one of canons and power, it is not clear who is the victor in this story. Brooks tells a story of the poem triumphing as it predicted, but in adopting its story and repeating it he seems to make its triumph his. As we have seen, it is very difficult to determine where Donne's story, or Donne's narrator's story, stops and Brooks's begins, and that confusion or collusion may be inseparable from its power – I will not try to say whose power. Perhaps in the end, the literary text is interesting because it doesn't have anything as defining as an identity. It occurs to me, however, that the critics who follow me in this collection of essays on the identity of the literary text may well reach identical conclusions. I only hope it will be by rather different, perhaps even original, routes that we reach our conclusions about the identity or absence of identity of the literary text.

NOTES

1 Stanley Fish, *Is There a Text in This Class?* Cambridge, Mass.: 1980, pp. 165–6.
2 Ibid., p. 14.
3 Ibid., p. 336.
4 Ibid., p. 165.
5 Wolfgang Iser, *The Act of Reading*, Baltimore, 1978, p. 96. See Samuel Weber, 'The Struggle for Control,' unpublished MS, University of Strasbourg 1981.
6 Stanley Fish, 'Why No One's Afraid of Wolfgang Iser,' *Diacritics*, 11:1 (Spring 1981), 7.
7 Jean-Paul Sartre, *Qu'est-ce que la litterature?* Paris 1948, pp. 55 and 58.
8 E.D. Hirsch, *The Aims of Interpretation*, Chicago 1976, pp. 2–3.
9 Ibid., p. 80.
10 Richard Rorty, *Philosophy and the Mirror of Nature*, Princeton 1980, pp. 344–5.
11 Roland Barthes, *S/Z*, Paris 1970, p. 9.
12 Barbara Johnson, *The Critical Difference*, Baltimore 1981, p. 4.
13 Idem.
14 Jacques Lacan, *Les Quatre Concepts fondamentaux de la psychanalyse*, Paris 1973, pp. 133 and 137.
15 Shoshana Felman, 'Turning the Screw of Interpretation,' *Yale French Studies*, 55/56 (1977), 190.
16 Ibid., p. 196.
17 Cleanth Brooks, *The Well-Wrought Urn*, New York 1947, p. 17.
18 Ibid., p. 15.
19 Ibid., p. 18.
20 Ibid., p. 193.

PART ONE

TEXTUALITY AND INTERTEXTUALITY

OWEN MILLER

Intertextual Identity

In this paper I attempt to define intertextual identity, fully conscious from the outset that in many ways the very expression is a contradiction in terms. If by identity we mean some fixed and stable essence, then it is very difficult to reconcile with intertextuality, which, both as term and concept, has built into it a sense of the provisionary and the unstable. The current vogue it enjoys in literary studies stems precisely from this provisionary and unstable status: it is a term in the process of becoming identified just as it confers on a literary work a variety of identities.

As a term intertextuality (and I shall use it throughout this study interchangeably with intertextual identity) addresses itself to a plurality of concepts. One might with some justice speak of it in the plural as *intertextualities* to cover the variety of ways it has been conceived in theoretical terms and deployed in methodological strategies. I have preferred, however, to retain the singular form to indicate that, although it is not a unified concept, its various forms enjoy what Wittgenstein would have called 'family relationships.' By this I mean that one notion of intertextuality may share with another certain common features, but there are few which are to be found in all notions of the word. In short, there is no constituent feature, satisfactory to all, which would allow us to define the term.

A second approach that might unify the different senses of the word and procedures it entails is to consider how intertextuality is defined in opposition to its historical forebear, source-influence studies. But like so many endeavours where disparate views are united against a common enemy, there is a tendency to overlook the internal contradictions and incompatibilities existing among the various factions drawn together by common cause. A further weakness of this tendency to define intertextuality in antithetical terms to source-influence studies (and many critical theories are guilty of this today) is to set up the latter as a straw man which is then easily demolished. Source-influence studies, like such notions as 'the traditional novel' or 'le roman lisible,' tend to be a mythic entity created by practitioners whose avowed aim, ironically, is to demystify.

Intertextuality, as Barthes would have said, is not an 'innocent' term. By this he would have meant that any claim for it which denies its ideological nature is intent on deceiving. Indeed much of the intellectual vigour enjoyed by the term stems from Barthes's conception of it and, rather than shrink from its ideological implications, we should engage them fully, which does not at all mean accepting them blindly. As an ideologically charged concept, intertextuality continues to acquire new meanings as various critics seek to define or refine it. Even here it partakes of a paradox. Its growth as a concept is the outcome of a very specific notion of 'text' which Barthes and Kristeva, among others, have sought to promote, while it, itself, has been instrumental in formulating the very notion of textuality. As Michael Riffaterre has pointed out, 'the very idea of textuality is inseparable and founded upon intertextuality.'[1]

Intertextuality comes into play when those approaches which insist on the text as a self-regulating unity and emphasize its functional independence are felt, for one reason or another, to be inadequate or untenable. Thus in many instances it has gained currency as an umbrella term, covering all and any 'external' relationships a text may have and embracing most conceivable ways of contextualizing it within a broader frame of reference. In the Anglo-American domain, where New Criticism, with its insistence on intrinsic factors, is on the wane, intertextuality is a welcome stimulus to literary studies. But therein lies one of its difficulties: its tendency to cannibalize every other aspect of the field. Part of the problem of defining intertextual identity has derived precisely from attempting to secure for the term a territory of its own, one which restricts its tendency to take over the allied fields of poetics and thematics.

A third approach (and it is the one I have attempted here) is to define the different sorts of intertextuality in terms of the central issues which they have had either to address or neglect. In this maze of competing views of intertextual identity, I have drawn on the notion of presupposition as a sort of Ariadne's thread. Whether I have slain the Minotaur or not is left to the reader's judgment, but the thread has at times proved a very tenuous guide. Distinctions exist between a philosophical and linguistic notion of presupposition.[2] It can and has been defined in many ways: as the conditions imposed by the user on an utterance, as a component of a statement's signification, and more recently as a particular form of speech act.[3] Those who have drawn on it theoretically to define a particular mode of conceiving textual relationships or used it methodologically in working with actual texts have by and large done so analogically rather than literally, though the shift between the two is often blurred and analogical usages are not always as rigorous as they would initially claim to be. The problem basically is that the notion of intertextual relationships as presuppositional has been used ambiguously both to establish the theoretical underpinnings of a particular position and, in a much more metaphorical way, as a heuristic device to deal with practical problems of textual analysis. The line between the two uses is not always clear.

INTERTEXTUALITY AS A RELATIONAL CONCEPT

To refer to text A as being the source of or exercising an influence on text B is really to refer to author A's intersubjective relationship with author B. Our very manner of speaking of source-influence studies (e.g. Hemingway's influence on Camus) betrays our fundamental ways of thinking about them as an author-oriented enterprise the nature of which the critic must uncover. Intertextual studies on the other hand are, above all, reader-oriented even if the reader is to be conceived, as by Roland Barthes, as 'une pluralité d'autres textes, de codes infinis, ou plus exactement: perdus ...'[4] It is the reader, then, who establishes a relationship between a focused text[5] and its intertext,[6] and forges its intertextual identity.

We can think of this relationship in several ways and to a certain extent any specific notion of intertextuality will tend to define itself in terms of the particular mode of interpreting the relationship. What proves to be a very thorny problem in this respect is finding a relational term which is consistent with a reader-oriented approach and avoids betraying an unconscious affiliation with an author-oriented one. One particularly productive way of defining the intertextual relationship is to think of it metaphorically as a form of citation in which a fragment of discourse is accommodated or assimilated by the focused text. Describing it in this way allows us to view the intertext as having two separate identities: (a) as an independent text functioning in its own right, which may be unknown, forgotten or even lost; (b) as an assimilated or accommodated version embedded in some way in the focused text.

A citational view of intertextuality gains some theoretical support if we consider presuppositions as basically relational terms, linking utterances. Indeed, it may be one of the strategic errors of current thinking of presuppositions to use the term itself in its nominal rather than verbal or adjectival form. We should perhaps conceive of the phenomenon more along the lines of 'x presupposes y' or 'y is presuppositional to x' rather than of 'y is a presupposition of x.' Naming an utterance a presupposition is merely a way of designating one of the statements in a manner which specifies its relational function to the other. However, the possibility of defining the term both as a noun and as a verb is of considerable value, on an analogical level, to a citational view of intertextuality in so far as it provides us with some theoretical justification for conceiving of the intertext as a discourse both embedded, in assimilated or accommodated form, within the focused text as well as existing as a separate entity, independent of the focused text.

However, if we go further and attempt to speak more precisely about the way this process of assimilation/accommodation functions within specific texts, we are confronted by one of the serious potential weaknesses of the citational view of intertextuality identity. If we have recourse, for instance, to such terms as imitation, parody, plagiarism, and even travesty to describe intertextual relationships (and it seems we must do so if the citational model is to have any practical value in dealing with actual texts), we bring into play an evaluative terminology which is difficult to sustain without implying some measure of authorial intentionality. We can of course seek to redefine such terms as parody in a more neutral manner, but we cannot deprive them entirely of all associations of intentionality[7] and thereby avoid weakening the definition of intertextual identity as a purely reader-oriented concept.

A somewhat different approach from that of the citational analogy is to stress the similarity or difference existing between the focused text and its intertext as a form of transformation mediated by some sort of invariant. As Laurent Jenny points out in an important study of intertextuality 'on ne saisit le sens et la structure d'une œuvre littéraire que dans son rapport à des archétypes, eux-mêmes extraits de longues séries de textes dont ils sont en quelque sorte l'invariant. Vis-à-vis des modèles archétypiques, l'œuvre littéraire entre toujours dans un rapport de réalisation, de transformation ou de transgression. Et pour une large part, c'est ce rapport qui la définit.'[8] But if the term 'transformation' reflects a neutral stance with respect to intertextual relationships, the terms 'transgression' and even 'réalisation' engage us irrevocably in value judgments. Two examples will illustrate how such a process works. In a discussion of the relationship between literature and 'its informing structures, myths,' Northrop Frye comments that 'at any given period of literature, the conventions of literature are enclosed within a total mythological structure, which may not be explicitly known to anyone, but is nevertheless present as a shaping principle.' He continues: 'In every age the most ambitious literary structures, such as the works of Dante, Milton, Victor Hugo or Joyce tend to be cosmological and hence nearest to suggesting what the total structure is like.'[9] In other words, what distinguishes La Divina Commedia and Ulysses from other works of their respective ages is that they offer a fuller and more complete realization of some mythological invariant and it is this which gives them their unique and distinguishing quality of being 'the most ambitious literary structures' of their time.

A somewhat different view of the text's uniqueness is provided by Michael Riffaterre, who argues that 'Le texte est toujours unique en son genre. Et cette *unicité* est ... la définition la plus simple de sa littérarité. Cette définition se vérifie instantanément si nous réfléchissons que le propre de l'expérience littéraire, c'est d'être un dépaysement, un exercice d'aliénation, un bouleversement de nos pensées, de nos perceptions, de nos expressions habituelles.'[10] In this case what constitutes 'le propre de l'expérience littéraire' is a particular text's capacity to transgress generic conventions, to achieve a uniqueness 'en son genre.' But the fact that the principle of defamiliarization, which dates at least from the Russian formalists and probably from Romantic aesthetics, is part of the current ideology of the text should not hide the fact that it is fundamentally a prescriptive as well as a descriptive notion of literariness.

Thus to assert a text's uniqueness with respect to other texts, in transformational terms, either as a fuller realization or transgression of some archetypal or structural invariant is not only to bring into play criteria of value but also to invoke a constitutive or essential notion of identity, very akin to that of the absolute self[11] which permeates Romantic aesthetics and forms one of the foundation-stones of the Romantic notion of originality. We may indeed wish to embrace the qualitative judgments about texts which a transformational or citational model of intertextual relationships involves. But if we follow such a course, we must also accept a fuller responsibility, one which leads us back to the two *bêtes noires* of source-influence studies – authorial intentionality and authorial originality – and thus to accepting a conception of intertextuality which is not entirely reader-oriented. I would suggest, however, that there is an alternative route, one in which intertextual identity is not concerned with establishing some sort of constitutive or essential property but rather with formulating a variety of relational procedures which would help us 'locate' a focused text, establish its co-ordinates so to speak. Such a view of intertextuality would draw heavily on the Derridean notion of relational identity,[12] though how it might be worked out and whether it would mean abandoning citational or transformational modes of describing relationships between texts is not clear to me at this stage.

AN OPERATIONAL MODEL OF INTERTEXTUALITY

One of the most vigorous attempts to develop the notion of intertextuality in opposition to source-influence studies is that of Jonathan Culler. 'The study of intertextuality,' he tells us, 'is not the investigation of sources and influences, as traditionally conceived; it casts its net wider to include anonymous discursive practices, codes whose origins are lost, which are the conditions of possibility of later texts.'[13] And elsewhere: 'we are faced with an infinite intertextuality where conventions cannot be traced to their source and thus positivistically identified. The notion of intertextuality names the paradox of linguistic and discursive systems: that utterances or texts are never moments of origin because they depend on the prior existence of codes and conventions, and it is the nature of codes and conventions ... to have lost origins.'[14] It is clear that Culler's intention is to forge a view of intertextuality much broader than that envisaged by source-influence studies, one that is consistent with the notion of the text which Kristeva, Barthes, Sollers, and others have developed. Such a view draws heavily on two basic principles: (1) a mosaic concept of the text as a series of quotations; (2) the inferential feature of presuppositions.

The mosaic concept of the text has been developed by Barthes in numerous writings. One expression of it is particularly pertinent here, since it addresses itself specifically to intertextuality. 'L'intertextuel dans lequel est pris tout texte, puisqu'il est lui-même l'entre-texte d'un autre texte, ne peut se confondre avec quelque origine du texte: rechercher les "sources", les "influences" d'une œuvre, c'est satisfaire au mythe de la filiation: les citations dont est fait un texte sont anonymes, irrépérables et cependant *déjà lues*: ce sont des citations sans guillemets.'[15] It is important to distinguish between the citational conception of the text being advanced here and the citational model of intertextuality discussed earlier. In the latter, we were involved with a metaphorical usage of quotation in which the intertext was considered as an embedded fragment within a new gestalt. The Barthian notion views the focused text (indeed all texts) as a mosaic composed entirely of fragments of linguistic matter quoted from anonymous sources, a collage of pieces of language brought into spatial proximity and inviting the reader to create some sort of patterning by forcing them to discharge some of their interrelational energy.

Such a radical view of the text envisages each sentence of the mosaic not only as creating intratextual patterns but also as gesturing towards its extratextual connections. It is here that the inferential feature of presuppositions becomes particularly pertinent. Since the source of these extratextual connections may be unknown (indeed one of assumptions of this notion of the text is that they are in fact not only unknown but unknowable), they can only be inferred in general terms, not located positively in specific, signed discourses. They function thus as presuppositions, since precisely what defines a presupposition is that it can be 'disconnected' from the utterance in which it is embedded by a process of inferential reasoning. Constrained only by the inferential capacities of a presuppositional nature, the intertextual relationships of any work of litera-ture[16] are theoretically infinite, since potentially any sentence of a text (or fragment thereof) may engender a series of presuppositional statements. If intertextuality is to engage us in such diverse considerations as 'explicit conventions of a genre, specific presuppositions about what is known and unknown, more general expectations and interpretative operations and broad assumptions about the preoccupations and goals of a type of discourse,'[17] there is a real danger that we will sit back and marvel at the promiscuity of such a concept while at the same time relinquishing any sense of its manageability as a methodological tool in analysing actual texts. If we are to make any real practical use of the notion of intertextual identity, we must put some tangible limits on its usage to ensure its productiveness with literary texts, while at the same time in no way denying the undoubted theoretical validity of a wider and more embracing definition.

In a sense this is already implicit in Culler's own position when he limits the inferential potentialities of the text to those concerns which are more properly literary. This itself seems a significant retreat from an even fuller notion of intertextuality envisaged, in theory at least, by Kristeva,[18] who conceives of it as a mode of integrating literary discourse with any other form of discourse, where no special status is accorded to literary or aesthetic values.

Another way of establishing limits might be to distinguish between logical and pragmatic presuppositions as Culler has done himself to advance his conception of intertextual identity. Pragmatic presuppositions are those that are defined as 'a relation between the utterance of a sentence and the context in which it is uttered.'[19] As Culler has shown, the investigation of pragmatic presuppositions is 'similar to the task which confronts poetics.'[20] It involves relating 'a literary work to a whole series of other works treating them not as sources but as constituents of a genre for example, whose conventions one attempts to infer.'[21] We are confronted here with the choice of whether we wish to deal with a notion of intertextuality which commandeers the whole field of poetics or whether we prefer that this notion have some coinage of its own. If we opt for the latter procedure, setting aside the analogical possibilities of pragmatic presuppositions while retaining those implicit in logical ones would suggest itself as a viable strategy.

The most debatable aspect of Culler's notion of intertextuality is his injunction that it is 'less a name for a work's relation with particular prior texts than an assertion of the work's participation in a discursive space and its relation to the codes which are potential formulations of that space.'[22] It is not clear to me exactly what theoretical objection could be raised by relating actual texts. It is one thing to maintain that an intertext may be unknown and quite another thing to assert that it is unknowable. Culler of course does not go this far, but his concern to work to some degree within the ideological framework established by

Barthes and others suggests that such an assumption at least lurks in his mind. Attempting to broaden the concept of intertextual relationships beyond the consideration of specific intertexts is laudable as a theoretical goal but should not preclude consideration of a specific intertext where to a reader's satisfaction one is in fact identifiable. I suspect that Culler's caution stems in part from his concern to evolve a theory of intertextual identity that is consistent with ideological strictures regarding source and origin and in part from a fear of falling prey to the ideological assumptions and methodological strategies involved in source-influence studies.[23]

The problem is that the source-influence approach, by its very procedures, entails a juxtaposition of actual texts and therefore implies a teleological model of intertextuality.[24] What above all characterizes the approach advocated by Culler is its avowedly operational nature, which best avoids source-origin problems and is most appropriate for developing the possibilities of presuppositional inference. If I am correct so far in my diagnosis, then the objection to a specific intertext is founded on the assumption that the unacceptable aspects of source-influence studies lie in the deployment of a teleological rather than an operational model. The position that I shall attempt to defend is that such an assumption is erroneous and that the ideological underpinnings of the source-influence approach (specifically those relating to authorial intentionality and originality) are not endemic to a teleological model but rather arise from a specific application of it. In pursuing this line of argument, my intention is to remove any theoretical objections to naming an intertext.

If we look closely at the underpinnings of the source-influence approach to intertextuality, we recognize that the basic methodological strategy is to establish a *necessary* relationship between the texts. If the source or influence is acknowledged by the author (as Henry James acknowledges Maupassant's 'La Parure' as a source of his own story 'Paste'), such studies take the form of a *demonstration* to clarify the extent of the 'debt.' In other cases where the source or influence is not acknowledged or confirmed by the author (such as James's 'borrowing' from Maupassant's 'Les Bijoux' also for 'Paste'), the strategy is to *prove*, through a juxtaposition of lexical, syntactic, and especially semantic features that the two texts are linked by necessity and not by chance. Thus the procedures relating the two texts are controlled by strategies which are functionally independent of a teleological model, specifically those of *demonstrating or proving* authorial intentionality and eliminating any possibility that one text's links with another are the product of a reader's personal engagement with the text.[25]

Once the primary goal has been achieved (that of establishing authorial intentionality), a second stage in source-influence studies becomes possible and characterizes most actual research of this genre. Again the problem is not with the teleological model *per se* but with the actual procedures followed within the framework of the model. The second stage consists of establishing *differences* between the texts. Here the rigour of the synonym is replaced by that of the antonym. The intention now is to demonstrate the *originality* of the influenced author and to re-establish the integrity of the influenced text. Once the elements have been shown to have been intentionally 'borrowed,' they must also be shown to have been successfully 'appropriated' by the focused text so that it functions as a new organic whole, independent of prior associations. Once the 'trade' has been completed, new 'ownership' must be clearly established.[26] What regulates the procedures at this stage is not the teleological model *per se* but the goal of establishing authorial originality, of asserting what Jean Ricardou has called the ideology of 'Expression.'[27]

One should add in fairness to Culler's position that, even if one grants that the objections held with respect to source-influence approach are unrelated to the deployment of a teleological model, such a conclusion in no way detracts from a preference for an operational one or from the advantages that such a model allows if one wishes to advocate a conception of intertextuality based on a mosaic notion of the text and on the inferential qualities of presuppositions. Nothing has been advanced here which favours a teleological model of inter-textual identity, which conceives of this problem exclusively in terms of relating two texts or of identifying the intertext. For this we must in the final section turn to Riffaterre's notion of 'obligatory intertextuality.'

CAUSALITY, TEMPORALITY, PRIORITY

'L'intertextualité est la perception, par le lecteur, de rapports entre une œuvre et d'autres, qui l'ont précédée ou suivie.'[28]

In this simple and succinct statement, Riffaterre has summed up the main elements defining intertextuality. One seemingly harmless element has been added, however, and must now be discussed: specifically that the intertext may chronologically follow the focused text. While this is perfectly consistent with any reader-oriented view of intertextual identity, it is not at all clear that it is consistent with many of the positions outlined to date, including Riffaterre's own notion of obligatory intertextuality.[29] One suspects that to take up the theoretical challenge posed by enlarging intertextual relationships to cover works which postdate the focused text would entail abandoning some fairly cherished positions and premises which, including an operational or citational model, seem founded on restricting the range of intertexts to those chronologi-cally prior to the focused text.

The danger of such a restriction in the composition of the intertext is that it not only curtails the reader's freedom but risks bringing implicitly into play one of the most devalued aspects of source-influence studies, namely the principle of causality. To assert that text B is the source of or influences text A is to imply that text B is explicable in terms of text A and that the latter is its point of origin. To restrict intentionally or implicitly the intertext on the basis of chronology is to open oneself to the objection that authorial intentionality has crept in the back door and that the restoration of meaning (or, as Ricoeur refers to it, 'the recollection of meaning') has become the dominant strategy of interpretation.[30]

Moreover, as Kant's famous justification of the principle of causality shows, it is difficult to speak of sequential order without invoking causality if only because, as Kant concluded himself, causality itself is an objective principle in nature. Whether one accepts this conclusion or not, restricting the intertext to chronologically prior works tends to conflate sequence and consequence, to fall into the error of *post hoc, ergo propter hoc* condemned by the Scholastics. Even Barthes's notion of anonymous quotation (which Culler takes up) escapes only tenuously being a causal phenomenon. One solution is to accept fully the notion of authorial intentionality, which would seem to be the direction being advocated by recent theorists of imitation, parody, plagiarism etc.[31] It seems significant that at least one, John Searle, has recently argued the case of intentionality on the very basis of citational intertextuality.[32]

Restricting intertextuality to chronologically prior works has of course several advantages that should not be overlooked. There can be no doubt that those who view intertextuality as a mode of introducing historical considerations might well look with less favour on a position which insists that intertextual identity is solely a product of reader participation in the text. Adherents of the phenomenological approach to literary history and textual identity would, on the other hand, find confirmation of their position in a range of intertexts freed from temporal strictures. The importance of intertextuality in defining a formal approach to literary history has been cogently argued by Tzvetan Todorov. Indeed it is significant that, in an earlier version of the same study, Todorov, citing Tynianov, argued categorically against an intertextual view of literary history.[33] In the revised version, again citing, paradoxically, Tynianov (who had argued that it was impossible to understand integrally a Dostoevsky text without referring to a prior text of Gogol), Todorov reverses himself completely on this point, arguing that any consideration of the relationship between poetics and literary history must take into consideration intertextual considerations, since 'si on ignorait la fonction parodique du texte dostoïevskien ... sa compréhension en souffrirait gravement.'[33]

Another substantial objection to de-chronologizing the notion of intertextuality is that it fails to make a clear distinction between intertextual and thematic identity.[35] To understand the issues raised by such an argument, let me develop it with an example. When T. S. Eliot brings together three texts to illustrate his sense of 'strange gods' inhabiting modern literatures, he would seem to be fulfilling Riffaterre's definition of an intertextual reading. 'It was almost by accident that I happened to read all of these stories in rapid succession. One is *Bliss* by Katherine Mansfield; the second is *The Shadow in the Rose Garden* by D. H. Lawrence, and the third *The Dead* by James Joyce. They are all, I believe, fairly youthful work; they all turn on the same theme of disillusion. … What is interesting in the three together is the differences of moral implication.'[36] Eliot's juxtaposition of these texts is certainly non-chronological. Even the order of his reading of them, as is explicitly indicated, is not a pertinent factor. Yet, in a sense, the perspective on each is the result of a relationship between them which draws attention to facets which unify them and those which distinguish them. The principle of selection is a common structural invariant (man-woman relationships in which one partner experiences a form of disillusion) and a dissimilar moral perspective; one that might be put crudely as (in the respective order Eliot mentions the stories) amoral/immoral/moral. Do we not therefore have here a case of intertextual identity providing the basis for Eliot, as reader, bringing these texts together?

What prevents our answering affirmatively is solely our intention to secure for intertextuality a field of operation which distinguishes it from thematics. If this is in fact our intention, then I would argue that intertextual identity implies some sort of ordering of the texts, whereby the focused text may function as figure to its intertext's ground. Thematic identity, on the other hand, fixes the ground outside the specific texts in a synecdochic fashion, that is as illustrating a more general concern, reflecting a sort of common denominator (differences of moral implication) to which they are subordinated. The texts from Mansfield, Lawrence, and Joyce are *organized* not *ordered*. None has any *priority* over the other except perhaps in an evaluative sense. This does not of course mean that Eliot might not have wished to read them intertextually and could not have done so if he had chosen some principle of ordering and priority which would have established a figure/ground relationship for such a reading.[37]

The question arises, of course, whether we can speak of ordering and of priority without being involved in that chain of reasoning which leads us from priority to temporality and finally to causality. The solution to this problem lies, I believe, in a reconsideration of the notion of presupposition as a condition of usage.[38] If I say: 'John has received more than adequate consideration,' I am presupposing that 'John has received some consideration' is a proposition with which my interlocutor already concurs and that the major point I am making is that 'the consideration is more than adequate.' Nothing suggests that my first proposition (John's getting some consideration) is temporally prior to the second, nor is there any sense that the former *causes* the latter, but I have, by the very phrasing of my initial utterance, built a sense of priority into the communicatory circuit whereby what I assume to be established allows me to make my major point. To clarify this problem let me consider a further example. If I ask 'Is John still smoking?' my question is addressed to what is happening now, about which I am inquiring, but it presupposes that my interlocutor has given prior assent to the proposition 'John was previously smoking.' The point I am making here is that certain utterances do, in fact, involve temporal sequence, but this is a feature of *some* presuppositions and not a constitutive feature of them *all*.

If the preceding discussion has some validity, then I believe that it is reasonable to define intertextuality (as Riffaterre has done) as the perception by the reader of relationships between a focused text and others, which have both chronologically preceded it and followed it. Intertextual identity, unlike thematic identity, involves some notion of a focused text (somewhat on the analogy of the focal point in an utterance containing a presupposition) and some notion of ordering or priority which the reader himself establishes in his engagement with that text. If we wish to bring questions of chronological order to bear (as is the case when we introduce historical considerations to our argument), we are free to do so within the framework of an intertextual reading but with the understanding that the chronological constraints we place on the choice of intertext are not a necessary or constitutive feature of intertextual identity.

OBLIGATORY INTERTEXTUALITY

One clearly successful attempt to reduce intertextuality to manageable proportions has been that of Michael Riffaterre, who has evoked a very useful distinction between 'aleatory' and 'obligatory' intertextuality. Aleatory intertexuality may be defined as the connection which a reader establishes between a focused text and a totally free, unrestricted range of other texts. These may be literary or non-literary, fragmentary or whole, in short any mode or form of discourse which he feels is pertinent within his own individually defined parameters. Obligatory intertextuality, on the other hand, imposes several important constraints on the connections the reader makes in his choice of intertexts and in his choice of relational procedures.

Il y a intertextualité obligatoire, lorsque la signification de certains mots du texte n'est ni celle que permet la langue, ni celle que demandent le contexte mais le sens qu'ont ces mots dans l'intertexte. C'est l'inacceptabilité de ce sens dans la langue ou dans le contexte qui contraint le lecteur à une présomption, à l'hypothèse d'une solution offerte dans un homologue formel du texte qu'il essaie de déchiffrer. L'objet n'est pas un objet de citation, c'est un objet présupposé.[39]

In this view, the identification of a specific intertext is not only admissible but an essential feature of intertextual identity. What signals the intertext as well as specifying it, is the notion of a *trace* discernible in the focused text, which testifies to the former's actual or potential existence without its being necessarily identifiable immediately. The trace left is of a cognitive nature, a form of unintelligibility which cannot be resolved at an intratextual level or by recourse to any possible institutionalized meaning of the trace. The reader is thus faced with an unresolved or an unsatisfactorily resolved aspect of the interpretation of the text which sets him in search of the appropriate intertext to resolve the problem.

My summary of the major facets of obligatory intertextuality does scant justice to the intricate theoretical reasoning which has led Riffaterre through several publications to elaborate this version of intertextual identity.[40] One can best understand its thrust by reviewing it in terms of the problems already analysed.

In the first place it is an explicitly non-citational approach and thereby avoids all problems of an evaluative nature, which appear endemic both to this approach and to a transformational one. Such a step is much more radical than might at first be imagined. What is new about most other versions of intertextual relationships is that they have envisaged alternative modes of conceiving of the connection between the *same* pairs of texts to which source-influence studies addressed themselves. Riffaterre's notion of obligatory intertextuality is a major departure from this position in so far as it operates on a very different principle from that which juxtaposes texts based on similarities or differences of syntactic, lexical, or semantic features, or those which are brought together on the basis of archetypal or structural invariants shared by two texts. It envisages unexpected alignments of texts while consigning such traditional relationships (such as those between the *Odyssey* and *Ulysses*) potentially to the aleatory category.[41]

Secondly, despite the reference in the passage quoted above, it is difficult to discern in what way Riffaterre's argument owes anything to a theory of presuppositions. In a sense one might say that the trace left by unintelligibility functions somewhat like the inferential aspect of presuppositions: it is an intratextual feature, embedded in the focused text, and pointing to intelligibility 'lying in wait' in another text. But though the idea that intratextual unintelligibility indicates intertextual intelligibility is a creative hypothesis (a 'présomption' to use Riffaterre's own word), it bears none of real inferential features of a presupposition which permit us logically to name that presupposition. One could argue that Riffaterre has utilized (somewhat metaphorically) one important feature of presuppositions that we have not yet dealt with, namely the cognitive relation between a presuppositional utterance and the utterance which contains it. If I say 'John has stopped drinking,' the statement 'makes sense' only if John was previously drinking. But here I am playing somewhat on the notion of 'making sense.' Presuppositions are not concerned with problems of intelligibility but with the truth and validity of an utterance. It is by a somewhat dubious sleight-of-hand that I turn the notion of truth into the notion of intelligibility through a semantic manipulation of the term 'validity.' Even then, to assert that a presupposition has to make sense for the proposition that includes it to make sense is a far cry from claiming that, if a proposition makes no sense, then that sense can be found by referring to its presupposition.

In Riffaterre's hands, the pragmatic feasibility of obligatory intertextuality is clearly demonstrated and fully justified by his extremely subtle analysis of several highly hermetic texts whose interpretational problems would seem insoluble without recourse to such a notion. But the analytic skill displayed in the actual textual analyses tends to make one overlook some of the problems which such a definition of intertextuality poses. Despite its undoubted methodological rigour (especially if our only alternative is the aleatory variety), obligatory intertextuality is in the final analysis a very limited way of looking at textual relationships. While many texts will signal through their traces of intratextual unintelligibility the existence of an appropriate intertext, one must wonder, realistically, how often there exists such an intertext or indeed, even if one should exist, what the possibilities are of actually locating it.[42]

On another level one might also ask whether the interpretational problems encountered by readers can all be accounted for by such a notion as unintelligibility. In addition to problems of this variety (which are undoubtedly posed by densely hermetic texts) other sorts seem equally at work, for which a more flexible notion of intertextuality might account. If we develop the major insight of the hypothesis (i.e. that we may read one text in the light of another), the way is open to us to address such concerns as the plurality of equally plausible interpretations with which literary texts often tend to confront us. Intertextual connections might strengthen one interpretation over another, help articulate a particular interpretation which intratextual features fail adequately to support, add, in short, to the potential polysemy of the text, while, at the same time, suggesting heuristic strategies on how to deal with it.[43]

The question, of course, is whether there is in fact any middle ground between the unmanageable category of aleatory intertextuality and the overly restrictive one of the obligatory variety. Does there exist a way to speak of a notion of intertextual identity which mediates between an overly text-oriented and an overly reader-oriented approach? I am not at all sure that such a theory would not be an illusion, but if it could be constructed it would have to arbitrate between a contingent and a necessary view of the text's relationship to its intertext. In doing so, it would have to rely on some theoretical argument which resembles Derrida's notion of 'supplément.' In *De la Grammatologie*, Derrida sets out to explain the logic of supplementarity as it relates to Rousseau's explanation of how education supplements nature. The concept of nature is something complete in itself to which education is but an addition. At the same time, paradoxically, nature is felt to be something incomplete and insufficient, which *must* be supplemented by education for it to be truly itself. Jonathan Culler has excellently summarized this notion as follows: 'The logic of supplementarity ... makes nature the prior term, a plenitude which was there at the start, but reveals an inherent lack or absence within it and makes education something external and extra but also an essential condition of that which it supplements.'[44]

If we substitute here the terms 'focused text' for 'nature' and 'intertext' for 'education,' we have very much the theoretical underpinnings of the position I am advancing. The text is in itself complete and the intertext merely an addition brought by a reader making, in his engagement with that text, connections with his own repertoire. Yet at the same time it can be felt to be incomplete, in need of some 'supplementary' text which reveals by its being brought to bear on the reading process as essential in the sense that it directs the reader along certain lines and enriches his experience. In one sense, the paradox in Derrida's notion of 'supplément' is more easily comprehensible within a literary context than in a discussion of nature and education. The sense of plenitude experienced by a reader of a literary text after a successful actualization of the text is perfectly reconcilable with the notions of successive actualizations being equally or more complete. We may say that our whole conception of literature as an institution depends on a sense of renewal in reading a text, by the same reader, and ultimately by different generations.[45]

One problematic consequence arises if we seek theoretical support for our argument in Derrida's concept of 'supplément.' In his analysis of nature and education, nature becomes the prior term, which in turn means that we must consider analogically the focused text as the prior term. In what sense therefore can we reconcile our previous comments about the priority of the intertext with a theoretical position which reverses that order? I believe that there are two ways of resolving this problem. The first is to suggest that there is a sort of ongoing dialectical order established by the reading process. We begin by attempting to interpret a text by treating it as a gestalt bringing words' normal associations to bear on those forged by a text, to establish some form of intratextual reading. At a second stage intertextual connections are made on the basis of initial engagement with the text and lead to a selection of pertinent intertexts. It is at this stage that the selected intertexts form the necessary ground in terms of which the focused text is read as figure. In this sense, then, we can argue that both text and intertext establish priority at different stages of the reading process.

The weakness of the above argument is that it tends to bring a temporal dimension back into the notion of priority, which ultimately raises as many problems as it resolves. Moreover, I am not sure that such an argument would successfully counter the objection that what I am describing is no more than another version of aleatory intertextuality, and to defend myself I would have to define the term *pertinent* in a way which disengaged it from the reader's whim and made it justifiable in terms of textual constraints.

My second argument, therefore, while approaching the problem somewhat differently, actually addresses the question of pertinence. To do this we must return to a consideration of presuppositions. If I say 'Pay me extra and I'll take on the job,' my interlocutor would have every right to assume that I meant also: 'If you don't pay me extra, I won't take on the job.' If this were not the correct implication to be drawn from my statement, my interlocutor would have every right to expect me to make this clear in a supplementary statement. Should the extra pay not materialize, I could always still claim that what I meant, by my original statement, was that paying me extra would secure my agreement immediately but did not categorically rule out my intended meaning; that, even without the extra pay, I was willing, though less enthusiastically perhaps, to make myself available. The implication drawn by my interlocutor is not a presupposition since it is not a *necessary* inference; it is not an inference which is intended but one assumed and supplied by my interlocutor. Thus, in a communicatory circuit, while a presupposition assumes a prior order to the focal point of an utterance by establishing a prior condition for its validity, an implication, being an inference supplied by an interlocutor and not a necessary part of the linguistic component of the utterance, comes afterwards. It is, in short, of a 'supplementary' nature.

In the context of an argument attempting to establish 'plausible' inter-textuality, the choice of intertext must be viewed as an implication rather than a presupposition. In other words, as a result of my intratextual interpretation of the text, I infer from it a *pertinent* intertext, that is one which I select from my repertoire and which seems to address itself to the interpretational problems which I have encountered. My selection is not a personal whim but one imposed to some degree (like an implication) by certain constraints of the text. In this sense my engagement with the text is prior to my selection of an intertext. The choice of an intertext functions as a supplement brought by the reader to facilitate additional meanings of the text, to which the text lends itself.

Of crucial importance, at this stage of the argument, is whether we are able to distinguish between the implications of an utterance and those interpretations of it which depend wholly on the context in which it is voiced. If when I say 'Pay me extra and I'll take the job' I mean 'If you don't pay me I'll join the opposition to ensure your downfall' only the context would ensure that the utterance is understood in this way. I am arguing here that a fundamental difference exists between an assumption which is inferable from the semantic content of an utterance and presumes normative conditions, and one which is totally unable to be inferred, except in the exceptional circumstances in which a specific speaker and interlocutor are able to generate other meanings pertinent only to them and to their context. If the distinction I have attempted to establish here is valid, then I believe it provides a theoretical basis for distinguishing a plausible notion of intertextuality (on the basis of implication) and an aleatory one which is wholly dependent on private and personal associations of a particular reader.

Does reconstituting the notion of intertextuality in terms of implication invite us to finally cut the umbilical cord linking us to one based on presupposition? I would suggest that, both as the heuristic device to analyse texts and as a mode of securing the underpinnings of a theoretical argument, presupposition has, at least in the theory on intertextuality, exhausted its potential. Where presuppositions seem of greatest value, namely in establishing a notion of priority which is neither temporal nor causal, they are not an absolutely necessary argument. One might in fact go as far as to say that, in certain cases, a presuppositional notion of priority constitutes a methodological impediment. The question of priority is after all a logical way of expressing a figure/ground relationship. To see the figure we must have secure ground; thus the security of the ground can be seen to be prior, in a sense, to seeing the figure. If we speak, however, of figure/ground relationships in spatial terms with the framework of a psychology of visual perception from which it originates, we are confronted by the phenomenon of reversibility: figure becomes ground and ground figure. Intertextuality viewed in this light takes on a new sheen. For if we speak literally of a focused text, we must envisage a reversal between figure and ground, between text and intertext as we reverse focus. The reversibility of figure/ground relationships in perception, we are told, is caused by perceptual fatigue on the part of the perceiver. Saturated with a static image, the human mind creates reversals to alleviate the perceptual fatigue. It would seem that we are not yet too fatigued to cease reading *Ulysses* in terms of the *Odyssey* and there are few readings which would reverse the figure/ground relationship of chronological order traditionally imposed on these texts. Thus we betray our unconscious reluctance to sally out from secure ground on which source-influence studies have left us. But a theory of intertextuality which would accept the full implications of the reversibility of focused text and intertext would challenge us to a great number of re-evaluations of the canon. It could equally lead us to think the problem of intertextual identity in more radical terms, and perhaps begin talking of intertextual alterity. We would thus be returning to Bakhtin's 'dialogical principle,' which inspired Kristeva in her initial formulations of the notion of intertextuality.[46] Here intertextuality would truly be seen as a relational concept, not a monologue but a dialogue, not a solo but a duet.

NOTES

1 Michael Riffaterre, 'Syllepsis,' *Critical Inquiry*, 6:4 (Summer 1980), 625.
2 See Richard Garner, '"Presupposition" in Philosophy and Linguistics,' in *Studies in Linguistic Semantics*, ed. Charles J. Fillmore and D. Terence Langendoen, New York 1971, pp. 23–42.
3 See Oswald Ducrot, *Dire et ne pas dire: principes de sémantique linguistique*, Paris 1972.
4 Roland Barthes, *S/Z* Paris 1970, pp. 16–17.
5 The use of this term is my own. Its particular relevance will become evident in terms of the notion of figure/ground relationships developed at the end of the study.
6 I have borrowed this term from Riffaterre, who uses it throughout his various studies of intertextuality. See specifically 'La Trace de l'intertexte,' *La Pensée*, 215 (October 1980), 4–18 and 'L'Intertexte inconnu,' *Littérature*, 41 (1981), 4–7. In its English version however, I have given it a plural, 'intertexts' to refer to several individual texts, while at the same time retaining the singular for those occasions when the term is ambiguously singular or plural. In earlier studies – e.g. Laurent Jenny, 'La stratégie de la forme,' *Poétique*, 27 (1976) 276 – some critics tended to use the term 'intertext' to refer to the focused text. Since Riffaterre's studies have gained currency as major statements on the question of intertextuality, usage has tended to solidify around his meaning of 'intertexte.'
7 See particularly the important contributions of Linda Hutcheon, 'Ironie, et parodie: stratégie et structure,' *Poétique*, 36 (1978), 467–77 and 'Ironie, satire, parodie,' *Poétique*, 46 (1981), 140–55.
8 Laurent Jenny, 'La Stratégie de la forme,' *Poétique*, 27 (1976), 257.
9 Northrop Frye, *A Study of English Romanticism*, New York, 1968, p. 5.

10 Michael Riffaterre, *La Production du texte*, Paris 1979, p. 8.
11 See Wylie Sypher, *Loss of Self in Modern Literature and Art*, New York 1962, pp. 19–41.
12 See Jonathan Culler's discussion of this notion with respect to Derrida in *Structuralism and Since: From Lévi-Strauss to Derrida*, ed. John Sturrock, Oxford 1979, p. 166.
13 Jonathan Culler, 'Presupposition and Intertextuality,' *MLN*, 91:6 (December 1976), 1383.
14 Ibid., p. 1382.
15 Roland Barthes, 'De l'œuvre au texte,' *Revue d'Esthétique*, 24 (1971), 229.
16 The use of the term 'work' instead of 'text' betrays no ideological intention but is used occasionally in this paper to provide lexical relief for the omnipresent 'text.'
17 Culler, 'Presupposition and Intertextuality,' p. 1388.
18 Julia Kristeva's seminal studies on intertextuality are to be found in 'Problèmes de la structuration du texte,' in *Théorie d'ensemble*, Paris 1968, *Semiotikè: recherches pour une sémanalyse*, Paris 1969, *La Révolution du langage poétique*, Paris 1974. As Culler notes in his critique of Kristeva, her actual textual analyses reveal a far less radical view than her theoretical comments might suppose. Indeed, as he notes, she speaks explicitly of tracking down sources.
19 Edward L. Keenan, 'Two Kinds of Presupposition in Natural Language,' in *Studies in Linguistic Semantics*, ed. Charles J. Fillmore and D. Terence Langendoen, New York 1971, p. 49.
20 Culler, 'Presupposition and Intertextuality,' p. 1394.
21 Ibid., p. 1394.
22 Ibid., p. 1382.
23 This seems to me clear in the following statement: 'To talk about similarities and differences between particular texts is a perfectly valid and interesting pursuit but it is not in itself a contribution to the study of intertextuality' (ibid., p. 1395). In addition, Culler's comments on Harold Bloom's 'anxiety of influence' tend to confirm my conclusions about his position.
24 I have adapted the teleological/operational distinction from Tzvetan Todorov, *Symbolisme et interprétation*, Paris 1978, pp. 159–61. Applied to intertextuality, an operational approach implies constraints on the nature of operations linking focused text and intertext (as, for example, do most of the approaches which use presuppositional theory). In such a model, the intertext is designated by features of the focused text (e.g. Riffaterre's 'trace' or Culler's use of the inferential quality of presuppositions). A teleological approach implies constraints on the specific choice of intertext. Certain models present a combination of these features (constraints on procedures and constraints on intertext). This would include source-influence studies but also Riffaterre's notion of obligatory intertextuality.
25 'Les Bijoux' appeared in 1883, 'La Parure' in 1884, and 'Paste' in 1922. The inadequacy

of source-influence studies is nowhere more amply revealed than in attempts to show that 'La Parure' (an acknowledged source) or 'Les Bijoux' (an unacknowledged source) are essential to the identity of Henry James's 'Paste.' In fact one is faced with the absurd situation, in the critical literature dealing with 'Paste,' that it is far easier to prove authorial intentionality with the unacknowledged source than to demonstrate it from the acknowledged one. The absurdity is compounded because James indicates very rarely in the prefaces that other literary texts are his sources. Thus one would tend to attribute some importance to his reference to 'La Parure' in the preface to *The Author of Beltraffio* (collected in *The Art of the Novel: Critical Prefaces by Henry James*, introduced by Richard P. Blackmur, New York 1953, p. 237). 'The origin of "Paste" was to consist but of the ingenious thought of transposing the terms of one of Guy de Maupassant's admirable contes ... It seemed harmless sport simply to turn the situation around – to shift, in other words, the ground of the horrible mistake, making this a matter not of false treasure supposed to be true and precious, but of a real treasure supposed to be false and hollow.' What James fails to mention is that 'La Parure' is itself a transformation of 'Les Bijoux,' which Maupassant had written a year earlier. Moreover juxtaposing either 'La Parure' or 'Les Bijoux' with 'Paste' in the traditional source-influence manner is not a particularly productive enterprise. James's claim that 'Paste' is an inverted structuring of 'La Parure' proves such a totally inadequate way of approaching 'Paste' that no critic has thought it worth while to pursue the comparison. While there are several points of comparison between 'Les Bijoux' and James's story, one is obliged to compare what is distinctly subordinate in the former to what is central in the latter. To deal adequately with the intertextual relationships between the Maupassant texts and 'Paste' would require a far different approach from that which source-studies have provided.

26 I have expressly used a commercial vocabulary to describe what happens in source-influence studies in order to indicate what seems to me to be its basic ideological underpinnings. Laurent Jenny has commented on how the French terms describing these studies are very much based on aquatic and liquid images. See 'La Stratégie de la forme,' p. 261.

27 The term is very much a feature of all of Ricardou's writings but in his *Nouveaux problèmes du roman*, Paris 1978, it is stated very cogently: 'L'idéologie qui actuellement domine, et notamment dans le secteur de la littérature, ressortit à ce que nous nommons le dogme de l'Expression et de la Représentation. Elle consiste en le credo suivant: toujours, à la base du texte, comme la condition de sa possibilité, doit, dans un premier temps, nécessairement gésir *quelque chose à dire*. Ou, plus précisément, ce que nous nommons un *sens institué*. Ensuite, dans un second temps, peut s'accomplir l'acte d'écrire qui ne saurait se concevoir autrement que comme la *manifestation du sens institué* ... si le sens institué concerne des aspects du Moi, le

manifestation est habituellement nommée une *expression*: si le sens institué concerne des aspects du Monde, la manifestation est communément nommée une *représentation'* (pp. 15–16).

28 Michael Riffaterre, 'La trace de l'intertexte,' *La Pensée*, no. 215 (October 1980), 4.

29 It is difficult to envisage, from Riffaterre's own examples of obligatory intertextuality, how it could be otherwise. Thus another constraint of the obligatory version (not mentioned by Riffaterre) is that of a chronologically prior intertext. The notion of an intertext which chronologically follows the focused text would seem, by definition, to belong to the aleatory category, discussed in the next section. Culler's constant references to the term 'prior' clearly indicate the chronological nature of his view of intertextual relationships.

30 See Paul Ricoeur's distinction between interpretation as 'recollection of meaning' and as 'exercise of suspicion' in *Freud and Philosophy: An Essay in Interpretation*, New Haven 1970, pp. 20–36.

31 See note 7.

32 See Searle's comment, in 'The Logic of Fictional Discourse,' *New Literary History*, 6:2 (Winter 1975), 319–32, that 'it is absurd to suppose a critic can completely ignore the intentions of the author, since so much as to identify a text as a novel, a poem or even as a text is already to make some claim about the author's intentions' (p 325); and his specific reference to Nabokov's parodic misquoting (in *Ada*) of Tolstoy as an example of utterances which cannot be conceived as fictional even though they appear in a fictional text. The ironic feature of Searle's position is that he is not arguing the Nabokov example as a case of authorial intention so much as he is using it to establish the very validity of authorial intention as a concept itself. If this is the case, then it would seem that the ideology of 'Expression' is not as dominant as Ricardou (see note 27) would have us believe.

33 Tzvetan Todorov, 'Poétique,' in *Qu'est-ce que le structuralisme?*, ed. F. Wahl, Paris 1968, p. 153.

34 Tzvetan Todorov, *Qu'est-ce que le structuralisme?, 2: Poétique*, Coll. Points, no. 45, Paris 1968, p. 193. Although the date of the original publication is retained for this single-volume edition, the actual text is a considerable reworking of the original one and appeared in 1973. One of the elements reworked is precisely this problem of intertextuality. It is significant, however, that here Todorov accepts fully the implications of authorial intentionality and originality which a citational mode implies. See also his more extended treatment of intertextuality in *Symbolisme et interprétation*, pp. 57–65.

35 This problem is raised, in passing, by Riffaterre in 'La Trace de l'intertexte,' p. 5.

36 T. S. Eliot, *After Strange Gods: A Primer of Modern Heresy*, London 1933, p. 35.

37 I am not suggesting of course that no figure/ground relation is in play here. Obviously the question of moral implications *is* a ground for the discussion of the

three texts which function as figures. What I am contending is that, in Eliot's consideration of the three texts, no one functions as a figure for the other two.

38 A full discussion of presupposition as a 'condition of usage' is to be found in Oswald Ducrot, *Dire et ne pas dire*, Paris 1972, pp. 26–62.

39 Riffaterre, 'La trace de l'intertexte,' p. 9.

40 As well as the publications mentioned elsewhere in this paper, see also an important aspect of Riffaterre's theory in 'Sémiotique intertextuelle: l'interprétant,' *Revue d'Esthétique*, 1/2 (1979), 128–50. In this study, Riffaterre makes use of Peirce's notion of 'interpretant' to suggest that certain texts (themselves, in a sense, intertexts) play a mediating role between a focused text and the intertext proper in order to resolve the particular problem of unintelligibility left by the trace.

41 For the *Odyssey* to be an intertext for *Ulysses*, it would be necessary to show that certain unresolved problems of unintelligibility in the latter are resolved by the former.

42 Riffaterre's examples are by and large drawn from poetic discourses and the very constrained nature of his model (the examples he gives are limited to very specific problems of the meanings of words) makes it difficult to see how it could address the larger interpretational problems which link a text like *Ulysses* to the *Odyssey* or how it would be conceivable to envisage intertextuality functioning across linguistic and cultural boundaries.

43 In a recent article, 'Syllepsis' (cited in note 1), pp. 625–38, by introducing the notion of undecidability, Riffaterre comes part of the way towards addressing these problems, but his notion of the intertext as a *necessary* element to complete what is basically incomplete remains. Thus his notion of undecidability still remains closer to that of unintelligibility than is consistent with the position I am advocating.

44 Jonathan Culler, 'Derrida,' in *Structuralism and Since: From Lévi-Strauss to Derrida*, ed. John Sturrock, Oxford 1979, p. 168.

45 Riffaterre's notion of obligatory intertextuality clearly implies that, on a cognitive level, the text is incomplete. See 'Syllepsis,' p. 627: 'Intertextual connection takes place when attention is triggered by … intratextual anomalies … in short, ungrammaticalities within the idiolect norm … which are traces left by the absent intertext, *signs of an incompleteness to be completed elsewhere.*' The italics are mine.

46 For a discussion of Kristeva's 'debt' to Bakhtin, see Smaranda Vultur, 'Situer l'intertextualite,' *Cahiers roumains d'études littéraires*, 3 (1981), 32–3.

PETER W. NESSELROTH

Literary Identity and Contextual Difference

In recent years, critics have questioned the old assumption that literary language, and especially poetic language, is different from ordinary language.[1] They claim that, when perceived in the proper way, ordinary language displays the same features as the language of literature. Stanley Fish, for example, argues that the formal characteristics by which we identify literature are foregrounded only when 'an interpretive community' applies to a given text a set of a priori conventions which will then *make it* a literary text. It is the reader who creates the poem, and not some immutable feature of the text. Thus, in a chapter entitled 'How to recognize a poem when you see one,' Fish tells us that he had left an assignment for a course in stylistics on the blackboard, and then told a class on seventeenth-century English religious poetry that it was a poem. The assignment read as follows:

Jacobs – Rosenbaum
Levin
Thorne
Hayes
Ohman?

It did not surprise Fish, nor would it anyone else, that the experiment was successful, since most of the names (Jacobs, Rosenbaum, Thorne, Ohman) have biblical connotations. Fish remains strangely silent about Hayes, although at one point he promises an explanation for it. The answer to the question of how we recognize a poem when we see one is not the 'common sense one of many literary critics and linguists,' i.e. 'the observable presence of distinguishing features': 'My students did not proceed from the noting of distinguishing features to the act of recognition that they were confronted by a poem; rather, it was the act of recognition that came first –they knew in advance that they were dealing with a poem – and the distinguishing features then followed.'[2] This seems to be a rather circular argument, for it was precisely the fact that the students were told that this text was a poem, both by the professor and by the vertical disposition of the names on the blackboard, with the compounding of the first two names resembling a title. For Western readers, these are all distinguishing features of poems. We know, at least since Dada, that it suffices to arrange random words in a poetic order to 'create a poem' (in Fish's sense of that expression, i.e. to make readers read it as such). It might not have been so easy if the names had been disposed horizontally, as a prose sequence; the list would not even have been long enough to make it appear as a prose poem. Although I do not completely disagree with Fish's position (I will try to show something analogous occurring with an Apollinaire poem), my point is that the framework of the argument has to be much broader, that the difference is not between ordinary *language* and literary *language* but between everyday *communication* and literary *communication*, and communication involves semiotic systems other than verbal language. This is a fact which Jan Mukařovsky had underlined as early as 1938.[3] If the experiment had been aural rather than visual, if the problem had been 'How to recognize a poem when you *hear* one,' Fish would have had much more difficulty in belittling the distinguishing features. When a poem (in the broadest sense, including nursery rhymes, political slogans, commercials, etc., as well as the 'higher' genres) is transmitted orally, Jakobson's poetic function will be dominant and attention will be focused on the form of the message. The poetic function does 'project the principle of equivalence from the axis of selection onto the axis of combination,'[4] there is a formal difference between 'I like Ike' and 'Vote for Eisenhower' or between 'Birds of a feather flock together' and, say, 'People who have similar shortcomings tend to associate with each other.' Those who, like Fish and Culler, claim that you can find equivalences just about anywhere if you look for them, can only prove it through written texts.[5] Although I seem to be defending the inherent difference of literary utterances, I am actually only putting into question the opposite argument, i.e. that either there is no difference or that the differences are simply a matter of perception. I would suggest, rather, that the concept of immanent difference is insufficient to explain literariness because it explains only the functioning of certain types of texts: those that are strongly marked by equivalences, parallel structures, and oppositions. The same reservation would apply to the criterion of indirection, as proposed by Riffaterre ('literariness transforms the obvious into the devious'; 'A poem says one thing and means another'), for there is no reason to assume that a poem had to say something indirectly, that it cannot mean what it says.[6] Indeed, the most hermetic poems are not the most difficult to interpret, since they will automatically require an explanation, while those which seem to say it all leave us speechless. My concern is with the literary status of *indifferent* utterances, utterances that *do not* project the principle of equivalence from the paradigmatic into the syntagmatic axes. What, in short, is the status of prosaic statement such as 'People with similar shortcomings tend to associate with each other'? This is, after all, the type of sentences that occurs with great frequency in literary discourse, especially in realistic genres. It is not merely a question of the function such sentences may have as negative or positive poles in a system of binary oppositions, a function which would allow the most banal of statements to appear as poetic, but of a discourse without any perceivable contrast, without unpredictability along the syntagmatic chain. The contrast may exist, of course, but beyond the limits of the utterance itself, with respect to literary (generic) categories rather than linguistic ones. For, if in oral communication the meaning of the message depends not only on its verbal components but also on the presence of the speaking subject and on the situation of the interlocutors, the written message depends on its framing, i.e. non-verbal context, title, signature, etc. This explains why two verbally identical texts can have completely different meanings when they are framed differently. The change is illustrated in the Borges fiction where Pierre Ménard, a nineteenth-century French Symbolist, decides to rewrite *Don Quixote* without actually copying Cervantes' novel, but by recreating the mental conditions of its production. Ménard does indeed reproduce a section of the work, and it is exactly the same as the original, although, as Borges tells it, Ménard's work is 'almost infinitely richer.' Written by a contemporary of Valéry and of William James, it has a completely different impact and effect.[7] Far from being only an expression of Borges' playfulness, we find in actual literary practice many examples of semantic shifts due to diachronic changes or to contextual transpositions. André Breton's poem *PSTT*, for instance, seems to reproduce the page of the Paris telephone directory where his name is listed.[8] Through its inclusion in a collection of poems, the reader is forced to seek out the features that make it an artistic composition, such as the name Breton as an invariant of the poem and the added signature (Breton, André) whose inversion parodies the style of the listings and, simultaneously, marks it as an original artistic creation. Or, less obviously, Lautréamont's plagiarisms from encyclopaedias of natural history, which are so well integrated into the narrative of *Les Chants de Maldoror* that, until fairly recently, they had not even been noticed. Yet they are sufficiently marked to have prompted a number of suspicious scholars to seek out their sources.[9]

Guillaume Apollinaire's calligram, *Lundi rue Christine*, uses a composition technique similar to plagiarism by borrowing, not from a specific source but from an anonymous collectivity, fragments of conversation overhead in a café, and mixing these with comments on the décor. They seem to be quotations without quotation marks, cut off from their speakers, as they would be perceived in the din of a Parisian brasserie:

Lundi rue Christine

1. La mère de la concierge et la concierge laisseront tout passer
2. Si tu es un homme tu m'accompagneras ce soir
3. Il suffirait qu'un type maintînt la porte cochère
4. Pendant que l'autre monterait.

5. Trois becs de gaz allumés
6. La patronne est poitrinaire
7. Quand tu auras fini nous jouerons une partie de jacquet
8. Un chef d'orchestre qui a mal à la gorge
9. Quand tu viendras à Tunis je te ferai fumer du kief

10. Ça a l'air de rimer

11. Des piles de soucoupes des fleurs un calendrier
12. Pim pam pim
13. Je dois fiche près de 300 francs à ma probloque
14. Je préférerais me couper le parfaitement que de les lui donner

15. Je partirai à 20 h. 27
16. Six glaces s'y dévisagent toujours
17. Je crois que nous allons nous embrouiller encore davantage

18. Cher monsieur
19. Vous êtes un mec à la mie de pain
20. Cette dame a le nez comme un ver solitaire
21. Louise a oublié sa fourrure
22. Moi je n'ai pas de fourrure et je n'ai pas froid
23. Le Danois fume sa cigarette en consultant l'horaire
24. Le chat noir traverse la brasserie

25. Ces crêpes étaient exquises
26. La fontaine coule
27. Robe noire comme ses ongles
28. C'est complètement impossible

29. Voici monsieur
30. La bague en malachite
31. Le sol est semé de sciure
32. Alors c'est vrai
33. la serveuse rousse a été enlevée par un libraire

34. Un journaliste que je connais d'ailleurs très vaguement

35. Ecoute Jacques c'est très sérieux ce que je vais te dire

36. Compagnie de navigation mixte

37. Il me dit monsieur voulez-vous voir ce que je peux faire d'eaux-fortes et de tableaux
38. Je n'ai qu'une petite bonne

39. Après déjeuner café du Luxembourg

40. Une fois là il me présente un gros bonhomme
41. Qui me dit
42. Ecoutez c'est charmant
43. A Smyrne à Naples en Tunisie
44. Mais nom de Dieu où est-ce
45. La dernière fois que j'ai été en Chine
46. C'est il y a huit ou neuf ans
47. L'Honneur tient souvent à l'heure que marque la pendule
48. La quinte major[10]

Here is Anne Hyde Greet's translation:

Monday in Christine Street

The concierge's mother and the concierge will let everyone through
if you're a man you'll come with me tonight
All we need is one guy to watch the main entrance
While the other goes upstairs

Three gas burners lit
The proprietress is consumptive
When you've finished we'll play a game of backgammon
An orchestra leader who has a sore throat
When you come through Tunis we'll smoke some hashish

That almost rhymes

Piles of saucers flowers a calendar
Bing bang bong
I owe damn almost 300 francs to my landlady
I'd rather cut off you know what than give them to her

I'm leaving at 8:27 P.M.
Six mirrors keep staring at one another
I think we're going to get into an even worse mess
Dear Sir
You are a crummy fellow
That dame has a nose like a tapeworm
Louise forgot her fur piece
Well I don't have a fur piece and I'm not cold
The Dane is smoking his cigarette while he consults the schedule
The black cat crosses the restaurant

Those pancakes were divine
The water's running
Dress black as her nails
It's absolutely impossible
Here sir
The malachite ring
The ground is covered with sawdust
Then it's true
The redhead waitress eloped with a bookseller

A journalist whom I really hardly know

Look Jacques it's extremely serious what I'm going to tell you

Shipping company combine

He says to me sir would you care to see what I can do in etchings and pictures
All I have is a little maid

After lunch at the Café du Luxembourg
When we get there he introduces me to a big fellow
Who says to me

Look that's charming
In Smyrna in Naples in Tunisia
But in God's name where is it ·
The last time I was in China
That was eight or nine years ago
Honor often depends on the time of day
The winning hand[11]

There are no problems of comprehension in this poem, at least not as far as each sentence or phrase is concerned. Only line 48 ('La Quinte major') is slightly unclear. Nor is the syntax particularly difficult. Yet it is the very simplicity of the components which disturbs its readers, almost as much as if it were Mallarmé, to the point of blocking interpretation. Here is Lagarde and Michard (the standard textbook for French literary education, the equivalent of the *Norton Anthology*): '*Ondes* groupe les textes des années 1913–1914. On y trouve les premiers "poèmes-conversations" qui, à l'époque, ont gravé la légende d'un Apollinaire mystificateur. Par exemple, *Lundi rue Christine*, fait de bribes de dialogue saisies dans la rumeur d'un café. Plus riches en conséquences sont les poèmes comme *Les Fenêtres* ...'[12] It is obvious that the mystification is produced by both the banality of the utterances and the absence of narrative continuity. Except for the first four lines, which seem to initiate a gangster novel, and the bit of gossip in lines 32–3 ('Alors c'est vrai / La serveuse rousse a été enlevée par un libraire') with its implicit melodrama, there are no stories. The easiest solution to the so-called mystery of the poem is, as usual, an appeal to authenticity. Jacques Dyssord, a friend of the poet, was there and tells us all about it: 'Le dernier souvenir que j'ai conservé de nos réunions avec Madsen et Apollinaire est celui d'une soirée passée vers la fin de 1913, dans un petit café découvert rue Christine par ce dernier. Je devais partir pour Tunis, le lendemain, et faisais mes adieux à mes amis. Nous étions les seuls clients de ce petit café, ce soir-là. Une servante aux cheveux de flamme, la figure semée de taches de son, nous servit des alcools, dans une salle noyée dans une lumière d'aquarium. Les propos que nous échangeâmes, vous les retrouverez dans un des plus beaux poèmes d'Apollinaire, écrit là, au courant du crayon, sur le bord d'une table. Avec leur point d'orgue, ils se prolongent tels quels, dans une sorte de clair de lune intérieur.'[13]

The poem is thus merely a realistic transcription of what could be heard and seen on a certain evening in a certain place.

A less naïve reading of this text is Philippe Renaud's in a chapter revealingly entitled 'Un nouvel état de la parole.'[14] It is less naïve because it attempts to pass from the literal to the literary, to 'make the poem' as Fish would say. I shall quote him at length, not to mock him, since his reading is both possible and plausible, but because it brings out the difficulty of interpreting a text that seems to say no more than what it says. About lines 25–8, ('Ces crêpes étaient exquises / La fontaine coule / Robe noire comme ses ongles / C'est complètement impossible'), Renaud writes the following:

Ce très court fragment est un monde d'indétermination: les possibilités de lecture sont très nombreuses et l'on a l'impression d'entrer dans le domaine mathématique des combinaisons et arrangements. Examinons l'hypothèse généralement admise, qui veut que la 'scène' se déroule dans une brasserie de la rue Christine, *ce qui est déjà une interprétation*: les choses ne sont pas simples pour autant. Le vers 25 peut être le propos d'un quidam, ou d'un compagnon d'Apollinaire, ou d'Apollinaire. Mais il peut aussi être une réflexion mentale de ce dernier. En fait, il en va de même des quatre vers. Ce qui paraît le plus plausible, c'est que le vers 25 est une remarque orale, que le vers 26 est une 'notation de décor' (Apollinaire voyant une fontaine de l'endroit où il est), est saisi au vol, et que le dernier est à nouveau une phrase entendue. Mais toute ces hypothèses sont discutables. A cela s'ajoute un effet singulier: en lisant:

La fontaine coule
Robe noire comme ses ongles

on peut se laisser prendre à l'impression que ces deux vers forment un tout, ce à quoi invite le rythme. Alors *robe noire* devient une apposition à *fontaine*, et l'on se trouve devant une métaphore étrange et fort belle, de type surréaliste. L'eau nocturne (c'est le soir puisque *trois becs de gaz* sont allumés), cette eau sombre et soyeuse est une robe fascinante, couleur d'ongles laqués de noir et semblables à des élytres d'insectes rares. Si l'on s'abandonne à cette image, on entre dans un climat de rêve d'où le vers 28 vous tire avec un réalisme froid, assez brutal, quelque chose comme: 'Mais vous rêvez, c'est complètement impossible!' La fonction de ce vers donc totalement changée, et avec elle, son ton.[15]

It is but a short step from a dream, induced by the surrealist image, to erotic fantasies, due I suppose to the well-known relationships of artists with their maids:

On peut de même rêver longuement aux sollicitations diverses qu'exercent sur l'esprit les vers 37 et 38:

Il me dit monsieur voulez-vous voir ce que je peux faire d'eaux-fortes et de tableaux
Je n'ai qu'une petite bonne

Pour nous, ces deux vers ont un curieux climat érotique mais qu'en sera-t-il pour d'autres lecteurs? L'interprétation de ce poème pourrait bien être révélatrice de l'inconscient du lecteur à un titre voisin de celle du test de Rorschach ... ou des objets bouleversants des surréalistes. Et ceci découvre un fait important: c'est le lecteur qui donne au poème un sens, ou qui, du moins, oriente ses éléments comme l'aimant la limaille de fer. Mais il ne peut être question de lui conférer ainsi un sens 'objectif,' valable pour tous, ni même un sens valable définitivement pour un seul lecteur.[16]

In fact, we might add that not only does the interpretation make the poem but that given any kind of indeterminacy or indecidability it will produce an erotic poem. Anne Hyde Greet elaborates on Renaud: 'Invitations to inspect engravings and paintings are notorious for the double meaning they frequently have.'[17] And Raymond Jean sees in line 5 ('Trois becs de gaz allumés') a reference to the 'seamy side of life' décor of the café.[18] That is in line with Michael Benedict, one of the English translators of the poem, who writes that 'The final phrase "la quinte major" is also slang for syphilis, a reference of course not foreign to this poem.'[19] This brings me to the only word in the poem whose meaning is not evident, simply because it contains an ungrammaticality. It is 'quinte major' rather than 'quinte majeure.' But this ungrammaticality facilitates the exegetical commentary: 'La *Quinte major*,' says Renaud, 'qui paraît dénué de sens et opaque si l'on ignore que dans certains jeux de cartes on appelle ainsi cinq cartes qui se suivent; mais dans ce cas, Apollinaire a glissé un écran supplémentaire en usant de *major*, forme vieillie de majeure.'[20] As could be expected, Renaud then goes on to suggest that the disposition of the lines and the stanzas can be compared to card configurations in fortune-telling: 'A propos de *Lundi rue Christine*, on peut encore établir une relation entre ce poème et la cartomancie; le dernier vers La Quinte major appartient au vocabulaire des jeux de cartes; rien ne s'oppose à ce qu'on pense que ces mots sont bien à leur place dans une brasserie; mais pourquoi alors ce *major* archaïque? On dirait qu'Apollinaire a voulu, par cet archaïsme, attirer l'attention sur ce vers et conférer à ces mots une dignité tranchant sur le reste du poème, une sorte de sollenité. Il serait assez curieux de comparer les strophes et les vers isolés de *Lundi rue Christine* à des cartes distribuées au hasard mais dont l'ensemble et les rapports mystérieux figureraient les "signes" d'une destinée.'[21]

It is quite true that *quinte major* is the archaic form of the card-hand *quinte majeure*. It appears as such in Molière.[22] But *quinte major* still existed at the beginning of the twentieth century and meant 'une bonne raclée,' a slap or a good licking, and this meaning would certainly also make sense in a French café, around 1913, with children being told to behave, or it could refer to *L'Honneur* of the preceding line.[23] I propose this, not as my own interpretation, but to increase the possibilities, to open up the work a little further ...

The difficulties that arise when critics attempt to assign a meaning to a text of this type stem from a confusion of two different semantic aspects: *meaning* and *significance*. This distinction was first used by E.D. Hirsch in *Validity in Interpretation*. For Hirsch, *meaning* is what a text meant originally, what the author intended it to mean, and *significance* what a text has meant subsequently, to later generations of readers.[24] I would bring at least one modification to this opposition: meaning is not what the author meant (although Hirsch makes a valiant attempt to defend the intentional fallacy) but rather the *literal* meaning which a statement or textual fragment has in its initial generic and cultural context. *Significance* is, then, what a text would mean in other historical periods, as a consequence of the reader's cultural evolution, or when it is *in a different verbal or situational context*. This is closer to Riffaterre's linking of the distinction to the two stages of interpretation: the heuristic and the hermeneutic. During the first, *meaning* is apprehended, ungrammaticalities noticed and rationalized (for example, understanding that a word is used metaphorically or metonymically instead of literally). *Meaning* is the 'information conveyed by the text at the mimetic level.' *Significance* occurs during retroactive reading, when what is being read is modified by what has been read before. The reader thus becomes aware of the 'formal and semantic unity, which includes all the indices of indirection' and when he perceives the text as one autonomous sign. 'From the standpoint of meaning' writes Riffaterre, 'the text is a string of successive information units. From the standpoint of significance the text is one semantic unit.'[25] I would, however, consider the constitution of the text into an autonomous sign as a step onto another level of interpretation, which could be called *the meaning of the form*. For a sign is never really 'autonomous,' since it enters into a system of relationships with other signs. A poem has a global meaning (the signified of the text as sign) and, like words within the linguistic system, it has a certain value within the whole system of poetry and of literature. *Lundi rue Christine*, for example, is one text within a group of poems, 'Ondes,' within a volume *Calligrammes*, a genre like *Méditations* or *Illuminations*.[26] Now, one of the formal characteristics of a calligram is fragmentation. We normally think of this feature as being purely typographical: words, syllables, and letters are so disposed as to make the text a pictorial representation of the topic, a *poème-peinture*. This is the case with the most famous of Apollinaire's calligrams, such as 'La Cravate et la Montre' (The Tie and the Watch) or 'Il pleut' (It is raining). In these poems, typography itself becomes the instrument for reducing the arbitrariness of the textual sign. But *Lundi rue Christine* stands out in the volume because it does not conform to that model, because its typographical disposition is conventional. How then does it conform to the requirements of the genre? I would suggest that the poem is a *printed sound calligram.* It works in opposition to, for example, the text entitled *lettre-océan* which represents an *explosion* of the phono-graphic material. There, letters and syllables, emanating from an emission centre, the Eiffel Tower, are broadcast visually in all directions. *Lundi rue Christine* is an *implosion* of the sound material of each of the speech utterances. The poetic word in French for *waves* is *ondes*, and in nineteenth-century poetry the word usually refers to water waves. But, as Michel Butor has shown, in the context of *Calligrammes* it means also, and primarily, radio waves.[27] The 'ondes' here are sound waves which can come from everywhere and everyone to meet *Lundi rue Christine*, not that day on that street, but in this poem. The chance encounter may even result in a poetic effect (line 10: 'Ça a l'air de rimer'). The page thus becomes the receiver, in the audio as well as in the literal sense, of messages whose source of transmission is unknown. The poem is the centre of a centripetal method of composition which, because it is inclusive, will, of necessity, produce a discontinuous discourse. The text incorporates into its own body fragments of speech that come from anywhere. Interpretation transforms the discontinuous into the coherent, but it does not 'make the poem.' Literariness is the result of reader/text interaction, it is a bipolar structure in which the text remains the grounded pole. The verbal components of a poem may or may not be different from what we find in ordinary language, but literariness is more than just literary language. It is a specific type of communication, and its analysis cannot ignore the contextual frame which defines it. The reading of *Lundi rue Christine* does not begin at the first line, or even with the titles of the section and the volume, but with the name *Guillaume Apollinaire*, whose semantic markers include 'modernism,' 'poet of twentieth-century technology and of a new dawn for mankind,' 'precursor of surrealism,' etc. These markers are, in fact, actualized in a prose poem by André Breton, a poem in the form of a news item headlined *Une maison peu solide* (A house with weak foundations), where a watchman named Guillaume Apollinaire saves, at the cost of his own life, a young child called Lespoir. The latter had almost died when the front of a building constructed in an irrational way (civilization ?) came crumbling down.[28]

The manner in which phrases are used in *Lundi rue Christine* brings out, through narrative discontinuity and through the isolation of each fragment, the literarization process of ordinary language: instead of having a referential function, as such utterances would in everyday communication, they acquire what might be called a *citational value*.[29] The *je* and *tu*, and all the other shifters which normally designate the speakers and their situation, represent in this poem only words that *might be used* in conversation, eclipsing any real or even imaginary referent. It would be wrong to think, however, that such an eclipsing of the referent occurs only in extremely fragmented poems like *Lundi rue Christine*, in texts fabricated with cut-off lines of dialogue and brief scenic descriptions. On the contrary, a literary text (so identified by the formal and cultural indices I mentioned above) automatically eclipses the referentiality of its words, including the shifters. It is not difficult, for example, to imagine famous statements like 'Aujourd'hui, maman est morte,' or 'Longtemps, je me suis couché de bonne heure' as lines in *Lundi rue Christine*. Such sentences guarantee both the 'effect of the real' and the fictionality of a work. They are realistic because they resemble what we say every day and they are fictional because, as statements within the context of literary communication, they are no longer subject to truth conditions. Their mimetic effect is not due to their capacity to refer to the objective world but to their ability to mimic a way of speaking which, because it is *not* different, produces verisimilitude. A text is framed by its title(s), its signature(s), and its disposition on the page, and these formal features, providing a distinguishing context for the verbal sequences, give the text its literary identity.

NOTES

1 In particular, Mary Louise Pratt, *Toward a Speech Act Theory of Literary Discourse*, Bloomington 1977.
2 Stanley Fish, *Is There a Text in This Class?: The Authority of Interpretive Communities*, Cambridge, Mass. 1980, pp. 325–6.
3 'Poetic designation is not, therefore, primarily determined by its relation to the reality signified but by the way in which it is placed in the contexture. This explains the well-known fact that a word or phrase-word which is characteristic of a certain significant poetic work, when transferred from its own contexture to another one, such as a communicative contexture, takes with it the semantic ambience of the work through which it has passed and with which it is connected in the collective consciousness.' Jan Mukařovsky, *The Word and Verbal Art*, trans. John Burbank and Peter Steiner, New Haven 1977, p. 60.
4 Roman Jakobson, 'Closing Statement: Linguistics and Poetics,' in *Style in Language*, ed. T. Sebeok, Cambridge 1960, p. 358.
5 See, for example, Culler's Jakobsonian analysis of a page from Jakobson's *Questions de Poétique* in *Structuralist Poetics*, London 1975, pp. 63–4.
6 Michael Riffaterre, *Semiotics of Poetry*, Bloomington 1978, and *La Production du texte*, Paris 1979. See my review of the two works in *Recherches Sémiotiques/Semiotic Inquiry*, 1:1 (1981), 81–7.
7 Jorge Luis Borges, 'Pierre Ménard, author of the *Quixote*,' in *Labyrinths, Selected Stories and Other Writings*, trans. J.E. Irby, New York 1964. pp. 42–3. On quota-

tions, see Antoine Compagnon, *La Seconde main ou le travail de la citation*, Paris 1979. On Borges, and on this story in particular, see pp. 370–80.

8 André Breton, *Clair de Terre*, Paris 1966, p. 49.

9 For a close analysis of this technique, see my 'Lautréamont's Plagiarisms; or, The Poetization of Prose Texts,' in *Pretext/Text/Context*, ed. R.L. Mitchell, Columbus 1980, pp. 185–95.

10 Guillaume Apollinaire, *Oeuvres poétiques*, ed. M. Adéma and H. Décaudin, Paris 1965, pp. 180–2. Quoted by permission.

11 Guillaume Apollinaire, *Calligrammes: Poems of Peace and War (1913–1916)*, trans. A.H. Greet, Berkley 1980, pp. 52–7. Quoted by permission.

12 Lagarde and Michard, *XXᵉ Siècle*, Paris 1968, p. 50.

13 Quoted in the Pléiade edition, p. 1081.

14 Philippe Renaud, *Lecture d'Apollinaire*, Lausanne 1969, chapter 3, pp. 313–30.

15 Ibid., pp. 316–17.

16 Ibid., p. 317.

17 *Calligrammes*, trans. Greet, p. 380.

18 Raymond Jean, *Lectures du Désir*, Paris 1977, p. 118.

19 Michael Benedict, *The Poetry of Surrealism: An Anthology*, Boston 1974, p. 26.

20 Renaud, *Lecture*, pp. 290–1.

21 Ibid., pp. 329–30.

22 Molière, *Oeuvres Complètes I*, ed. M. Rat, Paris 1959, *Les Fâcheux*, ii, 2, p. 416.

23 Renaud even suggests that line 47 ('L'Honneur tient souvent à l'heure que marque la pendule') could be a reference to a duel which Apollinaire was to fight the next day. *Lecture*, p. 304.

24 E.D. Hirsch, *Validity in Interpretation*, New Haven 1967, pp. 6–10.

25 Michael Riffaterre, *Semiotics of Poetry*, pp. 2–3.

26 The title *Calligrammes* is a neologism derived from *kalos*, meaning 'beautiful,' and *gramma*, 'letters.' It is thus a pedantic word for *belles-lettres*, a cliché which it renews by calling attention to the materiality of literary letters. See Ruth Amossy and Elisheva Rosen, 'Du titre au poème: une expérience surréaliste,' *Revue des sciences humaines*, 44:172 (October–December 1978), 153–71. See also their book *Les Discours du cliché*, Paris 1982, p. 135.

27 See the introduction to the *Poésie*/Gallimard edition of *Calligrammes*, p. 9.

28 Breton, *Clair de Terre*, p. 30.

29 As far as I know, only Richard Ohmann, particularly in 'Speech Acts and the Definition of Literature,' *Philosophy and Rhetoric*, 4 (1971), 1–19, has expressed a similar view of the problem. But the weakness of his approach is that it is grounded in speech-act theory, which is putting the cart before the horse, since we do not know what type of speech acts writing and reading really are. See also Samuel R. Levin, 'The Status of Nondeviant Expressions in Poetry,' in *The Semantics of Metaphor*, Baltimore 1977, pp. 128–31.

MICHAEL RIFFATERRE

The Making of the Text

I propose to attempt to show, in texts whose interpretation is difficult, that there is present a single factor which controls reading. This factor guides the reader to the significance. When substituted for the meanings the text shares with other texts, this significance gives the text its identity.

It is, for instance, hard to imagine a more confused and confusing textual identity than what confronts us in the Rimbaud poem beginning *O saisons, ô châteaux*! Interpretations range wildly: for some the poem is spiritual, mystical; for others it is a piece of erotic verse centred on an obscene *double entendre*. Yet the text's true nature is made clear enough by the hard-core difficulty itself. That is, indeed, this apparent ambiguity that offers two incompatible readings of the whole thing and leads the reader to the pertinent intertext. The intertext, in turn, gives a single, common significance to the separate meanings suggested by the poem's successive distichs.

There are two versions, with little difference between them. The one included in Rimbaud's last verse collection is on the left; the second version, incorporated into *Season in Hell*, is on the right:

O saisons, ô châteaux,
Quelle âme est sans défauts ?

O saisons, ô châteaux,

J'ai fait la magique étude
Du Bonheur, que nul n'élude.

O vive lui, chaque fois
Que chante son coq gaulois.

O saisons, ô châteaux!
Quelle âme est sans défauts?

J'ai fait la magique étude
Du Bonheur, qu'aucun n'élude.

Salut à lui, chaque fois
Que chante le coq gaulois.

Ah! je n'aurai plus d'envie:
Il s'est chargé de ma vie.

Mais! je n'aurai plus d'envie,
Il s'est chargé de ma vie.

Ce Charme! Il prit âme et corps,
Et dispersa tous efforts.

Que comprendre à ma parole?
Il fait qu'elle fuie et vole!

O saisons, ô châteaux!

Ce Charme a pris âme et corps
Et dispersé les efforts

O saisons, ô châteaux!

L'heure de sa fuite, hélas!
Sera l'heure du trépas.

O saisons, ô châteaux!

[O seasons, o castles! What soul is without its flaws? I have made the magical study of Happiness, that none can escape. Hurrah for him, every time his Gallic cock crows! But! I shall have no more desires, he has taken charge of my life. This magic charm! It has seized hold of me body and soul and cast my efforts to the winds. What does this speaking of mine mean! Before the Charm it flees, it flies! O seasons, o castles!]

Instead of the last question, about a meaning that slips away, the second version has a new distich: 'The hour of its flight, alas! will be the hour of death,' where 'its flight' must be referring to the end of happiness, rather than to the speaker's abandonment by the one whose cock crows in the first version.[1]

Most commentators are prone to wax lyrical about the 'climactic quality of this poem ... Rimbaud wants to have it all, eternity, beauty, but, like Macbeth, here upon this bank and shoal of time.' Thus R.G. Cohn, who wants to have it all too, assigning three meanings to the rooster: 'that piercing cock-crow, giving back all of sweet France to the boy waking to delight, also reminds us of the dawn of Christ's agony and the cock-crow which revealed Peter's frailty, original human fallibility and guilt.' John P. Houston would rather see the bird as 'the emblem of the poet's dangerous initiation: Gaul was a country of strange magic rites.' For others this is a poem about divine grace. A more exotic gloss assures us we are hearing of a quest for the wisdom of India.[2]

All of which windy symbolism is neatly deflated by earthy readers who point out that the phrase 'Gallic cock' had a risqué meaning in Rimbaud's native province. Let me add that you do not have to hail from the Belgian border region to detect ribaldry here; and the earlier draft of the poem is even more explicit: 'Every night his Gallic cock ...'[3] So there is no getting around it: you have to interpret the poem as a cynical song of sensual awakening, corresponding to Rimbaud's return to Verlaine's bed and board. Still, the spiritual strain is not to be dismissed, since the introductory paragraph preceding our verse in *Season in Hell* does quote two Latin allusions to the cockcrow of the Gospels, where the bird plainly symbolizes the soul's accession to the Light.

The two readings are thus mutually incompatible, and the text's significance is undecidable.[4] If, that is, the first version is regarded as a draft preparatory to the second, or the second is regarded as a mere quotation of the first (in which case it would be an example, an illustration livening up the prose of *Alchimie du Verbe*). The implied assumption of all commentators has been that this is the alternative.

What I propose instead is that *O saisons, ô châteaux!* actually contains two totally different poems within the same textual space (Rimbaud after all did keep them separate, each being self-sufficient). The reader shifts from one to the other when he receives a signal, the signal being the smallest, weakest, least noticeable unit of meaning in the text.

There are only two points of difference between the two versions: the rewrite of the final distich and the change from 'his Gallic cock' to 'the Gallic cock.' As for the modified distich, it retains an unchanged significance and its interpretation must remain the same in either case: be it question or statement, be it variation on the *verba volant* (*scripta manent*) motif or variation on the mortality theme, in both variants the speaker's poetic vocation or simply his existence expresses the frustration of the 'magique étude du Bonheur.' The change from 'son' to 'le,' on the contrary, affects the interpretation of the whole poem, even though it may seem minor. Its impact, in fact, is all the sharper because its lexical stimulus is so unimportant. Take the possessive, *his* Gallic cock, and the text is obscene; take the definite article, and obscenity vanishes. Because of the discrepancy between the general application of *rooster*, a bird emblematic of a nation, and the exclusive possessiveness of *his*, the humorously lurid meaning obtrudes itself upon our disbelief. Far from blunting recognition, the adjective sharpens it, since we have the myth of Gallic sexual liveliness, and the *esprit gaulois* is a salacious wit.

Should we not assume, then, that 'Gallic' precludes any spiritual reading? I think not, because the article generalizes the meaning of the *coq gaulois* phrase, and this generality permits another marking: the *exemplary*. The Gallic cock becomes an exemplar of the animal, just as the Hyrcanian tiger, in seventeenth-century literary discourse, is the most tigerish of tigers, though not necessarily resident in Asia Minor; just as the polar bear is the hyperbolic bear, the Roman eagle and Apollonian laurel are the eagle and the laurel tree *par excellence*. All this is a matter of convention rather than localization. The stereotyped epithet (dictionaries attach it to 'cock' on the same level as *fier* and *matinal*) is in fact perfect tautology, since the Latin *gallus* means both 'Gallic' and 'cock.' Twice named but with elegant variation[5] through the Latin pun, the cock now has the stature required for its other symbolism: awakening, especially moral awakening (attested in religious contexts ever since the poet Prudentius, and frequently extended to symbolize the Resurrection).

Thus two wholly different significances, two wholly different poems, emerge from the text, depending on whether we read *son* (his) or *le* (the). If the first, humour prevails, and the poem is about our bondage to the flesh, the body's potent but ultimately destructive sorcery. If the definite article is preferred, the tone is serious, introspective, lyrical: the cock-crow is the soaring of the soul at dawn, its blissful self-deliverance from this mortal coil. In the first reading the feathered creature is metaphorical, in the second symbolic. So powerful is this latent symbolism that it justifies *ex post facto* the introductory paragraph in *Season in Hell*:[6]

Le Bonheur! Sa dent, douce à la mort, m'avertissait au chant du coq, — *ad matutinum*, au *Christus venit*, – dans les plus sombres villes.

[Happiness! Its tooth, so sweet it almost makes you die, used to give me warning at cock-crow, – *ad matutinum*, just when they sing the *Christus venit*, – even in the gloomiest towns.]

The two references to Catholic liturgy do not compel a Christian reading of the poem, but they certainly do function as 'mystical' markers for a word already marked as exemplary by 'Gallic.' To sum up: we have a text identically repeated (with minor variants and endings differing but equivalent), yet the two are experiences completely different for the reader. Identical at the level of meaning, the textual reiterations are at variance with each other, indeed opposed to each other, at the level of significance, and they dictate diverging interpretations.

What enables the reader to distinguish between meaning and significance is thus an index so slight that it does not seem to be a carrier of literariness. To be sure, this index is not quite so simple as it looks: by itself, it only alerts the reader to something going on in the sociolectic hinterland of another word or phrase: the word or phrase it predicates. The index causes this word or phrase, which *is* a carrier of literariness (here 'Gallic cock'), to select among its potential intertexts the one that removes all ambiguity from the image that was undecidable.

If it is true that a single, solitary word makes the whole text what it is, why then, one may ask, have critics so uniformly failed to draw the obvious conclusion! They have seen the problem all right, the crux being so highly visible. But the crux blocks only the meaning; it is an enigma only within the context of the sociolect. Hence the common plight of commentators in such cases, for it is their misguided wont to look to the sociolect for linguistic reassurance when the text rattles them.[7] This flight, this attempt to cling to a linear rather than intertextual reading, undoes the text.

It has already become apparent from this discussion of Rimbaud's verse that no text can realize its own identity before the reader has related and perhaps opposed the text to its intertext. It is only after this intertextual relationship has been perceived that the literary work becomes more than a linear sequence of successive, discrete meanings. It is only then that it becomes interpretable as one unit of significance, thus achieving literariness.

But how can the work's semiotic and organic unity develop from the seemingly open-ended proliferation of the intertext? How does the text compel the reader to grasp its uniqueness by opposition to linguistic usage and to the sociolectic corpus? My example this time is a short poem of Francis Ponge's entitled *L'Huître* (The Oyster).[8]

We know from the context, that is from the collection it is part of, that we must regard it as a prose poem. But what justifies our final acquiescence? What is there in the text that we can objectively recognize as characteristic of the prose poem? Last of all, what is the connection between the poem's topic and its genre? What is the nature of the topic's poeticity? To make an oyster a poetic object is an endeavour that has a precedent in French literary history: the sixteenth-century genre of the *blason* consisted in minute and accurate depictions of natural or man-made objects. In his description Ponge glorifies in a supremely successful adequation of form and content, and certainly readers do expect this of poetic discourse in general, as opposed to the looser forms of everyday language. Indeed, adequation is obvious here so long as we realize that 'form' is meant to designate not the shape of the object described but rather a formal feature of the word for that object. The reader unavoidably notices a repetition, or variation, upon a visible model. Such a model determines the whole form of our poem: it is the title, the noun *huître*, whose sound is quite striking in isolation (there are no French words that rhyme with *huître*, save one, gone and forgotten – *bélître*). Further, this phonetic singularity is made typographically conspicuous by the circumflex on the *i*. Not only is this word unique in the language, with its *i* followed by the -*tre*, but there are precious few words in the entire lexicon ending in a vowel with a circumflex and the consonants -*tre*. There are two with *ê*, one with *ô*, none with *û*, and with *â* only one suffix -*âtre* which is used to form adjectives, always pejorative, negative and unpleasant.[9] *Vert* ('green'), for instance, becomes *verdâtre* ('greenish'); *gris* ('grey') becomes *grisâtre* ('dirty grey' of 'mouldy grey'). It is thus an inescapable feature of the text, insistently forcing upon the reader all sorts of -*âtre* adjectives: the oyster is *blanchâtre* ('whitish'); *opiniâtre* ('stupidly obstinate'), because it resists the gourmet's best efforts to crack it open and tries to snap back on his fingers; its flesh is a viscous *greenish* blob, with a *blackish* fringe:

L'huître, de la grosseur d'un galet moyen, est d'une apparence plus rugueuse, d'une couleur moins unie, brillamment *blanchâtre*. C'est un monde *opiniâtrement* clos. Pourtant on peut l'ouvrir: il faut alors la tenir au creux d'un torchon, se servir d'un couteau ébréché et peu franc, s'y reprendre à plusieurs fois. Les doigts curieux s'y coupent, s'y cassent les ongles: c'est un travail grossier ...

A l'intérieur l'on trouve tout un monde, à boire et à manger: ... les cieux [de nacre] d'en-dessus s'affaisent sur les cieux d'en-dessous, pour ne plus former qu'une mare, un sachet visqueux et *verdâtre*, qui flue et reflue à l'odeur et à la vue, frange d'une dentelle *noirâtre* sur les bords ...

[The oyster, about as big as a fair-sized pebble, is rougher, less evenly coloured, brightly whitish. It is a world stubbornly closed. Yet it can be opened: one must hold it in a cloth, use a dull jagged knife, and try more than once. Avid fingers get cut, nails get chipped: a rough job ...

Inside one finds a whole world, to eat and drink ... The [mother-of-pearl] skies above collapse on the skies below, forming nothing but a puddle, a viscous greenish blob that ebbs and flows on sight and smell, fringed with blackish lace along the edge ...][10]

Now this set of end-alike words, of rhymes, has been glossed by just about everybody else, aside from Ponge.[11] What I should like to add is that the negative connotations of the suffix contaminate words not by nature negative, and end up permeating the entire representation: everything becomes explicitly or implicitly disagreeable. The oyster refuses to be pried open, its shell flakes off, it cuts fingers and breaks nails. When you work on it you have to hold it in a cloth so it won't slip, but significantly this cloth is a *torchon*, a rag, usually none too clean. The special knife employed in this unequal struggle is dull and jagged; Ponge's term *pas franc*, if applied to a man, means 'insincere,' phony. True, the inner world of the oyster has a heaven, even two heavens, but one of them collapses on to the other, and the verb (*s'affaisse*) suggests a slow sinking that banishes the epic grandeur of the falling sky and is as revolting as the oyster's stickiness. True, again, Ponge tells us there is a whole world within the oyster, but his qualification – something to eat and drink too, *à boire et à manger* – is hardly objective. The two verbs do state the facts of the oyster, but the phrase itself happens to be proverbial. In common parlance, when you say a certain situation offers both food and drink, you mean it is a mixture of good and bad with a predominance of bad – an unpleasantly ambiguous setup. So it may fairly be said that the entire text is overdetermined by the shape of the title-noun, and that the connotations of that shape in the lexicon in turn overdetermine the whole semantic structure of the text. Both form and meaning develop the implication of the noun, rather than the nature of the thing. And the text is a variation on this one word. The extensive derivation from one given makes for its unity, while the variation in fact represents a constant, since we recognize an invariant factor common to all variants: the oyster's negativeness.

Now it is this type of derivation and the overdetermination not its components that gives the prose poem its generic identity, for it is what marks the difference between verse and prose poetry. In a versified poem formal unity is assured, if by nothing else, by the metre: that is by an established conventional system, existing before and outside of the poem itself. In a prose poem the unifying factor is generated by the text itself. It is a network of constant features built *ad hoc* and uniquely appropriate because they represent the poem's significance as well. Such is not the case with verse: metre *per se* remains independent of significance, though it may serve to underline it. The prose poem, on the contrary, indissolubly links up the recurring features of the paradigm of variants because these are overdetermined. No matter how many repetitions or variants the poem has, all of them derive from one word, all their mutual relationships are modelled upon the presuppositions this one word entails in linguistic usage. In effect, the whole poem is a transformation, a spatial expansion of the single word into sentences, and of these sentences into a text. Hence the unity: the diversity of forms is but a disguise of the initial given, endlessly reiterated and transmuted, but still identical. Hence too the epiphany of significance: the various separate meanings of each descriptive detail all share a common characteristic feature inherited from the given. This permanent feature inflects, orients the complex description towards a single dominating thought or colouration – the poetic significance.

It remains for us to understand the function of intertextuality in the genesis of this formal constant. Why should a descriptive poem, traditionally singing the praises of its subject, now turn to dispraise? Why is it so relentlessly negative, so serving up a delicacy that it becomes utterly unpalatable? Why poke us in the guts and turn our stomachs with a well-nigh physical nausea? One is tempted to assume that all this is rooted in usage. Our rising gorge corresponds to a number of commonplace negative connotations already alive and kicking in the imaginations of French speakers. A mollusc suspected of being hard to digest, often polluted, arouses heartfelt distrust. Oysters frequently go bad, they are viscous: the image of a prized delicacy elicits an ambivalent reaction – as if one had to suffer through an initiatory ordeal before arriving at gustatory bliss. This may appear to signal the integration of the object into human experience, annexation of the eternal thing to the inner world of reader-sensation and reader-psyche – and thus to reader-language.

This, I submit, would be a superficial interpretation. It might be valid perhaps for a non-literary text, but it ignores the fact that this text is a poem and that is identified as a literary praise. No irony is perceptible. The encomiastic structure is actualized through a negative mimesis. This, however, nowise deflects the praise, or does it constitute a parody of it.

Actually the pejorative mimesis and its laudatory semiosis are two complementary functions of the same sign system. The author himself senses a two-faceted phenomenon without being fully aware of its mechanism: witness his gloss on the poem's first oxymoron, *brillamment blanchâtre*, 'radiantly whitish,' a negative adjective with a positive modifier. By putting the two together, he says, 'I depart from the commonplace; I create a character (in the sense of a character in a novel) who is to be outside the norm, a hero at once brilliant and dull, an unconventional character, a complex of contradictions.'[12] But that is only a metaphor, not a full explanation. Had he gone further, he would have recognized that his oxymoron and the praise by dispraise are but special instances of something more general in the poetic, and doubtless in the human, unconscious: that is that the positive and the negative, in poetry, often the sublime and the abject, are the two sides of a single coin.[13] It is not by chance that French colloquial usage has only one word, *crachat*, both for 'sputum,' an extreme of loathesomeness, and for an ultimate of positive symbolism: a particular diamond-studded plaque, priceless as a material object (as a jewel), and as a spiritual object (as the emblem of an honour conferred upon the bearer, as the insignia of the highest rank in various national orders). It is not by chance either that the discourse of homiletics singles out in the Passion narrative sequence the episode of the soldiers spitting at the face of Jesus as *the* moment of sublimation.[14] The intertext of our poem is constituted by a descriptive system of the oyster. The system's components have positive markers. The text reverses these markers, a common intertextual transformation.[15]

The texts I have examined so far are short, though brevity by itself does not make it easier for us to identify significance. What then of long texts? How do we perceive the unity of a protracted narrative? Can we isolate, as we have in poetry, the factors that guide the reader's interpretation of a novel? Such factors, it seems to me, can be found in *mise en abyme* structures.[16] A *mise en abyme*, however, is not a text, but a fragment of the text, immersed in it and mirroring the whole. I shall therefore call it a subtext.

A subtext must be derived from the same matrix as the whole narrative, or from a matrix structurally connected with that of the encircling text. These subtexts operate as units of reading, so to speak, not unlike themes or motifs, except that a theme or motif has a matrix of its own, born elsewhere and existing before that of the larger text, so that theme or motif functions like a quotation, or borrowing – or rather, like an embedding in the syntax of the narrative. The subtext obtrudes on the reader as a segment that could stand alone and be remembered as a passage representing the whole and representing the author, as an episode may be remembered; only an episode is a link in a chain of events, while a subtext is no such thing, since it can be omitted without unravelling the fabric or obscuring the logic of the narrative. The subtext works like those units of reading or fragments or vectors in a reading sequence that Barthes calls *lexies*, except that Barthes's lexies depend upon the individual's choice, upon his ideological grids. The subtext, by contrast, is objectively defined and resists subjective, reader-initiated segmentation.

The subtext manifests itself, and its limits – in particular the connection between closure and incipit – are identified when the reader becomes retroactively aware that one textual component is echoing another component, formerly read and now remembered. The component from out of the past, thus recollected or reread with the eye of memory, takes on features not noticed during the first or primary reading, for they are noteworthy only because they are the first step or rung in a repetitive series. For the same logical reason that a rhyme is perceived only when the eye or ear has reached the second rhyming word, a narrative prolepsis is perceivable only after the fact: it carries nothing in itself pointing to its proleptic function, until the narrative sequence arrives at the consequences of the premises posited in the prolepsis. For the subtext to be identified, then, there must be homologues within the narrative from which flow recognizable, well-marked derivations constituting the formal and semantic constants any literary text must be able to show. When the reader does finally stumble upon one or more of such homologues, but a homologue whose shape and meaning indicate that the series is coming to an end – for instance, when this latest homologue reverses the order of components in the initial one – then the subtext closes.

Subtexts, however well defined by closure, are hardly ever solid, uninterrupted verbal sequences. The trouble with them – and it is a trouble that should make spotting them a chancy business – is that normally they overlap other subtexts, or are simply disseminated, as it were, throughout the novel: they are fragments loosely strung along the main narrative line. So it should be hard to figure out their identity: but it is not hard. A theoretically surprising fact, but there are reasons for it. The following example should offer some illumination; I take it from Proust. My subtext first comes to notice in *A l'ombre des jeunes filles en fleurs*, where it is already strewn through twenty pages of the Pléiade edition's small, tight print. Whereupon it vanishes, only to reappear in *Le Côté de Guermantes*, and much later on, in *Sodome et Gomorrhe*. All in all, a subtext sprinkled over about a thousand pages of an incredibly rich narrative. Add to this the fact that its interest is thin, the central figure a mere shadow, a supernumerary of the lowest order, a bellhop at the Balbec Grand Hotel. This paltry personage steps on stage, so it seems, only to sketch out a comic interlude. And yet no reader of Proust is likely to forget the boy's silent, walk-on part. The contrast is striking between the ostensible insignificance of an episode so trivial, a character so parenthetic, and the permanent imprint left on the reader's memory. Each fleeting reappearance strengthens the reader's feeling that some sort of whole is taking shape, stretched out over the slow, distracting expanses of the fiction. It is this very sense of contrast that triggers the reader's hermeneutic behaviour.

From the outset his attention is caught by an unusual description of the character as some kind of potted plant:

A côté des voitures, devant le porche ou j'attendais, était planté comme un arbrisseau d'une espèce rare un jeune chasseur qui ne frappait pas moins les yeux par l'harmonie singulière de ses cheveux colorés, que par son épiderme de plante.[17]

[Next to the carriages, in front of the lobby entrance where I was waiting, a young bellboy was planted like a shrub of some rare species. He was striking to look at no less for the singular harmony of his reddish hair than for his plant-like epidermis.]

This epidermis detail would probably be hard to take if we were tempted to linger on it. In the course of a normal reading it registers casually, a remark of a piece with the shrub image. Or it is like a whimsical comment before the fact, before the passage, on the next page, where the bellboy's idleness is called *immobilité végétale* (vegetable – plant-like – immobility). Next page, though, a *coup de théâtre* too, Proust gives his reader a jolt: instead of le *chasseur adolescent* we have le *chasseur arborescent*. Indeed, *arborescent* is read as a farcical translation of adolescent into vegetable code.

This startling image has been generated by a latent syllepsis, deriving as it does from the verb *être planté*, which applies as well to a person as to vegetation – we say he stood rooted to the spot in amazement, for instance. The verb is specially apt for a soldier on sentry duty, like our page-boy, a *planton* (orderly) – the French revealingly straddles the syllepsis. This implicit, or rather presupposed, syllepsis is susceptible of proof; it is real, not a figment of my imagination. In fact it is explicit in the first draft of the passage: there our verb is given two subjects, one human and one vegetal, and its relationship to each is equally literal, equally grammatical:

devant le porche étaient plantés un arbrisseau d'une espèce rare et un jeune chasseur

[in front of the lobby entrance were planted a rare species of shrub and a young bellhop]

Now the implied syllepsis cannot be anything but a game. The epidermal detail would still be fully explainable under the rules of the game: it is a pseudo-description derived from the 'wrong' meaning of *planter* with playful logic. Less easily explained is the jump from the first pun on *planter* to *chasseur arborescent*. Here what was to start with mere verbal whimsy seems to acquire the permanence of an Ovidian metamorphosis. Further, the youngster is reified, and this underscores the radical nature of his transformation: the narrative treats him as if he were a thing, and his portrait is saturated with a vegetable paradigm. Twenty pages later we come upon this fresh description, seemingly unmotivated:

Seul 'le chasseur', exposé au soleil dans la journée, avait été rentré pour ne pas supporter la rigueur du soir, et emmailloté de lainages, lesquels, joints à l'éplorement orangé de sa chevelure et à la fleur curieusement rose de ses joues, faisaient, au milieu du hall vitré, penser à une plante de serre qu'on protège contre le froid.

[the page-boy, exposed to the sun during the day, had been brought back indoors, so as not to have to bear the severity of the evening chill. He was all swaddled in woollens. These, combined with the orange weeping hair and the curiously rosy bloom of his cheeks, right in the middle of the glassed-in lobby, made you think of a hothouse plant being sheltered from the cold.]   (Vol. 1, p. 723).

At the very end, a return to reality: *faisaient penser* (made you think) seems to suggest that everything being said about the bellboy is just for fun. Yet this perfunctory correction notwithstanding, it is quite obvious that the text is actually describing a 'real' mutation from man to plant. This becomes clear from the rapid succession of the phrases 'exposed to the sun' and 'brought back indoors,' followed by the wordplay on the 'rosy bloom' in the boy's cheeks, and – still more strikingly – the strange *éplorement orangé de sa chevelure* (literally: the orangy weeping of his hair). For *éplorement* (being in tears) is not so human a touch as it should be. It has been attached to vegetation ever since the Romanticists resuscitated the dead metaphor 'weeping willow' (by changing *pleureur*, 'weeping,' into the stronger *éploré*, in tears; and by transferring the *éploré* to real descriptions of tree foliage). In phrases like *rameaux éplorés* (weeping branches) in Lamartine, and Musset's *feuillage éploré*, the *éplorement* image has taken on vegetal connotations: it bespeaks grief or sadness, but in botanical code.

I spoke of a genuine Ovidian metamorphosis. If proof were called for that such a metamorphosis had indeed occurred, I think the following would do. While the bellboy is still the *chasseur*, the name – his proper title – is already in quotation marks, as if that were the metaphor and *arborescent* the literal fact.

A thousand pages later, a clausula puts an end to the *chasseur* sequence. The signal closing it out is a cancellation of the metaphor that set the subtext going: Proust reverts to the initial syllepsis embracing *planton* and *plante*. We could ask for no more convincing evidence that the transformation from man to vegetable generates the sequence, or that this vast textual space has indeed been created by a transformation of its one lexical matrix:

L'aspect de la pelouse qui s'étendait derrière l'hôtel avait été modifié par la création de quelques plates-bandes fleuries et l'enlèvement non seulement d'un arbuste exotique, mais du chasseur qui, la première année, décorait extérieurement l'entrée par la tige souple de sa taille et la coloration curieuse de sa chevleure.

[The appearance of the expanse of lawn behind the hotel had been altered by the creation of several flowerbeds and the removal of not only an exotic shrub but of the bellboy who ornamented the outside of the entrance that first year with his supple flower-stem of a figure and the curious colouring of his hair.]   (Vol. 2, p. 773)

The humorous tone has been sustained throughout, and this by repetition of the same ungrammaticalities (such as the unlikely hair-colour), and the sudden literalization of descriptive metaphors: in the passage just cited, the boy's lithe physique and narrow waist become a plant stem, common enough in portrayals of elegant, youthful slenderness, but in this case how uncannily apt and accurate, since the key to it all is a literal acceptance of another cliché image: the adolescent as sapling. In short, a sequence of disseminated fragments has all along been displaying the constancy of feature, the unity of tone, and now the closure that characterize a literary text.

These textual characteristics show up even more sharply when we compare Proust's *chasseur* with other poetic transformations of adolescent into arborescent. For such mutation are not unusual: this is a literary motif. Take for example Chateaubriand's portrait of a young girl in *Les Martyrs* (1809):

Sa fille Cymodocée croissait sous ses yeux, comme un jeune olivier qu'un jardinier élève avec soin au bord d'une fontaine, et qui est l'amour de la terre et du ciel.

[His daughter Cymodocaea was growing up under his eyes like a young olive tree being raised with care by a gardener beside a water fountain – a young tree that is the love of earth and heaven.][18]

No subtext here, and no closure save the final apposition repeating in general terms the sentiment first expressed in a specific simile. It has been added to the basic line of the story. It also serves to trigger easy visualization – a picture of the girl pleasing through vague, since the simile clearly distinguishes woman from tree. They are both imaginable, but only side by side, distanced from each other by the very analogy that unites them: they must keep their separateness if the comparison is to work and if we are to be able to embroider in our minds on the theme offered to us. In the Proust text, on the contrary, the image of arborescence cannot lead to any acceptable visualization: each seemingly true-to-life detail invalidates the representation through the very mechanism that should solidify it: that is, through its preciseness and specificity. We cannot believe in or really conjure up the *épiderme de plante*, we cannot believe the bellhop has been carted back inside the hotel the way an inert object is carried; nor can we picture his hair as really orange. If we did we should probably question the author's common sense and the pertinence of this invented character, pointless, representing nothing but his own cuteness. And since we never do swallow this orangy vegetation anyway, but take it as a trick of pseudo-verisimilitude, we are left to wonder why the gauche precision was thought necessary. A cliché simile, *blond comme les blés* (wheat-blond) would have sufficed, without any departure from the text's deliberate bias towards the vegetable kingdom.

If the descriptive details, then, do not describe, or if they describe while at the same time telling us the description is not to be believed and cannot be accurate – there is only one way to decode them. They must be perceived as fanciful variation, as a verbal fugue upon *arborescent*. Thus upon a word that we already know has been born of yet another whimsy, the sylleptic reading of *planter*. This leaves us with a comic subtext. It also makes clear that the entire long-drawn-out unfolding is in fact one unit of significance, the textual equivalent of a single word, *arborescent*. Far from being an adventitious parenthesis within the fiction's continuum, a sort of make-believe descriptive hors-d'oeuvre, almost a hole in the novel's fabric, it turns out that the subtext, or rather the textual sign, actually functions like an embedding in the narrative sequence. Its relation to the story is that of a word to the grammar of a sentence.

Two factors must operate if the reader is to be able to discover the subtext's true identity. One is deictic, one hermeneutic. The deictic factor calls attention to the special nature of the subtext; it makes obvious that the subtext must be the key to a significance. The deictic factor here is the humour of an outrageous comparison. As for the hermeneutic factor, that is the nub of the outrage: the notion of modifying a noun of the human with an adjective of the vegetable, the impossible equation of man and tree. The subtext wants us to guess why a young man should be a potted plant.

And the text answers this question, fifteen pages after the subtext ends, in the voice of Baron Charlus. The old sodomite outlines a sentimental program, a strategy of desire:

Pour les meilleurs d'entre nous, l'étude des arts, le goût de la brocante, les collections, les jardins, ne sont que des *Ersatz*, des *succédanés*, des alibis. Dans le fond de notre tonneau, comme Diogène, nous demandons un homme. Nous cultivons les bégonias, nous taillons les ifs, par pis aller, parce que les ifs et les bégonias se laissent faire. Mais nous aimerions mieux donner notre temps à un arbuste humain, si nous étions sûrs qu'il en valût la peine.

[For the best of us, the study of the arts, collecting, gardening, these are only *Ersatz*, substitutes, alibis. From the bottom of our barrel, like Diogenes, we are asking for a man. We cultivate begonias, we trim yew trees – makeshifts – and because yew trees and begonias let us do what we like with them. But we should prefer to spend our time on a human shrub [*arbuste humain*], if we could be sure he was worth the trouble.]   (Vol. 2, p. 285)

We now understand why the subtext has been insisting upon the botanical epidermis: it corresponds to the type of detailed, slow-motion, close-up shot where the narrator's eye presses in nearer and nearer to his mistress's face; inch by inch he tells us how this scrutiny changes Albertine's smooth rosy skin into a coarse-grained epidermis. The nearer the nearness, the greater the desire; follow a kiss and further intimacies. Now we understand why the subtext has been accumulating metonyms of vegetality. Since this is not a progressive approximation of reality, since the mimesis is in fact overturned, made less and less convincing, the saturation must be a sign of semiotic transformation. All signs for the human must henceforth stand for the vegetal, so as to favour one seme of the vegetal's semantic makeup, its *immobility*. A transformation that would be paradoxical anywhere, but here the *plante/planton* relationship supplies at least a morphological basis for the new language of desire. The vegetable cannot walk away; the tree cannot escape; the potted plant cannot desert its loving gardener.

One recalcitrant detail is now illuminated; we discover that it is by no means the ultimate in authorial arbitrariness, it is in fact the clincher, the final proof that the subtext is logical. I am thinking of the orangish hair. It is not a colour, it is the surfacing of a synonym, or better, the hyperbole of vegetable movelessness. In French the orange tree is the potted plant *par excellence*, almost an antonomasia; the rich man is a Croesus, the *oranger* is *the* potted plant. It is also the shrub the gardener shelters most jealously from the frost – remember the *chasseur* all wrapped up in wool, the plant the hothouse is waiting for, as an alcove awaits the beloved.

The arborescent-adolescent is simply carrying *ad absurdum* the idea of rearing up the loved one in a cage – the program mapped out for Agnès in Molière's *L'Ecole des femmes*. The arborescent page-boy in fact prefigures the impossible dream of desire at last unthwarted, of total possession, in all senses of the word. Which is to say our *chasseur* hypostatizes the *La Prisonnière* books: the one subtext encapsulates in a comic playlet the significance of the entire novel. And the narrative, by the way, says the same thing still otherwise: the *chasseur* is sorry he has never been kidnapped by some wealthy female patroness, as his brother was, he regrets that he has not yet taken off for the greener pastures of the gigolo. And the *chasseur* and *Les jeunes filles en fleur*, the blossoming maidens of the novel's title – another human-vegetable equivalence – are both derived from the same matrix. The Baron Charlus makes that matrix explicit: *we should much prefer a human plant*. It might be true that our *chasseur* is only a male variant of the maids in bloom; but we know these girls are only male lovers in disguise. In either case, then, the book is repressing a portrayal of homosexuality; it is protecting the narrator's love from the spread of homosexual identification that engulfs all the other characters, all the other representation. And in either case self-censorship is at work; the only difference is in the censoring device. This device is a metaphor; women stand for men, plants for men. The first yields a likely, believable, socially acceptable mimesis – *les jeunes filles*. The second yields an unacceptable mimesis: hence the humour or farce of *arborescent*. But in both cases the vegetality seme remains the essential modifier, for it is the relationship of gardener to plant (not the similarity between man and vegetable) in which the simile is grounded. Once again, the identity of the text lies in the process of its creation: here the reader's compulsory retracing of the writer's steps as he composes, moving from image to subtext, from one subtext to the whole novel. And once again the process is triggered by the compound word that seemed destined to block it forever: compound, of course, because the verbal scandal that sets things in motion is not just *arborescent*, but rather the unholy union of a human noun and a vegetable adjective.

In each case examined, I have shown that a single word or phrase, a single sign, is indeed the key to the significance, and therefore the model for the making of the text as a literary work. In conclusion, I should like to stress a constant feature of this type of sign. Every time, the intertext is what provides the foundation of the text's unity and the text's identity (whereas the same intertext regarded as a source or as a mere thematic tradition would confuse the text with its homologues). Every time, the relevant significance is pointed to by some one difficulty insoluble at the level of the text itself: the crux indicates what reversal of markers or exclusion of components is needed for deducing text from intertext. The constant, and paradoxical, feature I am speaking about is that the significance of a literary text is to be found outside the text, and through a momentary eclipse of meaning.

NOTES

1 Arthur Rimbaud, *Oeuvres complètes*, ed. Antoine Adam, Paris 1972, III, 88, 946–9. The translations are mine.

2 R.G. Cohn, *The Poetry of Rimbaud*, Princeton 1973, pp. 236, 238; J.P. Houston, *The Design of Rimbaud's Poetry*, New Haven 1963, p. 183. For the other two interpretations, see Adam, pp. 946 and 948 fn. 3.

3 'chaque nuit son coq gaulois.' A second draft spells it out: 'Je suis à lui chaque fois / Si chante son coq gaulois.' Since these drafts were crossed out, we cannot use them to explain the reader's interpretation of the text, but we may still use them to prove that this perception is indeed consistent with Rimbaud's intention.

4 See my 'Interpretation and Undecidability,' *New Literary History*, 12 (1980–1), 227–42.

5 See W.K. Wimsatt, Jr, 'When Is Variation Elegant?' in *The Verbal Icon: Studies in the Meaning of Poetry*, New York 1960, pp. 188–99.

6 Commentators have acted as if this spiritual introduction must also fit the version of the *Derniers Vers* collection. This arbitrarily reverses the normal reading sequence. If there must be a link between the two poems, it will be from the first to the second, not the other way around. The reader marvels that Rimbaud should succeed in using obscenity to express a mystical yearning.

7 This, I believe, answers Jonathan Culler's objections to my approach in *The Pursuit of Signs: Semiotics, Literature, Deconstruction*, Ithaca 1981, pp. 94ff.

8 Francis Ponge, *Le Parti-pri des choses* (1942), reprinted in *Tome premier*, Paris 1965, p. 48.

9 This is not a fact known to lexicographers alone. The suffix is extremely productive. Its connotations are taught in French schools, and it constantly gives rise to *ad hoc* colloquial coinages.

10 Italics are mine. I am using the excellent translation by Beth Archer (F. Ponge, *The Voice of Things*, ed. and trans. with an introduction by Beth Archer), New York 1972.

11 See his detailed commentary in *Entretiens de Francis Ponge avec Philippe Sollers*, Paris 1970, pp. 107–15, esp. pp. 111–12.

12 Ponge, *Entretiens*, p. 109.

13 Cf. Julia Kristeva, *Pouvoirs de l'horreur: Essai sur l'abjection*, Paris 1980.

14 E.G. Léon Bloy, *Journal*, 1902, p. 89: 'le resplendissement surnatural de la face conspuée et souffletée de Jesus-Christ,' in which the simultaneity of *conspuer* and *resplendir* marks the transfiguration from the martyred Son of Man to Christus Rex. Cf. also the uses of *crachat, cracher*, as epic words to describe explosions, volcanic eruptions, the foam of waves, etc.; of *vomir* as a poetic description of cannon firing, etc.

15 Cf. the poisonous overtones of Zola's epic depiction of food in the Paris *Halles* throughout is novel *Le Ventre de Paris*. They do not detract from the efficacy of this description as a paean to its object.

16 See Lucien Dällenbach, *Le Récit spéculaire*, Paris 1977.

17 *A la Recherche de temps perdu*, Paris 1954, I, 706. all subsequent references to this edition are in brackets after the quotations. Translations are mine.

18 *Les Martyrs*, in *Oeuvres romanesques et Voyages*, Paris 1969, II, 108.

PART TWO

TEXTUAL DECONSTRUCTION

J. HILLIS MILLER

Topography and Tropography in Thomas Hardy's *In Front of the Landscape*

Take, as an example, Thomas Hardy's poem *In Front of the Landscape*. This is put as the opening text in *Satires of Circumstance* (1914). What is its identity as a text? If this identity arises from relations to previous and later texts and readers, among the most important of these relations are those to other poems by Hardy, for example to the other poems in Hardy's volume of 1914, or, more broadly, to all the poems taken together in *The Complete Poems of Thomas Hardy*. To call *In Front of the Landscape* an example of Hardy's poetry illustrates the falsification involved in assuming that Thomas Hardy is a single person or that his poems taken together form a coherent whole. The differences of *In Front of the Landscape* from any other poem by Hardy are more important, it may be, than any similarities. The poem tells the reader things about 'Hardy' she or he can learn only from this poem. If *Wessex Heights* dramatizes the relation the speaker has to the swarm of ghosts from the past when he sees them from the relative detachment of the hilltop, *In Front of the Landscape* describes what it is like, for Hardy, down there in the lowlands.

What is 'in front of the landscape' for the speaker of this poem is a great 'tide of visions,' memories of this or that person from his past. This so overwhelms and drowns him with its immediacy that it almost hides the scene behind. What should be there in the present is rendered ghostlike and insubstantial, as though the landscape were the mist and the mist the substantial reality. Scenes, objects, and persons from the past, 'miscalled of the bygone,' have more presence and solidity than anything present in the present. It is the presence and force of a great flood ramping over the land and sinking it:

> Plunging and labouring on in a tide of visions,
>   Dolorous and dear,
> Forward I pushed my way as amid waste waters
>   Stretching around,

Through whose eddies there glimmered the customed landscape
Yonder and near.

Blotted to feeble mist. And the coomb and the upland
Coppice-crowned,
Ancient chalk-pit, milestone, rills in the grass-flat
Stroked by the light,
Seemed but a ghost-like gauze, and no substantial
Meadow or mound.[1]

In Front of the Landscape is one of Hardy's most grandly rhythmical poems. It is unusually open in its expression of emotion. For once the metre does not seem an arbitrary framework into which certain material is pushed, trimmed to shape. The dactylic metre fits the thematic mood and the organizing figure, affirming that memories are like the inundating waters of great sea-swells, wave after wave. The reader will feel the swing and rise of the lines. This rhythm is punctuated by the rhyming of the last line of each stanza with the second line. Each stanza is like a wave finally breaking and crashing. The alternate long and short lines within each stanza give the rhythm of waters moving across a shallow tideland, building up in a slow mounting like a long indrawing breath: 'Plunging and labouring on in a tide of visions,' and then more rapidly dropping as it is exhaled: 'Dolorous and dear.' Within the complex wave movement of each stanza a new wave is preparing in the end-word of each fourth line: 'Stretching around,' 'Stroked by the light.' These have no rhymes within their own stanzas but hang there in the air, so to speak. They are responded to finally by the first and last short lines in the next stanza. The poem proceeds by way of a braided effect, in a complex rhythm of one wave that completes itself but always contains within itself the doubling or crossing rhythm of the next preparing wave. This interweaving is reinforced by frequent grammatical enjambment from one stanza to the next, as in the two stanzas quoted above. In the last stanza of all, the last two short lines rhyme: 'Round him that looms'; 'Save a few tombs?'

I have said that the poem is unusual among Hardy's in its rhythmical majesty. It is like some grand organ fugue. The poem is unusual also in its match of rhythm and theme, its frank yielding to the fallacy of imitative form. The rhythm is not only obviously meant to mime the movement of tidal waves but is also meant to mime what the figure mimes: the inundation of the poet by waves or visionary memories. There is no actual water named anywhere in the poem, only the figure of water introduced in the initial phrase 'tide of visions.' This is then made explicitly figurative in a simile later in the poem: – 'Yea, *as* the rhyme / Sung by the sea-swell, so in their pleading dumbness / Captured me these' (my italics). To put this another way, the words of the poem are themselves the incarnation of the tide of visions. The poem is a repetition once more, after the fact (since the poem is in the past tense), of what was itself a repetition of those earlier scenes. The figure of the waves is an element in a series projected backward from the present attempt to give experience form in poetry towards the past moment when the poet took his walk. It is as true to say that the figure of the waves names the musical, rhythmical, rhyming form of the poem itself as that it names the form the experience intrinsically had when it occurred.

In Hardy's poems, and in this one more obviously in many others, there is always some discrepancy between the rigid stanzaic pattern and the material put into it. Once the pattern is set up it goes on repeating itself from stanza to stanza, coercing whatever it is Hardy wants to say into taking that shape. The past experience is repeated in a new form that has its own intrinsic power of replication. This occurs, for example, whenever the poem is reread and its form takes shape once more in the mind of the reader. What *In Front of the Landscape* communicates is not the 'original original' experiences to which it refers and not the repetitions of those in the 'original' experience when the speaker took his walk and confronted his tide of visions. What the poem communicates is itself, its own form. The figure of the waves names that form.

The signs of this 'present' activity, the craftsmanship involved in the writing of the poem, include the artifice of the difficult stanza pattern and rhyme scheme. These are evidence of present choice and deliberate work to make the words fit. Another sign of poetic work, often present in Hardy's poetry, is a slowing down of the forward rhythmic movement of the poem in the counter-movement of a careful choice, one by one, so it seems, of words or phrases. Many of these seem slightly odd, unexpected, or out of place. The reader, if he is a teacher, may have a subliminal desire to write 'dic.' in the margin, until he has thought more about the lines and comes to see how right the word or phrase is: 'brinily trundled'; 'harrowed'; 'unreason'; 'wryness'; 'misprision'; 'corporate'; 'frilled'; 'scantly'; 'perambulates.' It is a feature of Hardy's poetry that he gets away with or even admirably exploits words which hardly any other poet would dare use at all. Often these words are harsh monosyllables slowing the line down almost to a halt, as word follows word: 'Cheeks that were fair in their flush-time, ash now with anguish.' Or the words may be polysyllables full of clogged consonants, technical or archaic words, words not in everyone's vocabulary, like 'brinily' or 'misprision.' This slowing-down by word choice is a counterpointed rhythm fighting against the swelling forward wave-like movement. The reader can see the poet feeling his way along the line, choosing word after word carefully, after much thought. He chooses each word not only for its more exact correspondence to the experience in the past he wants the poem to duplicate but for its creation of an integument of signs, there on the page. These will have a coercive power over the reader, as the notation of musical sounds in a score, when played aloud again, will, to borrow a formulation from *Tess of the d'Urbervilles*, 'lead' the listener 'through sequences of emotion, which [the composer] alone had felt at first' (chapter 13). It is impossible to tell whether these sequences of emotion were intrinsic to the original experience which the poem records or whether they are created by the formal properties of the poem as Hardy has happened to compose it. The reader has access only to the poem. He cannot compare it with anything which it might seem to copy.

The great tide of visions of which the poem speaks is made of scenes, such as the 'headland of hoary aspect / Gnawed by the tide,' or of objects – for example, 'Instruments of strings with the tenderest passion / Vibrant, beside / Lamps long extinguished, robes' – but most of all of persons with whom the poet had once been associated over the various times of his past life. These are, to borrow some fine phrases from *Wessex Heights*, 'shadows of beings who fellowed with myself of earlier days' (*Complete Poems*, p. 319). The sequence from musical instruments to lamps and robes continues with the fine irony of 'cheeks, eyes with the earth's crust / Now corporate.' The poet detaches parts of the bodies of those he has known and lists them as vanished objects like the rest. He thinks of them now as parts of the vast corporate body of the earth. Of that body we will all one day be members. These persons are now apparently all buried in the graveyard which is the goal of his long walk through the Wessex countryside:

> So did beset me scenes, miscalled of the bygone,
>> Over the leaze,
> Past the clump, and down to where lay the beheld ones.

It has been suggested by Hermann Lea that the scene of the poem is 'Came Down near Culliver Tree,' about three miles south of Dorchester. J. O. Bailey has observed that there is a chalk-pit nearby to match the one mentioned in stanza 2 of the poem, as well as many burial tumuli 'scattered in all directions from this point.'[2] The latter may be referred to in the last lines. Those lines imagine passers-by wondering who this dull preambulating form is who walks where there is nothing to see 'save a few tombs.' But the phrase 'where lay the beheld ones' must refer to a modern burial ground, perhaps the one southward in Weymouth, perhaps the ones northward in Dorchester or in Stinsford. Though all these old associates are now dead, this does not keep them from appearing before the poet as 'infinite spectacles,' 'speechful faces, gazing insistent.' These walking ghosts have so much solidity that they are 'hindering [him] to discern [his] paced advancement / Lengthening to miles.' The ghosts of the old associates apparently do not speak (though in one place he says he can 'hear them'), but they have 'speechful faces.' Their 'dumb pleading' is a double reproach. It is a reproach to the speaker for not having appreciated them sufficiently when they were alive and it is a reproach for his having in any case later on betrayed them.

> For, their lost revisiting manifestations
>   In their live time
> Much had I slighted, caring not for their purport,
>   Seeing behind
> Things more coveted, reckoned the better worth calling
>   Sweet, sad, sublime.

It appears to be a law, in this poem, if not necessarily always in Hardy, that what you have in the present as an actual physical presence you do not really have. The fact that something is there and that you possess it makes it seem worthless. It also makes it impossible to understand its 'purport.' The mind and feelings always look beyond or behind what is possessed now to what is not possessed. Those always seem more desirable, more valuable. What you have you do not have. You do not have it in the sense of neither understanding it nor valuing it. What you have and understand in the sense of 'reckoning' it as this or as that, 'sweet,' 'sad,' or 'sublime,' you do not have. Only later on, when they come back 'before the intenser stare of the mind,' intenser, that is, than the look of his 'bypast / Body-borne eyes,' intenser than any real stare at what is physically present, only when they come back as avenging ghosts, are they comprehended. Only then are they read, interpreted, deciphered, 'with fuller translation than rested upon them / As living kind.'

The irony of In Front of the Landscape is that the speaker is recalling a walk in which he committed again the crime he deplores. The real landscape is scarcely seen by the walker and not valued by him. His eyes, his attention, his feelings are all intensely focused on what in this case is not behind what is immediately present but in front of it, between him and it. He sees only what is not any longer the desired and as yet unpossessed future but the betrayed past. In either case, however, in either desire or regret, the detachment from what is actually there is almost total. It is as though Hardy goes through the world always out of phase. He dwells in anticipation or in memory. He never lives in other than a false appearance of the present. He always lags behind in his efforts to 'translate' the people and places he encounters. This anachronism can never by any means be put back into harmonious chiming. There is always a delay before the feedback, and the feedback always comes too late. While he is occupied in 'reckoning' at last the worth and purport of something he once had but undervalued, misread, he is already confronting a new scene which his preoccupation is leading him once more to misvalue and misread. He is thereby storing up for himself yet further times in the future when he will suffer again the pangs of retrospective understanding. It will then once more be too late. The effort of retrospection will then once more put swarms of ghosts like an almost impenetrable fog or like an obliterating flood between him and the real scene, the real present. That present he will once more misvalue.

On the one hand, then, the ghosts reproach him for not having understood and valued them when they were alive and bodily present, before his body-borne eyes. On the other hand, they also reproach him for having in any case betrayed them thereafter. The lines stating this are central to the poem. Their difficulty calls for commentary:

> O they were speechful faces, gazing insistent,
>> Some as with smiles,
> Some as with slow-born tears that brinily trundled
>> Over the wrecked
> Cheeks that were fair in their flush-time, ash now with anguish,
>> Harrowed by wiles.

The faces of the phantoms pass him in a beseeching procession, some 'as with' smiles, some 'as with' tears. The repeated 'as with' is odd. Does the poet mean that the ghosts do not really either smile or cry? Or does he mean that he could not quite make out their features? Or does he mean, as perhaps is most probable, that the speech of these 'speechful faces, gazing insistent' is the expressiveness of their features, so that it is as if they were speaking to him with their smiles or with their tears? The puzzle is a good example of the grammatical, syntactical, and lexical difficulty of Hardy's poetry. Overwhelmed by the great flood of their abundance, the reader hurries on from poem to poem, moving towards those generalizations which will allow him to encompass the whole. If he is at all a 'good' reader, he will nevertheless constantly be slowed down or even stopped by local difficulties. These must be brooded on and meditated over. They must be teased for their just meaning before the reader can proceed even to the next lines, much less to all the other poems.

If the faces of the ghosts are 'speechful' because they speak to him 'as with' their smiles or their tears, then when the poet says in the next stanza that he can 'hear them' he may mean that he reads their legible features as though they were audible sounds, not that the ghosts actually speak aloud. The lines of the smiles and the wrinkles that have been carved into the cheeks of the ghosts by their suffering, 'Harrowed' by 'wiles' in the literal sense of being trenched out as well as in the figurative sense of 'worn by fear or anxiety,' are deciphered as speaking signs. They are interpreted as 'insistent' messages of reproach, 'pleading dumbness,' beseeching demands for response from the poet whom they haunt. The pervasive image of the waves of waste waters is obliquely present in the image of the tears that 'brinily trundled / Over the wrecked / Cheeks.' It is as though the faces were battered ships aground in a storm dripping with salt water cascading down from the last wave which has just washed over them. If the poet is overwhelmed by a tide of visions, each separate ghost too swims bathed in the universal medium of the total simultaneous presence of all the scenes, places, objects, and persons from the poet's past. There is a congruence between the form of a book of Hardy's poems, or the whole volume of them taken together in *The Complete Poems*, and the poet's mind as he presents it in *Wessex Heights*, or, in a different way, in *In Front of the Landscape*. Both book and mind are capacious spaces filled pell-mell in profusion with an incoherent multitude of persons, scenes, and actions all going on at once side by side, without touching and without connection. Each is a detached fragment of a life story missing its context before and after.

If the stanza quoted above contains puzzles which slow down the reader or ought to slow him down, this is even more true of the following stanza:

Yes, I could see them, feel them, hear them, address them –
    Halo-bedecked –
And, alas, onwards, shaken by fierce unreason,
    Rigid in hate,
Smitten by years-long wryness born of misprision,
    Dreaded, suspect.

If the reader can guess what the poet means by saying he can 'hear' the ghosts when they do not speak, what is he to make of the claim that the poet can also 'feel' the ghosts? A ghost by definition is impalpable, and yet somehow the word seems right for the coercive intimacy, like an urgent touch, with which the phantoms appeal to him and 'capture' him in their 'pleading dumbness.' A formulation by Jacques Derrida in 'Télépathie'[3] is strangely apposite here. It is as though, by a species of telepathy, Derrida has written his sentence with this line of Hardy (which he has never read) in mind. He seems to have had a premonition of a critic's need, at some point in the future, to account for the strange presence of 'feel them' in Hardy's sequence. This is an example of the theme of Derrida's essay, which I have elsewhere discussed more fully in its relation to Hardy's poetry.[4] 'Before '"seeing" or "hearing,"' says Derrida, 'touch, put your fingertips there, or [it seems] that seeing and hearing amount to touching at a distance – a very old idea, but it requires the archaic to deal with the archaic.'[5]

The poet can see the ghosts, hear them in their pleading dumbness. He can even (therefore) feel them, as though seeing and hearing were touching at a distance, in this case a distance of years, or as if he were doubting Thomas palping the wound in the side of the resurrected 'halo-bedecked' Christ, or as if the ghosts were putting an importunate insistent hand on his arm. He can also 'address them,' presumably to plead with them in justification of his past actions towards them. The four lines which conclude the stanza are fundamentally ambiguous. It is impossible to be sure whether the 'onwards' and all that grammatically hangs from it – the series of four participles, 'shaken,' 'smitten,' 'dreaded,' 'suspect' – apply to the ghosts, as is most probably the case, or, as would be an equally possible reading of the syntax, whether the 'onwards' applies to the poet, the 'I' which is the 'subject' of the sentence:

> And, alas, onwards, shaken by fierce unreason,
>   Rigid in hate,
> Smitten by years-long wryness born of misprision,
>   Dreaded, suspect.

This can either mean that the procession of ghosts passes majestically and silently on, unappeased by the poet's appeal, unforgiving, or that the poet himself moves 'onwards,' as in fact he does, shaken, smitten, and twisted to wryness by the ghosts' misunderstanding of him. Even though the former is more likely, the latter remains hovering as a possibility for the reader (for this reader at least) as he tries to identify the reference of 'shaken,' 'smitten,' 'dreaded,' 'suspect.' Even if a decision is made about that – if the reader decides, for example, that it must be the ghosts who move onwards – the participles in all their violence remain undecidable in meaning. They oscillate between active and passive possibilities. Are the ghosts 'rigid in hate' because they are shaken by the 'fierce unreason' of the speaker who has taken them wrongly, twisted them to a 'years-long wryness' by his 'misprision' of them, or is their refusal to accept the explanation offered by the speaker's address to them a case of 'fierce unreason,' a taking wrongly of the speaker's treatment of them? It cannot be decided which. The power of the lines is the way they vibrate, affirming both possibilities, and neither unequivocally. Are the ghosts 'dreaded' by the speaker, 'suspected' by him, because they are so fiercely unreasonable and so bent on taking revenge? They would then take revenge by continuously haunting him, showing 'hourly before the intenser stare of the mind / As they were ghosts avenging their slights by my bypast / Body-borne eyes.' Or is it the speaker who is 'dreaded' and 'suspect' in the sense that the ghosts abhor him without reason, unreasonably blaming him for having taken them wrongly?

There is no way to tell, nor is there any way to tell whether the 'misprison' in question is the mistaking of the ghosts by the speaker, who took them wrongly in the sense of misprizing them when they were alive, 'caring not for their purport,' or whether the ghosts are twisted into wryness by *their* misprision of the speaker's attitude towards them. 'Misprision' – the word means etymologically 'taking wrongly,' from late Latin *minusprehendere*, from Latin, *minus*, less, plus *prehendere*, to take. 'Misprision' has lately been restored by Harold Bloom to its now archaic meaning of 'mistake' by his use of it to name the misinterpretation of the writings of an earlier writer by a later writer who is influenced by that earlier writer. Hardy too uses the word here to name a misreading of one person by another. Misprision is a misinterpretation of the signs presented by the face and features of others, whether fair in their flush-time or marked by lines of care and smitten to wryness. Misprision also has an overtone of 'misprizing.' Its strict modern meaning is a double one. It means either the misconduct or neglect of duty of a public official, for example in wrongfully appropriating public funds, or 'misprision of felony (or treason).' The latter is a term used in common law to define the offence of concealing knowledge of a felony or treason by one who has not participated in it. Both these meanings resonate in Hardy's line. The ghosts may be smitten to wryness by having been misappropriated by the speaker or by others, taken wrongly, or there may be some crime somewhere, some treasonous betrayal, either on their part or on the part of the speaker, which they have wrongly concealed or which they have suffered for because it has been wrongly concealed by others. In any case, there is a lot of guilt around somewhere. It is a guilt born of betrayal of trust. Both the ghosts and the speaker are suffering intensely for it. Exactly what betrayal is in question for each of the ghosts the reader is not told. He knows only that they were once fair and happy and that the speaker 'fellowed' with them. Later they were betrayed by him or by others, or thought they were betrayed. They suffered intensely for this, so intensely as to be left, even after death, with a fierce, implacable, unreasonable desire for revenge. No reason is given for these betrayals or for these misprisions. They just happened. By the time the speaker is able to appreciate the 'purport' of these persons now dead and enghosted, it is too late. Not only are they dead. They are wholly unforgiving, rigid in hate of him.

The phrase 'fierce unreason' may be given a wide application as an accurate description of many aspects of Hardy's poetry. 'Unreason': the word suggests an absence of *logos* in all its senses of reason, meaning, word, mind, measure, and ground. The word 'fierce' is as important as the word 'unreason.' It names the psychic and spiritual violence of Hardy's experience and of the experience the poems inflict on the reader. The relation between one person and another in Hardy's poetry, or in this poem at least, is the fierce unreason of a multiple betrayal. This betrayal has no reason and leads to a hatred exceeding reason. The poet himself is the victim of a fierce unreason which makes it impossible for him to remain of one mind long enough to be a single continuous self. At the same time he is unable to escape enough from his earlier selves to avoid being unreasonably persecuted by ghosts remaining in his mind from the acts of those earlier selves. He can be neither continuous with those earlier selves nor discontinuous enough to free himself from himself, and so he suffers from the fierce unreason of this anomaly. What David Hume describes objectively enough as a lack of substance and consistency in the self,[6] Hardy experiences as intense suffering born of the co-presence of continuity and discontinuity. He has the continuity of an elephant's memory and the discontinuity of a butterfly's inability to remain the same self for longer than the duration of a brief episode in his life. This inability has no reason or is given no reason. It is an unreasonable fact.

Fierce unreason defines well enough, finally, the local lack of reason, in the sense of single determinate meaning, in the verbal texture of Hardy's verse, however straightforward in meaning that verse first appears to be. The unread-able oscillations in meaning I have identified are born of syntactical, gram-matical, and lexical ambiguities. They impose on the reader a sense of fierce unreason, the lack of a firm ground in a single meaning, as he struggles to make univocal sense of what Hardy is saying. This local ambiguity is matched on a larger scale by the 'unreason' of the poems' inconsistency with one another, if Hardy is right (and he is) in what he repeatedly says, in his prefaces to individual books of poems, of his poems' lack of a coherent philosophy. They cannot be made to hang together, either individually or collectively. The poems too are cases of 'fierce unreason.' They respond to the reader's search for a compre-hensive logic with a violence of repudiation undoing all his attempts to 'translate' them into an order satisfying to the mind.

Hardy's use of the word 'translate' must be scrutinized more carefully as a translation to the last step in my interpretation of *In Front of the Landscape*. The word appears in the next to last line of the next to last stanza. The phantoms who haunt the intenser stare of the poet's mind, almost blotting out the real landscape behind, now 'Show, too, with fuller translation than rested upon them / As living kind.' This leads to the last stanza, with its altered rhyme scheme of closure and with its shift to an imagining of what the speaker must look like to others who see him on such walks and of what they must say of him:

> Hence wag the tongues of the passing people, saying
>   In their surmise,
> 'Ah – whose is this dull form that perambulates, seeing nought
>   Round him that looms
> Whithersoever his footsteps turn in his farings,
>   Save a few tombs?'

In Front of the Landscape seems in many ways compatible with *Wessex Heights*. Both are poems in which the speaker confronts swarms of ghosts from his past. He confronts also his own past selves and experiences the pain of being neither wholly different nor wholly the same, neither wholly continuous nor wholly discontinuous with himself. In *Wessex Heights*, however, the act of physically climbing the heights gives the speaker at least a partial detachment from those past selves and those past relationships. He knows 'some liberty' (*Complete Poems*, p. 320), a liberty like that of being not yet born or already dead and a revisiting ghost haunting others. *In Front of the Landscape*, on the contrary, offers no hope of liberation. The poet remains in the lowlands, haunted by implacable avenging phantoms. Neither the poet nor the poem gets anywhere, in spite of the poet's movement across the landscape. They get nowhere but perhaps to a better understanding of where he is. The poet remains in the same situation at the end as he was in the beginning. The poem can end only with a shift to the different perspective of the imagined watchers of his 'perambulations.' The poem does not record a movement towards liberation. It iterates rather the fact that no liberty is possible.

Something has happened in the poem, however. The poem itself has got written. This act is the covert dramatic action of the poem. This action is a shift from passive suffering to verbal praxis. This is the linguistic moment in this poem. The shift from 'experience' to 'language' is covertly signalled in the shift from the past to the present tense at the beginning of the penultimate stanza: 'Thus do they now show hourly before the intenser / Stare of the mind.' The stanzas until then are in the past tense. They record something which occurred to the poet at some time in the past, something he suffered. With the change to the present tense pathos becomes action. This action is within the poem. It is performed by its words. What takes place takes place within the space of the poem. It is translated there, carried over into the pages of a book.

This 'translation' is a successful defence. It is an impressive act of will to power over the ghosts. In the poem the ghosts are no longer intense presences which can almost palpably be felt. They are now no more than words. Though, for Hardy, ghosts in their literal form have power to hurt even more than sticks and stones, when they are turned into words, 'translated,' they will never hurt him. One motivation driving Hardy to write so many poems and to derive such satisfaction from it[7] is that the writing functions as a successful 'trope of defence' against all those reproaching and beseeching phantoms from his past. Writing is a 'trope' in the literal sense of turning, displacement, or transformation. 'Translation' – the word translates *translatio*. The latter is a traditional rhetorical term in Latin, for example in Quintilian's *Institutio Oratorio*. *Translatio* translates the Greek *metaphora*, 'metaphor.' The linguistic moment in this poem is a triple act of translation: the translation of the phantoms the poet's mind beholds into words; the translation of the phantoms into metaphor, the metaphor of the tide of visions which underlies and pervades all this poem; the translation or transportation of the phantoms into the formal order of the poem. They are transposed not just into words, but into words architecturally or musically ordered. Within this order all those ghosts and the scenes, objects, episodes which are their contexts can exist side by side, just as all Hardy's poems, in spite of their discord, exist side by side in Hardy's *Complete Poems*. This complex act of translation is not, as it first seems, a seeing clearly for the first time these people and their true 'purport.' It is a metaphorical transformation. It is a misreading or distortion, as all translation, for example from one language to another, necessarily is. In the act of defending himself from the reproach the phantoms make that they have not been seen clearly, that they have been misprized, Hardy commits again the crime of misprision from which he would defend himself. He commits it blatantly, out there in the open, on the page, where all who read may see. Therefore another poem in self-defence must be written. This commits the crime once more, and so yet another is necessary, *ad infinitum*. The poet never has a chance to catch up with his past transgressions. He cannot compensate for them, do justice to his past at last, pay off his debt to himself and to others, and wipe his slate clean. The act of compensation, the plea of innocence in response to the phantoms' recriminations, always turns into another act of self-incrimination.

This failure is also the triumph of the poetry. It is only by this constantly repeated act of misprision that Hardy can successfully defend himself and maintain his integrity. It is the integrity not of a self but of a grammatical function producing ultimately that disharmony of *The Complete Poems* Hardy so insists on in the prefaces. The individual acts of defence, turning perception into language, are more important than their hanging together.

It would appear at first that *In Front of the Landscape* depends on the experience of disjunction between the actual landscape and those mental visions which intervene for the speaker between his eye and the scene, blotting it to feeble mist. The poem, it seems, exemplifies that law of Hardy's experience which says you never have or prize what 'is' in the present, but always look before and after, and pine for what is not. The fundamental categories of the poem, it seems, are perception and interpersonal relations. The poem has to do with seeing and not seeing, and with struggles for power, by way of appropriation and misappropriation, between one person and another. The speaker cannot see the landscape because its place has been taken by the phantoms who exercise a coercive power over him, captivating him: 'so in their pleading dumbness / Captured me these.'

Is this in fact the case? If the full implications of the word 'translation' are accepted, the word 'misprision' is tipped toward that secondary meaning it can have of mistaking or misreading rather than of simply misappropriating. The speaker's original misprision of the phantoms was a mistaken interpretation of the signs they displayed, their 'purport,' what they said and what their features showed as legible tokens. The activity the poem first records as having taken place in the past and then, with the shift to the present tense, enacts within itself, is also an activity of 'translation.' This means it is mistranslation or misreading, a doing violence to the signs he sees. The signs now misread, however, are not merely, or not originally, those internal ones of memory. They are the tombs scattered around the landscape, perhaps initially the many prehistoric tumuli which dot the region where Hardy was walking, but also the graves of the dead friends, lovers, and relatives whose ghosts Hardy sees. He looks across the scene and then walks 'Over the leaze, / Past the clump, and down to where lay the beheld ones.' The passers-by who see him out walking know that he 'sees nought,' wherever his footsteps take him, 'save a few tombs.' The poet transforms those tombs. He translates them into the tide of visions the poem so eloquently names. Far from being detached from the landscape, the speaker's linguistic activity in the poem, like the past crimes of misprision he deplores, is based on taking features of the visual scene, in this case not faces but tombs, as signs, not merely as perceptual objects, as they are for the passers-by. These signs are then translated. This activity transforms the neutral notation of topographical description into what might be called a tropography. This tropography is the mapping of an act of figuration which is both Hardy's crime and his defence.

The poem, words on the page, is the monument or tomb of this act. The linguistic act of 'translation' is not a figure for perception. Perception is translation. This means the writing of the poem is not the record of the appearance of the ghosts. The writing is the act which raises the ghosts by turning dead signs into beseeching phantoms. The poem in turn, as the remnant of its writing, becomes dead letters once more waiting for some reader to 'translate' it again and to raise again the ghosts which inhabit it. In doing so the reader commits in his turn the crime of misprision which the poem both regrets and commits. In this case too, the linguistic moment has a momentum which leads to its repetition time after time, without hope of ever laying the ghosts once and for all.

Once again, as in passages by Wordsworth I have elsewhere discussed, but also in passages in Hegel and in Baudelaire,[8] among many others, in a tradition already present in the Greek pun on *soma/sema* (body/sign), the relation between a dead body and the mound or tomb above it, or between the corpse and the inscription on the tombstone above it, figures the complex relation between perception and language, or between language and its necessary material substrate – the stone, paper, or modulated air on which it is inscribed. The passers-by see the tombs as tombs, as harmless and insignificant matter. Hardy tells the reader in *In Front of the Landscape* that the robes, cheeks, and eyes of those he once loved are 'with the earth's crust / Now corporate,' and that others who 'had shared in the dramas' are now 'clay cadavers.' The dead are not just dead. They are turned to earth, incorporated in it, dispersed into the landscape. To see that landscape is to see the dead, or it is to see what they now are, harmless mounds on the earth. The 'intenser stare' of Hardy's mind resurrects those clay cadavers. It translates them back into what they were. It then transforms them into a 'tide.' This activity at first seems to be one of perception ('stare'). It then emerges as in fact an act of writing ('translation'). This act of translation is the writing of the poem itself. The poem is written as it were on or over those mounds, tombs, clay cadavers. The poem is a species of epitaph, an inscription on a tombstone, *sema* over *soma*.

There is more to be said of this act of inscription.[9] It is, as all epitaphs tend to be, also an act of invocation, an apostrophe or prosopopoia addressing the absent, the dead, and thereby raising the ghosts of the dead. Though prosopopoia overlaps with catachresis, as is evident from the way so many catachreses are personifications or anthropomorphisms, e.g. face of a mountain, leg of a chair, prosopopoia differs fundamentally from catachresis in a curious way. Though, as the word prosopopoia suggests (*prosopon* is 'mask' in Greek), personification gives a face to what no longer has one or never had one, it is at the same time an act of effacement or defacement, while catachresis makes things appear by naming them. Catachresis has to do with the phenomenal, the visible, the aesthetic in the Hegelian sense of 'shining forth.' Prosopopoia, on the other hand, always buries what it evokes in the apostrophic praise, like Antony speaking over the dead body of Caesar. Prosopopoia effaces what it gives a face to by making it vanish into the earth and become 'a body wholly body,'[10] *soma* without *sema*, or *soma* coming into the open as the material base of *sema*, as no longer overt personification but now effaced catachresis become mere literal name, like a tombstone with the letters worn away or a coin rubbed smooth, 'effaced.'

Hardy in *In Front of the Landscape* raises the dead from their tombs, where they have become 'clay cadavers,' their 'eyes with the earth's crust / Now corporate.' He is confronted and indicted for his betrayals by those 'speechful faces gazing insistent,' 'halo-bedecked.' At the same time this drama of personification has been dispersed unostentatiously or in effaced form through-out the whole landscape or in the literal words the poet uses to name the aspects of that landscape. The upland is 'Coppice-crowned,' as though it were a king's head, the light 'strokes' the landscape, and if one of the images from the past which rises to haunt the poet is 'the one of the broad brow,' the cliffs by the sea are named as 'a headland of hoary aspect / gnawed by the tide, / Frilled by the nimb of the morning.' 'Headland' is not metaphor. It is the 'proper' name for this topographical feature, though of course a cliff by the sea is not properly speaking a head. It is another personifying catachresis, and the reader may not even notice, so effaced is the linguistic action, so easy to take for granted, that the lines project into the landscape exactly the same image of a halo-fringed head, in this case that of an old man ('of hoary aspect') that the reader has already encountered in the description of the ghosts the speaker confronts as he advances through his tide of visions. These ghosts are no more than the embodiment or bringing into the open, like a photograph being developed, or an inscription in invisible ink being made to appear, of something already dispersed everywhere in the landscape in the ordinary language anyone could use to name it. To recognize this turns the ghosts back into language or disperses them back into the earth's crust. They are no more than a trick of words, and to see this is to lay the ghosts and to confront mere earth.

Moreover, the two lovers who once stood on the headland 'touched by the fringe of an ecstasy / Scantly descried' should have taken warning from the scene around them, for what is going on there is a grotesque horrible Dantesque scene of a halo-nimbed head being gnawed by some remorseless creature, apparently another head, as in Ugolino's gnawing of Ruggierri's nape in *Inferno* xxxii and xxxiii. If the sea can chew, it must have teeth, a mouth, eyes, a face, though the prosopopoia is evanescent, latent, once more effaced. This horrible drama pro-leptically figures the relation of mutual pain-giving which all human love, for Hardy, comes to in the end, even love like that between the two guilelessly glad friends who stood there on the headland touched by the fringe of an ecstasy. The image of the sea wearing away the land, as one head might gnaw at another, also figures the ultimate engulfment of each distinct shape or form, for example each living human body, by the shapeless matter which will eventually reincorporate it, as a cadaver is consumed, decomposes, and disperses into the earth. The figure, finally, figures the activity it itself manifests in effaced or scarcely manifested form, namely the effacement of the inaugural figures by which man takes possession of nature. These figures vanish into the innocently 'literal' language whereby, for example, we call a cliff by the sea a 'headland.' If *In Front of the Landscape* brings those 'dead metaphors' back to life, it also kills them again by exposing their base in baseless habits of language, projecting life where there is none. These habits no one, not even the greatest poet, with his matchless mastery of language, can either fully efface or fully control. He can neither do without that form of translation called prosopopoia, nor can he safely manipulate it for his own ends.

   In Front of the Landscape develops a tropographical ratio: as the perception transfiguring the landscape is to that landscape as it is in itself, neutral and harmless earth, so the poem as language is to its material base, the indifferent body which in one way or another is necessary to support any inscription, for example the paper on which Hardy's poems are printed. This ratio is a false or misleading one, since what appears to be the literal base of the metaphorical transposition, 'perception,' does not, it turns out, exist as such for Hardy at all. Perception is the figure and reading is the literal activity, in more senses than one, 'lettering' and 'real' at once, of which perception is the figure. Perception for Hardy does not literally exist. It is always already translation. It is an activity positing, reading misreading, transposing, dead earth as signs. For Hardy, the identity of the literary text is this proliferating act of translation. This act repeats itself before and behind within the poem. It is again repeated whenever you or I or another reads the poem.

NOTES

1 Thomas Hardy, *The Complete Poems*, New Wessex Edition, ed. James Gibson, London 1976, p. 303. The whole poem is printed following the notes.
2 J.O. Bailey, *The Poetry of Thomas Hardy: A Handbook and Commentary*, Chapel Hill, North Carolina 1970, pp. 261–2.
3 Jacques Derrida, 'Télépathie,' *Furor*, 2 (1981), 5–41.
4 In an essay forthcoming on Hardy's poem *The Torn Letter*.
5 Derrida, 'Télépathie,' pp. 15–16, my translation.
6 In 'Of Personal Identity,' section 6 of Book I, Part IV of *A Treatise of Human Nature* (1739).
7 The poet's second wife noted that her husband was never so happy as when he had finished writing another gloomy poem.

8 In 'The Stone and the Shell: Wordsworth's Dream of the Arab,' in *Moments Premiers*, Paris 1973, pp. 125–47. Paul de Man discusses related passages from Hegel and Baudelaire in an essay on Michael Riffaterre forthcoming in *Diacritics*.
9 I am indebted here to astute comments made orally by Patricia Parker when an earlier version of this essay was presented as a lecture at the University of Toronto.
10 Wallace Stevens, 'The Idea of Order at Key West,' in *The Collected Poems*, New York 1954, p. 128.

In Front of the Landscape

Plunging and labouring on in a tide of visions,
  Dolorous and dear,
Forward I pushed my way as amid waste waters
  Stretching around,
Through whose eddies there glimmered the customed landscape
  Yonder and near

Blotted to feeble mist. And the coomb and the upland
  Coppice-crowned,
Ancient chalk-pit, milestone, rills in the grass-flat
  Stroked by the light,
Seemed but a ghost-like gauze, and no substantial
  Meadow or mound.

What were the infinite spectacles featuring foremost
  Under my sight,
Hindering me to discern my paced advancement
  Lengthening to miles;
What were the re-creations killing the daytime
  As by the night?

O they were speechful faces, gazing insistent,
  Some as with smiles,
Some as with slow-born tears that brinily trundled
  Over the wrecked
Cheeks that were fair in their flush-time, ash now with anguish,
  Harrowed by wiles.

Yes, I could see them, feel them, hear them, address them –
  Halo-bedecked –

And, alas, onwards, shaken by fierce unreason,
    Rigid in hate,
Smitten by years-long wryness born of misprision,
    Dreaded, suspect.

Then there would breast me shining sights, sweet seasons
    Further in date;
Instruments of strings with the tenderest passion
    Vibrant, beside
Lamps long extinguished, robes, cheeks, eyes with the earth's crust
    Now corporate.

Also there rose a headland of hoary aspect
    Gnawed by the tide,
Frilled by the nimb of the morning as two friends stood there
    Guilelessly glad –
Wherefore they knew not – touched by the fringe of an ecstasy
    Scantly descried.

Later images too did the day unfurl me,
    Shadowed and sad,
Clay cadavers of those who had shared in the dramas,
    Laid now at ease,
Passions all spent, chiefest the one of the broad brow
    Sepulture-clad.

So did beset me scenes, miscalled of the bygone,
    Over the leaze,
Past the clump, and down to where lay the beheld ones;
    – Yea, as the rhyme
Sung by the sea-swell, so in their pleading dumbness
    Captured me these.

For, their lost revisiting manifestations
    In their live time
Much had I slighted, caring not for their purport,
    Seeing behind
Things more coveted, reckoned the better worth calling
    Sweet, sad, sublime.

Thus do they now show hourly before the intenser
   Stare of the mind
As they were ghosts avenging their slights by my bypast
   Body-borne eyes,
Show, too, with fuller translation than rested upon them
   As living kind.

Hence wag the tongues of the passing people, saying
   In their surmise,
'Ah – whose is this dull form that perambulates, seeing nought
   Round him that looms
Whithersoever his footsteps turn in his farings,
   Save a few tombs?'

PATRICIA PARKER

The (Self-) Identity of the Literary Text: Property, Propriety, Proper Place, and Proper Name in *Wuthering Heights*

I

The end of linear writing is indeed the end of the book.
Derrida, *Of Grammatology*

In 1957, Ian Watt began *The Rise of the Novel* by tracing the parallels between the growing popularity of the novel form and a number of contemporary Enlightenment phenomena – the realist epistemology of Bacon, Descartes, Hobbes, and Locke; the growth of Protestantism with its fondness for personal inventory and the measurement of time and progress in the sequential form of the journal or diary; economic individualism, with its division of labour and of private property; and the 'principle of individuation' enunciated by Locke:

The 'principle of individuation' accepted by Locke was that of existence at a particular locus in space and time: since, as he wrote, 'ideas become general by separating them from the circumstances of time and place', so they become particular only when both these circumstances are specified. In the same way the characters of the novel can only be individualized if they are set in a background of particularized time and place.[1]

This principle is connected in Locke – who also wrote a defence of private property – with the differentiating function of proper names, the very indicators of individual identity, since, as Hobbes maintained, a 'Proper Name' is 'singular to one only thing.'[2] Locke, whose work everywhere pervades the eighteenth century, established a principle in which individuality is linked to definitive placing – a place marked by the proper or 'appropriated' name which designates an individual identity and prevents its being confused with another ('and therefore in their own species, which they have most to do with and wherein they have often occasion to mention particular persons, they make use of proper names, and there distinct individuals have distinct denominations,' III.3.4). In literature, argues Watt, 'this function of proper names was first fully established in the novel,' with its attention to names as designating 'completely individualized entities' so as to 'suggest that they were to be regarded as particular individuals in the contemporary social environment.' Names point a finger, or single out, as Foucault observes in his discussion of the primacy of naming or denomination in the Enlightenment; they say, as the preacher does to Lockwood in his first dream at Wuthering Heights, '*Thou art the man!*'[3]

More recently than Watt, Patricia Drechsel Tobin, in *Time and the Novel*, has extended this exploration of the relation between the novel and the phenomenon of linearity in all its Enlightenment forms – the line of time, of language, of narrative, and of thought, the model which informs the linear structure of Puritan diary and capitalist ledger-book, of genealogy and chronological history, of division into discrete serial entities or binary oppositions, the continuation of the Aristotelian Law of the Excluded Middle into the post-Cartesian logic of succession and sequence. With Barthes, Foucault, and Derrida, Tobin associates this linear logic with syntax itself, the sentence moving like a miniature narrative from beginning to ending and thereby linking logic with closure. Derrida, in his discussion of the line and the book in *De la grammatologie* describes this linearity as 'the repression of pluri-dimensional symbolic thought' and makes a connection between linear writing, logic, scientific and philosophical analysis, and history itself understood as a line or irreversible progress. Foucault characterizes it as a shift from the Renaissance fondness for resemblance to a preference for classification and sequential or causal reasoning, from metaphor's paradigmatic verticality to metonymy – the syntagmatic and sequential. Discourse, he observes, is understood in the Classical *episteme* as 'a sequence of verbal signs,' a spacing out of the simultaneous into the successive, into a 'linear order' whose parts 'must be traversed *one after* the other.' It is the linear model which produces what Foucault calls the 'reciprocal kinship' between the 'chain of discourse' (Hobbes), epistemology as 'the chain of knowledge,' the conception of time as chronology or irreversible sequence, and the very Enlightenment preoccupation with progress. And it is this linear logic of Enlightenment thought, combined with the conception of time as chronological sequence, which informs the novel as well, linked so closely with chronology as to be arguably 'chronomorph,' even when it appears to be transgressing that order.[4]

Hugh Blair and others in the eighteenth century were concerned with the establishment of rules for language itself, its mastery according to the dictates of 'propriety' – a word still synonymous in this period with 'property,' in one of its senses – and with the decorum of proper place regulating the movement of tropes such as metaphor conceived of as 'improper' (Quintilian, *improprium*) or 'out of place.' Foucault provides a virtual paraphrase of the way in which what Blair calls language's 'gradual progress towards refinement' – where 'almost every object comes to have a proper name given to it' – is contrasted in the Enlightenment with the primitive mobility of words, before they could be assigned their proper places on the table or grid:

It is very probable that this mobility was even greater in the beginnings of language than it is now: today, the analysis is so detailed, the grid so fine, the relations of coordination and subordination are so firmly established, that words scarcely have any opportunity to move from their places. But at the beginning of human history, when words were few, when representations were still confused and not well analysed, when the passions both modified them and provided them with a basis, words had greater mobility. One might even say that words were figurative before being proper: in other words, that they had scarcely attained their status as particular names before they were being scattered over representations by the force of spontaneous rhetoric.[5]

We might keep this connection between the primitive paucity of words and their mobility in mind when we turn to Emily Brontë's *Wuthering Heights*, which involves a primitive setting seen through the eyes of a narrator whose name recalls Locke's, makes do with a curious paucity of proper names, and gives us Lockwood's own contrast between the story's more primitive setting and the civilized world from which he comes as that between 'setting a hungry man down to a single dish on which he may concentrate his entire appetite' and 'introducing him to a table laid out by French cooks.' (VII, 102).

Foucault's concluding discussion of the Enlightenment suggests that it is possible to see in the very grid of linearity, analysis, and proper placing the 'excluded' which was eventually to undo it:

if there is to be an articulated patterning of representations, there must be a murmur of analogies rising from things, perceptible even in the most immediate experience; there must be resemblances that posit themselves from the very start. ... If language exists, it is because below the level of identities and differences there is the foundation provided by continuities, resemblances, repetitions, and natural criss-crossings. Resemblance, excluded from knowledge since the early seventeenth century, still constitutes the outer edge of language: the ring surrounding the domain of that which can be analysed, reduced to order, and known. Discourse dissipates the murmur, but without it it could not speak.

For Foucault, it is the repressed violence of both nature and tropes which undoes the linear 'chain' of discourse and of knowledge: disorder in nature disrupting the 'general ordering of nature' and the 'ancient, enigmatic density' of words – the 'reappearance of language as a multiple profusion' – disrupting the order of language as a 'grid for the knowledge of things.'[6] *Wuthering Heights* is crucially situated within this history, not only because of its own preoccupation with proper name and proper place, but because in so many ways it recapitulates both the linear Enlightenment grid and its exclusions, the 'rise of the novel' and its potential unmaking. It may therefore be approached as one of those nineteenth-century texts which call into question – long before contemporary interest in this problem, which may be itself still an after-effect of the disruption of the Classical *episteme* – precisely the identity, or self-identity, of the text, by their simultaneous demonstration and undoing of the epistemological claims and ordering structures of the novel form.[7] In *Wuthering Heights*, this undoing involves both nature, which is placed outside the orderly 'house of fiction' in the binary opposition of nature and culture on which Lockwood's narrative partly depends, and the *unheimlich*, or uncanny, mobility of tropes such as metaphor traditionally described as 'alien,' part of the excluded which threatens the identity of that which seeks to control or master it.

II

We're dismal enough without conjuring up ghosts and visions to perplex us.
Nelly Dean, *Wuthering Heights*

the authoritarian demands put pressure on a narrative voice to turn into a narratorial voice and to bring about [donner lieu à] a narrative that would be identifiable. ...
Derrida, 'LIVING ON: Border Lines'

Wuthering Heights would seem to present us with a quintessential Enlighten-ment narrative in its own preoccupation with the claims of superstition and reason, primitive and civilized, and in the ambivalent middle position occupied by its secondary narrator, Nelly Dean, between belief in the supernatural and her own housekeeper's sense of order and proper place. The novel opens with a date (1801) inaugurating the text of a narrator who identifies himself in the opening line ('I have just returned from a visit to my landlord – the solitary neighbour that I shall be troubled with'), very soon after records his own proper name ('Mr. Lockwood, your new tenant, sir'), and then provides a second date (1802) at the beginning of chapter XXXII. The generic identity of the text, then, would appear to be that of the diary or journal – that sequential ordering of time and narrative that allies the novel with the linearity of chronology, genealogy, or history. Lockwood himself seems to belong on the side of enlightenment, as the master-narrator whose distance from the superstitious and supernatural phenomena he encounters gives the novel, in the view of some of its readers, a reassuring sense both of progress and of closure. The question of the identity of the literary text, then, when raised with regard to *Wuthering Heights*, involves at least two related issues: its generic identity – the novel form, with its dependence on chronology, spacing, the principle of individuation, and the designating function of proper names; and the identity, or self-identity, of a text which appears from the beginning to be the unified production of a single hand – authorized, as we now say, by the conferring of his narrative signature or proper name.

In approaching the question of the identity or self-identity of *Wuthering Heights*, we need to have recourse to a distinction from Maurice Blanchot, taken up again in a recent essay by Derrida which has precisely to do with the question of identity, and with the relationship between identity and placing. Blanchot distinguishes between the 'narrative voice' and the 'narratorial voice,' which in *Wuthering Heights* would be that of Lockwood himself, 'the voice of a subject recounting something, remembering an event or a historical sequence, knowing who he is, where he is, and what he is talking about.' The 'narrative voice,' by contrast, is, in Blanchot's phrase, 'a neutral voice that utters the work from the placeless place where the work is silent.' The narratorial voice can be located and identified – it has, says Derrida, and confers on the work, 'une carte d'identité.' But the narrative voice has no fixed place: it is both atopical and hypertopical, nowhere and everywhere at once. In Blanchot's terms, the neutral narrative voice is 'ghost-like,' a spectre which haunts the narratorial text and, itself without centre, placing, or closure, disrupts and dislocates the work, not permitting it to exist as finally completed or closed.[8]

This ghostlike atopicality and hypertopicality of something which resists definitive placing or closure may remind us in *Wuthering Heights* of its own principal ghost, that 'Catherine' who haunts Heathcliff after her death, overrunning all boundaries by being at once everywhere ('I am surrounded with her image! ... The entire world is a dreadful collection of memoranda that she did exist, and that I have lost her!') and no single, definable place ('Where is she? Not *there* – not in heaven – not perished – where?'). The novel itself, in fact, is full of ghosts, demons, and uncanny presences, from the 'Catherine' Heathcliff begs to 'haunt' him (XVI, 204), to the 'ghostly Catherine' Linton (IV, 75) of Lockwood's second dream in the room at the Heights he describes as 'swarming with ghosts and goblins' (III, 68), to Catherine's evocation of Gimmerton Kirk ('We've braved its ghosts often together, and dared each other to stand among the graves and ask them to come,' XII, 164), Heathcliff's affirmation of his belief in ghosts (xxɪx, 320), and his warning of the consequences of not burying him next to the open side of Catherine's coffin ('if you neglect it, you shall prove, practically, that the dead are not annihilated!' xxxɪv, 363). But this repeated reference to ghosts in the novel is also countered by their denial, from Isabella Linton's 'It's well people don't *really* rise from their grave' (xvɪɪ, 216) to Lockwood's concluding assurance against the superstition that the dead Catherine and Heathcliff 'walk,' when he visits their graves in the closing lines of the text ('I lingered round them, under the benign sky; watched the moths fluttering among the heath and hare-bells; listened to the soft wind breathing through the grass; and wondered how anyone could ever imagine unquiet slumbers, for the sleepers in that quiet earth'). The exercise of closure itself, by the master-narrator who confers on the text his own unifying identity and proper name, is linked with the laying, or denial, of ghosts, a forestalling of an uncanny return or 'advent,' a term the narrative several times repeats.

Wuthering Heights, then, offers the reader both the possibility of ghosts and their denial. But there is also in the novel a textual ghost, in Blanchot's terms, which inhabits and dislocates the identity conferred by Lockwood's narratorial order and its Enlightenment preoccupation with linearity, propriety, and proper place. All we have before us is Lockwood's text, but inscribed within it as its own uncanny other is an 'alien' text inhabiting it and disrupting its ordering structures – Lockwood's diary, Nelly Dean's genealogical history, and the very sequential process of reading which the novel form invites. Derrida speaks, in his discussion of the 'linear norm' and the 'form of the book,' of the undoing of the linear which takes place in the margins and 'between the lines.'[9] *Wuthering Heights*, with its own emphasis on marginal, competing, and heterogeneous texts – Catherine's manuscript writing, for example, inserted into the 'margins' or 'blanks' of 'good books' (ɪɪɪ) – itself provokes such a double reading, in which the text begins to lose the sense of coherent order or unified identity its organization under a single identifiable narratorial voice confers upon the book. It is, not insignificantly, to books that Edgar Linton repairs in the midst of his wife's delirious ravings (xɪɪ), and books which Lockwood piles up in a 'pyramid' to keep out a ghostly alien or 'changeling' who seeks to re-enter the house (ɪɪɪ). Reading itself – in the proper left-to-right order in which Hareton Earnshaw learns to decipher the inscription which will restore him to his property and rightful place – is part of the process, in this novel, of civilization and enlightenment. But in Derrida's terms, the 'text' – like Heathcliff both 'orphan' and 'alien' – works against the order and identity of the 'book,' and that which is in the margins or between the lines becomes part of the text's own 'subversive dislocation of identity in general.'[10]

Readers of *Wuthering Heights* have frequently commented on its apparent binary oppositions – nature and culture, good and evil, heaven and hell, primitive and civilized – and less frequently on the way in which it undermines this division in the very process of calling attention to it, as Shelley does in *The Witch of Atlas* with its opening reference to the Enlightenment division into 'those cruel Twins,' Error and Truth. Both logic and the logic of identity are founded, for Derrida, on the opposition of inside and outside which inaugurates all binary opposition – where each of the terms is 'simply external to the other' and the expulsion of one involves a domination or mastery, like naming itself which Nietzsche (speaking precisely of the opposition of 'good' and 'evil') links with a taking of possession or appropriation. But once expelled, the 'outside' functions as a ghost: the identical is haunted, as Foucault says of the Enlightenment table or grid, by what it excludes. The principal story in *Wuthering Heights* involves the usurpation of a house, or property, by a 'houseless' (IV, 78) alien, Heathcliff the outsider becoming master of the house, a guest who becomes host. What I will suggest is that Lockwood's own Enlightenment narrative – with the sense of unified identity it confers upon the book – is inhabited by a textual guest which threatens to become host, two terms used together in chapter III (68) at precisely the point where it is a question of Lockwood's having penetrated to the centre of the house and encountered a 'ghost.'[11] To look for the identity of the literary text may in this as in other nineteenth-century narratives be finally to discover a Ghost Story.

III

> Property was thus appalled
> That the self was not the same;
> Single nature's double name
> Neither two nor one was called.
> Shakespeare, *The Phoenix and the Turtle*

For Derrida, the self-identity of the text is intimately linked to 'propriété' in its widest sense. What must be emphasized, however, is that the complex of terms related to the 'proper,' a complex to which recent criticism has again called our attention, also engaged the Enlightenment, precisely in connection with the problem of identity. By considering the relation of property, proper place, and proper name in Lockwood's text to the question of its unified identity, we return to the context with which we began – the Lockeian principle of individuation, its relation to discrete chronological sequence or line and to the boundary-marking of individual identity through what Locke termed the 'appropriation' of the proper name. In the process, we will suggest the ways in which the two sides of the debate over *Wuthering Heights* – between formalist critics who emphasize its narrative structures and Marxist or sociological critics who emphasize its involvement with the laws of private property – converge in this novel precisely on the question of 'property' in its most radical or fundamental sense.[12]

Property and proper name are connected, first, in the figure of Lockwood himself: it is he who owns or masters his own text – as Hobbes says of the connection between Author and Owner (*Leviathan*, XVI) – and lends his name as the single unifying presence of a narrative which repeatedly calls attention to the importance of proper place, property, propriety, and proper name. The emphasis on place or position in Lockwood's text is everywhere – in the plot founded on the relation between the two houses, Wuthering Heights and Thrushcross Grange; in the sense of speech as placing characters by region or social class; and in Joseph's Pharisaical insistence on the Sabbath as an inviolable place in time. This is joined by a more specific focus on ownership, possession, and property, from Heathcliff's opening 'Thrushcross Grange is my own, sir' (I, 45), his reference to his own son as 'property' (XX, 242), Lockwood's uncertainty about who is the 'favoured possessor' of the female figure he encounters at the Heights (II, 55), and Earnshaw's finding the orphan Heathcliff without an 'owner' (IV) to the principal exchange of the plot, in which Heathcliff acquires the very property from which he had been excluded. Private property and its dividing lines are reduced to an extreme in the scene in which the 'divided' Linton children (VI, 89) almost rend a pet dog 'in two' in their struggle for possession – a sacrifice of whole for part which recalls the judgment of Solomon and its revelation of the logic, and limits, of property. The careful guarding of the Linton property at Thrushcross Grange against all trespass is epitomized in the elder Linton's charge to the little 'outlaws' Catherine and Heathcliff – 'To beard a magistrate in his stronghold, and on the Sabbath, too!' (VI, 90) – a charge whose biblical flavour recalls both Christ's trespass of the Sabbath and his breaking down of all barriers or partition walls (2 Corinthians 10:4, 'For the weapons of our warfare are not carnal, but mighty through God to the pulling down of strong holds').

'Property' in the sense of the establishment of boundaries – and the prohibition of trespass fundamental to a society based on the laws of private possession – appears as well in the frequency in the novel of images such as windows, thresholds, and gates which mark the boundaries between places, or between inside and outside. From the opening chapter, the novel's establishment of boundaries or dividing walls is intimately linked with the language of its narrator, whose syntax raises barriers even as he pushes through the gate which keeps him from the Heights ('I do myself the honour of calling as soon as possible, after my arrival, to express the hope that I have not inconvenienced you by my perseverance in soliciting the occupation of Thrushcross Grange') and whose convoluted speech contrasts pointedly with the abruptness of Heathcliff's replies and the Heights' own unmediated entrance ('One step brought us into the family sitting-room, without any introductory lobby, or passage'). Lockwood, indeed, presents himself in a series of episodes having to do with the interposition of barriers – his rebuffing of the young girl whose attentions he had encouraged, his interposing of a 'table' between himself and the dog whose fury he himself provoked (I), his piling up of books to keep out a ghostly 'Catherine Linton' (III) and rubbing her wrist against the broken glass of a partition which no longer divides. These apotropaic gestures provide our first introduction to the narrator who will both request and relate the housekeeper's story from the framed and mediated distance of Thrushcross Grange. In the midst of the chaos he himself has caused by baiting the dogs, Lockwood assimilates them to the biblical 'herd of possessed swine' and his hastening to interpose a table between himself and the fury he has raised proleptically enacts the function of the narrative which ensues, the casting out or distancing of demons too menacing to the enlightened mind, in a novel whose mediating perspectives and multiple narrations themselves both conjure and frame.

Lockwood's text, however, is remarkable for its emphasis not only on proper place, property, and boundary lines but also on trespass, transgression or crossing, or on boundary lines which themselves become thresholds. Heathcliff, the figure through whom Earnshaw will pass into Linton and back again, is pictured frequently at doorways or other places of crossing. And the novel is filled with crossings or exchanges of place which are frequently also reversals of position. Edgar and Isabella Linton's arrival at the Heights reverses the direction of Catherine and Heathcliff's trespass. Catherine and Isabella exchange places through marriage, the former moving from Heights to Grange when she marries Edgar and the latter, in her elopement with Heathcliff, moving in the opposite direction. The subsequent longing of each to return would map another crossing: Catherine in her delirium in chapter XII imagines a return to the Heights; Isabella in the very next chapter writes 'My heart returned to Thrushcross Grange in twenty-four hours after I left it' (XIII, 173). Heathcliff and Hindley change places as oppressor and oppressed; and the transformation of oppressed child into oppressive father which Kettle and others see as the central reversal of the novel is part of the general sense within it of things turning into their opposites or taking on the spirit of the place they exchange for another. Nelly remarks on the way in which Isabella and Heathcliff seem, after their marriage, to change positions ('So much had circumstances altered their positions, that he would certainly have struck a stranger as a born and bred gentleman, and his wife as a thorough little slattern!' XIV, 184). 'Crossing' is insisted on even at the purely verbal level – Nelly Dean's unsettling vision (XI) and Hindley's threatened burial (XVII, 221) at 'crossroads'; characters repeatedly responding 'crossly,' not bearing 'crossing,' or described as 'cross' (IX, 128; X, 134, 137); Nelly's warning Heathcliff, regarding Catherine, to 'shun crossing her way again' (XIV, 184); and even the name of Thrushcross Grange. The trope which is figured as a cross (chi, χ) is the figure of crossing known as chiasmus, the trope which Scaliger describes as creating 'a scissor formation in the sentence'[13] and this kind of scissor formation frequently provides the closest diagrammatic form for the exchange or reversals of place in the plot itself.

We could go on listing the novel's various forms of crossing or transgression, from the undercurrent of incest which would undermine the sequential authority of the genealogical line, to the crossing of boundaries between animal and human, nature and culture, responsible for the heightened intensity of the novel's language.[14] When Catherine's brow is described as suddenly 'clouded,' a dead metaphor comes once again to life, loosed from the tomb of the banal or familiarly 'proper,' and she becomes for a moment a novelistic Lucy, wrapped up in rocks and stones and trees. Language which should be dead – if we think of the Enlightenment strictures against the improper crossings of tropes – becomes in this novel alive and even violent, and the air swarming with 'Catherines' as Lockwood reads in chapter III may have its counterpart for the reader in the unsettling mobility of words which refuse to stay fixed in their single, or proper, meaning. 'Bridle' in the scene in which Nelly sees Isabella's dog suspended where 'a bridle hook is driven into the wall' (XII, 166) contaminates 'bridal,' as it stands as a menacing sign of Heathcliff and Isabella's elopement. Joseph's apparently peripheral and unreadable dialect is central to this kind of crossing, his 'gooid-for-nowt madling' (XIII, 180) combining both 'maid' and 'mad' just as his earlier 'marred' (180) crosses 'married' and 'marred.' Readers of the novel soon learn to translate the dialect forms into standard English, as part of the accommodation of 'primitive' speech to the civilized mind. But for a moment the words resist this standardization and their very ambiguity, blurring the line between dialect and the lexicon of civilized speech, contributes to the novel's sense of menace, of something undermining the boundaries of the age both of Enlightenment and of the Dictionary.

IV

Die Namen individualisieren nur zum Schein.
Stempel

The narrative of *Wuthering Heights*, then, combines proper place and property on the one hand and transgression or crossing on the other in a way which suggests that it is the very erection of boundary lines which creates the possibility of trespass, just as the sermon of Jabes Branderham in chapter III– with its proliferating partitions or dividing lines – has ironically to do with the forgiveness of 'trespasses.' It also calls attention to the activity of proper names – those names which in Hobbes and Locke distinguish individual identities and in Watt's description are inseparable from the principle of individuation integral to the novel form itself – in a way which may enable us to suggest how this crossing of boundaries undermines the identity of the text, the very partitions which Lockwood needs in order to produce a satisfying Enlightenment narrative or 'good book.' An interest in names and their relation to identities already marks the dizzying series of aliases or multiple designations in the Gondal saga, whose profusion of names or initials capable of reference to several different characters might suggest the accommodation involved for Brontë in moving to the more Lockeian assumptions of the novel form – each name in its place and a proper place for every name. *Wuthering Heights* seems to be alerting the reader to the function but also to the potential autonomy of proper names by its insistence on their detachability, their application to more than one person or the several names by which a single character may be called. For if the function of proper names is to be the boundary markers of individual identity and thus to contribute to the coherence and readability of the narrative,[15] these very instruments of order and identity are in this text unreliable instruments. The confusion which makes Lockwood feel 'unmistakably out of place' (II, 56) in the opening chapters results partly from the very ambiguity of proper names as indicators of place or property – of who belongs to whom – or of position in the genealogical grid, since 'Mrs. Heathcliff' could be both Heathcliff's wife and his daughter-in-law (II), the 'Catherine Linton' of Lockwood's second dream (III) either mother or daughter. Names in these opening chapters – including the 'Hareton Earnshaw' whose appearance as inscription on the Heights prompts Lockwood to desire 'a short history of the place' (I, 46) – are detached from clear or unambiguous reference and call out for histories, or explications.

Lockwood's confusion over names, identities, and proper placement reaches a climax in chapter III, which has itself strikingly to do with proper names and proper place, with both the establishment of boundary lines and their transgression. He finds on the window ledge of his room at the Heights writing which is 'nothing but a name repeated in all kinds of characters, large and small – *Catherine Earnshaw;* here and there varied to *Catherine Heathcliff*, and then again to *Catherine Linton'*:

In vapid listlessness I leant my head against the window, and continued spelling over Catherine Earnshaw – Heathcliff – Linton, till my eyes closed; but they had not rested five minutes when a glare of white letters started from the dark, as vivid as spectres – the air swarmed with Catherines. ... (p. 61)

When he rouses himself 'to dispel the obtrusive name' (p. 62), he finds yet another name ('Catherine Earnshaw, her book') introducing the marginal script – itself not in its proper place – which tells of the Sunday when Catherine and Heathcliff, compelled to 'square' their 'positions' for the appropriate Sabbath reading, throw the compulsory 'good books' (p. 63) into the dog-kennel, are threatened by Joseph with being 'laced … properly' for it, and then 'appropriate the dairy woman's cloak' for that crossing to the Grange which leaves a gap in the writing, taken up again only after the pair's crucial separation and Hindley's swearing to reduce Heathcliff to his 'right place' (p. 64). This pivotal chapter is virtually obsessed with names – the proliferating and disturbingly mobile 'Catherines'; the ghostly 'Catherine Linton,' called by Lockwood an 'appellation … which personified itself when I had no longer my imagination under control' (p. 69); the name 'Jabes,' like 'Zillah,' taken from a biblical genealogy (1 Chronicles 4:9) or list of 'Scripture names' like the one Catherine and Heathcliff are threatened with having to learn 'if they don't answer properly' (VI, 88); the cudgel 'denominated' a pilgrim's staff. But it is also preoccupied with the problem of proper place and with the erection, and crossing, of dividing lines or partitions: the blurring of the boundaries between real world and dream ('I began to dream, almost before I ceased to be sensible of my locality'); the pilgrim's staff as itself a sign that man is not in his proper place; the ironic echo of Christ's 'breaking down the wall of partition,' making the 'two' into 'one' (Ephesians 2:14) in the clergyman's 'house with two rooms, threatening speedily to determine into one'; the multiplication of the sequential 'partitions of discourse' in the *four hundred and ninety* parts' of Branderham's sermon, each devoted to different 'odd transgressions'; and even the linear partition of time, since the partitions of the Puritan sermon traditionally correspond to the ages of history between Creation and Apocalypse (an association which may explain why, in the dream, reaching the final 'head' or partition brings on eschatological echoes). The sermon is a virtual *reductio ad absurdum* of categorization and sequential division, in which something beyond enumeration or counting – the forgiveness of trespasses not 'seven times, but until seventy times seven' (Matthew 18:22) – is reduced to sheer enumeration, and the 'sin that no Christian need pardon' (p. 66) – blasphemy against the Holy Spirit (Matthew 12:31) – becomes instead transgressing a limit, the 'crisis' precipitated when Branderham reaches the '*First of the Seventy-First*' (p. 66). But the boundary between dreamer and dreamed is itself one of the partitions which here threatens to break down: Lockwood and the preacher become increasingly hard to distinguish as the dream moves towards mutual violence and Jabes' accusatory 'Thou art the Man!' – echoing a biblical application of a parable to its hearer, named and inscribed within a story he had thought himself outside (2 Samuel 2:7) – turns the focus back on Lockwood himself, as nomination becomes virtually inseparable from accusation.[16] The Lockwood who objects to the multiplied partitions of Branderham's sermon himself scrambles to erect a partition or dividing wall of books in the second dream, when the ghostly child threatens to enter the house through a window which no longer keeps the outside out; and the multiplication of the partitions of discourse Lockwood objects to in that first dream may have its counterpart in Lockwood's own preference as narrator for the sequential narrative partitions which keep names, times, and events in their proper place after this unsettling night.

It is significant that it is after this night that Lockwood both loses his way in the snow when it removes the indicative function of signs ('the swells and falls not indicating corresponding rises and depressions in the ground,' p. 73) and blots out the 'chart' in his mind with the 'line of upright stones' that formerly served as 'guides.' But it is also after this night that he requests the housekeeper's explanatory 'history,' which begins with a sorting out of proper names and, as in Foucault's description of classical discourse, 'sorts out' the simultaneous into the successive, into a 'linear order' whose parts 'must be traversed *one after* the other.'[17] Mrs Dean begins by describing Heathcliff as 'very near' – and then hastens to eliminate the ambiguity by adding that she means not 'close' but 'close-handed.' But the parsimoniousness of Heathcliff and the parsimony which is one of the senses of 'near' is shared by the extreme economy of names themselves ('Heathcliff' serving 'parsimoniously,' as Frank Kermode points out, as both Christian and surname),[18] a paucity emphasized by the novel's own striking juxtapositions – 'Catherine, Mrs. Linton Heathcliff now' (xxviii, 316), for example, containing the names of both rivals for this *second* Catherine's mother. The swarming and disembodied names of chapter iii, beyond Lockwood's control and endowed with an unsettling mobility, are themselves too compressed or 'near' – sheer parataxis or juxtaposition, without explanatory syntax or reference and with a power of combination neither logical nor chronological. It is only in the history provided by Mrs Dean, who presents herself as 'a steady, reasonable kind of body,' distinguished both by her housekeeping and by her familiarity with books (vii, 103), that the names are given their proper place within a genealogical line. Her history – which Lockwood insists proceed 'minutely' and which is accompanied by such emblems of chronos as the clock on the wall (vii, 102; x, 129) – moves in reassuring Enlightenment fashion in a single, irreversible direction from beginning to end, from the passionate Catherine and Heathcliff to the tamer, book-reading Cathy and Hareton, and imparts a sense of progress to the text as it moves to its ending. And yet, because Lockwood's request comes immediately after his disturbing night, the very linearity of the narrative, told from the

Linton property at Thrushcross Grange, links the mode of narration – the establishment of its boundaries or narratorial partitions, the assigning of a proper place to each proper name – with the boundary marking of property itself, and creates thereby the specifically narrative possibility of trespass, of something which transgresses both the linearity and the identity of Lockwood's text, even as it calls attention to his narrative *as* narrative, as both demand and need, a spacing or *espacement* of the unbearably 'near' into an order more accommodated to the civilized and enlightened – or novel-reading – mind. Logical and chronological are here inseparable; and what Barthes calls 'the chronological illusion' is part of the function of logic itself, the overcoming of repetition through syntax or narrative.[19] Sequence struggles to master repetition in order, as we say, to get somewhere. And what in chapter III is called 'nothing but a name repeated in all kinds of characters, large and small' is spread out over the characters of a housekeeper's history frequently read as a story both of progress and of enlightenment.

Nelly's tale performs its function and the two characters who could embody the obtrusive 'Catherines' are distanced by a generation. But there remains even in Ellen Dean's sequential narrative a sense of something which will not be accommodated to chronos or its logic – in the uncanny crossings, conflations, or reversals which transgress the categories of chronological time and sequence and even more strikingly within the activity of proper names themselves, the very markers of discrete identity. The novel's powerful, and disturbing, images of something that cannot be accommodated or contained – the 'oak in the flower-pot' and 'sea' in a 'horse-trough' (XIV) – have their counterpart in the sense of something resisting Lockwood's ordered narratorial frame. Even after Nelly begins her story, proper names are not wholly reliable boundary lines. Northrop Frye observes that the word 'identity' has a double aspect, identity *with* and identity *as*. The problem with proper names in this text is that they participate in this duplicity, disrupting by their repetition over several possible referents the very principle of individuation they exist to designate or mark.

The text's adherence to social conventions of naming – proper names in this society as indicators not only of identity but of proper social place – is as strict as its adherence to chronology or to property law: Heathcliff, for example, is degraded by a pointed distinction in the mode of naming ('You may come and wish Miss Catherine welcome, like the other servants,' VII, 94) and later ridicules his son for calling his own cousin '*Miss* Catherine' (XXI, 251). But if this novel observes the carefully articulated system of naming in which the form of address reflects distinctions of position, it also calls attention even after chapter III to the multiple names a single character can be called and conversely to the potential for ambiguity when, as with the 'Mrs. Heathcliff' Lockwood erroneously places in chapter II, more than a single character can be identified by the same name. In chapter VI, for example, Hindley is called variously 'Mr. Hindley,' 'young Earnshaw,' and simply 'Hindley,' depending on the socially appropriate form of address. But the first time he is called 'Mr. Earnshaw' ('I threw a shawl over my head and ran to prevent them from waking Mr. Earnshaw by knocking,' p. 88), the reader may receive a shock, since the former 'Mr. Earnshaw,' called in the previous chapter 'by name' (V, 85) in order to wake him, before they realize that he is not sleeping but dead, is now dead and his name, as in all forms of genealogical succession, now transferred to his son. The identity of the name momentarily effaces the boundaries of individual identity which the proper name should properly preserve.

The ambiguity of proper names is joined by the possible detaching of name from person or proper place, as in the spectral rising of disembodied 'Catherines,' the suggestion that the first Catherine's 'name' might be a substitute for her presence or 'voice' (XII, 158), or in the moment when that Catherine stares at her reflection ('"Is that Catherine Linton?"' p. 159), a moment in which the name – hers in any case only by marriage – is, as it were, detached from her person even before it is transferred to a second 'Catherine Linton' at her death. When Heathcliff says to Cathy 'I swear Linton is dying' (XXII, 266), the context, or narrative placing, indicates that he refers to his son. But that context's own references to a transferred name – '"Catherine Linton (the very name warms me)"' – and to exchange of place ('Just imagine your father in my place, and Linton in yours') make it possible to note that 'Linton is dying' could, out of its proper place, also refer to Catherine's father or to the progressive effacement of the Linton name itself. Names in this text frequently appear as a place or space to be filled, as the alien Heathcliff takes the name left vacant by an earlier, legitimate son, as the second Catherine Linton gets her name on the death of the first and fills the place of 'Miss Linton' after it has been vacated by Isabella's marriage, or as the initials 'C.' and 'H.' on the balls Catherine Linton and Linton Heathcliff find in a cupboard at the Heights (XXIV, 280) could as easily be filled by them as by 'Catherine' and 'Heathcliff,' or later by 'Catherine' and 'Hareton,' a possibility which would work against the narrative's carefully separated identities and times.

Names also participate in this text's transgressions or crossings. The curious mode of naming Hareton when he is first placed by Nelly on the genealogical grid – as 'the late Mrs. Linton's nephew' (IV, 75), rather than as the late Mr Earnshaw's son – subtly allies him with 'the house on which his name is *not* carved,'[20] just as the inscription 'Hareton Earnshaw' on the lintel or, in northern dialect, 'linton' of Wuthering Heights may suggest a crossing of families which will in the narrative be achieved only after Hareton's marriage to

Catherine Linton and their removal to the Grange. The potential chaos of sheer naming or categorization is part of the oppressive weight of Lockwood's first dream; but a similar chaos may be conjured from the alliances and associations names make independently of persons, almost as if they were engaged in a shadow play of combinations not permitted on the novel's more civilized surface, a mobility and transportability unsettling to the Enlightenment order or grid. Incest – the primal social trespass or crossing of boundaries – may be present not only in the uncertain relationship of Heathcliff and Catherine but in the promiscuous combination or confusion which remains open to names themselves, independent of genealogical or social placement.

Let us choose, for illustration, the most outrageous example. The female characters in the novel are variously called by their first and their family names, so that Isabella, for example, is also referred to simply as 'Miss Linton.' When she elopes with Heathcliff, Edgar Linton proclaims that she is to be thereafter 'only [his] sister in name' (xii, 170). At the only level which makes any logical sense, this phrase 'in name' is simply a formula for her disowning – a severing of a family tie in which the name will remain as the only trace of a former connection. But the other character who is, in the literal sense, his 'sister in name' is his daughter, a 'Miss Linton' who will also become, like Isabella, a 'Mrs. Heathcliff.' This might hardly be noticed if it were not for the novel's insistent reference to names as virtually autonomous entities, a reference, however, wholly plausible in the marrying and giving in marriage which form the principle exchange of the plot. When Isabella says in chapter xiii, 'My name *was* Isabella Linton' (p. 175), the phrase suggests what for a woman in a society where property relations extend to marriage is the repeated experience of detaching person from name, an exchanging of one name for another which Nelly reminds Heathcliff may involve a more radical change in identity ('"I'll inform you Catherine Linton is as different now, from your old friend Catherine Earnshaw, as that young lady is different from me,"' xiv, 185).

Frank Kermode points out that the three names Lockwood finds etched on the window ledge in chapter iii – *Catherine Earnshaw, Catherine Heathcliff,* and *Catherine Linton* – map in their textual order the novel's principal crossing or exchange, from left to right the story of the first Catherine and in reverse that of the second, a reading of the text in terms of *écriture* supported, I would add, by the housekeeper's own reference to 'retracing the course of Catherine Linton' (xvi, 202) after her death, by Lockwood's striking textual metaphor of the daughter as a potential 'second edition of the mother' (xiv, 191), and by Nelly's calling attention to the reverse order in which both Lockwood and the reader have been introduced to the two female figures who share the same name ('About twelve o'clock, that night, was born the Catherine you saw at

Wuthering Heights,' XVI, 201). This plotting of the history through the names is possible only through a reversal, a reading first in one direction and then in the other. The reader aware of the way in which things in this novel change places or seem to turn into one another – human into animal, civilized into violent, ghost into person, and person into ghost – might even perceive a lurking palindrome or verbal reversal in the name of the housekeeper herself – variously called 'Ellen' and 'Nelly' – a suggestion outrageous to readers of the naturalized *Wuthering Heights* preferred by Q.D. Leavis and others, but perhaps not entirely inappropriate for a character who, as go-between, meddler, and even 'double-dealer' (XX, 266) in the plot, also mediates as a kind of boundary-figure between superstition and enlightenment and moves as narrator in two directions, in towards the story in which she is involved and out towards her civilized listener.

V

It is, indeed, in the literal sense of the word, preposterous.
Coleridge, *The Friend*

Retracing or reversing the left-to-right order of reading involves an upsetting of the simple linear sequence of diary, chronology, or genealogy and calls into question the Lockwoodian text and its relation both to enlightenment and to the very idea of progress. The narrative is for the most part preposterous, in the still-current nineteenth-century sense of a reversal of proper order: it begins with the second Catherine and proceeds to the first. The dominating influence of mere sequence creates the illusion of proceeding away from the opening scene when in fact, or in chronology, it proceeds *to* it: the shock of hearing at the beginning of chapter XXV, 'These things happened last winter, sir' is the shock of the revelation that things which had seemed, in the familiar spatial metaphor, before us, are now just behind us, not distanced but close enough to overtake the present time. Even Nelly's carefully sequential 'history' includes episodes which upset its own partitions between discrete identities and times, disrupting both the linear order of the text and the certainty of chronological placing. In chapter XI, for example, Nelly tells of the apparition or uncanny return ('all at once, a gush of child's sensations flowed into my heart') at the crossroads pillar – itself inscribed with the initials of three possible directions – of Hindley himself as a child; then of finding when she hastens to the Heights that the apparition has preceded her, that what she thought was behind her now stands before her very eyes ('looking through the gate'), before she reflects that this child must be not Hindley but his son Hareton; and finally of her panic when, after her request to Hareton to fetch his father, Heathcliff appears. Hindley, Hareton, and Heathcliff are in this supernatural incident too 'near,' as the boundaries which should separate child from man, a child from his father, and individuals or discrete chronological times from each other here forsake even the housekeeper and send her back to the 'guide-post' ('feeling as scared as if I had raised a goblin,' p. 149), before the apparition, 'on further reflection,' fades into the light of common day. The scene is virtually the narrativization of a preposterous Wordsworthian copula – 'The Child is father of the Man' – a metaphor whose conflation of times and identities shocks, before the mind accommodates it logically and chronologically as a condensed analogy, and the conflation of times is spread out, or spaced, over what is called the 'natural' life of a single individual.

Yet another conflation of times, or separate parts of the text itself, occurs in chapter XII, where a delirious Catherine Linton experiences a collapse of the distancing space of time ('the whole last seven years of my life grew a blank! ... I was a child'), in which the years between the crossing of the moors which first separated her from Heathcliff and her marriage at nineteen to Edgar Linton drop away ('supposing at twelve years old, I had been wrenched from the Heights, and ... converted, at a stroke, into Mrs. Linton, the lady of Thrushcross Grange, and the wife of a stranger,' p. 163), an identification of historically separated times which may remind us of the aberrant 'identity with' of metaphor – a transgression of the boundaries of both logic and chronology which would provide the temporal counterpart of Catherine's own radical copula 'I am Heathcliff' (IX, 122).[21] But what is even more upsetting to both is this chapter's 'preposterous' textual recalls, its repeated echoes of Lockwood's encounters in chapter III: the snowy down plucked by a 'wandering' Catherine recalling Lockwood's 'wandering' in the 'snow'; the 'blank' of the disappearing space of years recalling the 'blank' filled by Catherine's marginal script, and the 'oak-panelled bed,' 'wind sounding in the firs,' and opened 'casement' of Catherine's delirium (XII, 162–3) recalling Lockwood's enclosure in the same bed at the Heights, the 'fir-tree' moved by the 'gusty wind' and the terrifyingly open casement window (III, 66–7). These echoes create the uncanny sense that the 'Catherine Linton' who in chapter XII is 'no better than a wailing child' (p. 162), sees herself as the 'exiled' and 'outcast' twelve-year-old of the crossing Lockwood reads about in chapter III, and imagines a return to the Heights through the graveyard 'ghosts' of Gimmerton Kirk, is the 'wailing child' ('still it wailed,' III, 67) or ghostly 'Catherine Linton' of Lockwood's second dream, who attempts to return to her 'home' after wandering on the moors for 'twenty years.' The two chapters, on rereading, contaminate each other preposterously, upsetting the ordered linearity of the narratorial text. The recalling of chapter III in chapter XII – a phenomenon common enough in the sequential process of reading in which a later chapter may recall an earlier one – here involves an uncanny, or preposterous, reversal, since the earlier chapter the later one recalls has its place, chronologically, almost twenty years after it.

The sense of fixed and inviolable place in time is also shaken by the uncanny sense of repetition in the return of the first Catherine in the second (whom Edgar Linton distinguishes from her mother by a difference in name) or by Joseph's calling Isabella (recently converted to 'Mrs. Heathcliff' of the Heights) 'Miss Cathy,' and saying that 'Hathecliff' will rebuke her for her tantrum (XIII, 180). The mind can accommodate the crossing by reference to Joseph's age or confusion; but the only character who is both 'Miss Cathy' and one whose tantrums will be punished not by Hindley but by Heathcliff is the *second* Catherine, a character who has already appeared to the reader and to Lockwood but who, in the story's chronology, is at that point not even born. Chronos in the myth devoured his children: the disruption of chronology in this novel allows children to come again.

Wuthering Heights refuses to let the reader forget that both the chronological sense of time and linear habit of reading depend upon sequence, on events maintaining a syntax, or proper sense of place. But Lockwood's encounter with the swarming and spectral 'letters,' the undercutting of the rational explanation of his first dream (merely a 'fir-tree') in the uncanny return of the second, Nelly's crossroads apparition, chapter XII's preposterous recalls, and Joseph's curious mistake are all episodes in which things refuse to keep their proper place. Tropes such as metaphor (Catherine's defiant 'I *am* Heathcliff' or the sheer parataxis of the juxtaposed 'Catherines') and *hysteron proteron* (the figure of reversal which Puttenham called 'The Preposterous')[22] unsettle the careful boundaries and spaced linearity of Lockwood's text and reveal its own strategies of closure or enclosure as precisely that. The impulse to enclose is finally so intimately connected with the psychology of the narrator whose diary it is that all forms of closure, of shutting off or containing – including the narrative itself – become suspect or inadequate to their task, like the coffins of gothic fiction which refuse to stay shut. A neutral and 'ghost-like' narrative voice inhabits and dislocates even Lockwood's final lines, which seem to promise a final forestalling of repetition, or uncanny return. What Foucault calls the return of both nature and tropes undermines the narrator's closing refusal to 'imagine unquiet slumbers, for the sleepers in that quiet earth': nature, in the 'soft wind breathing through the grass' and the 'moths fluttering among the heath and hare-bells'; and writing, or tropes, in the appearance there of buried names, 'Heathcliff' and 'Hareton,' the two oppressed children of the text itself. The curious absence of names in the description of the returning 'ramblers'

Lockwood hastens at this ending to 'escape' creates, if only for a moment, the illogical possibility that these ramblers are not the solid, second-generation Cathy and Hareton but the ghostly Catherine and Heathcliff, whom the country folk insist still 'walk.'

The endless debate over whether the novel's second generation constitutes a progress or decline in relation to the first may be precisely endless because the two sides are simply the opposite faces of a single coin – two possibilities within the model of the line. The second generation only approximately repeats the first; and it is this difference within repetition which constitutes both 'spacing' and the possibility of 'progress.' The novel proffers in familial and genealogical terms precisely the twinned questions of progress and enlightenment which so preoccupied eighteenth-century discourse. 'Reading' is part of the achievement of both enlightenment and progress in *Wuthering Heights*. But it is difficult to banish the suspicion that Cathy's civilizing of Hareton by teaching him to read is at least partly a project to forestall boredom, a way, as we say, of filling the time. The second-generation couple, who get together over the pages of an 'accepted book' (xxxii, 345) and whose domesticating of the Heights Lockwood approves, are still shadowed by the 'contrary' (xxxii, 338) activity of the first, if only in the margins which disrupt the 'good book' provided in this ending by Lockwood himself. W.J. Harvey writes that it is precisely the 'muting' of intratextual conflations or echoes 'by the intervening mass of the novel' which makes the difference, in *Wuthering Heights*, between it and the 'intolerable' or 'Gothic' reverberations which would have resulted if the echoes of one part of the text in another – the repetitions, for example, of that casement window from chapter iii – had been 'more closely juxtaposed.'[23] But *Wuthering Heights* manages to reveal this very spacing as a strategy of the novel form itself, an accommodation to its 'civilized' (Kermode) or 'bourgeois' (Macherey) reading public.

We have, finally, to honour both the naturalized novel – or the sense of naturalizing or of 'life' it produces by means of such spacing – and the uncanny conflations which disrupt both its unified identity and its linear structures. Lockwood is indeed, as several readers suggest, a surrogate for the reader and even Kermode's linear ordering is a form of Lockwoodian analysis – an ordering in sequence of the simple profusion of names in chapter iii, which fill the air like the snowy feathers of chapter xii. The very binary oppositions by which readers traditionally structure meaning are in this text both generated and undermined. The difference between Earnshaw and Linton, salvation and damnation, nature and culture, primitive and civilized, or (paradoxically) graves that join and windows that divide is finally a partition or dividing wall which does not really divide but is instead constantly crossed or transgressed by the novel's literal exchanges or by tropes such as metaphor which are 'beyond good and evil,' which appear amoral because as in any purely verbal exchange they proceed by a more, or less, than human logic. But at the same time as it undermines these partitions, the text does not allow any satisfying or simple identity *with*: Catherine's copular 'I *am* Heathcliff' suggests a unity beyond partition which in the novel nowhere appears. Metaphor itself involves a transgression of the boundaries of 'property,' but its radical union is, as Derrida would say, always already inhabited by difference. There is always 'partition': the binary oppositions in this text both break down and are regenerated, as the revolt against the proliferating partitions of discourse in Lockwood's first dream moves to the re-introduction of a partition in the second. Even the text's uncanny conflations – or the potential identification of one part with another – cannot be conscripted to a conclusive identity. The distance between Catherine's delirium in chapter xii and Lockwood's second dream in chapter iii is almost, but not quite, the twenty years of the ghost child's exile on the moors. The connection – neither logical nor chronological – remains and militates against logic, chronology, and the sense in both of progress, but cannot finally be forced to 'make sense.'

The identity of the literary text, both as unity and as a self-identity, guaranteed by the narratorial subject who offers the novel we read as his book, is in *Wuthering Heights* radically undermined: the text remains perpetually, and frustratingly, other to itself, forever inhabited by its own ghosts. The haunting of the narratorial text by something which escapes both identification and placing cannot simply be explained by recourse to the distinction between narrator and effaced author, to the substitution of one proper name – or one kind of mastery – for another. Indeed, we feel in reading Emily Brontë's novel the pertinence of at least one of her sister's prefatory remarks: 'the writer who possesses the creative gift owns something of which he is not always master – something that at times strangely wills and works for itself.'[24] Critics of *Wuthering Heights* as diverse as Fredric Jameson and Frank Kermode have remarked on its unsettling sense of automism, a staple feature of the Gothic as a mode which foregrounds the unsettling mobility of *things*. Brontë's novel, whose 'characters' are both the embodiments of a genealogical history and the unsettling graphic letters of chapter iii, suggests that something as apparently modern as the notion of a text writing itself may have a peculiarly Gothic pedigree. And the recurrence of the figure of the 'spectre' or 'ghost' in contemporary narrative theory may return us to the ghost narratives of the period we call post-Enlightenment – if we understand that 'post,' as we now do that of 'post'-structuralist, as still caught within the very structures it dismantles or undermines. *Wuthering Heights* calls into question not only private property but the very idea of the 'proper'; its violation is not only of moral proprieties but of novelistic ones. In the terms of one of its own most persistent figures, it demands a reading which seeks to raise more demons than it casts out.

NOTES

1 Ian Watt, *The Rise of the Novel*, 1957; repr. Harmondsworth 1963, p. 22, citing Locke's *Essay Concerning Human Understanding*, book III, ch. 3, sect. 6.
2 See Locke, *Essay*, III.3.2–5; Hobbes, *Leviathan*, part I, ch. 4; and C.B. Macpherson, *The Political Theory of Possessive Individualism: Hobbes to Locke*, Oxford 1962.
3 Watt, *Rise*, pp. 18–19; Michel Foucault, *Les Mots et les choses*, trans. as *The Order of Things*, New York 1973, esp. pp. 104ff.; Emily Brontë, *Wuthering Heights*, ed. David Daiches, Harmondsworth 1965, ch. III, p. 66. All subsequent parenthetical references to the novel are to chapter and page in this edition.
4 See Patricia Drechsel Tobin, *Time and the Novel*, Princeton 1978, introduction; Roland Barthes, 'An Introduction to the Structural Analysis of Narrative,' trans. Lionel Duisit, *New Literary History*, 6:2 (Winter 1975), 237–72; Jacques Derrida, *Of Grammatology*, trans. Gayatri Spivak, Baltimore 1976, pp. 85, 332; Foucault, *The Order of Things*, pp. 82–92; Eleanor N. Hutchens, 'The Novel as Chronomorph,' *Novel* (Spring 1972), 215–24; and Harold Toliver on 'Linear Logic' in *Animate Illusions*, Lincoln, Nebraska 1974. See also, on the ideological implications of form, Pierre Macherey, *A Theory of Literary Production*, trans. Geoffrey Wall, London 1978. The description of this 'linear logic' does not imply unawareness of writing in the Enlightenment which parodies or undermines it (the case of Sterne or Swift, for example).
5 Foucault, *The Order of Things*, p. 114. See also Hugh Blair, *Lectures on Rhetoric and Belles Lettres* (1783), lectures XIV and XV, with Dumarsais's *Les Tropes* (1729), part I and part II, i, on catachresis, and Rousseau's *Essai sur l'origine des langues*. I have discussed the relation between metaphor and the 'improper,' 'alien,' and 'out of place' in 'The Metaphorical Plot,' in *Metaphor: Problems and Perspectives*, ed. David S. Miall, Sussex 1982, an essay which includes an earlier version of some of the ideas developed here in relation to *Wuthering Heights*. It still remains an open question whether Foucault's characterization of the linear logic of Enlightenment thought can be said to fit all the texts of which he treats – or can be transported *tel quel* from a French to an English context. It can be observed, however, that many of the influential texts of the period we still refer to as the English Enlightenment have strategic recourse to a sequential narrative or genealogical history – in two cases, indeed, specifically in relation to property and the development of proper names.

William Blackstone, for instance, in the lengthy chapter on 'Property' in his *Commentaries on the Laws of England* (1765–9), begins his discussion by raising an anxiety about an owner's right to an exclusively private property when land was originally granted in common to all, but quickly proceeds to still that anxiety – or potential instability – by recourse to a sequential history, which moves from the fluidity of common property to the stability of private property, a property secured first by the institution of the 'house,' or permanent dwelling. Hugh Blair, in the *Lectures on Rhetoric and Belles Lettres*, provides a sequential narrative of the movement from figurative instability to the provision of 'proper' names, a history of progress away from the mobility of tropes like metaphor which his French authority Dumarsais had defined as living in a 'borrowed home' (*Les Tropes* x). The discourse of rhetoric, concerned with proper names, and that of economics, concerned with property, are here both in their generation of sequential histories and in their progress towards stability – a place for everything and everything in its place – strikingly similar. And both as well, in their common concern for placing and for partitions, seem particularly vulnerable to a specifically gothic plot, to a threat to the stability or inviolability of a 'house.'

6 Foucault, *The Order of Things*, pp. 119–20, 303, 298, and 304 respectively.

7 On identity understood as 'self-identity,' see the discussion of two differing conceptions of identity (as permanence amid change and as unity amid diversity) in *An Encyclopedia of Philosophy*, ed. Paul Edwards, New York 1967, sub. 'Identity'; 'Almost all the writers of the period under discussion, from Descartes to Kant, took the term "identity" to mean that an object "is the same with itself" (Hume).' The more particular sense of self-identity ('identité à soi') as used by Derrida involves as well the notion of self-presence. For readings of other nineteenth-century texts in relation to their own undermining of a unified identity and narratorial mastery, see, for example, Shoshana Felman on Henry James's *The Turn of the Screw* in 'Turning the Screw of Interpretation' and Peter Brooks's 'Freud's Masterplot: Questions of Narrative,' in *Yale French Studies*, nos. 55/56 (1977); Cynthia Chase, 'The Decomposition of the Elephants: Double-Reading *Daniel Deronda*,' *PMLA*, 93:2 (March 1978), 215–27; J. Hillis Miller, *Fiction and Repetition*, Cambridge, Mass. 1982; and Maria M. Tatar, 'The Houses of Fiction: Toward a Definition of the Uncanny,' *Comparative Literature*, 33:2 (Spring 1981), 167–82.

8 Maurice Blanchot, 'L'Absence de livre,' in *L'Entretien infini*, Paris 1969, pp. 564–6. The translations from it here are taken from Derrida's discussion of Blanchot's terms in 'LIVING ON: Border Lines,' in *Deconstruction and Criticism*, ed. Harold Bloom et al., New York 1979, pp. 104–7.

9 Derrida, *Of Grammatology*, p. 86.

10 Jacques Derrida, *Dissemination*, trans. Barbara Johnson, Chicago 1981, p. 86. See also pp. 103–4.

11 See Derrida, *Dissemination*, p. 103; Nietzsche, *Zur Genealogie der Moral*, First Essay, II; and, on ghost/host/guest, J. Hillis Miller, 'The Critic as Host,' in *Deconstruction and Criticism*, pp. 220ff. We are told at the end of ch. XVII, 'The guest was now the master of Wuthering Heights' (p. 222).

12 For the complex of terms related to 'proper,' see, *inter alia*, Derrida, *Of Grammatology*, pp. 26, 107–12, 244, and Derrida's long footnote on Marx's critique of the linguistic association of 'proper' and 'property' in *The German Ideology*, in 'White Mythology: Metaphor in the Text of Philosophy,' trans. F.C.T. Moore, *New Literary History*, 6:1 (Autumn 1974), p. 15. For a survey of Marxist criticism of Brontë's novel, including the work of Arnold Kettle, Raymond Williams, and Terry Eagleton, see Ronald Frankenberg, 'Styles of Marxism: Styles of Criticism. Wuthering Heights: A Case Study,' in *The Sociology of Literature*, ed. Diana Laurenson, Keele 1978. This survey necessarily omits Fredric Jameson's provocative short discussion in *The Political Unconscious*, Ithaca 1981, pp. 126–9.

13 Joseph J. Scaliger, *Poetices libri septem*, Lyons 1561, IV, xxxviii.

14 These have been discussed in, respectively, Tobin, *Time*, p. 41 and Mark Schorer, 'Fiction and the "Analogical Matrix,"' *Kenyon Review*, 11 (Autumn 1949).

15 See the discussions of proper names in, for example, Michel Butor, *Répertoire: Etudes et conférences 1948–59*, Paris 1960, p. 252; Jacques Lacan, 'L'instance de la lettre dans l'inconscient,' *Ecrits* I, Paris 1966, p. 252; Charles Grivel, *Production de l'intérêt romanesque*, Paris 1973, pp. 128–44; and Derrida, *Of Grammatology*, pp. 107–13.

16 On nominative and accusative, see Geoffrey Hartman, 'Psychoanalysis: The French Connection,' in *Psychoanalysis and the Question of the Text*, ed. Geoffrey Hartman, Baltimore 1978, pp. 94ff. Branderham's 'execute upon him the judgment written,' the 'concluding word' on which the assembly turns to violence, echoes the eschatological Psalm 149, while 'every man's hand was against his neighbour' and the final 'tumult' echo the vision of judgment in Zechariah. I have written in more detail on the relation between the partition of this sermon and the partitions of narrative and of time in 'Anagogic Metaphor: Breaking Down the Wall of Partition,' in *Centre and Labyrinth: Essays in Honour of Northrop Frye*, ed. Eleanor Cook et al., Toronto 1983, pp. 38–58.

17 Foucault, *The Order of Things*, pp. 82–3.

18 Frank Kermode, *The Classic*, New York 1975, p. 123.

19 Barthes, 'An Introduction to the Structural Analysis of Narrative,' pp. 251–4. We might remember, in relation to this markedly genealogical novel, the characterization of genealogy itself as a form of spacing in Nietzsche's *Zur Genealogie der Moral*.

20 Kermode, *The Classic*, p. 120. Other readings which have contributed to my argument here include, in addition to those of Hillis Miller and Fredric Jameson already

noted, Dorothy Van Ghent's pioneering study in *The English Novel*, New York 1953; Terry Eagleton's in *Myths of Power: A Marxist Study of the Brontës*, London 1975, pp. 97–121; Carol Jacobs's '*Wuthering Heights*: At the Threshold of Interpretation,' *Boundary 2*, 7:3 (1979), 49–71; David Musselwhite, '*Wuthering Heights*: The Unacceptable Text,' in *Literature, Society and the Sociology of Literature*, ed. Francis Barker et al., Proceedings of the Conference held at the University of Essex, July 1976, pp. 154–60; and Margaret Homans, 'Repetition and Sublimation of Nature in *Wuthering Heights*,' *PMLA*, 93:1 (January 1978), 9–19. Musselwhite speaks of the 'bracketting of Lockwood' which characterizes readings as otherwise divergent as those of Q.D. Leavis, 'A Fresh Approach to *Wuthering Heights*,' in *Lectures in America*, New York 1969, and Eagleton's chapter. We might add to this the reading of the ending of the novel as Brontë's capitulation to the conventional 'novelistic tradition' in Leo Bersani's *A Future for Astyanax*, Boston 1976, p. 221.

21 For the temporal form of copular metaphor ('A *is* B'), see Northrop Frye, *Anatomy of Criticism*, 1957; repr. New York 1966, p. 124.

22 Puttenham, *The Arte of English Poesie*, ch. 12. See also Derrida on the '*hysteron proteron* of the generations' in Freud's *Beyond the Pleasure Principle*, in his 'Coming into One's Own,' in *Psychoanalysis and the Question of the Text*, pp. 136–46.

23 W.J. Harvey, *Character and the Novel*, London 1965, p. 187.

24 See Charlotte Brontë's preface to the 1850 edition of *Wuthering Heights*, reprinted in the Daiches edition, p. 40.

PART THREE

HERMENEUTICS

CYRUS HAMLIN

The Faults of Vision: Identity and Poetry (A Dialogue of Voices, with an Essay on *Kubla Khan*)

It was a miracle of rare device,
A sunny pleasure-dome with caves of ice.

The following (imagined) dialogue attempts to explore the question of identity in the literary text in a manner which reflects, I hope adequately and productively, what I take to be a genuine quandary for criticism.

SCEPTIC: The identity of the literary text. What might that be? I can't imagine how a text could have an identity, nor how it could matter that the text is literary!

CRITIC: As usual, you're overreacting. It seems to me that a text is about as identifiable as anything else in our culture and that the distinction of literary texts should matter to critics. Do I have to remind you that textual criticism, within the prestigious domain of *philology*, was once a most sophisticated and self-confident enterprise? Have you forgotten what used to be called 'higher criticism'?

SCEPTIC: The old style of higher criticism was fine in its proper place, especially for the classics and the Bible, where editing texts and publishing critical editions could be a full-time job. We tend to take such things for granted now.

CRITIC: At least you acknowledge the legitimacy of editing texts, if only for a philology of earlier days. I hope you would also agree that the status of the text as scholarly artefact was first established by the discipline of philology, for instance in the editions of Homer by the scholars of ancient Alexandria. Behold now the splendid rows of books which fill the shelves of our university libraries, not to mention the more popular form of paperback and anthology volumes, which are supplied by bookstores to the general reader and assigned to students on the reading lists of our courses.

STUDENT: No one knows the tyrannies of a reading list so intimately as a student of Comparative Literature. Are you familiar with the kinds of bibliography imposed on us as recommended reading from world literature, reflecting whatever canons of taste and critical ideology may be currently in vogue, usually arranged by period and genre?

SCEPTIC: Do you maintain that the question of identity could be clarified by the uses of philology, best-seller lists, and the curricula of college courses?

STUDENT: Certainly not. My point would be that very few naïve readers still exist. Even beginning students quickly encounter avant-garde ideas about reading. The issue of *textualité* crops up everywhere in my field these days, and we all are made to pay homage to the problem of writing, which lately has seemed an exclusively French preserve.

CRITIC: Let me offer a thought here. We need to distinguish between two separate senses of text: first, there is the verbal construct, which in our bookish culture is usually secured in print as the product of editing and publishing; and, second, there are those functions which a text may legitimately serve for its readers, however varied and indeterminate. It seems to me that much recent avant-garde criticism, often under the vague rubric of 'post-structuralism,' has purposefully confused these two senses of text. We all know that there is a difference between the sign and what it signifies (even if powerful claims have been made for subsuming both *signifiant* and *signifié* under the heading of the sign), between the medium and the message (*pace* Marshall McLuhan), or between the literary text *as work* and the activity (or *energeia*, to use Wilhelm von Humboldt's term) through which it is produced and disseminated. I would argue that the term 'text' be limited to the former sense, as an artefact. In our supposedly literate, post-Gutenberg culture a complex relationship between text and discourse always pertains, even though the text may claim a priority, as theorists of textuality, such as Jacques Derrida, have argued. Speech acts for us would thus be a function of texts. Yet the text itself, as I am arguing, is never identical with the act of speaking. This claim would not in any way delimit the plurality of legitimate responses to a text, either hermeneutically through the act of reading or semiotically with reference to the code or system of signs which constitutes the language of a text (as *langue* in distinction from *parole*).

SCEPTIC: Now we've reached the point where the question of identity becomes interesting. Do we really only mean by that term the status of the text as object or artefact, as if identity were synonymous with *individuality*, or *specificity*, or even *character*? Let me outline briefly two quite separate theoretical contexts for the concept of identity, call them the *logical* and the *psychological*, which I borrow from an elaborate and authoritative survey of the philosophical history of the term by Dieter Henrich.[1]

The logical sense of identity is familiar in philosophy as a criterion of sameness, whereby one thing is itself by definition 'in itself the same.' The issue of identity was first established by the ancient Greeks in terms of the verb *to be* as copula for the predication of any subject. Leibniz clarifies the essential mathematical criteria for defining the identity of any two objects, if all the qualities of one are also found in the other. The furthest limit of this tradition, amounting to an onto-theological (or would it be: theo-sophical?) mysticism, is found in Schelling's *Identitätsphilosophie*, where God is argued to be manifested in all things, much as (so Hegel argued in his famous polemical response) the night where all cows are black. I doubt that there is much insight to be gleaned here regarding the status of the literary text.

The psychological sense of identity is a more recent development, constituting a kind of special instance for the logical sense when applied to the individual self. Identity thus becomes a principle of consistency or integrity for the person, in particular as a criterion of constancy through time and change. Identity may thus be regarded as a modern substitute for the traditional concept of *psyche*, whether we look to philosophical theories of the self (as in William James, argued by Henrich to be the originator of this view of identity) or to post-Freudian psychoanalytical views (as in the so-called psycho-biographies of Erik Erikson). We are all too familiar with this concept of identity, if only as a principle of crisis.

My basic scepticism begins here. I do not believe that either of these traditional senses of identity, the logical or the psychological, can be applied to the literary text. No criterion of sameness will do, unless we rigorously exclude all concern with verbal function, in which case perhaps the mere technological capability for reproducing copies of books with exactly the same text would constitute an identity. Nor can a text in any way resemble the personality of an individual human being, except through a dubious principle of analogy, whereby the author is identified with his work. Both these senses of identity, when applied to literary texts, lead inevitably to familiar romantic mystifications, through claims either for an organic unity or for a poetic individuality. I reject both these claims and propose that we abandon the concept of identity for the literary text.

STUDENT: Wait a minute. I have a question based on my reading of the later Heidegger, specifically the difficult essay entitled 'Der Satz der Identität.'[2] Heidegger there attributes to language the capacity to achieve an identity between thought and being, not only as an event in discourse, but also as a knowledge, as a conscious awareness in the mind which accompanies a speech act. To signify this cognitive dimension of discourse, the self-reflectivity of speech, he introduces an etymological pun on the term for event: *Er-eignis,* where the sense of 'ownness' in the root *eigen* is equated with the archaic sense of 'eyeing' something in the verb *eräugnen*. Heidegger thus grounds the identity of speaking in the self-reflective movement of language itself, essentially as a dialectical or hermeneutical function (terms which the late Heidegger would not accept) of thought in and through the act of speaking. He also introduces the notion of a 'leap'(*Sprung*) which occurs for thought within 'the resonating domain or preserve' (*der in sich schwingende Bereich*) of language as it is spoken, whereby man and Being enter into a 'belonging together' (*Zusammengehören*) within the 'essential light' (*Wesenslicht*) of the event. It seems to me that Heidegger here retrieves the concept of identity as essential for language, or at least for authentic speaking and thinking, if not for the literary text as such.

SCEPTIC: Though I have little patience with such obscurity, I agree that Heidegger's oracular pronouncements belong, however obliquely, within the main stream of philosophical thinking about dialectics and hermeneutics.

STUDENT: It has also been suggested to be that the term *Sprung* might here signify more than a leap of thought, even though the primary force of his metaphor concerns the movement of the mind through darkness, as along an uncertain forest path, into the sudden brightness of a clearing. *Sprung*, however, might also indicate a kind of break or fault, a gap or fissure in the totality of Being, within which thought moves, from which it originates, and towards which its inquiries strive as to a goal or end. The fault or flaw, as in the perfection of a crystal or a sculpture, would open up a perspective on that which otherwise would be concealed and self-contained. Self-reflection would thus be achieved as a distancing or an interruption in the sustaining vehicle of the mind. More specifically, with regard to language as this vehicle, which Heidegger also called 'the house of Being' (*das Haus des Seins*), such faults would provide the possibility of reflection through figurative rupture or the discontinuities of discourse.

SCEPTIC: This reading of the term *Sprung* seems dubious to me, yet it is an eminently Heideggerian misreading. It recalls his use of the term 'rift' (*Riss*) in the earlier essay 'Der Ursprung des Kunstwerks,'[3] where he discusses the cognitive structures of the work of art. Perhaps we here approach a proper sense of the violent, conflictual relation of texts, as constructs or fabrics of language, to thought, where a sense of division or separation is crucial between signifier and signified, or between message and signal. Such conflict or opposition seems incompatible with traditional notions of vision, or truth, especially in Heidegger's own sense of truth as *Unverborgenheit* (from the Greek *alētheia*). Yet this sense of conflict yields a crucial model for hermeneutics, in particular for the forms of language which impose interpretative responses upon the mind through the act of reading.

CRITIC: Well, now I've heard extreme positions on identity outlined by the two of you, based largely on the authority of borrowed philosophical arguments. I'm not persuaded that literary criticism, or even literary theory, would profit from such models, especially if we are concerned primarily with the practice of interpreting texts.

Let me outline my own position. I would maintain that the crucial criterion for any discussion of identity in a literary text derives from the nature of language itself as a system of signs and from the essential functions of discourse. Every statement in language necessarily involves two separate and simultaneous acts of mediation: on one hand, an act of representation, which establishes a relationship between the verbal code and the world to which it refers; and, on the other, an act of communication, which establishes a relationship between a speaker and his audience.[4] This twofold function of discourse will also apply to every literary text through the act of reading. With regard to such functions identity in a strict sense is impossible, since meaning is constituted through a twofold structure of interrelationships that depend upon polarities of opposition and differentiation. The act of representation requires a distinction between the system of signs and the frame of reference (between the code of signifiers and the range of signifieds); and the act of communication requires a distinction between speaker and audience (between addresser and addressee). The text *as text* thus stands within a fourfold dynamic structure of implicit relationships, which are sustained by opposition and difference. I would be inclined to locate that 'resonating preserve' of language, as Heidegger called it, within this dynamic structure; just as I would also argue that this polarity of mediations, or 'crossings-over,' constitutes the essential *meta-phoric* dimension of poetic discourse. To be translated into such metaphoric resonance is the purpose , goal and end (*telos*) of every literary text. I fail to see how the concept of identity as traditionally defined could be applicable here.

SCEPTIC: We seem dangerously close to agreement, even if what we agree on is to deny any identity to the literary text.

STUDENT: That sounds like an admission of defeat.

SCEPTIC: Not quite. The time has come, which I regard as critical to any good argument, to return to the Greeks. My own predilection for scepticism is borrowed from the spirit of Socratic inquiry, which underlies our dialogue. But we can also learn from the arguments of the philosophers.

Aristotle provides a fundamental insight into hermeneutical consciousness in that peculiar work *Peri Hermēneias*,[5] where he asserts that 'spoken sounds are symbols [*symbola*] of affections in the soul, and writing [*ta graphomena*] of spoken sounds.' Aristotle uses the terms *symbol* and *sign* synonymously, as in the sentence immediately following the statement just quoted, where he argues that signs (*sēmeia*) designate the relation between spoken words and whatever in the mind (or *psyche*) they stand for or signify. These remarks are too brief to establish a comprehensive semiotics or even a psychology of language; but a fundamental hierarchy is nonetheless clear: written words stand for spoken words and spoken words stand for thoughts, feelings, or whatever within the mind. This hierarchy could be reformulated with terms appropriate to our own discussion: the text represents or signifies discourse, which represents or signifies the message or the meaning. In effect, Aristotle lends support to our challenge against the identity of the text. In so far as the symbolizing or signifying functions of language involve a semantic differentiation or a hierarchy of figuration, the concept of identity is out of place.

STUDENT: Aristotle's hierarchy reminds me of the more familiar discussion of imitation by Plato in the *Republic*.[6] We all recall the attack against the poets in Book x, where poetry is accused of being an imitation (*mimesis*) which is two degrees removed from the truth of ideas. The painter imitates an object, such as a couch (596c–597b), which is itself, according to Socrates' argument, an imitation of an idea or form (*eidos*). This hierarchy of imitations could be regarded as analogous to the hierarchy of figuration in Aristotle. The difference between them corresponds to the basic duality of interrelationships (just outlined by our friend the Critic) inherent to language in its functions as a system of signs: the act of representation, which would be the Platonic model of mimesis; and the act of communication, which would be the Aristotelian model of hermeneutics.

CRITIC: Plato himself may have anticipated this duality in his use of the term *mimesis*, in a manner which suggests that Aristotle might have been indebted to his teacher (as so often in his work) for the hierarchy of figuration outlined in his *Peri Hermēneias*. Consider the passage in *Republic* III where the education of the guardians is discussed with reference to stories that could be told and music that could be performed. The term *mimesis* is used there, not as a principle of representation, but as a criterion for expression and response in the soul. Particularly important is the discussion of rhythm and harmony in relation to speech (*logos*) and the figures of diction or style (*ho tropos tēs lexeōs*; 400d–402e). These attributes of music are said to follow the manner of speaking just as speech follows the disposition, or *ethos*, of the soul (*ho tēs psychēs ēthos*). There is a principle of ethical correspondence at work here, developed at some length in the dialogue, that beautiful forms in music and art, not to mention poetry and discourse in general, will only be produced by beautiful minds.

STUDENT: The converse is also argued as a principle for what might be called aesthetic education, where the beautiful forms of art and music will have a corresponding affect upon the minds of those who respond to them. *Mousikē* is offered as a model of *paideia* through its influence upon the soul by imitative (*mimetic*) response (401c–e). Could this claim be important for the question of identity?

SCEPTIC: There is no doubt that Plato's argument has been enormously influential throughout the history of Western aesthetic theory. The entire neo-Platonic and Christian tradition from Plotinus and St Augustine through Dante to the Romantics could bear witness to this influence. The ultimate outcome of Plato's claim would be found in Schelling's *Identitätsphilosophie*, specifically in his *Philosophie der Kunst*. The legacy of Plato imposes a humanistic valorization of the arts for education. The centrality of literature and criticism in the curriculum of our universities still bears witness to this legacy. Even if is sounds like heresy, I would like to challenge its basic assumptions as misleading and, in its mystical and sentimental extremes, as downright dangerous.

CRITIC: That statement sounds rather hostile and provocative to me. Do you truly intend to reject the basic humanistic values inherent to the tradition of Plato?

SCEPTIC: Far from it. I fully agree with Plato's basic model for mimesis as a hierarchy of production and influence, of creation and reception. But I regard this model as the basis for a theory of figuration, rather than a theory of identity, whereby the creation and reception of art involves an essential process of metaphoric transformation. Modern hermeneutical theory, which is probably more indebted to Plato than it acknowleges, has demonstrated that interpretation depends upon a cognitive and reflective distance in aesthetic experience. The appropriate relationship between the mind and the work of art is that of conflict or even negation. Any principle of identity applied to the interpretation of art yields an anti-hermeneutics. Critical judgment itself depends upon such a principle of difference, or tension, or opposition.

CRITIC: You seem to be using Plato against himself, or at least your reading of the *Republic* is directed against the traditional reputation of Plato and Platonism. Perhaps your views are coloured by modern theories concerning the nature of the sign and the place of metaphor in poetic discourse, which you merely project retrospectively upon Plato.

SCEPTIC: I do not deny the influence of modern theory on my thinking, nor do I diminish the complexity of influence, which makes our own views merely another instance in the continuing tradition of Plato. But I also believe in the legitimacy of a revisionary reading of Plato's text based on whatever fresh insights we may bring to it.

CRITIC: Let me offer yet another instance of such insight specifically with regard to lyric poetry, which may throw further light on our discussion of identity. I have in mind a recent essay by the German scholar Karlheinz Stierle on identity in the lyric.[7] He develops a theory of transference or, as he puts it, *transgression* as the constitutive feature of lyric discourse. Initially he uses the term *Überschreitung* ('crossing-over') as an etymological equivalent for the Greek *metaphora*, and I surmise that *transgression* may be intended as a synonym. The implications of this term for the status of the figure seem less neutral and innocent to me, as Stierle himself seems to achnowledge, when he speaks of the lyric as 'anti-discourse.'

STUDENT: What interests me in Stierle's essay are the several connections he makes with related positions among contemporary theorists, especially in France. Beginning with Roman Jakobson's definition of the poetic function in his essay 'Linguistics and Poetics,' Stierle proceeds to distinguish between the text as verbal structure and discourse as *praxis* or event within a specific speech community and in accord with specific conventions and contexts of communication, referring to arguments by Michel Foucault and Pierre Macherey.[8] Stierle's notion of identity in the lyric seems to depend entirely upon discourse as event.

CRITIC: I surmise that this basic structuralist and post-structuralist distinction between verbal form and the functions of discourse is crucial for Stierle's theory of figuration as transgression.

SCEPTIC: How does that lead us back to the question of identity?

CRITIC: Stierle's insistence on the priority of metaphor as transgression in the lyric corresponds roughly to the claims you were making with reference to Plato's hierarchy of influence and exchange in the procedures of discourse. Metaphor as transgression is essentially a challenge to the concept of identity, especially if identity is restricted (as I think Stierle intends) to a criterion of integrity or coherence in discourse as speech act or event.

STUDENT: Can you further clarify what is meant by transgression?

CRITIC: Stierle offers two practical distinctions for what he has in mind: first, the disruption (*Aufhebung*, probably not in Hegel's sense) or the calling into question of the linearity of discourse; second, the superimposition of multiple contexts of discourse upon each other.

SCEPTIC: He also challenges the notion that there could be any literal sense, as distinct from figurative functions, in lyrical discourse. The status of both the object as referent and the subject as lyrical self is seen as problematic. Looking to the example of Rousseau and Romantic poetry, he cites the function of landscape as a symbolic image. The lyrical self is described with reference to the tradition of Petrarch as a constuct of intersecting verbal contexts within a single moment, such that a specific, seemingly subjective mood is conveyed. The plurality of figurative discourse thus depends upon a principle of coherence projected upon the sensibility of a subject which is acknowledged, implicitly at least, to be the construct of that figurative complex. What this amounts to is a theory of reflectivity in the lyric as the direct outcome of a plurality of figurative discourse. This theory has important implications above all for the hermeneutics of reception through the act of reading. The principle of lyric transgression would thus indicate a specific formal device in the language of lyric which imposes upon its reader a conscious awareness of that language as form and of the specific procedures through which it conveys a meaning or mood. Stierle thus challenges the concept of identity in the lyric by claiming an inherent hermeneutical reflectivity through figurative transgression.

STUDENT: I fail to understand what you mean here by reflectivity and how it might be related to lyrical figuration.

SCEPTIC: I understand your difficulty, and I hasten to place the blame on myself rather than Stierle. Perhaps I can indicate something of what I have in mind with reference to Hegel's concept of reflectivity in the *Science of Logic*.[9] Crucial for Hegel's project is the identification of the movement of thought with movements of language, specifically a movement of abstraction in language which constantly reflects upon itself and thus always knows what it is doing (or saying, or thinking) as it proceeds and is capable of articulating this advancing knowledge in and through Hegel's text. The key to this process, as I see it, is Hegel's fundamental insight into the relationship between language and thought as tension or opposition, indeed as *negation* in Hegel's specific sense of the term. The dialectical movement of thought through language is thus defined by negativity as the negation of the negative, whereby thought turns upon itself and becomes conscious of itself. This negativity of the dialectic is the basis, as I read Hegel, of thought's ability to reflect upon itself.

STUDENT: What does all this have to do with the identity of the literary text?

SCEPTIC: The figurative forms of discourse as transgression which, as Stierle argues, constitute the poetic text impose a cognitive task upon the reader, which is directly analogous to the negativity of dialectical thinking in Hegel. The transgressions of lyrical discourse thus impose the challenge and the capacity of reflectivity upon the mind of the reader, which is the basis of all hermeneutical consciousness.

STUDENT: I still fail to understand what you mean by negativity. But it does occur to me that transgression in Stierle's sense comes very close to what Heidegger referred to as the *Sprung* of discourse, either as a leap or as a fault. Perhaps Hegel stands silently behind both notions.

SCEPTIC: At any rate it should now be apparent that the forms of figuration in lyrical discourse are radically opposed to any model of visionary fusion or (to use Coleridge's term) the coalescence of subject and object, as traditionally associated with Romantic theories of the imagination as the basis for identity.

CRITIC: If any of this abstruse speculation is to be valid for me, it will depend upon the outcome of specific interpretive readings. We need an example, a demonstration in practice.

STUDENT: You cannot fault Stierle on this point, since the latter part of his rich essay consists of a detailed and highly innovative reading of Hölderlin's ode *Heidelberg*. Would you like to summarize that reading?

CRITIC: Not at all. Let me offer instead an experiment in critical reading, using a familiar text from English Romanticism, which is not usually associated with theoretical questions in criticism. I refer to Coleridge's *Kubla Khan*, a poem which enjoys a reputation comparable to Hölderlin's 'kunstlos Lied.' A fresh look at this poem in the light of our discussion may prove instructive, even for students of Coleridge.

'MINGLED MEASURE' IN *KUBLA KHAN*[10]

Sameron adion asō: but the to-morrow is yet to come.

Kubla Khan occupies a special place among English Romantic poems. Few texts have received so much critical attention, and few of the major Romantic lyrics make so persuasive a claim for what might be called visionary or inspired discourse. Romantic poetics privileges the powers of the imagination. This holds true for Coleridge above all. *Kubla Khan*, however problematic its status as text, seems to demonstrate with consummate eloquence and authority that singular poetic quality. Yet precisely because of this claim as poetry and because so much is at stake for a theory of poetry to which this text bears witness, *Kubla Khan* remains a challenge for criticism. No more crucial instance comes to mind for the question of identity in poetry.

. . . .

Despite the claim of the original published text to be a fragment and despite the biographical circumstances of its composition, as described in the prose preface which accompanied that publication (discussion of which is here omitted), *Kubla Khan* can and does stand on its own as a poetic statement, complete and self-sufficient. Nor can the organization of its language be denied a latent sense of coherent and unified design as a potentially conscious or even self-conscious work of art, despite the author's apparent denial of such design and such consciousness to himself at the occasion of writing the poem. It may even be argued, as has been done,[11] that the form of statement in the poem opens up at least the possibility of a transcendental response (in Kant's sense of the term as self-reference or self-reflection), whereby the act of reading the poem engenders in the mind of the reader a conscious awareness of the language as such, both in its design and in its self-reference. The outcome of such a reading – this is my central point, which has not, so far as I am aware, hitherto been made – is a complex transformation from a literal to a figurative or symbolic function for the poem as discourse. *Kubla Khan* thus becomes a paradigm for poetic discourse in general. A critical reading involves an act of recognition, whereby a hermeneutical consciousness of the poem is achieved as poetic function. The identity of the text – if the term has any validity at all – must be found in the dynamic process through which this hermeneutical consciousness is achieved for the reader. It includes above all a tension between vision and reflectivity, established by discontinuities of discourse within the language of the text. These discontinuities impose a sense of transgression (in Stierle's sense) or *Sprung* (in Heidegger's sense), a figurative crossing-over which opens up a reflective, self-referential dimension to the poem.

1.   *The Poem as Event: 'Quietly Shining'*
What is the principle of organization for *Kubla Khan*? Much attention has been devoted by critics to irregularities of form, which to some might strengthen the case for the poem as visionary reverie, a speaking which does not know what it is saying, totally lacking in formal design. The stanza divisions show no formal principle of length, thus suggesting convenient demarkations of statement, as if the stanzas were paragraphs in a narrative. Yet the final stanza does indicate a significant turn in the movement of the poem, which justifies consideration of the text as if it were a composition in two movements.

The first movement focuses almost exclusively on the pleasure-dome of Kubla Khan and the exotic setting in which it is located. Certain shifts of focus and variations of tone may nonetheless be perceived, which allow the text to be arranged on the analogy of a classical sonata-allegro form in music (which I shall not attempt to justify further here), as follows:

Exposition: lines 1 to 11
Development: lines 12 to 24
Recapitulation: lines 25 to 30
Coda: lines 31 to 36

A basic distinction is made throughout this movement between art and nature. The pleasure-dome is a man-made construct, exotic and elaborate, whereas the setting in which it is located is defined as a landscape through which the sacred river flows from its source in a fountain that bursts forth from a hidden cavern or chasm to its final destination in the 'sunless sea' (5) or 'lifeless ocean' (28). Little attention is actually paid to the pleasure-dome itself, apart from the initial assertion that it was built by the decree of the Khan. Descriptive material in the latter part of the exposition focuses entirely upon the landscape of the enclosed space within walls and towers, which consists of gardens and forests. A sense of symmetry and order is achieved here, where verbal form appears to imitate what it describes: art encloses nature. A quality of harmony and repose is attributed to the enclosure, which yet partakes of the life and power of nature: 'fertile ground' (6) is 'girdled round' (7). The pleasure-dome is mentioned again in the recapitulation, but there the focus is not the dome itself, but its shadow, reflected upon the moving surface of the river as it flows past. A curious displacement of concern thus occurs away from the palace of the Khan, first to the landscape which contains it and then to the surface of the river which reflects it.

The delineation of landscape remains curiously indeterminate. The river's course occupies the centre in highly schematic manner, as a force ('turmoil,' (17) and a sound ('tumult,' 28), projected upon both origin and destination, which constitute the limit of reference for this life. In the development an exotic and momentous significance is attributed to the act of bursting forth, through which the fountain emerges from 'that deep romantic chasm' (12). It is called 'a savage place' (14). Several figurative associations are superimposed upon the fountain, so that it assumes a complex significance as place and event. The place is given a supernatural aura: 'as holy and enchanted / As e'er beneath a waning moon was haunted / By woman wailing for her demon-lover!' (14ff.). The force of the fountain is attributed to nature as an animate, if not a sentient being: 'as if this earth in fast thick pants were breathing' (18). Fragments of earth thrown up by the fountain are compared to natural and rustic activity: 'like rebounded hail, / Or chaffy grain beneath the thresher's flail' (21f.). This sequence of similes opens up a pluralistic perspective, more general and fantastic than the place itself. The tone of the evocation is also made personal and emphatic by an exclamation: 'But oh' (12); by a demonstrative: 'that deep romantic chasm' (12); and by an apostrophe: 'a savage place!' (14). These various verbal devices evoke a sense of design and intention to the poet's statement.

The movement of syntax is convoluted and accumulative in its rhetorical affect, as indicated by the use of repeated exclamation points and colons. Within this complex sequence, however, a spatial perspective is also established upon a middle ground, as if we ourselves were located within the pleasure-dome. This occurs through terms of position: 'amid' (20) and ''mid' (23), and interruption: 'intermitted' (20), enhanced by a sense of dramatic immediacy in the repeated adverb 'momently' (19 and 24), which offsets the sense of temporal and historical distance in the consistent use of narrative past tense. As the poem advances from development to recapitulation a marked shift of rhythmic cadence and phonetic patterning occurs, which resembles a kind of eddying (a favourite image of Coleridge) and which signals the movement within the poem from event to reflection upon the event. To offer one instance among many: an alliterative pattern of repeated consonants across two rhythmically balanced phrases within a single line evokes a sense of measured flow which is attributed to the river:

> Five miles meandering with a mazy motion (25)

This line introduces the recapitulation, where phrases are repeated from the opening of the poem ('to a lifeless ocean,' 28, is a variant of 'to a sunless sea,' 5). Recognition of this repeated material thus occurs within a rhythmic and phonetic cadence of resolution and ceremonial reduction to the complex dramatic movement of the poem. A heightening of focus and accent is also achieved in the recapitulation through syntactical ellipsis and delay, so that the main subject of this continuous statement ('the sacred river,' 26) assumes a sense of climax, semantically and rhythmically. The pattern of rhyme across these lines also achieves a kind of balance and interaction which complements the effect of reflective eddying: *motion – ran – man – ocean*. The movement of the language at various formal levels thus forces the mind of the reader to turn back upon itself in company with the recapitulation of statement.

The figure of the emperor is also reintroduced at the end of the recapitulation. Initially he was invoked as the originating cause for the pleasure-dome; now through a subtle shift of reference he functions as an effect of or a response to his creation. At the beginning of the poem his role seemed to echo that of God as creator in Genesis, causing the palace to come into being by mere decree. Now we are told that the Khan hears the voices of his ancestors communicating a prophecy of war. What does this shift of roles signify? Presumably these voices are conveyed by the sound of the river, both in the tumult of its bursting forth and in its final sinking into the lifeless ocean. The emperor thus hears a sound 'from far' (29) which is interpreted as the murmuring of spectral voices. Such a response also suggests a symbolic substitution, whereby the river is associated with the course of human life from birth to death. Recognition of this substitution further opens up a sense of analogy between the role of the emperor in his interpretive response and our own role as readers interpreting the poem. The response of the Khan thus serves as a hermeneutical signal for the task of interpretation as such. The emperor was identified initially as creator, a kind of surrogate for the author of the poem (even if that association was not explicit), and now has been transformed into a mere recipient, a kind of auditory exegete, responding to the sounds which reach him as the effect of his own creative act. By recognizing the analogy between this shift of roles and our own hermeneutical task as readers we also may identify the fundamental structural design of the poem as a communicative strategy, whereby the act of reading the text accompanies the movement of the poem through a sympathetic imitation: from descriptive inquiry towards interpretive response. This shift also suggests how we as readers may relate to the poet as author, in a relation *not* of identity but of reciprocity, which is appropriate to the dynamic, dialectical form of communication itself.

On the basis of this perceived relationship as communicative strategy, we may locate in the coda a further strategy of figuration and self-referential resonance. There is a twofold focus here. First, the image or 'shadow' (31) of the pleasure-dome is reflected upon the surface of the river as it flows past. To *float midway* (32) is to attain the privileged status of the symbol, where temporality is transcended or, in Hegel's sense, sublated. Second, the sounds of tumult from the river in the origin and completion of its course are transformed into a 'mingled measure' (33) in the manner of a musical harmony. Senses of sight and sound are thus conjoined: presumably for the emperor, as for the poet and for the reader of his poem. To perceive and enjoy this experience requires a shared dwelling within that pleasure-dome as symbolic space, which conveys both the vision of reflected resonance and the mingled measure of harmonious sound. The poem itself thus becomes identical with this space through symbolic transference and the self-reflective turn of figuration. The meaning achieved at this moment within the poem involves for the reader an act of self-recognition, since the hermeneutical response of his own mind is included within the symbolic reference of the poem's statement. The couplet which concludes the coda constitutes the climax and fulfilment of the poem as a whole, in so far as it conveys to us our own experience as readers within the hermeneutical consciousness attained by our reading of the poem:

> It was a miracle of rare device,
> A sunny pleasure-dome with caves of ice!   (35f.)

The poem may now by understood as *event*, in Heidegger's sense: *Er-eignis*, both as 'en-*own*-ment' and as 'en-*eye*-ment.'

What can be made of the 'caves of ice'? At one level the validity of the phrase is apparent. The indeterminate copula ('it was') includes both the pleasure-dome itself and its reflected image upon the surface of the river. The mingled measure from fountain and cave is superimposed upon this ambivalence of a resonating preserve. As a symbol of art it is a fixed and unchanging value within a dynamic movement and a mingling of sounds: *Dauer im Wechsel.* Yet equally we may refer this phrase to the poem itself as artefact or verbal construct, which like a 'cave of ice' is inhuman and lifeless. The image thus sustains a sense of art as pure reflectivity, an ambivalent paradigm for vision as both shine and sheen (in the dual sense of the term *Schein* defined by both Schiller and Hegel).[12] Here also that sense of poetry as verbal event is affirmed in Heidegger's sense of a resonating preserve ('der in sich schwingende Bereich'), where the moment is realized and known. The opposition of sunlight and ice, established by balanced phrases as a reciprocity of identity and difference, conveys the deepest paradox of what Coleridge understood to be the poetic imagination. Readers of Coleridge will recall another symolic image, equally powerful and precisely correlative to this, where reflected light is revealed in a fixed and frozen form. This occurs at the end of *Frost at Midnight* in the image of the icicle, frozen water drops, dangling from the eaves of the poet's cottage, which is seen through the window in the wintry night: 'quietly shining to the quiet moon.'

2. *The Poem as through a Glass: Darkly Reflecting*
The critical moment of figurative transgression in *Kubla Khan* occurs at the outset of the final verse paragraph of the poem. It is a moment of categorical reversal, of disruption, disillusionment and deconstruction, of crossing-over in the most radical sense. Reference shifts, on one hand, to the 'damsel with a dulcimer' (37), conjured apparently out of the poet's own memory; and the poet introduces himself, on the other, as first-person pronominal subject for the first time in the poem. All apparent concern with Kubla Khan and his pleasure-dome is abruptly abandoned by arbitrary displacement. This transgression from descriptive subject matter to the subjective self was anticipated by the strategies of reflective figuration which preceded it. The movement of the poem may thus be perceived as an advance beyond its moment of visionary climax through a disruptive response, which sustains and completes the symbolic action of the poem in the manner of a dialectical negation. The full import of this movement for the hermeneutical reception of the text needs further consideration.

What is the relation of the damsel to the pleasure-dome? How does the vision here claimed by the poetic self as something once seen relate to the development of his previous description into poetic event? More specifically, within the temporal continuum of the poem as fictional historical narrative, how is the assertion of a particular moment of experience – 'once' (38) – to be referred back to the remote setting of the opening movement? It is presumably no accident that an identical form of indeterminate generic statement with the verb *to be* occurs both at the end of the first movement and near the outset of the second: 'It was ...' (35 and 39), both times at the beginning of a line. Given the remoteness of Kubla Khan and his world to the poet and the position he occupies as speaker in both time and space, the question of relationship between description and vision becomes extremely problematic. An awareness of this problem is central to the hermeneutical design of the final movement.

The subject of the damsel's song is Mount Abora, which remains unrelated, except through patterns of sound, to Xanadu and the river Alph. Yet, through a displacement of discourse into the subjunctive mood of a condition contrary to fact, a hypothetical analogy is established between the song of the Abyssinian maid and the poet's own poem. May we therefore associate the damsel's song with the simile used earlier of the 'woman wailing for her demon-lover' (16), whose manner was associated with the 'savage place' (14) of the river's birth? The common denominator is vision, and the medium of communication in each instance would be 'symphony and song' (43), received once by the poet 'in a vision' (38) and now to be revived 'within me' (42) through a recreative act of the poetic imagination. The automatic and inevitable consequence of such a recreative act, we are told, would be a 'music loud and long' (45). Even more, to achieve such music of vision would be to 'build that dome in air, / That sunny dome! those caves of ice!' (46f.) What does this mean?

Such allusion to the earlier focus of the poem on the pleasure-dome involves a radical opposition to the project of its own discourse. Earlier the pleasure-dome and caves of ice were evoked as image and as paradigm, recalled and reconstructed within the descriptive language of the poem as fictional event. The final couplet of that movement established a reflective, hermeneutical perspective of self-reference, as if 'it was' (35 and 39) had become 'this is.' Now all possibility of such realization is removed into a subjunctive alternative: 'if only.' The poem thus seems to undo everything it earlier achieved. Equally important for a hermeneutical reading of the poem is the assertion that a reconstruction of sunny dome and caves of ice, the possibility of which is implicitly denied, would not be a reflection or shadow upon the surface of the sacred river or a mingled measure of murmuring spirit voices, but rather an aerial palace suspended impossibly in the sky like some cloud, signifying the distance and insubstantiality of poetic vision or imaginative Schein. How does this second dome relate to the first?

The two constructs appear initially to oppose each other, as description opposes vision, or as reality (event) opposes idea (image). Upon reflection, however, we perceive that the two are identical, both within the fictional or poetic world of the poem and within the mind of the recreative imagination, regardless of the recipient of that recreation: Kubla Khan, the Abyssinian maid (as she sings to her dulcimer), the poet (as he speaks in and through his poem), and ourselves (as we read this text). The only difference – and it is the crucial difference for hermeneutical consciousness – resides in the affect of that figurative transgression which occurred in the movement from one section of the poem to the other. The shadow of the dome was initially affirmed as a figure of capable imagination, the product of a willing suspension of disbelief; reference to it latterly involves displacement through several levels of negation or deconstruction, so that it serves as a conscious, indeed a self-conscious, sign for the poem itself, not as it has been achieved, but as it might be in an ideal instance. The content of that sign, its transcendental referent, is thus the norm for poetic vision, performing in the manner of a transcendent signified for the discourse of the poem as a play of signifiers, against which the actual movement of that discourse may be measured as negative instance (in Hegel's sense of the negative).

How appropriate, finally, that the language of the poem shifts its focus at the end through a further ironic displacement to a hypothetical recipient for such visionary song. This recipient turns out to be, as the last playful surrogate for the identity of the text, the reader of *Kubla Khan*, indeed we ourselves, at least within a figure of hermeneutical response. About that poet singing of his vision in a fine frenzy, whose voice until now has been tacitly accepted as the vehicle for the entire text of this poem, we ourselves are made to utter the concluding lines (49–54) as a warning to dissociate ourselves from the madness of his vision. Everything which constituted the fiction of the pleasure-dome as event and even the damsel's song as vision has now collapsed into a hyperbole of affect. We share in it only vicariously through a distancing of perspective, a dissociation of sensibility, which we ourselves impose – or rather: the final lines of the poem do it *for us*. The poet's state of mind as he produces his visionary song is relegated to a kind of madness, manifested by such clichés as 'his flashing eyes' and 'his floating hair' (50). The exclamation by this hypothetical audience of 'all who heard' (48) even assumes the rhetorical form of a second-person address in the imperative mood. In effect, we are giving commands to each other, indeed to all readers. The effect of such a statement, as further enhancement to the thematic reflectivity of our hermeneutical consciousness, is that the poem speaks directly to us in our own voice, so that our position and attitude are categorically differentiated from those of the poet. The discourse of the lyric, through a final transgression, thus dispels all sense of presence and breaks all sense of poetic illusion. Where are we left at the end but in the real world, beyond the limits of vision, outside the magic circle which we ourselves have drawn about the poet, to separate us from all possible exchange with that lunatic mind which fed on 'honey-dew' (53) and drank 'the milk of Paradise' (54)? Our compensation must be that the language of the poem has also moved with us to the outside, thus sharing in the breakdown of its vision, indeed causing it through an imperious usurpation of our own voice. The implications of all this for the concept of identity are disturbing.

It may now be instructive by way of conclusion to this essay on the poem to consider briefly the prose preface which Coleridge included with the initial publication of the text in 1816. Whether or not this preface reports accurately the biographical circumstances in which the poem was composed may be of less interest than the ironic thematic association of the situation there described with the hypothetical status of the poet as visionary within the poem. The opium dream in which the poem is said to have been composed may thus be identified with the frenzy of vision attributed to the poet at the end of the poem. Also important is the use of water images to describe the failure of the poet's vision when he endeavoured to write down his dream after waking up. Following the interruption by his visitor, he asserts, 'all the rest [of the vision] had passed away like the images on the surface of a stream into which a stone has been cast, but, alas! without the after restoration of the latter.' He then quotes a passage from his poem *The Pains of Sleep*, which was included in the initial publication just after *Kubla Khan*, where a similar image of concentric circles upon the surface of water is used to signify the disruption of a vision, like the breaking of a spell. The hope is there expressed that the smoothness of the surface will soon return, re-establishing the lost vision as in a mirror or a glass. May we not refer this image of the reflecting surface of water to the central symbol of the poem itself: 'The shadow of the dome of pleasure / Floated midway on the waves' (31f.)? Such continuity must be more than accidental and suggests, further, that the apparent fragmentary status of the written text may contrast with the vision it seeks to recapture in the way that the smooth surface of the water relates to the concentric rippling which results when the surface is disturbed.

A thematic analogy may also be perceived between the dissociation of the reader from the poet at the end of the poem and the interruption of the act of writing by the arrival of the visitor from Porlock on business in the prose preface. To refer both these moments of disruption to the act of reading may go beyond any apparent intention on Coleridge's part, although within the poem it seems unavoidable as analogy *for the reader*. Yet such ironic transformations are precisely appropriate to the dialectical movement of thought: through moments of projected vision towards a position of reflective self-awareness by means of a cognitive response to patterns of figurative transgression and the breakdown of vision. Not unrelated to this strategy of ironic dissociation is the initial assertion in the preface that the author is only publishing his fragment 'at the request of a poet of great and deserved celebrity' (whom scholars inform us was Lord Byron), and that, as far as the author is concerned, the text serves 'rather as a psychological curiosity, than on the ground of any supposed *poetic* merits.' Do we not perceive a bit of tongue in cheek here? Yet that request by a fellow poet, perhaps in analogy to the decree of Kubla Khan for the construction of the pleasure dome, shifts the burden of *authority* away from the poet himself, who nonetheless remains the source of the vision represented in the fragment, and attributes the claim for publication to what must be regarded as a response to a *reading* of the text, including presumably a hermeneutical consciousness of what the text is capable of communicating concerning that vision which the poet claims to have been lost.

These several levels of related paradoxical distinctions between vision and reflection, both in the text of the poem and in the prose preface, serve to enhance and sustain that hermeneutical consciousness in the reader, which I take to be the ultimate communicative purpose of such texts. The meaning of poetic vision thus remains always and only accessible to our interpretive understanding, as Coleridge well knew, from the distance of a disillusionment, like the circles upon the surface of the water or the faults in a crystal, a sense of absence or distance rather than presence, indeed as an image of a paradise which has always just been lost at the moment it is glimpsed. The measure of identity for a reader of poetry, as a reflective knowledge to be achieved, is the radical breakdown and destruction of the principle of identity itself.

AFTERTHOUGHTS

CRITIC: Will this do? I hope such a reading helps clarify some of the practical implications for literary criticism to be drawn from the theoretical issues which arose in our discussion of identity.

STUDENT: I am grateful for it. You have shown how our shared quandary about identity in a literary text could yield productive insights for the actual encounter with poems and the production of a hermeneutical consciousness through critical reading.

CRITIC: Are there any changes to be made in our earlier theoretical pronouncements?

STUDENT: Several concepts are now clearer to me. I begin to understand how Heidegger's notion of *Er-eignis* could apply to the hermeneutical reception of a text as an event in discourse. I also see how the notion borrowed from Stierle concerning the discourse of lyric as a transgression can apply to the communicative functions of figurative or metaphoric language in poetry.

CRITIC: Anything else?

STUDENT: There is one area of our discussion that did not enter at all into your reading of *Kubla Khan*. I refer to the polemical point developed from Plato and

Aristotle concerning the ethical value or pedagogical affect of literature, specifically with regard to the impact of poetry on the mind. Is this not implicitly an issue even for *Kubla Khan*, especially if we agree that the text exhibits a communicative design intended to elicit a hermeneutical response? CRITIC: I am puzzled. What you say about the omission of an ethical concern in my reading is true, especially recalling the apparent impasse of our challenge to traditional humanism in education. But I fail to find evidence in this text that would clarify what its function might be for education or for the general ethics of reading.

SCEPTIC: Let me once again perform my role as sceptic and offer a critique of your reading. The issue, as I see it, does not depend upon what this poem says about ethical values, but rather upon what it does *not* say. I will have to elaborate what I have in mind more fully.

I do not believe this poem to be so politically naïve as it seems. What are we to make, for instance, of Kubla Khan himself as a model for creation by decree? His historical reputation, which I assume was familiar to Coleridge, speaks for itself. He is the extreme instance of an oriental despot or tyrant, a Mongol warrior emperor, who achieved his power and domination through vast destruction and military violence. What sort of pleasure-dome does such a monarch build? If it serves the poem as a model for paradise, should we ignore the fact that it must have been built upon human blood and sweat, violence and oppression? Nothing is said in the poem about this, unless a profound, even tragic irony is intended in the allusion to ancestral voices heard by the emperor prophesying war. What war might this have been, unless a direct outcome of the emperor's policies of violence and oppression? I think such considerations can and should affect our reading of the poem. The shadow of the pleasure-dome upon the water as a cave of ice may signify a more sinister political implication than your reading suggested. Could such dark allusions also be reconciled with your claim that the pleasure-dome serve as paradigm for art?

Consider also the historical context of the dates associated with the composition and publication of this poem. The prose preface ascribes the composition to the year 1797 and it was finally published in 1816. These dates neatly bracket the public career of Napoleon Bonaparte. Coleridge himself, as is well known, had strong political opinions concerning developments in Europe from the French Revolution to the Restoration after Napoleon's fall. Evidence could probably be assembled to support the claim that the poet regarded Napoleon as a military tyrant in the manner of a Kubla Khan. But we do not need to impose any explicit or even hypothetical political design upon the poem. My point would be that the historical context of the poem is itself sufficient to allow readers to make this connection between the two emperors. A latent ideological perspective on the political status of Romantic poetry is thus opened up on the poem, whether the author intended it or not.

If we take such an analogy between internal and external historical and political contexts for despotism seriously, what affect would there be upon our reading of *Kubla Khan*? An answer is provided only indirectly from the text, again from the evidence of what remains unspoken. The norm of visionary song evoked by this oriental pleasure-dome is signalled by the damsel with her dulcimer. She can hardly serve as a spokesman for the political events of the Napoleonic era. But we also associated the damsel's song with the earlier simile of the woman wailing for her demon-lover. Does that simile suggest a valid model for poetic inspiration? I think not. The woman's wailing must signify either an unfulfilled sexual desire or a lament for some kind of exotic ravishment. We are either in the domain of psychopathology or the strange gothic world of the ghost-ballad.

The politics of an oriental despotism are thus supplanted by a peculiarly inhuman model of ethical relationship, which can only have negative implications. Visionary song, however we interpret the damsel and the wailing woman, is clearly antisocial. The lyrical outburst of the damsel is also the direct cause of an emotional frenzy in the poet, when he attempts to recall the vision she conveyed. Our response as hypothetical audience to all this must be repulsion, as the final lines insist with regard to our attitude towards the poet. This yields a model of incompatibility, indeed a radical alienation, which must be regarded as the exact opposite of the Classical norm of aesthetic education. You recall our discussion of Plato's argument in *Republic* III, where the beauty of art and music is asserted to be the memetic outcome of a corresponding disposition in the soul, just as the proper affect of such beauty upon the mind of its recipient was argued to be a sympathetic or imitative transformation, in the manner of an aesthetic education. Nothing of all this is implied for the response to *Kubla Khan*. Coleridge's text imposes a radical revision of the Classical norm regarding beauty and its affects. This constitutes a blatant challenge to the ethical values of art, just as extreme in its way as the political implications of a paradisal garden built by the decree of an oriental despot.

To read *Kubla Khan* does not in any way improve or edify the mind, except by categorical negation and opposition. The act of reading affects an abrupt disruption even for a recollection of vision. Our function as readers, so you argued, is to break the spell of vision. My point would be that such a breaking – remember Heidegger's *Sprung*? – constitutes a catastrophe, in the original Greek sense of a reflective turning back upon itself by the mind. The consequence is a categorical destrucion of all the affects of beauty. The value of art, by the example of this poem, must be understood in purely negative terms.

To achieve this insight requires the substitution of an ethical criterion, however negative, for any aesthetic norm. Remember that we are left outside the magic circle of vision; we move through the poem as a figure for paradise only to leave it behind. We recognize, finally, the figures of language in the poem to be the empty, lifeless, and inhuman structures, like caves of ice, for a pure reflectivity, which has no further ethical value *for us* (i.e. for the human community) than the fact that it knows itself to be thus isolated and bereft and obliges us to share that knowledge. Such knowledge is the very opposite of the traditional, humanistic edification claimed for art. It is also the basis of my fundamental scepticism concerning any claims for the identity of the literary text.

Let me conclude. The garden of vision, whether we associate it with Eden or Elysium, is beyond our access here in the fallen world. We are all subject, including the poet, to the violence and suffering of politics and time. The best that art may communicate to us is the semblance of beauty (the *Schein* of *Schönheit*), an illusion of vision, which we can and do and must see through as an elaborate fiction. The ethical, political, and even ideoligical value of art resides precisely in the act of seeing through the fiction. We must be very careful in drawing any lessons from our experience of art, with which to make claims either for the conduct of our lives or for the education of our souls. Can we agree that such issues of ethical value need to be considered?

CRITIC: Considered by whom? I acknowledge the importance of these political and ethical issues for questions of value and ideological commitment, especially where they remain unspoken within the text. But I would also argue for suitable limits to the powers of criticism, in so far as the basis of judgment must always be the language of the text. What lies beyond or behind the text in silence may also lie beyond the certainty of our grasp. This is no longer a question of identity so much as propriety. Forgive my caution.

STUDENT: Let me plead at the last for an appropriate balance between what is proper to criticism and what is important for political and ethical judgment. My concern as student of literature remains with the value of literary study for education. Despite your attack on traditional humanism, I still regard Plato to be our best guide for the educational effects of critical reading, above all through the example of his dialogues as a norm for such reading, indeed as an implicit norm for the development of a hermeneutical consciousness. Your comments on *Kubla Khan* may challenge the traditional assumptions concerning the value of literature for edifying the mind and guiding us to the truth and the light. There is no doubt in my mind, however, that the enlightened study of poetic texts, whatever the outcome for our understanding, will continue to be central to the procedures and the purposes of higher education.

SCEPTIC: Agreed. And in that spirit of conclusion let me quote the line from Theocritus' first Idyll, which Coleridge used in part (and slightly garbled) in the prose preface to *Kubla Khan* and which stands as motto to the essay here. The shepherd-poet addresses the Muses: 'I will sing you a sweeter song another day.'[13]

NOTES

1 Dieter Henrich, '"Identität" – Begriffe, Probleme, Grenzen,' in *Identität*, ed. Odo Marquard and Karlheinz Stierle, *Poetik und Hermeneutik*, 8, München 1979, 133–86. The examples cited in the paragraphs which follow are borrowed from Henrich's authoritative argument.

2 Martin Heidegger, 'Der Satz der Identität,' in *Identität und Differenz*, Pfullingen 1957, pp. 13–34. The discussion of *Er-eignis* occurs on pp. 28f.; the phrase 'der in sich schwingende Bereich,' on p. 30; and the concept of *Sprung* on p. 32. The following statement is summarized here: 'Im Er-eignis schwingt das Wesen dessen, was als Sprache spricht, die einmal das Haus des Seins genannt wurde. Satz der Identität sagt jetzt: Ein Sprung, den das Wesen der Identität verlangt, weil es ihn braucht, wenn anders das Zusammen*gehören* vom Mensch und Sein in das Wesenslicht des Ereignisses gelangen soll' (p. 32).

3 Martin Heidegger, 'Der Ursprung des Kunstwerks,' in *Holzwege*, 3rd ed., Frankfurt 1957, pp. 7–68. The essay appeared separately as a Reclam paperback, Stuttgart 1960, with an important introduction by Hans-Georg Gadamer. The concept of *Riss* is developed in the final section of the essay, 'Die Wahrheit und die Kunst,' esp. pp. 51ff.

4 The position outlined here derives in large part from the important essay by Roman Jakobson, 'Linguistics and Poetics,' in *Style and Language*, Cambridge, Mass. 1960, pp. 350–77. Also important for my thinking on such theoretical issues are the views of I.A. Richards, notably in his essay 'Toward a Theory of Comprehending,' in *Speculative Instruments*, Chicago 1955, pp. 17–38, and 'The Future of Poetry,' in *So Much Nearer*, New York 1968, pp. 150–82; also Richards's discussion of Jakobson's essay, 'Factors and Functions in Linguistics,' in *Poetries: Their Media and Ends*, The Hague 1974, pp. 1–16. I have outlined my view of Richards's theory in a commemorative essay, 'I.A. Richards (1893–1979). Grand Master of Interpretations,' *University of Toronto Quarterly*, 49:3 (Spring 1980), 189–204.

5 The text of Aristotle is cited from the bilingual (Greek and English) edition in the Loeb Classical Library: Aristotle, *The Organon*, trans. Harold P. Cooke, Cambridge, Mass. 1938, pp. 114f.

6 Plato, *Republic*, 2-volume bilingual (Greek and English) edition in the Loeb Classical Library: Plato, vols. v and vi, trans. Paul Shorey, repr. Cambridge, Mass. 1970. I have also consulted the translation of the *Republic* by Allan Bloom, New York 1968.

7 Karlheinz Stierle, 'Die Identität des Gedichts – Hölderlin als Paradigma,' in *Identität*, pp. 505–52. The discussion of transgression occurs in section 1, 3 of the essay (pp. 513–23). Particularly important for my argument is the following statement by Stierle: 'Das "Poetische" der Lyrik geht hervor aus der unaufhebbaren Einheit von formaler Artikulation auf der Ebene des Textes und reflexiver Funktion des Diskurses im Hinblick auf ein Subjekt, das in seiner emotiven Gestalt nicht mehr aufgeht, sondern zum Fluchtpunkt wird für eine Pluralität simultaner Kontexte' (p. 521).

8 Michel Foucault, *L'Ordre du discours*, Paris 1971, and Pierre Macherey, *Pour une théorie de la production littéraire*, Paris 1966. Stierle discusses these works in relation to his own theory on pp. 510–13 of his essay.

9 Hegel, *Wissenschaft der Logik*, part II (Zweites Buch: Das Wesen; Erster Abschnitt: Das Wesen der Reflexion in ihm selbst; Erstes Kapitel: Der Schein), ed. Georg Lasson, Die philosophische Bibliothek, vol. 57, repr. Hamburg 1966, pp. 7–23. Invaluable for the study of this text is the detailed commentary by Dieter Henrich, 'Hegels Logik der Reflexion. Neue Fassung,' in *Die Wissenschaft der Logik und die Logik der Reflexion*, ed. Dieter Henrich, *Hegel-Studien*, *Beihefte*, vol. 18, Bonn 1978, pp. 204–324. Valuable material on the concept of negativity is also contained in the volume *Positionen der Negativität*, ed. Harald Weinrich, *Poetik und Hermeneutik*, 6, München 1975. I do not claim any competence to address Hegel's text directly. The value of the concept of negativity for literary theory is briefly discussed in my essay 'The Hermeneutics of Form: Reading the Romantic Ode,' *Boundary 2*, 7:3 (Spring 1979), 1–30, esp. pp. 6f.

10 In order to reduce the length of the present essay for inclusion in the current volume on the Identity of the Literary Text, a section of about seven pages in typescript was omitted from the discussion of *Kubla Khan* (the lacuna is indicated by the line of dots). What I have omitted is a brief survey of the publication history of the poem and the history of its critical reception. This material, however important for a reassessment of the poem in the context of Coleridge scholarship, did not seem essential to the discussion of identity. The complete text of the essay will be published in a collection of my essays forthcoming under the title *The Hermeneutics of Form*. The poem and its prose preface are printed following the notes.

11 Kenneth Burke, '"Kubla Khan," Proto-Surrealist Poem,' in *Language as Symbolic Action: Essays on Life, Literature, and Method*, Berkeley 1968, pp. 201–22; esp. pp. 209f.

12 The basic ambivalence of the term *Schein* for aesthetic theory was first perceived by Schiller in his letters to Körner in 1793, which have come to be known as the *Kallias-Briefe*, since he there outlines plans for an essay on the theory of beauty to be entitled 'Kallias.' The letters are printed together in the volume of *Theoretische Schriften*, in the edition of Schiller's works, ed. Fricke and Göpfert, München 1959, V, 394–433. For Hegel on *Schein*, see note 9 above. I have discussed this

ambivalence in an earlier essay, 'The Temporality of Selfhood: Metaphor and Romantic Poetry,' *New Literary History*, 6 (1974–5), 169–93, esp. pp. 174f.
13 Theocritus, *Idylls*, I, 145: ἐγὼ δ᾽ ὔμμιν καὶ ἐς ὕστερον ἅδιον ᾀσῶ.

Kubla Khan: or A Vision in a Dream

Of the Fragment of Kubla Khan
The following fragment is here published at the request of a poet of great and deserved celebrity, and as far as the Author's own opinions are concerned, rather as a psychological curiosity, than on the ground of any supposed *poetic* merits.

In the summer of the year 1797, the Author, then in ill health, had retired to a lonely farmhouse between Porlock and Linton, on the Exmoor confines of Somerset and Devonshire. In consequence of a slight indisposition, an anodyne had been prescribed, from the effects of which he fell asleep in his chair at the moment that he was reading the following sentence, or words of the same substance, in 'Purchas's Pilgrimage:' 'Here the Khan Kubla commanded a palace to be built, and a stately garden thereunto. And thus ten miles of fertile ground were inclosed with a wall.' The author continued for about three hours in a profound sleep, at least of the external senses, during which time he has the most vivid confidence, that he could not have composed less than from two to three hundred lines; if that indeed can be called composition in which all the images rose up before him as *things*, with a parallel production of the correspondent expressions, without any sensation or consciousness of effort. On awaking he appeared to himself to have a distinct recollection of the whole, and taking his pen, ink, and paper, instantly and eagerly wrote down the lines that are here preserved. At this moment he was unfortunately called out by a person on business from Porlock, and detained by him above an hour, and on his return to his room, found to his no small surprise and mortification, that though he still retained some vague and dim recollection of the general purpose of the vision, yet, with the exception of some eight or ten scattered lines and images, all the rest had passed away like the images on the surface of a stream into which a stone has been cast, but, alas! without the after restoration of the latter:

> Then all the charm
> Is broken – all that phantom-world so fair
> Vanishes, and a thousand circlets spread,
> And each mis-shape the other. Stay awhile,
> Poor youth! who scarcely dar'st lift up thine eyes –
> The stream will soon renew its smoothness, soon
> The visions will return! And lo, he stays,
> And soon the fragments dim of lovely forms
> Come trembling back, unite, and now once more
> The pool becomes a mirror.

Yet from the still surviving recollections in his mind, the Author has frequently purposed to finish for himself what had been originally, as it were, given to him. Σαμερον αδιον ασω: but the to-morrow is yet to come.

As a contrast to this vision, I have annexed a fragment of a very different character, describing with equal fidelity the dream of pain and disease.

Kubla Khan

In Xanadu did Kubla Khan
A stately pleasure-dome decree:
Where Alph, the sacred river, ran
Through caverns measureless to man
   Down to a sunless sea.
So twice five miles of fertile ground
With walls and towers were girdled round;
And here were gardens bright with sinuous rills
Where blossom'd many an incense-bearing tree;
And here were forests ancient as the hills,
And folding sunny spots of greenery.

But oh that deep romantic chasm which slanted
Down the green hill athwart a cedarn cover!
A savage place! as holy and inchanted
As e'er beneath a waning moon was haunted
By woman wailing for her demon-lover!
And from this chasm, with ceaseless turmoil seething,
As if this earth in fast thick pants were breathing,
A mighty fountain momently was forced:
Amid whose swift half-intermitted Burst
Huge fragments vaulted like rebounding hail,
Or chaffy grain beneath the thresher's flail:
And mid these dancing rocks at once and ever
It flung up momently the sacred river.
Five miles meandering with a mazy motion.
Through wood and dale the sacred river ran,
Then reached the caverns measureless to man,
And sank in tumult to a lifeless ocean:
And 'mid this tumult Kubla heard from far
Ancestral voices prophesying war!

The shadow of the dome of pleasure
Floated midway on the waves;
Where was heard the mingled measure
From the fountain and the caves.
It was a miracle of rare device,
A sunny pleasure-dome with caves of ice!

A damsel with a dulcimer
In a vision once I saw:
It was an Abyssinian maid
And on her dulcimer she play'd,
Singing of Mount Abora,
Could I revive within me
Her symphony and song,
To such a deep delight 'twould win me,
That with music loud and long,
I would build that dome in air,
That sunny dome! those caves of ice!
And all who heard should see them there,
And all should cry, Beware! Beware!
His flashing eyes, his floating hair!
Weave a circle round him thrice,
And close your eyes with holy dread:
For he on honey-dew hath fed,
And drank the milk of Paradise.

HANS ROBERT JAUSS

The Identity of the Poetic Text
in the Changing Horizon of Understanding

INTRODUCTION

Since the 1960s, the renewal of literary hermeneutics has brought to the foreground of methodological reflection a notion which the historico-philological disciplines have always presupposed, but which has rarely ever been developed methodically in its own terms. The notion I am alluding to is that of horizon, which constitutes all creation of meaning in human behaviour and in our primary understanding of the world both as historical limitation and as the condition of possibility of any experience.

The level of understanding to be achieved in order to bridge the historical distance between the alien horizon of the text and the interpreter's own horizon did not become problematic as long as the notion of *Geist* from German idealism or the ideal of precision from positivism appeared to guarantee for interpretation an unmediated access. The historicist paradigm, however, recognized the limitations of the interpreter's point of view and thereby established the qualitative difference between past and present as a hermeneutical problem. It considered the problem of understanding the alien horizon as being resolved if only the interests or biases of the interpreter were excluded. Thus, the scope of historical understanding was radically diminished, being limited to the undifferentiated reconstruction of past life in the horizon of its historical distinctness. The renewed critique of historicism, led for the most part by Gadamer, has brought to light the objectivist illusion of this one-sided hermeneutic and has insisted that the past event cannot be understood without taking into account its consequences, that the work of art cannot be separated from its effects. The very history of effects and the interpretation of an event or work of the past enables us to understand it as a plurality of meanings that was not yet perceivable to its contemporaries. If the horizon of our present did not always already include the original horizon of the past, historical understanding would be impossible, since the past in its otherness may only be grasped in so far as the interpreter is able to separate the alien from his own horizon. It is the task of historical understanding to take both horizons into account through conscious effort. To believe that it is possible to gain access to the alien horizon of the past simply by leaving out one's own horizon of the present is to fail to recognize that subjective criteria, such as choice, perspective, and evaluation, have been introduced into a supposedly objective reconstruction of the past.

The recent trend towards historical knowledge, provoked by the success of the structural method, can be distinguished from classic historicism mainly through a methodological consideration of the historicity of understanding. Such an understanding requires that the horizons of the past and the present assert themselves as the central problem and achieve once more the complete hermeneutical triad of understanding, explanation, and application. Such a requirement has established the notion of horizon as a fundamental concept in both literary and historical hermeneutics. It poses the problem of understanding what is alien by insisting on the distinctness of the horizons not only of past and present experience, but also of familiar and culturally different worlds. One may state it as the problem of aesthetic experience when the horizon of expectation, evoked in the contemporary experience of the reading of the literary text, is reconstructed. It may also be conceived as a problem of intertextuality when one considers the function of other texts that constitute the horizon of a literary work and gain new meaning by this transposition. As well it encompasses the problem of the social function of literature mediating between the horizons of aesthetic and everyday experience. Historical knowledge may also be approached as the problem of the transformation of horizons, a perspective which arises when the teleological or evolutionist theory of tradition is invalidated and when, even in the arts, historical processes are drawn into the dialectic of appropriation and selection, conservation and rejuvenation. Finally we encounter the problem of ideological criticism when we have to elucidate the latent horizon of concealed interests and repressed needs that seems to challenge today the humanist trust in the transparency of communication in our dealings with art.

This sketch of the history of the problem might well be expanded to include other disciplines, the implications of which we will only briefly allude to here. Most disciplines have recently begun to question the hermeneutical presuppositions of their theoretical foundations and have raised explicitly or implicitly the notion of horizon: as a thematic field in the sociology of knowledge and its theory of relevancies (Schütz), as frame of reference that ultimately conveys meaning to actions and perceptions in the theory of science (Popper), as a presupposition of reasoning in the analysis of logical language (Frege), in generative semantics (Brekle) and in linguistic pragmatics (Wunderlich), as the isotopic level in structural semantics (Greimas), as the cultural code in semiotics (Lotman), as the situational context in the theory of speech-acts (Stierle), as the intertext in structural stylistics (Riffaterre), and finally as the language game in analytical language-philosophy, which, in Wittgenstein's later period, ultimately makes all understanding of meaning possible and thereby succeeds in replacing what was, until then, a precise world-portraying aspect of language.[1]

My own contribution to this change in the history of science was the attempt in *Literaturgeschichte als Provokation* (1967) to introduce the notion of horizon as an instrument in literary hermeneutics. By returning to it now I intend to re-examine the biases and lacunae of this enterprise, using my own work to test it. Rather than seeking to resolve problems raised by my critics, I shall attempt to summarize my argument by addressing myself to those examples in my critical work where the problem of bringing into play the notion of horizons focused on new aspects which as yet cannot claim to have been solved.

DIALOGICAL UNDERSTANDING IN LITERARY COMMUNICATION

Recent interest in aesthetic theory relating to the problem of the experience of art and its communicative function, to the experience of other historical periods and other cultures, and to the understanding which it brings of temporal remoteness and unfamiliarity has once again brought to the fore the problem of the circularity of literary communication and, at the same time, its dialogical nature.

Just as the producer of a text becomes also a recipient when he sets out to write, so the interpreter has to bring himself into play as reader when he wants to participate in the dialogue of literary tradition. A dialogue consists not only of two interlocutors, but also of the willingness of one to recognize and accept the other in his otherness. This is even more true when the other is represented by a text which does not speak to us immediately. Literary understanding becomes dialogical only when the otherness of the text is sought and recognized from the horizon of our own expectations, when no naïve fusion of horizons is considered, and when one's own expectations are corrected and extended by the experience of other.

The recognition and acceptance of the 'dialogicity' of literary communication brings into play in more than one way the problem of otherness: between producer and recipient, between the past of the text and the present of the recipient, between different cultures. Today hermeneutical reflection and semiotic analysis compete as methods to grasp the otherness of a text that is unfamiliar to us. Neither the continuum of meaning of history nor the universality of semiotic systems can claim to have a better guarantee of understanding. In this respect one might appropriately recall Schleiermacher's axiom: that non-understanding is the rule rather than an exception when we come to deal with speech which is unfamiliar to us. The question to which literary hermeneutics must address itself, when faced with the otherness of a text, is how to bridge the gap between otherness and speechlessness.

Because of the aesthetic distance of the spectator, one cannot resolve the problem by asserting that the literary work will open up, as it were, by itself. For this reason precisely, Bakhtin's claim to base understanding on the 'dialogicity of the word' went beyond contemplative hermeneutics. If, in a literary dialogue spanning different temporal moments, an embodiment of the experience of others becomes possible, the aesthetically mediated otherness has to include something identifiable which can also be discerned in the alien text. The topical interest in historical anthropology can be explained by this line of argument. Although it was taboo, until only recently, even to formulate the question of 'anthropological constants,' anthropology, which developed historically a theory of human needs or an archaeology of knowledge, and reconstructed the knowledge of elementary distinction and orientation of past worlds, has regained today an unchallengeable validity. Literary communication has the advantage that agreement about the work of art and the understanding of oneself in the alien object attains transparency. Literary hermeneutics can therefore take heart from the fact that its object – the experience of men in a productive and receptive relationship with art – makes available what is hidden by religious ritual from the uninitiated and repressed or concealed by a political or judicial document. It is characteristic of the aesthetic object that it conserves and, at the same time, reveals the historically other, since it not only allows the representation of subjective experience of the world but also makes it available within the framework of art as experience of itself in the experience of other. This brings us back to our question: to what extent is dialogical understanding an aid to us and what are its limitations when it has to make accessible art and literature in their temporal or spatial, historical or cultural otherness, thereby involving them in the progressive dialogue of aesthetic communication?

Theology may (as Magass explains with reference to Rosenzweig and Buber)[2] consider experience in conjunction with a theory of types of speech or speech-acts elucidating in turn the problem of dialogical understanding in otherwise exceptional cases. 'Dialogicity' is characteristic of the Christian religion in a particular way, specifically as the speech situation of I and Thou between God and Man. This I-Thou relationship is constituted as early as God's address and call to man in Genesis 3:9: 'Adam, where are you?' The dialogue between God and man initiated by this sentence is dominated throughout the rest of the Old Testament by the vocative, which awakens man from mute elements by the articulation of his name as an individual and makes of him a partner in the covenant. This dimension of question and answer distinguishes the Christian origin of dialogue from the 'idealism of productive notions' that inhabits a monological world. The first monologue by God in the Bible (*And God said: Let there be light*) is drawn into the story of the creation, enabling us to deduce a theological triad of speech-acts. The *dialogue*, as a mode of revelation, occupies a middle position between the *tale* as the mode of creation and song or *hymn* as praise, leading to the *I* and *Thou* being transcended at a third stage by the liturgical paradigm of *we*. Thus dialogue in the end fades in the song and silence of the Sabbath. What remains an open question is how this theological triad is represented, functionally, in types of speech beyond the Bible, or whether every tale is an attempt to produce order akin to that ordering of elements which Genesis 1 seems to suggest, or whether dialogue, by definition, transgresses or breaks through established orders, or finally whether there exist ways to open and close a dialogue other than that of God and man with its beginning in the vocative and its end in a contented silence ('those that are separated still have to talk, the reunited can be silent – one keeps silent because all is said and done' – but one can also keep silent as a protest!).

Theological hermeneutics studies both the ideal form of the dialogue which achieves transcendence in contented communication and in forms of disintegrating 'dialogicity.' The Christian dialogue, which refers in the Last Supper to taking, giving and sharing, to the Revelation, may degenerate into an unchristian polemic about the mass – into a *Religionsgespräch* ('because the participants only wanted interpretations') or into apologetics, which in its crudest form degenerates into a catalogue of invectives, turned by the heretic opponent against himself, culminating in a refusal to engage in a dialogue. The progressive dogmatization of the *ecclesia militans* is revealed also in subtler ways of refusing a dialogue: in contempt for any searching on the part of both the *curiositas* and the *novitas*, confirmed by catechisms with fixed answers to the only questions which are allowed and crowned by the dialogically closed confession of faith that expresses 'political intolerance of otherness and an incompatibility with dialectic.' We might ask the theologian whether such a pattern is inevitable or whether it can only be explained historically in terms of the history of Christian apologetics and of the risk that the profession of faith (reinforced by the text which is spoken in unison in the first person) would become monological. At the same time, the speech-act of confession does not have to prevent dialogue in any way since it can sometimes open it up or initiate it again. We might question whether dialogically open forms of religious confession do, in fact, exist?

The 'master dialogue,' which is usually determined by the superiority of the one participant over the other, e.g., the teacher over the pupil, needs from a theological point of view a third perspective, the absent present in the person of the authoritative third, which can be represented as participant by Scripture or by the binding direction of Christ. In the formulation of the New Testament, the 'master dialogue' is characterized by several stages: the *conversatio*, which seeks to relate the dialogue to the local circumstances; the *quaestio*, which reveals the deficiency or despair that a teacher may feign when he actualizes the past or delivers the questioner from an all-powerful past; the *interpretatio*, in which the rabbi becomes the giver of the gift or reaches agreement by a masterly maxim. Literary hermeneutics up until now has paid little attention to the 'master dialogue.' It can no longer be dismissed simply as repressive canonization, but must begin to be understood in its literary forms and interpreted as a medium for the creation of experience (e.g., by learning, in sequences of questions and answers).

Moreover, there is a considerable difference between the 'master dialogue' in the New Testament and the Platonic dialogue. In the former the conversation is directed all the time by the teacher, the authoritatively pre-existing meaning is concretized by explanation in terms of the present situation, whereas the latter is a free conversation proceeding through digressions of question and answer, in which meaning is primarily constituted as a result of a joint quest through the mastery of the unknown. This typological opposition might certainly be modified by looking at it in new and interesting ways. Is it possible for the New Testament dialogue to regain openness by removing constraints from the pupil's questioning and by demanding that the master explain the Scripture from the point of view of the present situation and thereby reinterpret it differently? The effectiveness of the two rival forms of dialogue is beyond doubt, but their reception in the history of European literature seems to have almost completely escaped modification.

As long as the *philosophy of art* remained under the influence of the work-aesthetic, it has envisaged 'dialogicity' as being primarily revealed in a dialogue of poets who soar above the chain of tradition of mediocrity into timelessness, thus opening eyes to the genesis of great works, viewed as a dialectic of imitation and creation, of constitution and revision of the aesthetic canon. To engage the recipient of literature in dialogue with its producer, to recognize the latter's part in the establishment of meaning and to ask how the work of art might be a whole, both closed in upon itself and open, and yet dependent on interpretation, would require a turning away from contemplative hermeneutics and its substantialist notion of the work. A long-unknown but extremely informative document relevant to the movement towards modern-day aesthetic theory has been introduced into the discussion by Bonyhai.[3] It deals with an important but little-known forerunner of the contemporary hermeneutics of art and literature, Leo Popper, and demonstrates his importance in the history of science by revealing his various insights, specifically his pioneering theory of 'double misunderstanding.' A more personal and historical reason for Leo Popper's obscurity is the success of his contemporary, friend and opponent Georg Lukács, whose *Heidelberger Philosophie der Kunst* (written in 1912–14 and published in 1974) was openly a reworking of the former's ideas, after which their paths quickly separated.

Popper and Lukács's common point of departure was an attempt to overcome divinatory hermeneutics, the aesthetics of expression and the theory of empathy. Aloys Riegel's notion of *Kunstwollen*, which would effortlessly become part of the work in accordance with the artist's intention and thus constitute the norm for adequate understanding by the recipient, indicates very clearly the opposing position they challenged. Popper opposed this brand of hermeneutics with a new hermeneutic which sought to recognize and justify the problem of inadequate understanding as the condition and characteristic of all understanding of art. His theory of 'double misunderstanding' is in fact an aesthetic of non-identity, founded on the notion that the work of art does not so much reveal, monologically, a transcendental meaning (in which both the will of the artist and the understanding of the observer disappear), but creates rather a double gap between the intention of the writer, the finished work, and its significance for the observer. In this way the constitution of meaning may be seen as a never-ending process between the production and reception of the work. An essentially analogous theory of the 'open work' was argued at about the same time, but independently, by Paul Valéry. In Valéry's view the product of an author's aesthetic activity cannot be completely finished by him. The finished work is much more the illusion of the recipient, but also the beginning of his necessarily inadequate interpretation ('mes vers ont le sens qu'on leur prête'), reintroducing thereby the never-ending process of productive understanding. Thus Bonyhai rightly claims that Popper's theory indicates the beginning of a development which leads from the monological work-aesthetic to dialogical understanding, to the hermeneutical history of influence, and finally to the reception aesthetics of the present.

Lukács's evolution towards a 'synthesis of sociology and aesthetics,' even in its later materialistic drift towards the theory of mimesis, retains a platonizing tendency, and may already be identified by his adaptation of Popper's premises.

Lukács explains the notion of double misunderstanding as the duplicity of the work of art that transcends life and man's yearningly familiar attitude to it, that separates the creative from the purely receptive attitude and at the same time ultimately sustains the distinction between the historicity and timelessness of the work of art. Popper's until now unpublished *Dialog über die Kunst* illustrates the basic difference between his position and that of Lukács, and casts an interesting light on the crossroads at which aesthetic theory found itself at the beginning of this century.

Their dialogue begins with the introduction of the opposition between closed and open works of art. Lukács interprets these as two fundamental possibilities of art, the moment of wish (Rodin's *Paolo et Francesca*) or that of fulfilment (Rodin's *Le Baiser*). Consequently, the theory of double misunderstanding, which Popper relates to two moments of non-identity in productive and receptive understanding, is separated into two different types of art and is qualified historically, since Lukács's distinction implies from the outset (with its dichotomy of the last or limited and the penultimate or unlimited) the historical and typological opposition between classical and romantic notions of art. To Popper's reply that the closed/open distinction must prove its validity in the wholeness of the form, Lukács refers (as he will do even in his later work) to the classical principle of the adequacy of form and content, thus attributing open works of art to the contemporary avant-garde and insisting that only the most recent art has used this medium, 'this breaking off, this desertion.' Popper counters this argument by revealing the romantic substratum (the unfulfilled as the only ending) of Lukács's presentation of modernism as fragmentary, and opposes it with the contention that the notion of completedness is no longer an ontological quality which lends the work expression, but is born out of man's desire for completeness (which he himself has to create) in the face of matter and ultimately of nature, where man finds himself confronted with 'only transitions, never closure itself.'

Thus the diametrically opposed positions of the debate concerning the work of art may be summed up in Lukács's formula: 'in its finishedness unfinished' and in Popper's: 'in its unfinishedness finished.' Popper implicitly undermines the original distinction: the work of art is in its unfinishedness *finished*, because 'art creates out of the penultimate, a last,' meaning that 'through art we take from nature what nature itself takes from us in our lives: unendedness.' In Popper's view, art is a-cosmic, 'the formula of people in things,' i.e. the work of art is finished in its *unfinishedness*, because, whether it is open or closed, it attains its closedness only when the recipient is involved in it: 'The ultimate end of the work of art is the recipient.' Lukács on the other hand retains his own distinction by justifying it transcendentally: the work of art is in its finishedness *unfinished*, because 'it relates the temporal to the eternal,' which is another way of saying that the 'question involves an absolute' and presupposes the 'great answer,' under which yoke man struggles without realizing it. In this way the recent theory of the open work offers the hermeneutics of art a choice. From Popper's viewpoint the work opens itself to the recipient and directs aesthetics towards the dialogicity of communication, while from that of Lukács it leads to the transcendental, regaining for aesthetics the Platonic feedback of a timeless absolute which, by its monological truth, grants the recipient little more than the role of contemplative understanding.

In the area of *philosophical hermeneutics*, Gadamer has defined dialogicity as the prerequisite of all understanding, both of foreign speech and of a temporally alien text. As a result of his work, the Platonic dialogue comes to be viewed as a hermeneutical model, where meaning is constituted not by a monological explanation but by a dialogical search for understanding, achieved by bringing experience into the open: 'The dialectic of question and answer has always preceded the dialectic of explanation. It is the former which has made an event out of understanding.'[4] To understand something means to conceive it as an answer, or, more precisely, to test one's own opinion against the opinion of the other through question and answer. This is true for the understanding of both an unfamiliar text and another's speech. One part of the hermeneutical project is to recuperate the text which has become alien through temporal distance and reinsert it 'in the living presence of dialogue, constituted originally as question and answer.' The expression 'to enter into conversation with the text' remains metaphoric since the interpreter himself has to embody the role of the other before the text can speak, answer a question, or be understood ultimately as a 'question to me.' Just as a traditional text becomes a question only for a questioning person, the 'dialogue with the past,' if it is not to become a victim of the one-sidedness of traditionalism or 'actualism,' demands an appropriating understanding to become completed, i.e. one which takes into account both the alien horizon of the text and the interpreter's own horizon (a process which is often misunderstood in the ocular metaphor of 'fusion of horizons').

The other concern of the hermeneutical project consists of elucidating the 'dialogicity' of understanding involved in a conversation, where one's own speech enters into an unmediated relationship with speech which is alien. Gadamer defines such understanding, in an actual conversation, as 'to understand-oneself-in-an-object' and thereby forges a relationship between the understanding of a text and understanding which occurs in a dialogue. But this obscures a second (equally original and interesting) aspect of dialogue: the understanding of the other in his otherness. It is clear that the understanding-of-oneself-in-an-object may also entail, in a dialogue, an understanding of the otherness of the interlocutor. However, such is not always the case and there undoubtedly exists, as well, an understanding of the other through dialogue, where agreement about the object is deemed irrelevant. In his criticism of the hermeneutics of empathy (which he sees foreshadowed in the psychological explanation of Schleiermacher) Gadamer has attributed interest in the understanding of alien speech to the fascination with the 'dark thou.'[5] Schleiermacher's shift from the problem of understanding texts to that of understanding speech as such requires a hermeneutics of dialogicity to replace the understanding-of-oneself-in-an-object with the understanding-of-oneself-in-the-other, as of equally important epistemological interest. Since literary hermeneutics has as its real point of departure the understanding of the aesthetic experience of a work of art (in the *how*, not the *what* of what is said) and does not therefore require agreement about an object, the aesthetic and literary writings of Mikhail Bakhtin offer, without doubt, an innovative approach to the question of how the otherness of other may be disclosed by literary speech.

Bakhtin's aesthetic theory can be viewed, in its hermeneutical premises and implications, as occupying a similar place in the theory of science to that of Popper and Lukács; specifically in relationship to the movement away from the aesthetics of expression and the theory of empathy which dominated the years after the turn of the century.[6] One of Bakhtin's points of departure is Wilhelm Worringer's *Abstraktion und Einfühlung* (1918), which views (in line with Theodor Lipps's theory of empathy) aesthetic activity as an act of self-expression, where the 'I' loses itself in the outside world so as to produce the work of art in the objectification of what has been experienced: 'Aesthetic enjoyment is objectified self-enjoyment. To enjoy aesthetically is to enjoy myself in a sensible object which is different from me and to feel myself in it.'[7] From this model Bakhtin borrowed the act of self-expression, but saw it as a twofold counter-current movement. Empathy as a movement outside, in order to put oneself knowingly and consciously in the position of the other, has to be followed by a turning-back on oneself, which makes the experienced identification through distancing or 'finding oneself outside' (*vnenachodimost*) into a productive and once more receptive aesthetic experience.[8] Empathy constitutes a necessary transitory stage and does not represent the goal of aesthetic experience. A prior identification with the other is necessary in order to attain, by means of the withdrawal of oneself, a position of aesthetic eccentricity (Plessner's notion comes very close to Bakhtin's *vnenachodimost*), making it possible, in turn, to experience the other in his difference and oneself in one's otherness. The reciprocal nature of experience of the alien and experience of the self is the decisive innovative aspect of Bakhtin's reformulation of the theory of empathy. It not only asserts that human consciousness is inherently dialogical ('The consciousness of oneself is always experienced against the background of the consciousness that somebody else has of one'),[9] but also that aesthetic experience is characterized by its capacity to facilitate (if not render possible) the experience of oneself in the experience of the other:

I cannot imagine myself as contained in my own external form, as surrounded and expressed by it. ... In this sense it is possible to say that man depends in an aesthetically absolute way upon the other and his seeing, remembering, gathering and synthesizing activity, because only this can give him an externally finished personality; this personality does not exist, when the other does not create it.[10]

This audacious theory of the dialogical nature of consciousness, which Bakhtin developed in an early essay (only recently published), has hermeneutical implications and is the basis of his later *Esthetika slovesnogo tvorchestva*. The basic theses developed in this essay are as follows: dialogue as initial form of human language; language as social event of linguistic interaction; a fundamental opposition between speaking (hearing) and writing (reading); the dialogical principles of the open truth and the monological principle of the closed truth; the three categories of the direct word, the represented word, and the word that is focused on alien speech; the historical genesis of the multivocal expression in Socratic dialogue, its subversive survival in the Menippean satire and the polyphonic novel (whereas official monologism reinforces constantly univocal aspects of discourse); prose as the place of the bivocal expression; poetry as the medium of the word (without witnesses) about oneself and the world. Bakhtin's *Esthetika slovesnogo tvorchestva* with its antithetical characterizations of the dialogical principle offers a framework of categories which makes possible a new definition of the communicative function of types of speech and literary genres. As well, Bakhtin ultimately broadened his notion of dialogue into a model with three stages.

Dialogue has to find its own truth in understanding a reply and is therefore, in principle, uncompletable. This notion is illustrated by the history of the conflict of interpretations in the unending dialogue maintained with the art of the past. Such dialogue presupposes the higher authority of the third or 'super-addressee,' 'whose absolutely perfect understanding is postulated either in the metaphysical distance or in temporally distant historical times. ... In different periods and in different world-views this super-addressee and his ideal answering and understanding are expressed in distinct ideological ways (God, the absolute truth, the judgment of the impartial human conscience, the people, the judgment of history, science etc.).'[1] We already know this third stage from theological hermeneutics. It is no longer an ultimate guiding authority, but an ultimate 'absolutely perfect' understanding super-addressee who, as the postulated third, is always present (but also absent) in the dialogue between text and interpreter – between the alien voice and the interpreter's voice – and functions as the guarantee of any possibility of understanding. This rather beautiful but peculiar secularity betrays an embarrassment in *Esthetika slovesnogo tvorchestva*. Bakhtin designed his aesthetic theory of otherness initially from the point of view of aesthetic production alone, considering the counter-current movement of self-expression and the experience-of-oneself-in-the-other. Only in his later writings did he begin to develop them further, from the point of view of reception.[12]

Thus he did not address himself to the hermeneutical problem of what makes it possible for the reader to understand the text in its otherness or what the reader at a second stage has to invest in this dialogue from his own experience in order to allow his understanding to enter into a dialogue with the text and its earlier interpreters. Bakhtin's aesthetic of otherness, which has so effectively revalidated the dialogical principle of the poetic word, requires a hermeneutical basis to account for the historical continuity of dialogical understanding.

If one agrees with Bakhtin's idea (which I arrived at without any knowledge of his works by approaching it from the perspective of an aesthetics of reception), that the experience of art is an excellent way to experience the alien 'you' in its otherness and, with that, one's own 'I' enriched by it, one cannot expect that the understanding-of-oneself-in-the-other, through aesthetic communication, needs anything more than the counter-current movement of empathy and its withdrawal in self-reflection (*vnenachodimost*). When a work of art is excellent, it is capable of representing and disclosing the alien 'I' as subject and when especially the polyphonic word of the novel, according to Bakhtin's brilliant interpretation of Dostoevsky, can represent and disclose alien speech in its own speech, the recipient is unable to bridge the hermeneutical difference from the otherness of the text and therefore from the 'alien speech in speech' except by an aesthetically mediated self-reflection. If the understanding of literary texts is not to be allowed to degenerate into a free-floating production of differences (a danger posed by the fashionable theory of 'intertextuality,' which Julia Kristeva's abridgment of Bakhtin's dialogic is not able to avoid),[13] then the understanding-of-oneself in the otherness of the text and the everyday-understanding-of-oneself when one speaks and another replies have to be anchored in a prejudgment of what has already been said and understood together, and what is still operative. Although Bakhtin's dialogical principle illustrates the difference of polyphony between grammatical persons and 'speech-distance,' it still seems, so far as I can discern, to presuppose the transparency of the poetic word and fails to take into account, really, the hermeneutical difference between the intention of the author, the meaning of the text, and its significance for the reader. This hermeneutical difference of the text (which begins from the very outset when the hearer or reader of the discourse does not necessarily picture the same thing as the speaker or the writer) increases as a function of historical distance. It may also become more acute when it is used consciously in ideology or unconsciously in the poetic text, thereby developing into the problem of the deceptive use of indirect speech. Bakhtin's dialogical principle can only do justice to these aspects of the otherness of the text when it is supplemented by other modes of understanding and when access to the understanding-of-oneself in other is achieved through constructing hermeneutical bridges.

Another hermeneutical bridge is already implied in Bakhtin's thesis of the character of the word as answer, in so far as the word only becomes an answer when it responds dialogically to a question. This makes the dialectic of question and answer into a genuine hermeneutical instrument to transgress the dialectics of its own horizon, to question the alien horizon of the other, and to take up again the dialogue with the text which may only respond a second time when the text is once again engaged. However, not every literary text has the hermeneutical structure of the word as answer. This is especially true for poetry. Here the attitude towards the world which is revealed in the lyrical voice may become by itself a hermeneutical bridge of the understanding-of-oneself in other, since such openness of speech towards the subjective world-experience delineates, according to Ricoeur, the character of the text fixed in a written form. The literary word distinguishes itself from the purely informative or utilitarian one in so far as the significance of the text can be detached both from the intention of its producer and, simultaneously, from the pragmatic limitation of a speech situation, thereby gaining semantic autonomy which may also reveal itself to a later recipient in the fullness of meaning of a world that is seen differently. One may doubt whether the semantic autonomy of the poetic word, as it is defined here, does not still presuppose some sort of prejudgment about the 'world' which is peculiar to Western culture and would therefore be unsuitable in bridging the gap to the otherness of different cultures. Here the understanding of alien speech may be helped by this sort of prejudgment, based in anthropology and having recourse to the forgotten stock of myths, and which in turn makes it possible to construct a bridge of understanding between various figures and configurations of the imaginary. Since, according to Blumenberg, the mythic world experience always brings about the supposed otherness of an 'original condition' and, at the same time, actualizes itself in the 'Albeit am

Mythos,'[14] aesthetic understanding may begin where the imaginary envelops the forms and configurations of myths with the aura of completeness, thereby satisfying an aesthetic need. If it is true that completeness is the (or at least *one* strong) reason for fascination with the imaginary, then in the 'anticipation of completeness' lies, according to Gadamer,[15] what amounts to a privileged possibility of understanding, determining in its turn the understanding-of-oneself-in-the-other; this understanding comes about when, in the gradual emancipation of the subject, the other is accepted precisely as completeness and contingency-as-individual, when the other becomes idealized in literature and is raised to the real problem of dialogical understanding.

MY OWN WORK: A RETROSPECTIVE AND PROSPECTIVE GLANCE

My initial incentive to examine the problem of the horizon of expectation of the reader for whom the literary text was originally written was the result of my study of a literature that is very distant and strange to us. The limits of traditional philology very quickly became apparent. This approach held that a work which had become foreign could be understood either literally or through interpretation by disregarding the distance in time and by studying the text alone, or by returning historically to its sources and compiling factual knowledge about its time. It was medieval literature in the vernacular, more precisely its characteristic animal epic, which blossomed in the twelfth century, that presented me with the foreign horizon of a closed past as the barrier against understanding. The literature of the Middle Ages, because of the break in continuity created by the Renaissance, has been endowed with a high degree of otherness. By comparing it with the literature of antiquity, which, until recently, remained canonical in the history of Western education, hermeneutic reflection encounters if not a less significant problem then a different one. The fact that medieval literature might serve as an example for contemporary research precisely because of this otherness was obscured by the philological research of the 1950s with its insistence on the practice of interpreting 'from sources,' a procedure which was unexpectedly and massively legitimized by E. R. Curtius's *Europäische Literatur und lateinische Mittelalter* (1948), considered at that time to be paradigmatic. This encouraged the positivists, who were as philologically exact as they were aesthetically blind, to reduce the humanistic motto *ad fontes* to an interest in sources for their own sake and to claim that even the least significant discovery made by their pursuit contributed to the proof of the unbroken, albeit latent, continuity of the 'indispensable' heritage of antiquity, in which the Middle Ages served as a link in a 'golden chain of literary tradition' and lost almost completely any historical independence. The famous interpretation of Villon which Leo Spitzer, in his provocatively titled *Etude ahistorique d'un texte*, had used as early as 1938 in fighting for an aesthetic approach in opposition to the objective search for sources was barely influential at all. The ideal of serious research was Italo Siciliano's *François Villon et les thèmes poétiques du moyen âge* (1934), which pushed reliance on sources so far that it found for almost every element of Villon's revolutionary poetry an antecedent in the universal repertoire of previous poetry.

The implicit presuppositions of this search for sources were promoted by Lansberg as a principle for the study of tradition,[16] developing thereby Curtius's program for a historical topology founded on a rhetoric that was equated with literature. The substantialist postulate was that every new literary work not only potentially presupposed the *summa* of the complete previous literary tradition but ultimately varied the archetypical substance of tradition to create only the appearance of historical innovation. Such a theory and metaphysic of tradition is based upon the allegedly humanist conviction that, 'in a book, literature is timelessly present,'[17] thus making of the philologist the real reader for whom the text is written and who, as 'super-reader,' best understands the writer. Only the philologist, then, is capable of recognizing, through the later horizon of a more complete if not universal knowledge, the sources from which the author not only consciously but also unconsciously creates his work. Hermeneutically, the study of tradition, as it was understood at this stage, remained completely virginal: the philologist as super-reader naïvely presupposed that the later horizon of his knowledge existed in the earlier horizon of the creation of a work. Hence the distance in time (and also the limitedness of future historical horizons) disappeared in the timeless present of great literature, and even minor literature remained in the 'unbreakable chain of the tradition of mediocrity.'[18]

The hermeneutical innocence of this uncritical research in philology was simultaneously challenged about this time by Guiette and Nisin in France and by Bulst in Germany, in the paradoxically formulated statement: no text was ever written to be read and interpreted philologically by philologists or historically by historians. This stance raised the basic problem of a new literary hermeneutics by attempting to eradicate the fallacy that the text is as immediate to the philologist as – according to Rank – every epoch is to God, and to deny the necessity of recovering the meaning of the text for the reader as the actual addressee. This hermeneutical project entailed a twofold problem. On the one hand the reconstructed intention of the author could no longer constitute the final word on the understanding of the text, though the author still had to have some controlling function. On the other hand the reading experience of a reader of the past could only be reached through the actual reading of the reader of the present. This meant that the difference between past and present horizons of the reading had to be brought into play in the interpretation itself.

The critics that I alluded to earlier did not yet have a methodological solution for this twofold problem. Bulst[19] leaned towards distinguishing between the subjective experience of reading and the objective investigation of the genesis of the text and doubted whether it was possible to reconstruct the experience of a past reader if it were not expressly stated. Guiette[20] tried to rehabilitate the unmediated enjoyment of medieval texts by interpreting the Artus-novel as a fascination with darkness, with the 'not yet dissolved,' and the poetry of the troubadours as a fascination for a 'poésie formelle,' a conscious pleasure in unending variation. In this way he discovered specific aesthetic attitudes that were implied by these and other literary types, but failed to recognize how far this discovery depended on a later point of view: the modern prejudgment of anti-romantic poetics which developed with Verlaine and Mallarmé. To Nisin, in his (undeservedly neglected) book La Littérature et le lecteur (1959),[21] we owe the disclosure of the latent Platonism of academic philology, its belief in the timeless essence of classic works and in the neutral point of the observer. Nisin's pioneering work towards a hermeneutics of reading insisted that the literary work had to be viewed like a musical score, and could only be realized through an act of reading. Genuine understanding of an aesthetic text requires also that the philologist integrate this explanation and his critically evaluative reflection with his primary experience as a reader. This requirement is not merely a way of sanctioning a purely subjectivist reading; the text continues to oppose an arbitrary attitude on the part of readers. The literary work as score becomes an instance of understanding in so far as the reader, in his returning for a second reading or in the second realization of what has been read in the experience of the whole, verifies in the wording of a text what seemed to him to be a possible sense in his first aesthetic observation. The deficiency of this theory is that Nisin makes of the spontaneity of the first reading (which seems to transfer the reader immediately into the unknown of another world of the imaginary) an absolute. To this extent his theory is limited; the sens vécu of a text of the past is not available any longer without the mediation or the translation by a philologist or without historical understanding. That there 'is no virginity in aesthetic experience' (since one cannot understand any work of art without bringing to it a past and can only judge its aesthetic value by contrasting a literary work as an unknown with the horizon of already known works) had already been stressed by Picon in his aesthetics of literature.[22] But how was one to avoid the fallacy of a pure, spontaneously emotional reception of literature, without relegating interpretation to the primary experience of the reading? How was one to make clear the sense of prejudgment which already governs the spontaneous reading of a text, and what did one have to do to gain access to the sort of experience which the historically first addressee may have had in his reading?

These were the questions I attempted to come to grips with in my *Untersuchungen zur mittelalterlichen Tierdichtung* (1959). The medieval *Reineke Fuchs*, revived by Goethe, alienates the reader of our time specifically because of the so-called 'anthropomorphisms' of its animal characters, in other words because of human attributes, chivalric gestures and courtly speech, fictitious behaviour in short, which can be understood neither mimetically (as observable life of animals in nature) nor allegorically (as spiritual meaning of their 'natures'). In the history of the criticism of the *Roman de Renart* since Jacob Grimm, this peculiar mixture of human characteristics and animal form was resolved in various ways, though the romantic distinction between nature-poetry and art-poetry as latent paradigm remained operative even in the historico-positivist interpretation. As the shapes of the loosely connected tricks were seen as naïve, as the nature-poetry of an original agreement between man and animals, one could postulate behind the anthropomorphic traits (which were considered to be later aberrations) the pure form of original animal fairy tales. However, if one considered the animal characters as time-conditioned disguises of epic heroes, it was possible to see the feud between Renart and Ysengrim as the satirical art form of an animal epic, which, as parody of the chivalric epic and mirror of the feudal society, used the animal form as representative of eternal folly or as a form of decorum. By their contradictory one-sidedness, both paradigms of interpretation disregarded the obvious question,[23] namely, what the analogy of animal being and human nature played out in the *Roman de Renart* may have meant to the addressees for whom this work, begun in 1176, was written. Might the answer to this question not be linked to the pleasures which the medieval reader experienced in the novel's animal tricks and might this not also explain why this work, by Pierre de Saint-Cloud, had so many limitations? What could explain the inexhaustible interest in continuing the fable of the 'real beginning of why the wolf and the fox are mortal enemies,' in revising again and again the opening of the trial at the court-day of the lion, and in making the oldest animal epic in the French popular language into the unending adventures of the rake in the feudal kingdom of the animals, a story which along with *Tristan* and the *Roman de la Rose* alone survived the fall of medieval literature?

An answer to these questions was suggested by the fact that Pierre de Saint-Cloud, author of the oldest part (II–va) of the *Roman de Renart*, made, in his prologue, the typical declaration: 'I bring something that has never been said!' and then proceeded to name both single works and genres in previous literature which were to be overshadowed by his new work and which were well loved by his audience: *Troja* and *Tristan* and consequently the ancient and chivalric novel, the poetic farce (*fabliau*) and the chivalric epic (*chanson de geste*). From this canon, from further reference to already known facts and especially by viewing it as continuing the work of a predecessor (the Latin *Ysengrimus* by Magister Nivardus) unmentioned in the prologue, I was able to infer the horizon of expectation of the contemporary public, which the author evoked in order to contrast it with the novelty of his work. The textual analysis that was based on this insight indicated that the writer had, indeed, fulfilled his announcement in the prologue in the tale itself. He returns to the expectations that he evoked earlier, satisfies or disappoints them implicitly, and sometimes even explicitly and critically, when he wants to parody the chivalric epic or when he wants to make a travesty of the casuistic aspects of courtly love. This fact enables the later interpreter to reconstruct the prejudgments of the original addressee even when the distance in time is great and to trace out the difference between retrospective expectation and prospective experience which is progressively constituted in the reading. It is this transformation of horizon which the text must have brought into play for the public of the *chansons de geste* and courtly poetry, about 1176. The enjoyment of the new genre of fox's nasty tricks appears and reappears in so far as the reader interprets the 'anthropomorphisms' as signals prompting him to recognize in the animal figures an element of human nature. Thus the 'unheard-of war of two barons' may be read as an imitation of heroic poetry which for the first time questioned the elevated ethics of the chivalric world and the ideals of courtly love by clearly showing as playful satire the less than ideal, indeed purely human, nature of men in the projections of its perfection.

My attempt to interpret this medieval text from the horizon of expectation of its contemporary public opened new vistas to modern understanding. I do not at all deny that this reconstruction of the otherness of an aesthetic experience which has become alien to us presupposes the hermeneutical anticipation of an anthropological theory. It was Lipps's phenomenological analyses of the *Natur der Menschen* that made me see that the animal, with 'its character written across its face' and marked by an 'unbroken relationship with its nature,' allows us to recognize in the character of man the natural substratum of his spiritual being.[24] Though this theoretical anticipation surely cannot engender the spontaneous experience of a first reader, it can disclose the attitude implied by the text, which initially makes it understandable as a condition of possible meaning. The spontaneous reading experience of a historically alien and distant reader has no hermeneutical value, and it is an illusion to try to reconstruct it as such, since spontaneity can never be completely covered by reflection. A misguided attempt of this sort also fails to see that aesthetic experience is, by nature, an observation which is mediated and therefore intensified; it cannot consequently be absorbed by emotional spontaneity. However, such a theoretical anticipation, especially when it brings into play (as is the case here) prospects of a vague, yet to be developed, generalization based on phenomenological anthropology, at least opens up these mediations, making aesthetic experience on the whole communicable, systematically as the attitude which the text implies and historically as a series of prejudgments which are evoked with the transformation of the horizon of expectation and experience and made accessible for interpretation.

The new significance brought to the *Roman de Renart* arises certainly from a modern perspective: an inquiry into the historical and literary genesis of individuation. It is therefore not just the projection of a modern interest, but succeeds also in disclosing an experience of the character and nature of people that was new in the everyday life of the twelfth century. It is accomplished by consciously removing the horizon which historically actualized the theoretical anticipation. The work of Pierre de Saint-Cloud reveals, as an anti-heroic parody of chivalric and courtly ideals, a complete world of characters removed from historical change, and establishes at the same time a negative hero, Renart, who, outwitting others by taking advantage of their less-than-ideal and all-too-human nature, with the wit of the rake becomes the first character with individuality. Although this innovation would not have been recognized or interpreted by the majority of the contemporary addressees, there exists extra-literary evidence which demonstrates that it might well have been understood. The threshold of individuation, which is apparent in the earlier parts of the *Roman de Renart* to later interpreters, is also historically mentioned for the first time by Otto von Freising, who by *persona* not only means the interchangeable mask, role, but also implies the uninterchangeable *individualitas* of worldly people.[25]

The threshold metaphor indicates for historical hermeneutics that the transition from the old to the new did not have to happen only once or, for all contemporaries, at the same time. In order to go beyond the field of experience of medieval life, which seemed hardly changeable, the Christian understanding of the world, hitherto limited to its closed horizon of the future, had to transgress the prohibition of *curiositas*. Licence to break the charm of the ideal norms of chivalric and courtly living and to portray human nature on the other side of good and evil in its imperfect ordinariness was obviously easier to achieve by means of the fiction of the animal kingdom. Thus, literary hermeneutics is able to participate in historical understanding in its own way and to show, through the transformation of the horizon of aesthetic experience, what for the contemporaries of a past world was still a latent need, wish, or presentiment of the future, and what may only be made conscious in its still-incalculable significance by the history of interpretation.

While the work of the medievalist introduced me to the hermeneutical problem of the lifting of horizon and led me to argue against the traditionalism of positivist philology, my initial attempt to turn these insights into a blueprint for a reception-aesthetic of literature (*Literaturgeschichte als Provokation*, 1967) grew out of a somewhat different situation. The concept of a new literary history, which would extend the short-circuited relationship of author and world in order to include the recipient and would raise the latter, as reader or public, to a mediating position between past and present, had to be asserted in the face of the discredited ideal of objectivity of the old literary history and of the claims of objectivity made by both sociological and structuralist opponents of historical understanding. The central feature of this position was the transformation of horizons, a paradigm which was introduced into modern literature. It was to be illustrated in certain ideal cases in works such as *Don Quixote* and *Jacques le fataliste* that 'evoke the reader's horizon of expectations, formed by a convention of genre, style or form, only in order to destroy it step by step – which by no means serves a critical purpose only, but can also once again produce poetic effects.'[26] In this transformation of horizon between preliminary expectations and the indicated new experience, I discerned the principle of aesthetic mediation in the literary historical process, leading by an actual transformation of the canon to a revision of our ideas about all past works. This idea of the transformation of horizons allowed me also to see the artistic character of a work as related to implicit aesthetic distance (i.e. the distance of expectation and experience, tradition and innovation) and to contrast its constitutive negativity with the affirmative character of the norm-sustaining trait of consumer literature.

My formulation of this paradigm was undoubtedly influenced (though to some degree unconsciously) by the opinion of the Russian formalists that aesthetic innovation is the agent of literature's evolution, and by Adorno's aesthetics of negativity, according to which the autonomous work can only acquire a social function by a certain negation of the existing norms. The flagrant modernist bias of this first paradigm of reception aesthetics reflects the position I took in my inaugural lecture at Constanz, which generated an unexpected and lively polemical debate.[27] My attempt to respond to my critics allowed me to develop this first project for a reception aesthetics step by step in a dialogue with them and to test it practically. The next stage was to introduce the notion of a horizon of expectation as a device for the analysis of the experience of the reader:

The analysis of the literary experience of the reader avoids the threatening pitfalls of psychology if it describes the reception and the influence of a work within the objectifiable system of expectations that rises for each work in the historical moment of its appearance, from a preunderstanding of the genre, from the form and themes of already familiar works, and from the opposition between poetic and practical language.[28]

Directed against those who thought that an analysis of the reader's experience ended inevitably in the subjectivism of individual reaction ('so many readers, so many interpretations') or in the collectivism of a sociology of taste, this stance made it possible to conceive of literary experience in the objectifiable difference between normative expectation and norm-creating experience; it was therefore more internally literary. It had the advantage of leaving out of consideration what, in such a transformation of horizons, had to be ascribed to the influence of the text and what was appropriated by the initial and subsequent addressees. This posed the problem of distinguishing, in the process of literary history, between the two aspects of the relation between text and reader, i.e. *effect* as that element of the actualization of meaning which is determined by the text and *reception* as that which is determined by the addressee. In opposition to the notion that a literary tradition constitutes itself spontaneously as a passive synthesis of a 'fusion of horizons,' it became necessary to stress the event-character of a literary work as a moment of a process, in which two horizons are always at play in an active synthesis of understanding. In other words, the horizon of expectation evoked by the work confirms or transcends the horizon of experience introduced by the recipient.

The active participation of the reader in the historically progressive actualization of meaning (the possibility of its 'productive reception' – Sartre) was also left unclear so as not to present literary history as autonomous of the historical process but rather to stress its *Partialität*, where its own relation to general history had to be seen in order to grasp its social function and history-making energy: 'The social function of literature manifests itself in its genuine possibility only where the literary experience of the reader enters into the horizon of expectations of his lived praxis, preforms his understanding of the world, and thereby also has an effect on his social behaviour.'[29] Directed towards the theory of mimesis, which Lukács had once again brought into favour but which had hardened into the closed circle of the aesthetics of production and representation, my final 'Constanzer' thesis insisted on the precedence of the norm-constituting function of literature over the representational one. What was left open was the question of how the horizon of the experience of practical life might be included, if not by the mute determination of economic forces then by the primary attitudes of people concerned, by latent interests, needs, and wishes. What also remained to be considered was its relationship to the horizon of aesthetic experience. Such a relationship could only be elucidated with the provocative stance I took at the end of *Literaturgeschichte als Provokation*. Here I insisted on the expectation that literature today, as in the past, might renew the 'consolidated observation' of things and destroy the taboos of prevailing morality. This necessitated transposing reception-aesthetics, constituted from an internally literary point of view, into the force field of a social praxis and inquiring if and how the historical actualization of a literary work, through the passive or the productive reception of its reader, reacts to a social situation, assesses its contradictions, and attempts to solve them projectively. This meant, above all, responding seriously to the ideological and critical suspicion that literary tradition does not have the privilege of developing in complete freedom but may be enforced so that one does not merely presuppose the transparency of literary communication between people and time-periods, but seeks to recover it in the face of the tendency of tradition to annex everything which is heterogeneous to the harmonic classical canon.

For the majority of my critics,[30] the theses which I developed in my inaugural lecture at Constanz were not sociological enough. There were others, however, who considered them too sociological, claiming that my attempt to found a new reception aesthetics failed to go beyond a hermeneutical and function-analytical sociology of reception, thereby missing what was aesthetic in the reader's experience. Petrovic has asserted that, by engaging in what he acknowledges as an absolutely necessary critique of the dominant ontology of art relating to the notion of the work in classic aesthetics and to that of mimesis in orthodox Marxist aesthetics, I have moved to the other extreme of a theory of literature, sacrificing along with the work its aesthetic value as object of reception and thereby reducing aesthetic experience to the transformation of the social norms of taste. But taste is only the condition of possibility of literary communication, not its content nor even its result. Literary communication really becomes aesthetic experience (and this renders comprehensible its difference from pragmatic experience) when its constitution is sought in the 'materialization of the aesthetic object' both at the level of the pre-reflective reception of aesthetic meaning (*aistheton*) and at the reflective level of aesthetic judgment, when it is finally characterized as the specifically aesthetic activity of the producing and receiving subject.[31] I considered it a rare yet encouraging coincidence of scientific work that Petrovic had asserted *de facto* in his critique (read at a symposium in Belgrade in 1976) the continuation of the first paradigm of my reception-aesthetics and had outlined what was lacking in the theory of aesthetic experience. I myself had addressed these problems, meanwhile, in my second university lecture at Constanz (entitled *Apologie der ästhetischen Erfahrung*) and developed them further in the *Theorie und Geschichte der ästhetischen Erfahrung* (1972; published in 1977). I shall therefore only briefly summarize this book.

My purpose was to define the particular nature and everyday function of aesthetic experience (1) historically, as process of its liberation from the authority inherited from Platonic aesthetics, and (2) systematically, in its three basic forms of productive, receptive, and communicative aesthetic experience, otherwise known historically as the triad of *poiesis, aisthesis,* and *katharsis,* whose common fundamental attitude constitutes aesthetic pleasure. This point of departure made it possible to consider aesthetic experience at work not initially in the manifestations of autonomous modern art which rejects all enslavement, but already present in the practical (i.e. religious and social) functions of older art. Thus it was possible to bridge the gap, opened up by the reigning aesthetics of negativity, between pre-autonomous and autonomous, 'affirmative' and 'emancipatory' art. This revision of the modernist bias of my first project began therefore with a critique of the aesthetic theory of Adorno, and necessitated rehabilitating the notion of 'pleasurable understanding' as the determining factor in aesthetic reflection and aesthetic judgment, demanding a consensus, as a specific social effect of aesthetic communication, despite the fact that the latter has been blocked in the age of the mass-media and the culture industry.

My contribution to research in literary hermeneutics is represented by several essays. *Racines und Goethes Iphigenie* (1973) was written to confront the Marxist theory of literature and illustrates the basic problem of literary hermeneutics: the limitedness of the historical horizon of understanding and the dialogical nature of production and reception in the processes of literary communication.

In order to reconstruct the original provocatory effect of Goethe's *devilishly human risk,* which was obscured by the transformation of horizon from historical to aesthetic classicism and by the incorporation of the neo-humanist ideals of education in specific instances, it was necessary to remove the first 'concretization' (that of Hegel), of the near horizon of French classicism and of the alien horizon of Greek tragedy. It thus became possible to interpret the new *Iphigenie* as Goethe's answer to Racine and as a new version of the classical myth, in which Iphigenia's *outrageous deed* achieves man's liberation from his mythic entanglement with nature. But this victory over the mythic meteronomy is ultimately attained in Goethe's play at the expense of a new myth, that of all-redeeming pure womanhood, and turns the end with Thoas into a false solution in terms of modern understanding. It is here that one confronts the problem of the possibilities and limitations of an actualization of the classic work. After reconstructing the temporally alien horizon and considering those normative interpretations ('actualization') in the history of the reception available to the modern understanding, literary hermeneutics faces the problem of application and is able to complete in its own manner the triad of understanding, explanation, and application. I reconsidered this problem in *Klassik-wieder modern?* (1977) and explored it in terms of contemporary theatre, where it revealed itself initially in avant-garde experiments and, more recently, has had a broader effect both in literary production and in the practice of staging. The specific issue at stake is how a classic work may be decanonized, how it may be introduced into the horizon of contemporary experience, countering any pretence of timeless validity and being rejuvenated on the modern stage in such a way that the link between past and present experience is not broken, as it undoubtedly is in a naïve actualization or rigorous historicization. A 'rejuvenating' reception requires that the fusion of horizons not be silently presupposed but be consciously achieved as a dialectic mediation of the past and present horizons in a new actualization of meaning. The new *Mary Stuart* of Hildesheimer and *Die neun Leiden des jungen W.* by Plenzdorf were signs of a change in literary history, in that they transgressed the taboo of the untouchable text and the unchangeable form of classic works; it is precisely because of this that they succeeded in reviving classics which were already considered to be dead. What they achieved was applied hermeneutics, i.e. the historical distance between text and present is presented to the observer and the familiar horizon of the classic is merely quoted, firstly to bring to the observer's attention the real otherness of a past world, and then to disclose the other meaning of the past experience which has again been brought to the observer's attention in the continuous confrontation of self with other. In this way, by the renewed interplay with a separated past, a horizon of new experience is revealed to contemporary understanding.

I have attempted to solve the hermeneutical problem of how the transformation of the horizons of expectation and experience in the inner horizon of literature may influence the outer horizon of everyday life. The process of transformation involves three stages. In *La Douceur du foyer* (1974) I made use of the theory of the constitution of social reality from the sociology of knowledge to illustrate the communicative function of poetry in the transmission, internalization, legitimization, and transformation of social norms. I used specifically the example of the Second Empire bourgeois family's expectation of happiness at home. The sociology of knowledge developed by Schütz and Luckmann contributed a perspective which had not been explored by historical studies, even after their transformation into social history. I am referring to a historically applicable theory of the perspectivist organization of everyday reality, the pre-orientation of the experience of environment (i.e. the here-and-there of reality), the present situation (i.e. the reciprocally generated present) and the flow of time, and the horizon of limited spheres of meaning (*Subsinnwelten*) of human behaviour. The transcendental scheme of the organization of the social world alone was not enough to comprehend the past horizon of predominantly latent attitudes and norms but, by fulfilling an anticipatory theoretical role, it made it possible to look for the latent horizon of expectation of the historical view of life in 1857 within the pattern of contemporary poetry, and to describe it as a system of literary communication which makes visible what remained self-evident and therefore latent in the routine and the pressure of everyday life. The sociology of knowledge did not inquire into the status of aesthetic experience in the social praxis. Aesthetic experience remained hidden as long as it was located as a *Subsinnwelt* among other sub-meaning-worlds and as long as one failed to realize that its specific social function begins at the point where aesthetic experience illuminates, in fiction, the unshakeable horizons and ideological legitimizations of other (e.g., religious, political, professional) sub-meaning-worlds, and where it makes possible communication with the world, within whose limits the other lives, thereby making it possible for new expectations of the seemingly immovable horizon of a social order to open up.

The limit-situation of aesthetic experience, as compared with the other functions of action as defined here, justifies the hermeneutical priority of the approach offered by reception aesthetics. When one seeks to reconstruct the social situation out of derivative knowledge drawn from historical and economic sources, one indeed easily succeeds in finding, in the mirror of 'literary evidence,' confirmation for what one already knows historically. The responsive character of literature may only be recognized when one uncovers its mediations which, principally, become transparent in the medium of literary experience and intelligible in lifting the horizon. Goethe answers Rousseau's *Julie* with his *Werther*, although he fails to mention anywhere the provocative model of his admired predecessor. The fact that the French and then the German *Catechism of Sentimentality* responds to the resulting social situation only becomes a problem again when one reconstructs the horizon of literary expectations transmitted in Germany by *Die Leiden des jungen Werthers* and by the enthusiastically received *La Nouvelle Héloïse*. My analysis of horizon led then to the thesis that the unexpected success enjoyed widely by both books created not only literary but also social norms. The *homme sensible* incarnated in the figure of Rousseau's couple and in Goethe's *Werther* as a 'German Saint-Pierre' appeared to offer a solution for the self-alienation of bourgeois existence diagnosed by Rousseau in his first and second *Discours*. The dissatisfaction which Goethe may have felt about Rousseau's solution can be concretized in the way in which he picks up the contradictions of his predecessor, who effortlessly conceals the *ménage-à-trois* in the utopia of Clarens, and solves it by qualifying the proclaimed autonomy of consciousness, with the result of *sickness unto death*. This transformation of horizons makes it also possible to show how different the social substratum of the bourgeois institutions of status, family, religion, and work were and how they were experienced before and after the threshold which divides French enlightenment and German idealism.

My concluding essay, *Der poetische Text im Horizontwandel der Lektüre* (1980), sought to meet Gadamer's demand to develop fully again, for poetry, the triadic unity of the hermeneutic process. If the horizon-structure of aesthetic experience is the superior hermeneutic bridge enabling one to understand a text from the past in its otherness and to bring it into contact once again with the horizon of personal experience, it has to be possible to discover by hermeneutical reflection in reading itself what is really aesthetic about the aesthetic experience and thereby what makes historical understanding possible. My interpretation of Baudelaire's second *Spleen* poem is an attempt to separate the act of the aesthetic observation and that of explicatory understanding, which, in reading, are always mutually supportive. I approach this problem methodologically by withdrawing the still-open horizon of a first reading from the retrospective horizon of a second one. This allows the reader to follow, in the first stage of the analysis, the constitution of an aesthetic observation in the process of happening and to describe it as an effect of both the poetic structures and the still-open expectations of significance of the text. In the second stage of the analysis the aesthetic experience of the first reading, with the return of the end and the accomplished whole to the beginning of the poem, may become the horizon of an explicatory understanding, creating out of its conjectures and unanswered questions a context of meaning. Since this meaning fails to distinguish between what is implied by the text and what is brought to bear by the interpreter, a third stage of analysis has to reintroduce the distance in time initially omitted and reconstruct the author's intended meaning as a historical alternative, thereby elucidating the personal prejudgment from the point of view of the history of reception which determines the interpreter's horizon of interpretation. At this stage the validity of personal interpretation must be tested by inquiring whether it permits us to understand the text in a new and different way and whether it takes into account the work of predecessors. This last requirement alone can give literary hermeneutics its specific purpose which, according to Marquard, is to fight the battle of interpretations in such a way that it does not end in a political duel of life or death. In the horizon of the aesthetic experience, different meanings do not necessarily result in contradiction. Literary communication opens up a dialogue, in which the only criterion for truth or falsity depends on whether significance is capable of further developing the inexhaustible meaning of the work of art.

NOTES

1 References in the article *Horizont* in *Historisches Wörterbuch der Philosophie*, Basel and Stuttgart 1974, especially pp. 1204f., by M. Scherner; see also Karlheinz Stierle, 'Sprechsituation, Kontext und Sprachhandlung,' in *Handlungstheorien-interdisziplinär*, ed. H. Lenk, München 1980, I, 439–83 and Michael Riffaterre, 'Interpretation and Undecidability,' *New Literary History*, 12 (1981), 227–39.

2 In his essays 'Der Religionsphilosophische Aspekt des Dialogischen,' 'Der grosse Sabbat – oder vom Ende des Dialogs,' and 'Episkopales und Pastorales zum Dialog/zur Dialektik,' in *Dialogizität in Prozessen literarischer Kommunikation*, Konstanzer Kolloquium 1980, ed. R. Lachmann (to be published shortly by W. Fink Verlag, München).

3 In his article 'Leo Popper (1886–1911) und die moderne Hermeneutik,' in *Dialogizität*, ed. Lachmann, which discusses the appendixes of the then unpublished *Dialog über die Kunst* (written by Popper, who represented with A and B the positions of himself and Lukács). I have used the names in the rest of this paper.

4 Hans-Georg Gadamer, *Wahrheit und Methode*, Tübingen 1960, p. 447. English translation: *Truth and Method*, translation ed. Garrett Barden and John Cumming, New York 1975, p. 429.

5 For the latest Schleiermacher research and for a critique of the primacy of the understanding-of-oneself in the object, in which 'the being of the other as other disappears,' we refer to M. Frank, *Das individuelle Allgemeine-Textstrukturierung und -interpretation nach Schleiermacher*, Frankfurt 1977, pp. 20–34, esp. p. 33.

6 I rely here on Mikhail Bakhtin, *Problems of Dostoevsky's Poetics*, trans. R. W. Rotsel, Ann Arbor 1973 and *Die Ästhetik des Wortes*, trans. Sabine Reese and Rainer Grübel, Frankfurt 1979; see also Tzvetan Todorov, 'Bakhtine et l'altérité,' *Poétique*, 40 (1979), 502–23 (included in his book, *M. Bakhtine et le principe dialogique*, Paris 1981, pp. 145ff.).

7 Wilhelm Worringer, *Abstraktion und Einfühlung*, München 1918, p. 4.

8 'The first movement of the aesthetic activity is one of empathy: I have to perceive his perceptions, learn them, even live them, I have to occupy his place, even identify with him ... . But is this total merging the final aim of the aesthetic activity? ... ? Not at all! The really aesthetic activity has not even started. ... And the aesthetic activity only begins when we return to ourselves and to the position outside the

other and shape the contents of our emphatic experience and raise it into a finished completeness.' 'Avtor i geroi v esteticeskoj dejatel'nosti,' written around 1924, published in Mikhail Bakhtin, *Esthetika slovesnogo tvorchestva*, Moscow 1979, quoted from pp. 26–8 passim, from an as yet unpublished German translation by A. Sproede.

9 Bakhtin, *Problems*, p. 213.

10 From the already quoted German translation of 'Avtor i geroj v esteticeskoj dejatel'nosti,' pp. 39–41 passim.

11 Mikhail Bakhtin, 'Problema teksta-Opyt filosofskogo analiza,' *Voprosy literatury*, 10 (1976), 149f. (Quoted from R. Grübel's introduction to Bakhtin, *Die Ästhetik*, p. 48, revised from the Russian original.)

12 My definition of aesthetic enjoyment as 'enjoyment of self in the enjoyment of the alien,' or as 'experience of oneself in the possibility of this being different' (Jauss, *Ästhetische Erfahrung und literarische Hermeneutik*, München 1977, p. 59), which I formulated in a critique of Geiger rather than of Worringer, almost coincides with Bakhtin's model of *vnenachodimost*, all the more because it implies the same criticism and development of the already quoted formula of Worringer.

13 The abridgment lies in the moment of the voice, which makes polygraphy take the place of polyphony, while at the same time the subject of the other disappears out of the 'dialogue of the text with itself.' See R. Lachmann in his essay 'Bachtins Dialogizität und die akmeistische Mythopoetik als Paradigma dialogisierter Lyrik,' in *Poetik und Hermeneutik XI* (unpublished).

14 H. Blumenberg, *Arbeit am Mythos*, Frankfurt 1979.

15 H.-G. Gadamer, 'Vom Zirkel des Verstehens,' in *M. Heidegger zum 70. Geburtstag*, Pfullingen 1959, pp. 24–35.

16 Henriquez Ivan Lansberg, *Handbuch der literarischen Rhetorik*, München 1960; see also the programmatic essay by his pupil W. Babilas, *Tradition und Interpretation*, München 1961.

17 E. R. Curtius, *Europäische Literatur und lateinisches Mittelalter*, Bern 1948, p. 22. English translation: *European Literature and the Latin Middle Ages*, trans. Willard R. Trask, Princeton 1973, p. 14.

18 Curtius, *Europäische Literatur*, p. 404. English translation, p. 400.

19 'Bedenken eines Philologen' (1954), in *Medium Aevum Vivum*, Festschrift for W. Bulst, ed. Jauss and D. Schaller, Heidelberg 1960, pp. 7–10.

20 *Questions de littérature* (1960/72); see also Jauss, *Alterität und Modernität der Mittelalterlichen Literatur: Gesammelte Aufsätze 1956–1976*, München 1977, pp. 411–27.

21 See also my review in *Archiv für das Studium der neueren Sprachen*, 197 (1960), 223ff.

22 See my review in *Philosophische Rundschau*, 4 (1956), 113ff.

23 With the exception of L. Olschki, K. Vossler, and L. Spitzer, whose controversy I tried to solve with my interpretation; see Jauss, *Alterität*, pp. 106ff.

24 Hans Lipps, *Die Menschliche Natur*, Frankfurt 1941, p. 19/25. See also Jauss, *Alterität*, p. 201.

25 According to A. Borst in *Poetik und Hermeneutik VIII*, p. 638.

26 Jauss, *Literaturgeschichte*, p. 176.

27 For this I refer to 'Die Partialität der Rezeptions-ästhetischen Methode', special issue (*Rezeptions-ästhetik-Zwischenbilanz*) of *Poetica*, 7 (1975), to *Rezeptions-ästhetik – Theorie und Praxis*, ed. R. Warning, München 1975 (his critical introduction summarizes the theory up to 1975), and especially to Manfred Naumann's critique in Naumann et al., *Gesellschaft, Literatur, Lesen*, Berlin 1973. See also B. Pinkerneil in *Methodische Praxis der Literaturwissenschaft*, ed. D. Kimpel and B. Pinkerneil, Kronberg 1975, pp. 60–8, and S. Petrovic in *Teorijska Istrazivanja*, ed. Z. Konstantinovic, Beograd 1980, pp. 63–74.

28 Jauss, *Literaturgeschichte*, pp. 173ff.

29 Jauss, *Literaturgeschichte*, p. 199.

30 See Pinkerneil, *Methodische Praxis*, p. 67.

31 Petrovic, *Teorijska Istrazivanja*, pp. 63ff.

PAUL RICOEUR

The Text as Dynamic Identity

Any discussion of identity – including text-identity – is fated to pass between two pitfalls: that of taking identity in the too narrow sense of *logical* identity, or of indulging in the delights of the game of sameness and difference after the model of Plato in the *Sophist* and the *Parmenides*, to say nothing of Heidegger's cryptic treatment of *Identität und Differenz*. My purpose is to follow an intermediary course between the Charybdis of logical identity and the Scylla of the identity of identity and difference, by speaking of the *dynamic identity* of the text. Along this 'third way,' I intend – hopefully – to keep, on the one hand, something of the logician's quest for minimal criteria of *identification*, without yielding to his claim that identification amounts to the non-contradictory, tautological acknowledgment of some atemporal entity; and, on the other hand, to remain open to a radical reassessment of our notion of identity, without yielding to the lack of concern for criteriology among the modern pre-Socratics. My notion of the dynamic identity of the text should both reflect something of the pleas of each camp and resist their opposite strategies of intimidation.

I would like to take two preliminary liberties. Allow me first to take my starting-point in the field of inquiry which is presently mine, that of *narrativity* at large, including historical as well as fictional narrative. Allow me further-more to focus on the structuring function of *plot*, following Aristotle's *Poetics*, which includes under the term 'plot' not only the argument of a narrative, the intrigue in the narrow sense, but also the characters, the theme, the point of view or narrative voice – in short all the components of the *integrative* process which establishes a narrative as an imitated action one and complete.

It is the dynamic identity of the structuring process of emplotment which I want to put to test in this paper, with the hope that, in spite of the deliberate narrowness of my starting-point, this investigation will release some broader vista from which to survey the act of poetic composition that Aristotle called *poiesis* and will also give us access to those features of *poiesis* which support procedures of identification compatible with its various modes of historicity.

I shall proceed in the following way. I shall assemble my remarks around four nuclear propositions or theses which, taken together, are intended to delineate what I would like to call *dynamic identity.*

1 *My first thesis is that emplotment is the paradigm for all 'synthesis of the heterogeneous' in the narrative field.*

As you may have noticed, I say emplotment rather than plot, in order to underscore the process character of plot itself. Already in Aristotle's *Poetics*, all the definitions pertaining to the *mythos* (i.e. the fable, the fictional story) of tragedy and epic are substantives derived from verbs: the fable – the plot – it is said, is 'the arrangement [*sustasis, sunthesis*] of incidents in an action one and complete.' It is this definition which I want to expand in order to equate it with the narrative field at large. For this purpose, I want first to underscore the *mediating* function of the plot. It is this mediating function which is implied in the concept of a 'synthesis of the heterogeneous.' This concept actually summarized several singular traits pertaining to the 'configurational act' which makes a temporal whole of the story told.

Staying close to Aristotle's definition of the *mythos* of tragedy and epic, we may say that plot, as emplotment, *mediates* between scattered events or incidents (*ta pragmata* in Aristotle's *Poetics*) and the whole story. In this regard, we may say either that plot draws an intelligible story *from* the various events or incidents, or that it makes these events or incidents *into* a story. (The reciprocal prepositions 'from' and 'into' characterize the plot as mediating between these events or incidents and the told story.) An event, accordingly, must be more than a singular occurrence and be qualified as event by its contribution to the advance of a plot. A story, on the other hand, must be more than a mere enumeration of events put in a serial order: it must organize them into an intelligible whole which always allows one to ask about the 'theme' of the story.

Secondly, emplotment brings together such heterogeneous features as circumstances, agents, interactions, ends, means, and unintended results. Emplotment provides these heterogeneous elements with the ambiguous status of a concordant-discordant whole. We gain a synthetic comprehension from this composition in the act of 'following a story' (Gallie) – or better, in the act of 'retelling' the story (Mink) – to the extent that in this second reading we are less prey to the unexpected and more attentive to the way, as Marx would have put it, human beings make their history in circumstances they themselves have not made, and – I would add – with results they have not intended. The French historian Paul Veyne may consequently define plot as the dynamic unity of goals, means, and contingencies. It is this dynamic unity which is at stake in the process of identifying the 'what' of the story told. Identity is the answer given to the question: telling 'what'?

Thirdly, from another point of view, emplotment mediates the temporality proper to poetic composition. This temporality interweaves the two temporal components: on the one hand, the pure, discrete, and interminable succession of what we may call the story's incidents which constitute the episodic side of the story; on the other hand, the aspect of integration, culmination, and closure brought about by what Louis O. Mink calls the configurational act of narrating. This act consists in 'bringing together' the incidents of the story, in creating a configuration from a succession. This third trait has to do with the twofold structure of human time. Time is both what passes away and what endures. The creation of a temporal whole is precisely the poetic way of mediating between time as passage and time as duration. What we try to pinpoint is the temporal identity of what is enduring in the midst of what is passing away.

2 My second thesis concerns *the epistemological status of the intelligibility displayed by the configurational act of emplotment. My claim here is that narrative intelligibility shows more kinship with practical wisdom or moral judgment than with theoretical reason.* This thesis entails an important corollary concerning the relation between contemporary narratology and the intelligibility proper to emplotment. I see narratology as a *simulation* of narrative intelligence by means of a second-order discourse belonging to the same level of rationality as the other sciences of language. *This priority of narrative intelligence over against narratology as a rational discipline is the core of my second thesis.*

Before considering this dependence of scientific narratology on narrative intelligence I want to focus on the very term *intelligible.* Aristotle was the first to underscore the capacity of poetry to 'teach,' to convey meanings endowed with a certain kind of universality. The very act of configuring the plot makes it typical and understandable in spite of, or thanks to, the singularity of its 'heroes' designated by 'proper names.' This typification of the story allows poetry to be connected with this other kind of intelligibility, that of ethics, which Aristotle called *phronēsis. Phronēsis* tells us that happiness is the coronation of excellence in life and in praxis, but it does not tell us in which ways this state of affairs can obtain. It is poetry which shows us how shifts in fortune – mainly reversals from fortune to misfortune – are nurtured by actual practice. But it shows it in the hypothetical mode of fiction. Nevertheless, it is through our acquaintance with types of emplotment that we *learn* how to link excellence and happiness.

This kinship between narrative intelligibility and *phronēsis* – as opposed to *theōria* – suggests that the universals yielded by plots are not those of theoretical knowledge and science. They are universals of a 'lower' order appropriate to the configurational act at work in poetic composition. One of the ways of characterizing the intelligibility proper to emplotment is to unearth another kinship, this time a kinship with Kant's theory of judgment. This kinship has already been anticipated by the description of emplotment as 'grasping together.' Now 'grasping together' is judging, in the Kantian sense of judging, which consists not so much in joining a subject and a predicate as in placing some intuitive manifold under a rule. This is precisely the kind of *subsumption* that emplotment executes by putting events under the rule of a story, one and complete.

In order to preserve the force of the Aristotelian distinction between *phronēsis* and *theōria*, I suggest that we assign the operation of emplotment to the mode of synthesis that Kant called *schematism*, which is itself the intelligible kernel of the *productive* imagination. According to Kant's *Critique of Pure Reason*, it is the business of the schematism to generate the rules which may be systematically ordered at the level of philosophical discourse. The *schematism* has such power because the productive imagination itself performs a basically synthetic function. It connects the level of understanding and that of intuition by generating new syntheses, both intellectual and intuitive. In the same way, emplotment generates a mixed intelligibility between what can be called the *thought* – the theme, or the topic of the story – and the intuitive presentation of circumstances, characters, episodes, changes of fortune, etc. We may thus speak of a *schematism* of the narrative function to characterize the work of intelligibility proper to emplotment. It is at this intermediary level of *schematism* that we identify a plot. To continue with the model of the *schematism* which Kant held to be the matrix of the categories of understanding, we could say that it is thanks to this potential intelligibility that singular plots lend themselves to typologies of the kind construed by Northrop Frye in the *Anatomy of Criticism*. Such typologies, to my mind, reflect a sustained familiarity with the singular works of our narrative tradition or traditions and constitute the *schematism* of narrative function, in the same way that the singular plots express the productive imagination at work at the concrete level of poetic composition.

Such is the way in which we may transpose into more modern terms Aristotle's contention that poetry teaches universals. These universals are not those of theoretical thinking but those of the *schematism* of the narrative function. They are learned only by *reflecting upon* the self-structuration of our narrative tradition (or traditions). In this sense, they still belong to the cycle of productive imagination with its potential of intelligibility, and not to that of theoretical reason. This kinship with productive imagination constitutes a part of our concept of dynamic identity. We identify a plot as a product of productive imagination and accordingly as a potential *schema* delineated in the narrative field.

The corollary of this thesis is that narratology, as it is practised with the accuracy and intellectual mastery that we admire in the works of Roland Barthes, Gérard Genette, Tzvetan Todorov, Claude Brémond, and, above all, A. J. Greimas proceeds from a shift of strategic levels: by emphasizing the logical constraints at work at the level of deep structures constitutive of the 'grammar' of narrative, narratology shifts the scientific interest from the level of message to that of code. One may then wonder whether what we call emplotment is not just the surface configuration of the text and, accordingly, whether narrative intelligence is not simply a derivative mode of understanding grounded in some more fundamental operation pertaining to a rationality deprived of any irreducibly narrative character.

My contention is rather that it is the kind of rationality put to task by the logical analysis of narrative constraints that is derived from narrative intelligence. To my mind, narratology's aim is to *simulate*, by means of a second-order discourse, what we have already understood at the level of the schematism as the narrative function. This relation of simulation cannot be found in the linguistic disciplines which have provided structural poetics with a powerful model, because a phoneme or a lexeme has a *cultural* status prior to its delineation by the linguist; linguistic science is not concerned with objects already entangled in the networks of symbolic elaboration. It challenges no other symbolic practice in which its object would already have appeared as a distinct cultural object. With narratives, the situation is quite different: narratology is preceded by a previous cultural creation which displays an intelligibility of its own. In this respect, the rationality of narratology is parasitic upon the intelligibility of narratives themselves. An example: in narratology we are accustomed to speaking of diachrony and synchrony. But these categories, characteristic of the new rationality of narratology, imply a fragmentation of the apparent unity of the cultural object, in order to establish, thanks to this fragmentation, a new combinatory system following rules foreign to the strategy of emplotment. It is for the sake of this new rationality that narrative time is now expressed in terms of diachrony, subordinated to the synchrony of the models which rule the narrative logic to be installed. What is called the 'chronological' aspect of narrative must now be derived from its 'logical' dimension. As Roland Barthes says in his *Introduction to the Structural Analysis of Narratives*, the task of this analysis is 'to dechronologize the narrative content and to submit it to what Mallarmé called ... the primordial lightnings of logic.' But the 'chronological' dimension which is accounted for here already proceeds from the transformation of the product of poetic formation into the object of a science which entails its own practice of initiation. In this way, the very attempt to transform the cultural object into an object for structural analysis implies that narrative time is held as 'chronological illusion.' It is the substitution of analytic rationality for narrative intelligence which requires that narrative time recede to the status of chronological illusion. To my mind, it is the task of a hermeneutic of narrative time to show that narrative logic is a second-order discourse which borrows from the narrative intelligence that it claims to generate, and that it enjoys the same epistemological status as Kant's transcendental logic as regards the schematism of the productive imagination.

For example, it can be shown that in Propp's *Morphology of the Folktale* the definition of the thirty-one 'functions,' whose chain constitutes *the* Russian folktale, relies on the definition of the function as contributing to the progression of the tale as a whole and, in this sense, to its emplotment. The grasping of the plot as a self-structuring whole controls the operations of segmentation and concatenation constitutive of the analytical approach. I can only hint at this conflict between a teleological grasping of the tale as a system of parts and whole and a mere external and mechanistic concatenation of abstract segments, by the following enumeration of symptoms: the notion of 'initial situation'; that of a 'preparatory part'; the role of 'villainy' as that function which provides the tale with its dynamics; the description of a bundle of functions as a 'quest'; the function of closure assumed by the last function ('at this point, [Propp says] the tale draws to a close'); finally the assertion that a given tale is constituted by one or more 'moves' (xod): 'this type of development is termed by us a move (xod): each new act of villainy, each new lack creates a new move.' This concept of 'move' is the most striking example of the hidden role played by the teleological approach to the folktale as plot in the distribution of functions along the unilinear series of elementary functions.

In concluding this second section of my paper I want to make it clear that the analytic procedures characteristic of a rational approach to narrative texts are absolutely legitimate. And I am the first to admire the works of the French structuralists whom I quoted earlier. The problem is not that of what is right or not right, but of the self-understanding of the discipline under consideration. Is the so-called logic of narratives an autonomous discipline? Or does it reformulate in a second-order discourse what has already been understood at the level of the first-order discourse, that of the poetic composition constitutive of emplotment? As one may surmise, the identity of the text means two different things according to whether one relies only on the procedures of segmentation and combination of a narrative logic or if one refers – as I think we should do – the reconstruction of the text by analytical procedures to the dynamic identity secured by the poetic act of configuration. My wager would be to consider the recourse to analytic procedures as a detour which starts from a naïve understanding, follows the long path of explanation, but for the sake of a more mature understanding, leads to a 'learned' understanding – or, sometimes, maybe, to a *docta ignorantia*.

3 *My third thesis is that this narrative schematism, in turn, is constituted by a history which shares all the characteristics of a tradition.* By this I do not refer to the inert transmission of some dead depository, but the living transmission of an innovation that can always be reactivated through a return to the most creative moments of poetic composition. This phenomenon of traditionality is the key to the functioning of the narrative paradigms and, accordingly, to their identification. The constitution of a tradition relies upon the interplay between innovation and sedimentation. It is to sedimentation that we can ascribe the paradigms which constitute the typology of emplotment of which we just spoke. They – or rather their schematization – stem from a sedimented history whose genesis has been obliterated.

This sedimentation obtains at several levels that require us to accurately discriminate our use of the term 'paradigm.' Thus, Aristotle displays his analysis of emplotment at three levels which are so to speak 'levelled off' in the *Poetics*. He first presents a *formal* concept of plot, as the discordant concordance of any story encompassing peripeties, i.e. contingencies within a temporal order of any kind. Then, he develops the *generic* concept of the Greek tragedy, specified by the reversal from fortune to misfortune, by the role of pitiful and frightening incidents, by the tragic flaw of a character otherwise distinguished by excellence and the absence of vice or wickedness, etc. This 'genre' has more or less ruled the further development of dramatic literature in the West. Thirdly, there is something paradigmatic in singular works, such as the *Iliad* and *Oedipus Rex*. To the extent that the causal link prevails over mere succession – the 'because of one another' over against the 'after one another' – the arrangement of incidents itself becomes a *type* which yields a universal. In this way our narrative tradition has been informed not only by the sedimentation of the *form* of discordant concordance, but by that of the tragic *genre*, and finally by that of *types* generated at the level of singular works dealt with as paradigmatic. If we hold as paradigmatic the *form*, the *genres*, and the *types*, we get a hierarchy of paradigms which are born from the work of productive imagination at these several levels.

The *identification* of a given work starts with this multiple recognition of the underlying paradigms. But the *identification* of a work is not exhausted by the identification of its sedimented paradigms. It also takes into account the opposite phenomenon of *innovation*. Why? Because, paradigms, being generated by a previous innovation, provide guidelines for further experimentation in the narrative field. These change under the pressure of innovation, but they change slowly and even resist change, by virtue of the process of sedimentation. Innovation, then, remains the opposite pole of tradition. There is always room for innovation to the extent that what is ultimately produced, in the *poiesis* of the poem, is always a singular work, *this* work. Paradigms are a kind of grammar, ruling the composition of *new* works, new before becoming typical. Each work is an original production, a new existent in the realm of discourse. But the reverse is no less true: innovation remains a rule-governed behaviour. The work of imagination does not start from scratch. It is connected in one way or another to the paradigms of a tradition. But it can enter into a variable relation to these paradigms. The range of solutions is widely deployed between the two poles of servile repetition and calculated deviance, passing through all the degrees of 'déformation réglée.' Folktales, myths, and traditional narratives in general stand close to the pole of repetition. This is why they constitute the privileged kingdom of structuralism. But as soon as we move beyond such traditional narratives, deviance becomes the rule. The contemporary novel, for example, may in large part be defined as an anti-novel, to the extent that contesting ruling paradigms prevails over merely varying their application.

Furthermore, deviance may work at all levels: in relation to types, to genres, finally to the very principle of discordance. The first kind of deviance – deviance from type – seems to be constitutive of any singular work. Each new work deviates from each previous work. Less frequent are changes of genre: this amounts to the creation of a new genre, for example that of the novel by opposition to drama and to romance, or that of historiography by opposition to chronicle. But the most radical rejection is that of the formal principle of discordant-concordance. We may leave open the question of the breadth of the space of variation allowed by the formal paradigm. But we may already surmise that when the rejectionist becomes the schismatic, to use Frank Kermode's terms, there is no longer any narrative form to identify.

At any rate, the possibility of deviance is included in the relation between sedimentation and innovation which constitutes tradition. Under the extreme form of the schism, deviance is only the opposite of servile application, and 'déformation réglée' remains the general axis around which the modalities of paradigm-changes get distributed. Such variation confers upon productive imagination a historicity of its own and keeps alive the narrative tradition. If this analysis is correct, the *identity* of a work is nothing other than a point of equilibrium between the process of sedimentation and the process of innovation, and implies a twofold identification, that of the paradigms that it exemplifies and that of the deviance that measures its novelty. This twofold identification brings the notion of identity close to the borderline where identity and difference merge. But, as I said, I shall not let myself be swallowed by this conceptual whirlwind. Let it suffice to notice that our notion of *dynamic identity* has never been deprived of dialectical tensions: first between the unity of the configurational act and the episodic manifold that it gathers; secondly between the intelligibility of the universals 'taught' by the plot and the concreteness of the goals, the means and the contingencies which the configurational act grasps together; and finally between the identifiable paradigms sedimented in the tradition and the identifiable deviance which makes the 'newness' of a new work.

4 *The identity of the narrative text is not confined to the so-called 'inside' of the text. As a dynamic identity, it emerges at the intersection between the world of the text and the world of the reader. It is in the act of reading that the capacity of the plot to transfigure experience is actualized. The act of reading may play this role because its own dynamism is grafted upon that of the configurational act and brings it to completion.*

There are three stages in this fourth thesis. First, it speaks of an 'intersection' between two kinds of worlds. By the world of the text I mean the world displayed by the fiction in front of itself, so to speak, as the *horizon of possible experience* in which the work displaces its readers. By the world of the reader, I mean the actual world within which *real action* is disclosed. It is a world in the sense that action occurs in the midst of 'circumstances' which (as the term suggests) 'surround' action; or to use an expression of Hannah Arendt in *The Human Condition*, action occurs in a 'web of relationships' in the midst of which the agent is disclosed in speech and action. It is this 'disclosure of who' which implies a world as the *horizon* of the circumstances and the interactions which constitute the proximate web of relationships for each agent.

For literary criticism this world of action is the 'outside' of the text, as opposed to the 'inside' of the text. As the 'outside' of the text it is irrelevant to its mode of inquiry. My contention is that this undialectical distinction between 'inner' and 'outer' is not self-evident, but results from the extrapolation of features appropriate to sub-phrastic entities such as words, lexemes, and phonemes to works of discourse – i.e. to verbal expressions equal or longer than the sentence. It is for linguistics, as the science of these shorter entities, that the so-called actual world that we call the 'real' is an 'extra-linguistic' entity. The 'outer' world is 'outer' only for a treatment of language which establishes it as a self-contained set of entities, all of whose relationships are immanent. But it is the methodological decision, constitutive of linguistics as a science, of dealing with language as an 'inside' without an 'outside' which makes all consideration of this 'outside' irrelevant. For a hermeneutics which does not take this undialectical separation between the 'inside' and the 'outside' of the text for granted, the problem is rather to understand how language keeps *mediating* between man and world, man and man, man and himself, even when the poetic function, as Roman Jakobson points out, increases the gap between signs and world. This threefold *mediation* of referentiality (man and world), of communicability (man and man), and of self-understanding (man and himself) constitutes the major problem of a hermeneutics of poetic texts. What I call the intersection between the world of the text and the world of the reader is only one aspect of this hermeneutical problem.

I would like to claim that the previous description of the identity of the narrative text as a *dynamic* identity may help bridge the gap between the work's world and the reader's world created by the extrapolation of linguistics into poetics. To my mind, the capacity of fiction to transfigure experience is included in the very nature of the configurational act. How? The second half of my fourth thesis says that it is the dynamism of this configurational act that the act of reading resumes and completes. Nothing confirms this better than the two previous features by which we just characterized fiction in theses 2 and 3, i.e. *schematization* and *traditionality*. Both traits help us to dispel the prejudice which opposes the 'inside' to the 'outside' of the text. This opposition is closely related to the conception of a static and closed structure of the text. The notion a structuring *activity*, displayed in the operation of emplotment, transcends this dichotomy. Schematization and traditionality are already categories ruling the interaction between the operative function of writing and that of reading.

On the one hand, received paradigms provide structure to the *expectations* of the reader and help him or her to acknowledge and identify the formal rule, the genre, or the type exemplified by the story told. They provide guidelines for the encounter between the text and its reader. In other words, *they* rule the capacity of the story to be followed – what Gallie called its 'followability.' On the other hand, it is the act of reading which, as it were, 'accompanies' the configuration of the narrative and actualizes its followability. To follow a story is to *enact* or *re-enact* it by reading. If, therefore, emplotment may be described as an act of judgment at the level of productive imagination, this is so to the extent that emplotment is the joint work of the text and its reader, in the same way that Aristotle called sensation the common work of the 'sensed' and the 'sensing.'

Furthermore, it is the act of reading which accompanies the interplay between the innovation and the sedimentation of the paradigms that schematize emplotment. It is in the act of reading that the recipient plays with narrative constraints, generates deviances, takes part in the fight between novel and anti-novel, and enjoys the kind of pleasure that Roland Barthes called 'pleasure of the text.'

Finally it is the reader who completes the work to the extent that, according to Roman Ingarden in *The Structure of the Literary Work* and Wolfgang Iser in *The Act of Reading*, the written work is indeed a guideline for reading, but nevertheless an unfinished work which presents holes, lacunae, 'places of indeterminacy,' and even, as in Joyce's *Ulysses*, challenges the capacity of the reader to configure on his own a work that the author seems to have defigured as much as he could. In this extreme case, it is the reader, literally forsaken by the work, who alone carries the burden of emplotting it. The act of reading is accordingly the *vector* of the transfiguration of the world of action under the auspices of fiction. It may play this role because the effect caused by the text on its recipients is an intrinsic component of the actual meaning of the text. The text as text is a set of *instructions* which the individual or public reader *complies* with in a passive or creative way. But the text becomes a work only in the interaction between text and recipient.

I am well aware of the difficulties raised by this thesis. The differences between Iser's theory of reading and Jauss's theory of reception witness to these difficulties. Iser proceeds from the amendment of Ingarden's analyses of the indeterminacy and concretization of literary works; Jauss from the amendment of Gadamer's theses on the history of effects, the fusion of horizons, and the logic of question and answer. Iser lays stress on the response of an individual reader in the process of reading, while Jauss focuses on the response of a public at the level of its collective expectations. In a sense, a theory of reception presupposes a theory of reading, since it is through the process of reading that the text reveals its *Appelstruktur*. But in another sense, a theory of reading presupposes a theory of reception, to the extent that individual reading is prestructured by cultural expectations. In this way, a reception aesthetics may rescue the theory of reading from the danger of 'psychologizing,' by including individual reading within the broader process of constituting a literary *history* – a history which could balance and even challenge and provoke literary theory, Marxist or structuralist. (The title *Literaturgeschichte als Provokation* speaks for itself.) I agree that a theory of reading and/or reception has to avoid the two pitfalls of 'psychologizing' and/or 'sociologizing.' But these two dangers are the price to be paid for a hermeneutics of the work in which the text completes its travel in an act which, in turn, has no other function than to *mediate* between two worlds, the work's world and the reader's world.

We must therefore take a third step: it is not enough to say that a theory of reading and a theory of reception presuppose one another, to the extent that, on the one hand, the individual reader shares the expectations already sedimented in the public which guides his or her reading, and that, on the other hand, these public expectations result from the indefinite set of individual acts of reading. We must still include this circular relationship between private reading and public reception within the broader circle constituted by the reciprocal relation between the work's world and the reader's world. In other words, we have to relate the problem of the *communicability* of the work to that of its *referentiality*, i.e. its capacity to 'reshape' reality. Once more, what has to be shattered is the opposition between an 'outside' and an 'inside' of the text. For this purpose, it would not be enough to put side by side, or to combine in a simple, eclectic way, a structuralism of the 'inside' and a psycho-sociology of the 'outside' of the text. The task of hermeneutics is to accompany the structuring activity which starts in the midst of life, is invested in the text, and, thanks to private reading and public reception, returns to life. An aesthetics of reception is unable to deal exclusively with the problem of communication without involving that of reference. What is communicated, ultimately, beyond the 'inner' meaning of a text, is the world that it projects and the horizon it constitutes. The reader reciprocally receives this pro-position or pro-ject of a world according to his or her finite capacity to respond, which is in turn delineated according to a situation which is limited and yet which opens on a world's horizon.

PART FOUR

ANALYTICAL CONSTRUCTION

LUBOMÍR DOLEŽEL

Literary Text, Its World and Its Style

The identity of the literary text is a semantico-pragmatic problem. If we consider the text in its form of expression, the question of identity as a theoretical problem does not arise; as a graphemic, morphological, syntactic, and contextual structure the text is finished, fixed, and unchangeable after the last touch of the author's hand. Textual criticism which deals with dubious, controversial, or uncertain versions of literary works is a discipline with a purely practical goal: to establish the definitive, authoritative form of the text.[1]

In its semantic and pragmatic aspects the text appears as a signifying system, as a 'pregnant' semiotic object which has to be processed by its recipients. There is no way of recovering the text's meaning other than by the procedure of interpretation. The paradox of interpretation is given by the fact that in the very process of recovery, the text's meaning is pluralized and, consequently, the identity of the text is undermined. One and the same form of the text can be read, interpreted, 'concretized' in many different meanings. While the literary text controls fully its form of expression, it does not seem to control its meaning, or, at least, does not seem to control it with sufficient authority.

EPISTEMOLOGY OF LITERARY SEMANTICS

In this essay, the problem of semantic interpretation of literary texts will be approached from the position of general text theory.[2] This epistemological position can be summarized in the following assumptions:[3]

1 Reading as the primary mode of text-processing leads to many different interpretations of one and the same text, or, at least, to many possible variations of a core meaning. The characterization of the reader's interpretation as a merger of the world of the text and the world of the reader (Valdés, 1980, p. 99) explains this fact very aptly. In the operation of reading, the meaning of the

literary text is recovered by an unlimited number of individual readers in many different cultural, social, historical contexts. While recognizing the plurality of readers' interpretations as a necessary fact of literary communication, we have to ask whether *interpretation in reading* is the only mode of the recovery of the text's meaning. In the final account, the problem of interpretation is crucially linked to the fundamental epistemological question of literary study: is reading, a practical activity based on skills and experiences, the only access to literary texts, or is it justified to claim that an analyst (critic, theoretician) with his theoretical and methodological apparatus has a privileged access to literary texts? The answer given by general text theory and literary semantics is quite definite: a strict distinction has to be made between the theoretical activity of the analyst-interpreter and the practical activity of the interpreting reader; while the former is a source of knowledge about literary texts, the latter cannot yield theoretical knowledge; on the contrary, the practical activity has to be explained by a theory of reading.[4]

2 Literary semantics is an empirical theory. It is clear today that speculative theoretizing about interpretation has reached a dead end; speculative arguments in favour of particular concepts of interpretation are now as repetitive and predictable as well-explored chess-game openings. Empirical theory and empirical study is the only way towards a renewal of literary semantics and of literary scholarship in general.

An empirical theory of meaning in literature is a theory which defines a system of concepts – a general model of meaning – which can be used to formulate semantic interpretations of particular literary texts. The foundations of the empirical theory of interpretation have been recently attacked by Fish (Fish, 1980). In fact, Fish repeats an old argument against any empirical theory of literary texts by claiming that there is no interpretive procedure (i.e. no theory) which is 'independently specifiable': 'The construction of the grammar and the construction of the poem [the poem's interpretation in common parlance] are going on at the same time' (Fish, 1980, p. 263). It seems that Fish has in mind *ad hoc* 'grammars' constructed and tested on a very narrow empirical base. Most theories of text semantics are developed on a general level, quite often linked explicitly to highly abstract models of logical or linguistic semantics. Whatever the empirical or theoretical background of text models, there is no denying the fact that text interpretations (and all text descriptions) are expressed in terms of a model. The purpose of models as tools of empirical study is to provide us with a metalanguage for descriptions. What has to be emphasized, however, is the fact that the encounter between an abstract model and a concrete text is not a mechanical 'application' of the model, its reiteration and reaffirmation; rather, this confrontation is a complex epistemic procedure which results not only in the identification of the text constituents in terms of the model, but also, and primarily, in the discovery of their specific relationships, patternings, functions, modifications, etc., within the specific totality of the text. Needless to say, in its encounters with texts the model is tested in its scope of validity and effectiveness. However, the main result of the confrontation is a description or interpretation of a concrete text, which provides *knowledge about the text not contained in the model itself*, i.e. knowledge not derived (in the logical sense) from the model. This is the reason why (to use examples discussed by Fish) a model of case grammar or action theory can lead to knowledge about specific features of agency in a poem by Keats or in a novel by Golding.[5]

3 The ultimate target of literary semantics is the discovery of the literary text in its *individual identity*. A literary text is identical with itself by being different from all other literary (and non-literary) texts. Text identity is analogous to personal identity, both being constituted by a set of specific, permanent, and recognizable features differentiating one individual from all others. We have to emphasize, however, that 'individuality' does not mean 'singularity' ('uniqueness') (Wellek-Warren, 1948, p. 7); therefore, the focus on individual identity does not prevent literary semantics from pursuing the study of similarities and shared (invariant) features of literary texts and text classes.

In its insistence on the individual identity of literary texts, literary semantics transcends the function of pure theory and assumes a significant cultural role. The present consumeristic society is characterized by its egocentric appropriation of nature, history, foreign cultures, and other human values. A reader transforming the rich variety of texts into *his own* interpretation performs a consumeristic operation. The consumeristic operation forces him into a monotonous, dull, one-text world which, being his own closed world, does not provide any semantic, aesthetic, or ethical challenge. In such a world, texts are just mirrors in which the man of the end of the second millenium discovers again and again his own bored face. In this situation, literary theory has a clear choice: either to justify and reinforce the consumeristic attitude to literature, or to challenge it by opening the view towards the multitude and variety of literary texts.

TWO PILLARS OF THE TEXT'S IDENTITY

Literary semantics offers two basic arguments in favour of the individual identity of the literary text. (1) A literary text has an individual identity because it constructs its own restricted, circumscribed fictional world. (2) A literary text possesses individual identity because it displays its own idiosyncratic literary style. A circumscribed fictional world and an idiosyncratic literary style seem to be also relatively stable in the variety of readers' interpretations: most readers will probably agree on the basic constituents and overall shape of the fictional world; they will also be able to differentiate (intuitively) the literary styles of various writers, especially those with prominently idiosyncratic styles.[6] The text's fictional world and literary style seem to offer strong resistance to modifications, transformations, and distortions. For our purpose, however, the main significance of the two concepts is the possibility of defining a correlation between the fictional world and the literary style. Consequently, the problem of the identity of the literary text can be placed and discussed in the framework of a unified empirical semantic theory postulated above (p. 190). In the core of my argument, I will advance specific suggestions for the development of such a theoretical framework; necessarily, these suggestions will be relatively brief and somewhat lopsided.

FICTIONAL WORLD

By the text and through the text a fictional world is constructed which we refer to or talk about in the same way as we refer to or talk about the actual world. While I wish to avoid plunging into inconclusive ontological controversies, I have to express my belief that a theory of *fictional* literature is possible only if a fundamental distinction is made between semiotic worlds constructed by texts (and by other semiotic systems) and the actual world existing independently of any text.

The empirical test of the formation of the fictional world is the possibility of truth-valuation of statements which describe the world. This procedure has been well explored in logical and semiotic theories of fictionality. Thus, for example, Woods speaks about the 'bet-sensitivity' of statements about fictional worlds: We would win a bet on the statement 'Sherlock Holmes lived on Baker Street,' while we would lose by betting on 'Sherlock Holmes lived on Berczy Street' (Woods, 1974, p. 13). Statements with positive truth-value describe the constituents, the shape, the extent, etc. of the corresponding fictional world of a particular text. The procedure of truth-valuation makes it possible to decide what exists and what does not exist in a fictional world.

Truth-valuation of statements about fictional worlds is an elementary procedure of semantic text interpretation. It is a *model* interpretive procedure and its study leads to formulating theses which are of general import for the theory of interpretation. Let me state four such theses:

1 Statements about a fictional world can be assigned truth values only when

the world is already available, i.e. when it has been constructed by its text. Statements *about* fictional worlds are to be strictly distinguished from sentences of the original text *constructing* the world; while the former are within the scope of truth-valuation, the latter are not. With respect to the original text sentences, statements about fictional worlds represent a *paraphrase*.[7] Thus, for example, the statement 'Emma Bovary committed suicide' is a paraphrase of a segment of Flaubert's text performing the construction of that event. Flaubert is the author of the original text, an interpreter is the author of the paraphrase. It makes no sense to ask whether Flaubert was right or wrong, whether he was telling the truth or lied; by his text he was constructing a world which had not existed before. It is, however, possible, indeed, necessary to ask whether the interpreter's paraphrase is true or false, i.e. whether the world which the interpreter *reconstructs* corresponds to the world which the text *has constructed*.

From the specific consideration of the truth-valuation of the paraphrase, the first general thesis on interpretation can be derived: *Interpretation requires paraphrasing the original text; it is possible to devise specific evaluation procedures whereby the correspondence of the paraphrase to the original text will be assessed.*

2 If we claim that it is possible to assign truth values to statements about fictional world, we have to provide a criterion of truth-valuation. Obviously, there is only one criterion available, namely a recourse to the text itself. If we want to know what is true or false about the actual world, we have to inspect this world; if we want to know what is true or false about a fictional world, we have to inspect the text which has constructed this world.[8] Specifically, we have to discover which sentences of the text are authenticated, i.e. have the performative force of constructing facts of the fictional world. Authentication is the source and explanation of fictional existence. It is a purely textual procedure, a component of the text's semantic structure; it represents the most powerful semantic restriction imposed on the world by the text. By the procedure of authentication, the text shapes and controls its world.[9]

Discovering authentication as a base of truth-valuation leads to our second general thesis on interpretation: *The inspection of the text, particularly of its semantic structure, is the necessary criterion of validity in interpretation.*[10]

3 While claiming that the peculiar shape of a fictional world is determined by the set of authenticated sentences of the literary text, we do not mean to say that only explicit sentences participate in the world construction. The fictional world is constructed not only by explicit (manifest) components of the text, but also – and sometimes quite significantly – by its implicit semantic constituents. A literary text is a totality of the manifest (i.e. explicitly expressed) and the

derived (i.e. implicit) meanings. Correspondingly, the fictional world is a structure incorporating both domains constructed explicitly, and domains constructed by implication. In particular cases, the opposition between the two domains becomes the dominant feature of the world's structure; such is the case of Kafka's novels where the implicit domains of the Court (in *The Trial*) and of the castle (in *The Castle*) function as inaccessible, mysterious, but most powerful black holes.

Contemporary text semantics has tremendously enriched our understanding of implied meaning, especially in the theories of presuppositions (for a summary, see Lyons, 1977, II, 592–606), 'sous-entendu' (Ducrot, 1972), pragmatic implicature (Grice, 1975), etc. Modern text semantics has put an end to arbitrary guesses about implicit meaning in literary texts by postulating: (a) that this meaning is triggered by specific signals given in the manifest text (hints, allusions, ellipses, etc.); (b) that the inference of implicit meaning from explicit meaning is governed by a set of specifiable procedures. Since inference of implicit meaning is linked to explicit meaning, the text preserves the control of its world, while allowing the construction of specific world domains by implication.

This reflection leads to our third general thesis on interpretation: *Text meaning is a totality of explicit and implicit components; implicit meaning is not guessed, but derived by controlled inference procedures from the meaning of the explicit text components.*

4 Even if we provide for implicit text components to participate in the fictional world construction, we will discover that only some possible statements about fictional worlds are decidable, while others are, by necessity, undecidable. The question whether Emma Bovary committed suicide or died a natural death can be answered, while the question whether she had or did not have a birthmark on her left shoulder is undecidable and, in fact, meaningless.[11] The vast truth-value gaps which are easily discovered in any description of fictional worlds lead to the claim that fictional worlds are by necessity *incomplete*. Incompleteness might be the essential property differentiating fictional worlds from the actual world (Heintz, 1979, p. 94).[12]

If incompleteness is a necessary property of fictional worlds, then gaps are essential components of their individual structure. A fictional world is circumscribed no less by its empty spaces than by its populated areas. The task of literary semantics is to locate the empty domains and to determine their function in the overall structure of the fictional world.[13] Literary interpretation which postulates the filling-in of gaps ('blanks') is a reductive procedure, since it transforms the multifarious incomplete worlds of fiction into uniform structure of the complete (Carnapian) world.[14]

The fact of the necessary incompleteness of fictional worlds leads to our final thesis on interpretation: *Procedures of semantic interpretation should reveal the specific locations and functions of gaps in the overall structure of the fictional worlds, rather than reduce the variety of incomplete world structures to the uniform structure of a complete world.*

I have stated at the beginning that the identity of the literary text is made problematic by the possible plurality of the readers' interpretations. An investigation of a specific interpretive procedure, i.e. of truth-valuation of statements about fictional worlds, has led to the outline of a theory of interpretation which preserves the individual identity of the literary text.[15] It should be emphasized that this theory is not suggested for the purpose of ending conflicts of interpretations; it is not a recipe for single, definite, solely 'correct' interpretations.[16] Its main aspiration is that of any other epistemological reflection: to formulate a set of explicit assumptions, so that rational criticism of the theory is made possible. There is no doubt in my mind that the conflict of interpretations cannot be resolved by weighing particular interpretations, but by examining the underlying interpretive principles.[17]

LITERARY STYLE

The concept of style in general, and of literary style in particular, is hardly a rigorous concept. However, it has been useful in literary study and beyond by expressing the intuition of an organized, regulated, consistent individuality or specificity. I am tempted to define literary style in terms which, at first glance, appear almost contradictory: *Literary style is an ordered set of global regularities of texture,*[18] *determining conjointly the idiosyncrasy of the literary text.* Under this definition, style does not appear as a random collection of isolated, local features, but as a fundamental organizing force operating in the text.

Global regularity of texture (in distinction to a local pattern) operates throughout the text and, therefore, can be described in any sufficiently representative text sample.[19] A *semantic* global regularity of texture can be expressed in terms of intensional function. Intensional function is the regular matching of elements of the fictional world with expressions (devices) of the texture. In other words, *intensional function* is a function from fictional worlds to textures. As such, the concept provides a common ground for our theory of text identity: it unites the peculiar fictional world of a text with the characteristic features of its literary style.[20]

Let me first demonstrate, for the sake of clarity, the operation of the simplest, i.e. a two-value intensional function (see schema 1). The fictional world is here

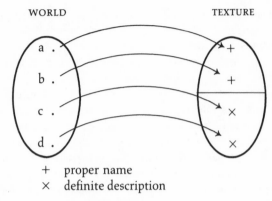

+   proper name
×   definite description

SCHEMA 1   Two-value intensional function

represented by the set of its individuals (agents), distinguished from each other extensionally (for example, by lower-case letters of the alphabet), but not named by natural language expressions. It is assumed that the process of naming consists in assigning to each individual of the fictional world either a proper name (such as *Odysseus*), or a definite description (such as *the king of Ithaca* or *the hero of Homer's poem 'The Odyssey'*).[21] If the assignment of the two kinds of name is regular and consistent throughout the text, then we will say that a two-value intensional function of naming operates in that text. Such is the case of Defoe's *Robinson Crusoe*: three individuals of its world are assigned proper names – *Robinson, Xury,* and *Friday* – while all other agents are named by definite descriptions only: *my father, the Portuguese captain, the English captain's widow, Friday's father,* etc.

Natural language offers more than two alternative modes of naming individuals, or, to put it more clearly, within the basic categories of proper names and definite descriptions stylistically differing subcategories can be distinguished. Thus, for example, a significantly different stylistic effect is achieved if we call somebody by his last (proper) name than if we call him by his first (proper) name. Since the repertoire of the alternative name categories is more than two, higher-value intensional functions of naming can be expected to operate in literary texts.

In order to demonstrate how a literary text reveals its individual identity in a complex intensional function, I will proceed to examine the regularities of naming in Kafka's *The Trial*. This novel – and Kafka's work as a whole – has been a challenge to interpretation since its posthumous publication.[22] Unfortunately, *The Trial* has shared the fate of many works of modern literature in having been subjected almost exclusively to the ideological mode of interpreta-

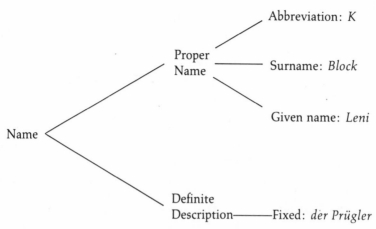

SCHEMA 2 Categories of naming in *The Trial*

tion (cf. Politzer, 1965); the interpreters have been discovering (or rediscovering) in the text merely their own systems of thought. The study of the stylistic regularities of the text is pursued in direct opposition to such self-serving modes of interpretation.

The first observation about the texture of *The Trial* is the fact that various categories of names are assigned to the agents of its world with surprising consistency and exclusiveness. An intensional function of naming indeed operates in Kafka's text.[23] The intensional function selects from a set of alternative categories of names, specified in schema 2. I shall focus on three fundamental aspects of the text's literary style, which are generated by the intensional function of naming:

1 The hierarchy and relationships of agents in the 'private group.' It is obvious that the protagonist of the novel is singled out from the set of all agents by his exclusive proper name, an abbreviation: *Joseph K.* or *K.* or *Herr K.* In this non-standard 'surname' Kafka follows a venerable tradition of literature with its *X.Y.*s, *N.N.*s, etc. Critics have been attempting to seek an interpretation of this name in isolation. While we could pursue this course – suggesting, for example, that the abbreviation makes the protagonist a purely literary (fictional) figure – the function of the name revealed in the whole system of naming is much more significant. By his unique name, the protagonist forms a one-member class, differentiated and isolated from all other individuals of the fictional world.

At the same time, the intensional function of naming leads to the formation of a class of agents who are named by standard proper names. At a closer inspection, this class can be interpreted as the *private group* of the protagonist; its members enter into clearly specified relations and interactions with the hero in his lonely conflict and quest. A set of male characters, named consistently and exclusively by surname only – *Huld, Tittorelli, Block* – can be said to act as K.'s 'helpers' and 'informers'; in such a way, they are involved in the hero's quest to penetrate into the inaccessible world of the Court. At the same time, *Block*, a standard surname of a defendant, testifies to the fact that K.'s abbreviation is a sign of his exceptionality within the set of the accused.

An interesting split can be observed in the set of the female characters belonging to the hero's private group. K.'s mistresses have no surnames, but first names only: *Elsa, Leni*.[24] In contrast, the inaccessible female is named consistently by a polite form of the surname: *Fräulein Bürstner* (Miss Bürstner). It is interesting to note that in their most intimate moment (at the end of chapter 1), Joseph K. wants to call Fräulein Bürstner by her first name, but realizes that he does not know it. This lack of the first name is no less significant for the semantic interpretation of the novel than is the polite surname under which this remote *femme fatale* is consistently and exclusively known.[25]

2 The domain of institutions. Two social institutions, the Bank and the Court, are constructed in *The Trial*. In spite of their fundamental semantic oppositions – the Court being an invisible world with a random, irrational mode of operation, the Bank a visible world with a highly rational and efficient mode of operation – the two institutions are linked on the level of texture: their agents are designated consistently and exclusively by fixed (permanent) definite descriptions. *Der Direktor* (the director), *der Direktor-Stellvertreter* (the vice-director), *der Diener* (the servant), and so on are names for the members of the Bank's hierarchy. The set of the Court's representatives, designated by fixed definite descriptions, is much larger: *der Aufseher* (the supervisor), *der Untersuchungsrichter* (the examining magistrate), *der Gerichtsdiener* (the Court attendant), *der Prügler* (the whipper), *der Richter* (the judge), *der dritte Richter* (the third judge), *der Gefängniskaplan* (the prison chaplain), and so on. The designation for *der Angeklagte*, which can function as a definite description, links with this mode of naming; it is used for several minor characters, but in the case of Joseph K. and Block it serves as a secondary name of major characters.

Both the negative and the positive sides of naming by fixed definite descriptions are semantically significant. On the negative side, the agents of the Bank and of the Court are deprived of a standard mode of naming, a proper name. On the positive side, the fixed definite description designates the function or position of the agent in the hierarchy of his institution. The agents are presented as institutional roles, rather than as private individuals; their individual identity has been absorbed by their institutional role.

As can be seen, the intensional function of naming contributes substantially to the structuring of the fictional world of *The Trial*; in particular, it reinforces the split of the world into a private and a public (institutionalized) domain. In the private domain, the agents are designated by standard proper names, typical of human individuals. The exclusive non-standard name of the protagonist (an abbreviation) expresses the uniqueness of this character. In the public domain, the agents, designated by their positions and responsibilities in the institutional hierarchy, appear as roles without true individuality. At the same time, by associating the agents of the Bank with the agents of the Court, this mode of naming bridges the deep semantic contrast between the two institutions; they now appear as two opposite modes of one and the same activity, the institutionalized social activity alienated from and imposed on private individuals.

Two minor details confirm this description of the semantic splits and linkages generated by the intensional function of naming: among the Bank's employees, three insignificant clerks are assigned proper names: *Rabendsteiner, Kullich, Kaminer*. On the side of the Court, Joseph K.'s wardens are also known under their first names *Franz* and *Willem*. This mode of naming corresponds to the relationship which these agents assume with respect to the protagonist: they are drawn into the hero's private group, following him not only in their 'roles' but also in their 'human' interest. The case of the protagonist himself is more significant in this respect. As a private citizen he is named *Joseph K.*, while in his institutional roles he is assigned fixed descriptions: he is *Herr Prokurist* (Herr Assessor) in the system of the Bank, and *der Angeklagte* (the defendant) in the hierarchy of the Court. Thus the one-member set represented by the protagonist is an intersection of all the three domains of the fictional world of *The Trial*, i.e. the private domain and the institutional domains. The pivotal position of *Joseph K.*, alias *Herr Prokurist*, alias *der Angeklagte* in the structure of the fictional world and in the story of *The Trial* is confirmed by the text's style.

3 Suspicious executioners. It is striking to discover that the two gentlemen who appear in the last chapter of *The Trial* to kill Joseph K. are not named in accordance with the intensional function controlling the assignment of names in this text. If the court has its *judges, magistrates, whippers, wardens,* and *prison chaplains*, it could be expected to have its well-appointed and properly named *executioners*. However, the naming of the two gentlemen from chapter 10 remains in the vague mode of unstable descriptions; in the narrator's text, they are designated as *zwei Herren* (two gentlemen), *die Herren* (the gentlemen), and *seine Begleiter* (his companions); in K.'s inner monologue, they are *alte*

untergeordnete Schauspieler (old, minor actors), *vielleicht ... Tenöre* (maybe ... tenors). (K. even asks one of them in which theatre they perform.)

This absence of the expected mode of naming could be explained away as an exception, if it was clearly established in the text that the gentlemen are representatives of the Court. However, unlike the wardens of chapter 1, they do not claim to act according to a commission (*Auftrag*); they make just a silent sign in answer to K.'s rather indefinite question. The association of these agents with the Court is expressed neither explicitly nor by the semantic indicator of naming. Thus the text forces us to acknowledge that the identity of K.'s killers is uncertain. Should we assume that they are not at all connected with the Court? Should we interpret K.'s 'execution' as an event which was not 'ordered' by the Court? A positive answer to this question would bring a new aspect into the semantic interpretation of *The Trial*. If K.'s execution cannot be traced to the Court, then it is a random, unmotivated event coming from another, unknown realm. Such a twist in the line of the story would indicate that Kafka wrote not only *The Trial* but also, in the last chapter, a parody of it, specifically a parody of the rules governing its fictional world. We know that the Court's proceedings and decisions are purely random and arbitrary; consequently, any random and arbitrary event, if its origins are not specified, will be interpreted as originating from the authority of the Court. The final event of K.'s tragedy has been interpreted as such without question. Our investigation of the modes of naming in the texture of the novel suggests that this interpretation is far from self-evident. We are faced with a textual fact which forces us to contemplate a new interpretive hypothesis: in Kafka's fictional world, there exists a higher degree, absolute, non-institutionalized randomness represented by 'freelancing' agents. A systematic stylistic analysis of the text reveals its potential: it is a challenge to the habitual interpretations offered by readers and critics.

This paper is based on the claim that a circumscribed fictional world and an idiosyncratic style represent the strongest warranties of the individual identity of the literary text. In the course of our discussion, it became obvious that the two pillars of the text's identity are not randomly selected features; rather, they are theoretically linked by the concept of intensional function, a function projecting the fictional world onto a specific texture. Furthermore, it quickly became apparent that the problem of the individual identity of the literary text has to be tackled in close association with the problem of semantic interpretation, owing to the fact that the identity of the literary text is undermined by the plurality of the readers' possible interpretations. The development of the concept of fictional world has led to the formulation of four general theses on interpretation. The investigation of the literary style of a concrete text (Kafka's

The Trial) has demonstrated the validity of our second and most important thesis on interpretation: text analysis is the only reliable route leading to verifiable semantic interpretations. In analysing Kafka's text with respect to the regularities of naming, we have discovered basic patterns of its semantic organization, justifying a specific interpretation. Moreover, a strange deviation from the regularity has forced us to reconsider the standard interpretation and to propose a new interpretive hypothesis.

A meticulous attention to the text, discarding no details as insignificant, is the essential method of literary semantics, as it used to be in classical hermeneutics. The authority of the text cannot be replaced by intentions of ghost authors or by readings of ghost readers or 'interpretive communities.' The literary text will reveal its secrets to those who are willing to listen to it with concentrated attention and devoted humbleness.

NOTES

1 There is one problem of the text's identity which is located on the level of material form, one arising in connection with the possible 'reproductions' of literary texts. In this respect, literature stands between the visual arts (original–copy) and the performing arts (score–performance). Margolis (1980, pp. 51–76) discusses the problem in terms of the type/token relationship, using 'identity' and 'individuation' as synonymous designations of this aspect. Although there is a similarity between interpretation and performance (Margolis, 1980, p. 116f.), 'individuation' under different reproductions is to be clearly distinguished from 'identity' under different interpretations.

2 The traditional discipline of interpretation, hermeneutics, at least in its empirical branch, has moved very close to text theory in Ricoeur's project: 'Hermeneutics is the theory of the operations of understanding in their relation to the interpretation of texts.' Its basic concern is 'the elaboration of the categories of the text' (Ricoeur, 1981, p. 43).

3 I am leaving aside two assumptions of literary semantics, which are indispensable in any general discussion, but are not essential for the topic at hand: (a) the postulate to treat meaning in literature as an aesthetic phenomenon; (b) the necessity of differentiating the primary ('literal') and the secondary ('transposed') levels of meaning.

4 The general framework of this theoretical assumption is discussed in Doležel, forthcoming. To prevent misunderstandings, we have to mention that the analyst cannot, of course, bypass reading; however, his mode of reading has specific characteristics given by its final, cognitive goal. It is desirable to introduce different terms for the

practical and theoretical procedures of interpretation. Such a differentiation – which is beyond the aims of this paper – would be the first step in a general terminological revision, attacking the burdensome polysemy of the term 'interpretation' (for a brief survey of its uses, see Juhl, 1980, pp. 3–10).

5 In his alternative epistemology of 'affective stylistics' Fish proposes to shift the focus of attention 'from spatial context of a page and its observable regularities to the temporal context of a mind and its experiences' (Fish, 1980, p. 91). It should be noted that this is an invitation to a purely mystical trip, unless some methods of direct access to the 'mind and its experiences' are specified. If we recognize that, at present, the only sufficiently reliable access to the reader's mind is his own spontaneous or elicited texts, then we are back where we started: instead of interpreting literary texts, we have to interpret the reader's texts (or the texts of interpretive communities).

6 This situation justifies Booth's suspicion that 'most readers most of the time read most parts of most works in identical ways' (Booth, 1976, p. 412). This suspicion seems to be borne out by preliminary empirical investigations of readers' interpretations, indicating that the scope of individual variety is restricted: 'Reading and responding to poems is not entirely an idiosyncratic and subjective experience, ... substantial agreements may be found regarding matters of structure and meaning' (Fairley, 1979, p. 349).

7 To make the distinction between the sentences of the original text and the paraphrase statements quite explicit, Pavel has designated the latter as *ersatz sentences* (Pavel, 1976).

8 It has been correctly noted that the 'absolute certainty' of fictional facts 'is never completely reached in non-fictional narratives' (Ryan, ms.).

9 For a detailed discussion of the theory of authentication, see Doležel, 1980a.

10 There is no denying that there is an author behind every text, but it is dubious or tautological to claim that the author's intentions provide the criterion of validity of interpretation. The author does not communicate as a physical persona, but rather as the constructor of a fictional world and as the idiosyncratic source of a literary style.

11 I am modifying an example given in a recent study of this problem (Heintz, 1979).

12 Fictional worlds share the property of incompleteness with dream worlds (cf. Parsons, 1980, p. 209).

13 For a brief demonstration of such an analysis, see Doležel, 1980b.

14 If Iser's 'blanks' (including 'missing links') are understood as 'the implicit' which has to be 'brought to light' (Iser, 1978, p. 169), then they fall under the scope of our thesis 3; the filling-in by implication will not destroy the incompleteness of the fictional world. We have to emphasize, however, that the domains constructed by implication are of a different semantic character from those constructed by the explicit text.

15 In fact, we can observe how the specific problem of truth-valuation merges with the general problem of interpretation in theses 3 and 4.

16 Even if we had a generally accepted theory of interpretation, single interpretations would be impossible in the most interesting case, i.e. in the case of ambiguous or polysemic texts. While for some ambiguous texts the process of disambiguation is available, there exist texts (or maybe whole genres) which cannot be disambiguated into exclusive or alternative meanings, but where several complementary meanings coexist (cf. Eco, 1980).

17 The formulation of an explicit theory of interpretation will be deemed irrelevant by those who practise interpretation not as a cognitive but rather as a poetic enterprise, as an extension of the constructive power of literature: a poetic text is interpreted by writing another poetic text. There is no doubt that poetic interpretation might offer interesting insights into the meaning of literary texts, but such insights, it should be remembered, are gained purely by chance. The purpose of a theory of interpretation, not unlike any other theory, is to circumvent the randomness of discovery.

18 'Texture' is used here as a technical term for designating the explicit wording of the original text together with its implicit component.

19 I am leaving aside the fact that stylistically non-homogeneous literary texts exist; in such a case, global regularities operate only throughout differentiated segments of the text.

20 The theoretical background of the concept 'intensional function' is explained in Doležel, 1979.

21 The intensional difference (i.e. the difference in sense) between proper names and definite descriptions has been substantiated by Linsky: 'Two correferential singular terms cannot be identical in sense if one is a rigid designator [the case of proper names] and the other is not [the case of definite descriptions]' (Linsky, 1977, p. 68).

22 For a very helpful survey of Kafka criticism, see Beicken, 1974 and Binder, 1979.

23 A study of the system of naming (in terms of intensional function) represents a radical departure from the habitual approach to names in Kafka's work. The proper names are studied in isolation and with the assumption that they represent crypto-grams to be deciphered; the names of Kafka himself and of persons important in his life are supposed to be 'hidden' in these cryptograms. Rajec's survey of these guesses (Rajec, 1977) demonstrates quite clearly the arbitrariness and sterility of this 'method.'

24 The naming of K.'s mistresses has a 'realistic' motivation, as observed by Jaffe (1967, p. 94): the subjects of K.'s erotic interests are females of lower classes.

25 This lack of the first name is a good illustration of the incompleteness of fictional worlds, stated in thesis 4. Fräulein Bürstner inhabits a world where individuals might lack first or other names. There is no base for inference and, therefore, her first name cannot be derived (filled in).

Feigning in Fiction

I

It has long been a commonplace that literary texts are by nature fictional. Such a classification clearly distinguishes them from those texts which, according to current terminology, are regarded as expository or factual because they have a referent outside themselves. The opposition between reality and fiction is an elementary item of what the sociology of knowledge has come to call tacit knowledge – a term used to designate that storehouse of beliefs that seem so soundly based that their truth may be taken for granted. But convenient though the distinction may be, is it in fact as cut and dried as it seems? Are fictional texts truly fictions, and are non-fiction texts truly without fictions? The implications and ramifications of this question are such that it is greatly to be doubted whether our tacit knowledge will be able to help us overcome the difficulties.

A piece of fiction devoid of any connection with known reality would be incomprehensible; consequently, if we are to attempt a description of what is fictional in fiction, there seems to be little point in our clinging to the old fiction vs reality concept as a frame of reference: the literary text is a mixture of reality and fictions, and as such it brings about an interaction between the given and the imagined. This interaction produces far more than just a contrast between the two, so I suggest we discard the opposition of fiction and reality altogether and replace this duality by a triad: the real, the fictional, and what I shall term the imaginary. It is out of this triad that I see the text as arising: it cannot be confined to its real elements; nor can it be pinned down to its fictional features, for these in turn do not constitute an end in themselves but are the medium for the appearance of the imaginary.

In this triadic relation lies not only the justification for our study of the fictional but also our best means of approaching such a study. The opposition between fiction and reality presupposed a tacit knowledge of what each of them consisted of, with fiction being basically characterized by the absence of those attributes that made reality real. This somewhat questionable 'certainty' simultaneously obscured a central problem that has bedevilled modern epistemology. The form of the problem was bequeathed to the modern world by Cartesian thinking: how could something exist which, although actual and present, did not have the character of reality?[1]

Herein lies the heuristic justification for replacing the customary antithesis by the triad of the real, fictional, and imaginary, which will provide us with the background against which we may grasp the specifically fictional element of the fictional text. The fiction/reality antithesis cannot but exclude a most vital dimension of the literary text, although this is undoubtedly permeated by a vast range of identifiable items, selected from social and other extratextual realities. Their transportation into the text does not make them fictional, although they are not represented just for their own sake. Instead, this reproduction of items brings to light purposes, attitudes, and experiences that are not part of the reality reproduced and hence present themselves as products of a fictionalizing act. This act of fictionalizing cannot be deduced from the repeated reality and so clearly brings into play an imaginary quality which links up with the reality reproduced in the text. Thus the fictionalizing act converts the reality reproduced into a sign which endows the imaginary with an articulate gestalt.

The triadic relationship between the real,[2] the fictional,[3] and the imaginary[4] is basic to the literary text, and from it we can extrapolate a special quality pertaining to the fictionalizing act. Whenever realities are transposed into the text, they turn into signs for something else, which indicates that their original determinacy has been outstripped. As this is brought about by the fictionalizing act, its basic quality begins to emerge: it is a crossing of boundaries, nothing short of an act of transgression. This in turn links it to the imaginary, which according to our ordinary experience tends to manifest itself in a somewhat diffuse manner, in fleeting impressions defying our attempts to pin it down to a concrete and stabilized form. It may suddenly flash before our mind's eye in an almost arbitrary apparition, only to disappear again or to dissolve into quite another form. 'The peculiar quality of fantasy,' says Husserl, 'is its self-will. And so ideally it distinguishes itself by its absolute arbitrariness.'[5] The act of fictionalizing is therefore not identical to this protean potential of the imaginary, for it is a guided act, imbued with direction, and aiming at something which in turn endows the imaginary with an articulate gestalt – a gestalt that is quite different from the fantasies, projections, daydreams, and other reveries that ordinarily give the imaginary a direct route into our experience. Here, too, we have a stepping beyond limits, as we pass from the diffuse to the precise.

The act of fictionalizing endows the imaginary with a determinacy which it could not otherwise have, and the imaginary thus takes on an essential quality of the real, for determinacy is a minimal definition of reality. This is not to say that the imaginary now *is* real, although it certainly assumes an appearance of reality in the way it intrudes into and acts upon the given world.

We can now see two distinct processes that are set in motion by the act of fictionalizing. Reproduced reality is made to point to a 'reality' beyond itself, and the imaginary is made to take on a determinate gestalt. In each case a boundary crossing occurs: the determinacy of reality is exceeded, the diffuseness of the imaginary is transformed. Consequently, extratextual reality merges into the imaginary, and the imaginary merges into reality.

The text, then, functions as the point at which the interplay between the real, the fictional, and the imaginary emerges.[6] Although each component of the triad fulfils a different function, the act of fictionalizing is of paramount importance: it brings about a transgressing of boundaries both of that which it organizes (external reality) and of that which it converts into a gestalt (the diffuseness of the imaginary). It leads the real to the imaginary and the imaginary to the real, and it determines to what extent the given world is to be reformulated, a non-given world is to be formulated, and the formulations and reformulations are to be accessible to the reader's experience.

Given this situation, then, the old antithesis between fiction and reality is revealed as inadequate and even misleading, for as tacit knowledge it implies a system of references that can only be invalidated by the transgressing operations of the fictionalizing act. Our task now is to elucidate relations, not to define positions; there is no longer any need to assume the transcendental stance that was necessary whenever the opposition between fiction and reality had to be defined. The triad rids us of such a burden, especially if one thinks of the latter-day fate of epistemology which, in struggling to grasp the nature of fiction, ended up by having to recognize its own premises as fictions and, in the face of its ever-increasing dependence on fictions, had to forfeit its ambitious claims to being a universal explainer.

II

On the basis of this triadic relationship, we may now focus on the act of fictionalizing, which on closer inspection appears in fact to comprise three separate acts. These can be distinguished from one another according to the functions each is meant to perform, so that there are several interacting functions that bring about the merger between the real and the imaginary. It is, however, a basic characteristic of each act that it crosses a boundary of some kind.

As the product of an author, the literary text indicates a particular attitude with which the author has directed himself to the world. As this direction does not exist in the given world to which the author refers, it can only take on a form by being inserted into that world. The insertion in turn takes place not by plain mimesis of existing structures, but by a process of breaking them down. Every literary text inevitably contains a *selection* from a variety of social, historical, cultural, and literary systems that exist as referential fields outside the text. This very selection is itself a step beyond the boundary, in that the elements of reality are lifted out of the respective system in which they fulfil their specific function; this applies to both cultural norms and literary allusions that are incorporated in every new literary text.

Now this fact has several consequences. Owing to the inroads made into the various systems, the systems themselves move into focus and can be discerned as the referential fields of the text. So long as they remain organizational units of the given world, fulfilling their regulative function, they are taken for reality itself, and thus stay unobserved in the background. The act of selection, however, deconstructs their given order, thereby turning them into an object for observation. Observability is *not* a component part of the systems concerned, it can only be brought about by the act of selection. Thus the referential fields of the text are thrown in to relief, and this happens precisely through dislocating specific elements of the system by transposing them into the literary text. Systems as referential fields of the text are highlighted by the subversion of their patterning. The elements that are now incorporated into the text are not in themselves fictional, but their selection is an act of fictionalizing through which existing systems, as fields of reference, can – paradoxically – be separated from one another precisely because their boundaries are transgressed.

The observation of the referential fields gets its perspectival slant by each of the fields being split into elements that are either actualized by the text or remain dormant within it. While the chosen elements initially spotlight a field of reference, thus opening it up for perception, they bring in their wake all those elements that the selection has excluded, and these form a background against which the observation is to take place; it is as if that which is present in the text must be judged in the light of that which is absent. Thus the act of selection places defining limits on the chosen elements only in order to overstep these limits so that the present may be examined through the absent, and the absent may make its mark upon the present.

This process has the character of an event, as it defies referentiality. There are no preconceived rules governing selection, which arises out of an impenetrable choice made by the author of the text. This choice can be pinpointed only by means of the selections made, and these, in turn, reveal the attitude adopted by the author to the given world. If the act of selection were governed by a set of rules given prior to the act, then the act itself could not be qualified as one of transgressing existing boundaries, but would just be one form of actualizing a possibility within the framework of a prevailing convention. The specific form of the selective 'event' can be perceived through that which it produces. It marks off the referential fields from each other and turns them into clearly distinguishable structures whose borderlines are crossed in such a manner that existing relations are wiped out and the chosen elements are extended into new patterns. These elements are therefore differently weighted from when they had their place in the respective system. Deletion, extension, weighting – these are all basic 'Ways of Worldmaking,'[7] as outlined in Nelson Goodman's recent book.

These operations point to a purpose, although this is not formulated in the fictional text itself. Thus selection as a fictionalizing act reveals the intentionality of the text. It encapsulates extratextual realities into the text, turns the elements chosen into contexts for each other, and sets them up for observation against those elements it has excluded, thus bringing about a two-way review: of the present through the absent, and vice versa. This provides an angle from which the interrelationships are to be perceived. The whole process brings to the fore the intentional object of the text, whose reality comes about through the loss of reality suffered by those empirical elements that have been torn away from their original function by being transposed into the text.

If we can confine our discussion in this way to what the text *does*, rather than what the text is meant to do, we shall relieve ourselves of the perennial bugbear of critical analysis, namely: what was the author's actual intention?[8] The desire to penetrate the author's mind – as expressed and followed in so many lecture-halls and seminar-rooms – has led to countless investigations of the author's psyche, with results that can at the very best only be pure speculation. If we are to uncover an intention, our best chance lies not in the study of the author's dreams, philosophy, eating, and sleeping habits, etc., but in those manifestations of intentionality expressed through the selection of extratextual systems to be found in the fictional text. If the proper study of mankind is man, surely the proper study of fiction is texts, and the intentionality of a text will best be found in the way it breaks down and distances itself from those systems to which it has linked itself. The intention, therefore, is not to be found in the given world; nor is it simply something imaginary; it is the preparation of an imaginary quality for use – and this use, in turn, remains dependent on the given factors within which it is to be applied.

Selection, then, is an act of fictionalizing, in so far as it marks off from each other the referential fields of the text by both spotlighting and overstepping their respective limits. Out of this operation arises the intentionality of the text, which is to be identified neither with the system in question nor with the imaginary as such (for its determinacy depends largely on those extratextual systems to which it refers).

It is, rather, a 'transitional object' between the real and the imaginary, and it has the all-important quality of actuality. Actuality is the basic constitutive feature of an event, and the intentionality of the text is an event in the sense that it does not end with the delineation of referential fields, but breaks these down in order to transmute their elements into the material of its self-presentation. The actuality lies in the way the imaginary takes effect on the real.

III

Within the text itself there is a complement to selection as an act of fictionalizing, and this is the act of combination. The different elements that are combined range from words and their meanings, through encapsulated extratextual items, to the patterns in which characters and actions, for instance, are organized. Combination, too, is an act of fictionalizing, with the same basic mode of operation – the crossing of boundaries.

On the lexical level this is to be seen, for instance, with neologisms such as Joyce's coining of benefiction. Here, with the combination of benefaction, benediction, and fiction, lexical meanings are used to derestrict semantic limitations. The lexical meaning is faded out and a new meaning faded in by way of combination; this establishes a foreground and background relationship which allows both a separation of the individual elements and a continual switching of the viewpoint between them. In accordance with whichever reference forms the foreground or background, the semantic weighting will be shifted, Indeed it is the very instability of the references that produces the whole oscillating semantic spectrum, which cannot then be identified with any of its lexical components.

A similar derestricting effect can be seen in rhyming strategies such as Eliot uses in Prufrock:

Should I, after teas and cakes and ices,
Have the strength to force the moment to its crisis?[9]

Through their consonance, the rhymes lay stress on the semantic divergence. With similarities signalling their non-equivalence, the combination here functions as a means of revealing what is different in what is similar. Again we have foreground-background structure: the crisis is trivialized, and the ice cream can take on a hitherto unsuspected significance. The end effect with this, and many similar strategies, is a heightening of the semantic potential; the combination is so structured that the foreground-background balance can be tilted virtually at will.

These attributes on the lexical level are also to be found on the levels of selected extratextual items and textual patterns organizing the constellation of characters and their actions. Here the semantic potential is heightened to the level of a continually unfolding event. Generally the narrative text will contain semantic enclosures that are built up from selected outside items and are clearly delineated by the schematic presentation of the characters (the goodies and the baddies). But here, too, we have a basic foreground-background relationship, because as a rule the hero will step beyond the restrictions of these semantic enclosures,[10] so that the relevance of the respective field of reference will fade in and out of focus, giving rise to a whole network of possible combinations that are not to be found in the individual, given patterns of the text.

Combination as an act of fictionalizing has long been regarded as a basic feature of poetry, distinguishing it from reality. Bacon, for example, describes poetry as a process of combining 'which may at pleasure make unlawful matches and divorces of things ... it commonly exceeds the measure of nature, joining at pleasure things which in nature would never have come together, and introducing things which in nature would have never come to pass.'[11]

The extent to which statements of this kind appear to be commonplace can be gauged from the echo of Bacon's words in Locke's *Essay*, where he condemns as 'fantastical' such secondary ideas as are not to be found in nature, despite their occurrence in human communication. Of them he says: 'those are *fantastical* which are made up of such collections of simple *ideas* as were really never united, never were found together in any substance: v.g. a rational creature, consisting of a horse's head, joined to a body of human shape, or such as *centaurs* are described.'[12]

For Locke as for Bacon, a basic condition of poetry is the continual process of separating and combining in a manner not to be found in nature; with Locke even more clearly than with Bacon, this is the condition for producing something fantastical that seems to threaten the reliability of the epistemological process. These statements are solid evidence that the fictionalizing act of combination can retrieve such a degree of determinacy that the imaginary impinges upon the real.

The fictionalizing act of combination produces relationships within the text. The relating process, just like the intentionality which comes to light through the selecting process, leads to the emergence of 'fact from fiction.'[13] The relating process takes on this extraordinary 'factualness' through the degree of its determinacy and also through its effect on those elements which it relates. It is not, however, a quality of those elements, and so it does not share their independent reality, even if its determinacy does arouse the impression that it has a reality of its own. The 'factualness,' then, lies not in what it is, but in what it produces. As we have already seen with the foreground-background link between the chosen and unchosen elements, the overall process of relating not only alters the positions involved in each combination but also excludes other positions. As each relation achieves stability through what it excludes, it creates its own background of unchosen positions. These are, as it were, the shadow cast by the realized combination, helping to give it its shape; thus that which is absent is made present. But if the realized combination draws its life from that which it has excluded, the fictionalizing act of relating thus clearly brings about a co-presence of the realized and the absent, and this in turn causes the realized relations to be undermined, and makes them sink back into the shadows of background existence, so that new relations can come to the fore, gaining stability against this background. Thus the relating process oversteps the inherent limits of each position, links positions together, but then – in accordance with the intentionality of each particular text – causes the realized link itself to be overstepped by those possibilities which it has excluded.

It goes without saying that the relating process functions in many different ways. However, if we are to grasp the peculiar nature of the fictionalizing act, there are certain categories of relating that require special attention. In particular there are three levels of derestriction or boundary-crossing that can be discerned in the fictional text.

Firstly, there is the relating process that is concerned with selection of extratextual conventions, values, allusions, quotations, etc. within the text. 'Fiction can hold together within a single space a variety of languages, levels of focus, points of view, which would be contradictory in other kinds of discourse organized towards a particular empirical end.'[14] The contradictory elements of the text take on their articulate form through the relations that are established, but it is difficult to describe these sysematically because the relating process does not follow any predictable rules. On the contrary: 'The force, the power of any text, even the most unabashedly mimetic, lies in those moments which exceed our ability to categorize, which collide with our interpretive codes but nevertheless seem right.'[15] The fact that such connections appear to be convincing without being guided by any overall regulative code is due mainly to the manner in which the linked-up elements are made to extend beyond the borders of their previous validity. The revaluation becomes plausible, not least because it is continually fed by relating norms and conventions as these are lifted out of their original context and thus recoded.

This process is most evident in narrative literature, where the characters represent different norms whose value is disclosed by the relating process only in order that their inevitable limitations should serve as the starting-point for their being transgressed.

A second level of relating is to be seen in the organization of specific semantic enclosures within the text. These give rise to intratextual fields of reference, themselves brought about by the relating of the external items encapsulated in the text. Generally, these fields of reference provide the occasion for the hero to step over their boundaries, even though in principle this ought not to be possible. Such a boundary-crossing is, in Lotman's terms, a subject-creating event, which is a 'revolutionary element' in so far as it breaks down 'established classification.'[16]

This structure applies just as much to poetry as to narrative fiction, for the lyrical self is the intersecting point of the schemata that are drawn into the poem from various forms of extratextual discourse. Initially relations between the selected discourse schemata will be graduated, but they must then be exceeded if the lyrical self – as their intersecting point – is to assume its individual gestalt.[17] Like the hero of the novel, the lyrical self can emerge only by breaking out of and thereby moving beyond the semantic topography established in the poem. Thus there occurs a transcoding of those values arising from the organization of semantic enclosures within the text. Such encroachment on the semantic system built up in the text itself bears the character of an event, for the 'reference' of the ensuing semantic phase is the derestriction of that determinacy initially produced by selection and combination.

The 'actions of fictional characters interest us to the extent that they represent possibilities of relation. Fiction, in this case, is not just the *accomplishment* of relating things, but it is also a *representation* of possible relations or a communication concerning possible relations.'[18] The capacity of the relating process actually to go so far as self-presentation is an indication of the vast range of relations possible between elements, and also of the extent to which elements set up in different networks of relationships may be transformed.

The third level of relating is the lexical one which we have already discussed. This consists of the derestriction of lexical meanings through their reciprocal influence on one another: 'meanings vanish in favor of certain relationships.'[19] On this level, we can see in the fictionalizing act of combination a very special use of language. The literal meaning of words is faded out in just the same way as their denotative function. The relating process manifests itself in the derestriction of lexical meanings, encroachment on semantic enclosures, and ultimately recodings and transcodings, but it is not itself verbalized in order to be grasped in explicit statements. Consequently, relating – as the product of an act of fictionalizing – is manifested by way of the effects it conveys through language, although these effects are not themselves given linguistic expression.

Language's function of denotation is transformed by the relating process into a function of figuration. But even if the denotative character of language is expunged in this figurative use, the latter is still not devoid of references. These, however, are no longer to be equated with existing systems; their target is expression and representation. If we follow Goodman's suggestion,[20] and take expression and representation as the reference for figurative language, we shall come to two conclusions:

1   The reference is not itself of a linguistic nature; nor does it exist as objective data that would merely require denotative language to designate them. Therefore this form of language outstrips the denotative function in order to indicate, through its figurations, the linguistic untranslatability of its references.

2   At the same time – owing to its figurations – it makes its references conceivable. Thus language dwindles to an analogue which merely contains the conditions that will allow a reference to be conceived, but cannot be identical to that reference. Thus we may discern a strange ambiguity in the function of this figurative language: as an analogue it permits and conditions conceivability, and as a sign it denotes the linguistic untranslatability of that which it refers to.

The fictional quality manifested in the relating process can now be pinpointed. Combination as a fictionalizing act endows the imaginary with a specific form according to the relations to be established. This form of the imaginary eludes verbalization, but at the same time it can never dispense with language, for language points to what is to be concretized, and it also enables the concretization to be shaped and thus fed back into existing realities.

In this context, it is well worth noting that Jeremy Bentham, who was the first in the empirical tradition of philosophy to attribute a positive value to fiction, saw its existence as being anchored in language: 'To language, then – to language alone – it is, that fictitious entities owe their existence; their impossible, yet indispensable existence.'[21] The reason why fiction owes its 'impossible existence' to language is explained by Bentham with the following basic definition: 'By a fictitious entity, understand an object, the existence of which is feigned by the imagination – feigned for the purpose of discourse – and which, when so formed, is spoken of as a real one.'[22] Through language, then, fictions take on their appearance of reality; this reality comes about by way of the concrete gestalt with which the fictional endows the imaginary, which in turn can only become effective through its concrete form. As fictions can only have their existence in language, they assume their reality through the manner in which they subvert the lexical meanings of words, expunge the function of denotation, and signal the linguistic untranslatability of that to which they refer.

It is true – as Bentham said – that fictions owe their existence solely to language, but this 'impossible, yet indispensable, existence' is so constituted that it borrows the quality of reality from language in order to render conceivable something that language cannot comprise. The relating process is a basic mode of fiction – a mode that functions through language, although it is never given linguistic expression itself. Here, too, Bentham is illuminating: 'Once introduced upon the carpet, the fictitious entity called relation swells into an extent such as to swallow up all the others. Every other fictitious entity is seen to be but a mode of this.'[23]

I V

We have so far noted two fictionalized acts pertaining to the fictional text – those of *selection* and *combination*, each of which entailed the boundary-crossing of the literary and socio-cultural systems on the one hand and intratextual fields of reference on the other. As the focus shifted from selection to combination, an increasing complexity became all too evident. Combination occurred on two levels at once. Through the relating process fields of reference had to be produced from the material selected, and these fields, in turn, had to be linked up with each other, thereby being subjected to a reciprocal transformation. This differentiation is complicated still further by yet another fictionalizing act, which is the fictional text's *disclosure* of its own fictionality.

Literary texts contain a whole range of signals to denote that they are literature and therefore not reality. These signals, however, generally do not point to a contrast with reality as much as to the fact that fiction's 'otherness' cannot be grasped from stances which prevail in our everyday reality. It would take too long to run through the whole repertoire of signals by which literature discloses its own fictionality. What must be stressed, though, is that they are not exclusively to be pinned down to and equated with linguistic signs in the text, and all attempts made in this direction have proved unsuccessful. For these signals can become significant only through particular, historically varying conventions shared by author and public alike. Thus the signals do not invoke fictionality as such, but conventions, which form the basis of a kind of contract between author and reader, the terms of which identify the text not as discourse, but as 'enacted discourse.'[24] One of the most obvious and most durable of such signals is the literary genre itself, which has permitted a wide variety of contractual terms between author and reader. Even such recent inventions as the 'non-fiction novel' reveal the same contractual function, since they must invoke the convention before renouncing it.

The implications of the disclosing process are extremely far-reaching. It is a commonplace that fiction is not confined to literature: fiction plays a vital role in the activities of cognition and behaviour, as in the founding of institutions, societies and world-pictures.[25] The difference between all these and the literary text is that the latter reveals its own fictionality. Because of this, its function must be radically different from that of other activities that mask their fictional nature. The masking, of course, need not necessarily occur with the intention to deceive; it occurs because the fiction is meant to provide an explanation or a foundation, and could not do so if its fictional nature were to be exposed. The concealment of its fictionality endows the explanation provided with the *appearance* of reality, which is vital because the fiction functions as the constitutive basis of this reality.

In philosophical discourse – particularly within the empirical tradition – this state of affairs is highly conspicuous. Whenever fiction is focused upon in order to outline its achievement, the self-disclosure of its fictionality is never even considered as a possible feature of fiction. On the contrary, from Bacon to Vaihinger, fiction is being treated as if it constantly attempted to veil its true nature, in consequence of which epistemology took it upon itself to unmask it. For fictions to be useful they have to be recognized for what they are, and as long as their fictionality remains hidden, it has to be uncovered. This unmasking tendency prevailed in philosophical discourse long after the usefulness of fictions had been fully acknowledged.

Vaihinger put together a voluminous work proving that virtually everything that had ever been thought in science and philosophy was fiction. But none of the fictions that he exposed led him to recognize the special attribute of the literary fiction – namely, that it discloses its own fictionalizing. Regardless of their judgment and evaluations, it is undeniable that philosophers from Bacon to Vaihinger are constantly preoccupied with exposing the fictionality of fiction, even in those cases where they fully recognize the importance of fiction, in gaining access to the 'real' world. Herein lies the dilemma of philosophical discourse in its attempt to gain a cognitive grasp of that which seems to constitute cognition. The necessity to unmask fiction even when its heuristic value is not in question, and to prevent it from pretending to be reality, harks back as far as Bacon, who equated fictions with idols in the sense that by veiling their true character they begin to assume the character of real objects.[26] Reified fictions, however, are dangerous, as they eclipse an insight emerging at the threshhold of the modern world that there are things which not only elude but defy representation. To equate an expanding world with forms of its representation would be a fatal self-imprisonment of man in his own conceptions. Even Vaihinger sees himself obliged to unmask the model of the atom as a useful fiction so that he can destroy the long-held belief of the physicist that atoms exist and that therefore the atom model represents an objective reality.[27] The problem for him and others who concern themselves with fictions is that on the one hand he must acknowledge their practical function, but on the other hand he must deny their reality in order to prevent their usefulness from assuming the character of reality. If the necessity to unmask fictions in spite of their acknowledged usefulness is basic to philosophical discourse, two consequences are bound to ensue: (1) the ambivalence of an epistemological approach, which exposes fiction for what it is, and yet endorses its usefulness, without questioning how that usefulness comes about; and (2) the constant need for philosophical discourse to restore to fiction the essential attribute that it must be *known* to be fiction in order to *be* fiction.

If this restoration can only be accomplished by unmasking the fictionality, the problem arises of what the transcendental stance could be from which one can distinguish between the fictional and the real, as well as justify such a distinction. And would not such a position itself be a fiction that has not yet acknowledged its own fictionality? This is a problem that does not apply to the self-disclosing fictional text. Even if the apparent reality is felt to be identical to the reality of the outside world, the only unmasking to be done will be that of the reader's *attitude* to the fiction, not of the fiction itself. It is even possible for literature itself to point up the processes that lead to these attitudes. For instance, in Fielding's *Tom Jones*, Partridge takes a performance of *Hamlet* for reality and not a play, and in view of the dreadful goings-on he finds it necessary to intervene.[28] In *A Midsummer Night's Dream* Shakespeare himself provides a perfect example when the artisans act their play and remind their audience that they need not be afraid of the lion, which is not a real one but is being played by Snug the joiner. The unmasking here does not concern the fictionality of the text, which is clear to everyone, but the naïvety of an attitude which cannot distinguish between fact and fiction, and therefore cannot register the signals of the fictional convention.

Our glance at the role of fiction in philosophical discourse has brought out two things: (1) Self-disclosure of fictionality appears to be a basic attribute of fiction, but – should a fiction fail to self-disclose of its own accord – it has to be unmasked. (2) When a fiction signals its own fictionality, it will necessitate an attitude different from that adopted towards fictions that hide their fictionality. The philosopher's hunt for fictions is accompanied by the desire to ensure that they should not become objects of the 'reality' they represent; similarly, the self-disclosing of the literary text proves that, as fictionalizing, it is not identical to that which *it* represents.

It is time now to remind ourselves that the fictional text does contain a large number of identifiable items from the outside world as well as from previous literature. These recognizable 'realities,' however, are marked as being fictionalized. Thus the incorporated 'real' world is, so to speak, placed in brackets, to indicate that it is not something given but is merely to be understood *as if* it were given. In self-disclosing its fictionality, an important feature of the fictional text comes to the fore: it turns the whole of the world organized in the text into an 'as-if' construction. In the light of this qualification (implicitly accepted the moment we embark on our reading), it is clear that we must and do suspend all natural attitudes as adopted towards the 'real' world, once we are confronted with the represented world. This is not present for its own sake; nor is its function exhausted merely by its denoting an outside reality. Just as the incorporated 'real' world is bracketed off, so too are our natural attitudes.

Here we can see a first vital difference between the literary fiction and the fiction that masks its fictionality: in the latter, our natural attitudes continue. Indeed it may even be a function of the masking to leave natural attitudes intact, in order that the fiction may be construed as a reality capable of explaining realities. But where the world and our attitudes are fenced off, that world cannot then be an object in itself; it must be the object of whatever kind of study or manipulation the text is geared to. Reality, then, may be reproduced in the fictional text, but it is there in order to be outstripped, as is indicated by its being bracketed. Whenever bracketing occurs, a purpose makes itself felt which can never be a property of the world represented, not least because the represented world is built up out of a selection of items from the world outside. In this overarching purpose the pragmatic function of the fictional work is adumbrated – for fictions are inextricably tied to their use. The reality represented in the text is not meant to represent reality – it is a pointer to something which it is not, although its function is to make that something conceivable.

This function has been characteristic of literature at least since the Renaissance. It is in the pastoral works of that time that fiction first takes itself as its own subject matter. There are indications in the pastoral poems, romances, and dramas that the rustic life of the shepherds represented in them is not meant to signify a pastoral world, but is itself a signifier for something else. Spenser makes it quite clear that what he is 'feigning' in his eclogues aims at bringing to light a hidden 'secret meaning.'[29] The rustic world represented is not what is aimed at, and so the world bracketed off in the fictionalizing act is made to lose its reality in order that the hidden reference may emerge as a new and present reality. And this process has remained common to all fiction ever since.

In order to understand it more fully, we might perhaps take a closer look at the 'as-if' construction mentioned above. As Vaihinger points out, the conjunctions signify 'that the condition set up is an unreal or impossible one.'[30] The world occurring in the fictional text is judged as if it were a reality, but the comparison is only implicit – what is in the text is linked up with something it is not. 'Thus equating something concrete with the necessary consequences of an impossible or unreal case is the claim articulated by these conjunctions ... thus an impossible case is to be made up, the necessary conlusions are drawn from it, and, equated with these conclusions, – which ought themselves to be equally impossible – are claims which do not issue forth from the existing reality.'[31] The 'as-if' construction serves to 'equate an existing something with the consequences of an unreal or impossible case.'[32] If the fictional text combines the represented 'real' world with an 'impossible' one, the resultant representation will lead to the determinacy of something that by nature must be indeterminate. This, then, is the imaginary which the acts of fictionalizing mediate through the world represented in the text. In Vaihinger's words, again: 'wherever an imaginative comparison or a comparison with something imaginative takes place, and this comparison is not merely an empty game of ideas but has a practical purpose through which the comparison may lead to consequences, the conjunctions "as-if" take their rightful place, because ... they compare an existing something with the necessary consequences of an imaginary case. Here it must be emphasized that this imaginative activity must have some practical use, some purpose: only if this is so will the consequences emerge from that imaginative function; it is not a question of aimlessly accepting an unreality as real.'[33] And so if the 'imaginative' attains its gestalt in the purpose, clearly the represented world cannot constitute that purpose but is, rather, the point of comparison which enables the pragmatic dimension of the text to become conceivable.

This function is fulfilled by the represented world in so far as representation itself is of a dual nature: it may have a denotative or a figurative reference. The concreteness of the represented world appears to denote a given world, but we have seen from our study of the fictionalizing acts of selection and combination that in fact it cannot be identical to any given world as it has arisen out of a prevailing intentionality and a relating process. Consequently, the world represented in the text is neither totally denotative nor totally representative of any given world. This may be one of the reasons why in semiotics these fictional worlds of the text are sometimes termed self-referential. If self-referentiality is due to a fading out of the denotative function, then the iconic signs assume a figurative reference. The given boundaries of the world represented have to be exceeded in order to turn this world into an analogue for what is to be conceived, thus bringing the 'as-if' to full fruition. Taking into account that the world represented is in itself the product of fictionalizing acts, the 'as-if' in once again overstepping this emergent world highlights the transgressing of boundaries as the basic quality of fictionalizing. The acts described so far are geared to each other, allowing for a graded reformulation of given realities and thereby enabling us to grasp both these realities and the process of their reformulation.

The importance of the distinction between a denotative and a figurative reference in representation is strikingly illustrated by Dürrenmatt's criticism of Giorgio Strehler's production of his play *Der Besuch der Alten Dame*. Dürrenmatt claimed that Strehler had blundered by presenting the scene in the station, like all the other scenes, as realistically as possible. He complained that this striving after realism could only destroy his play, because he had filled it with allusions that were meant constantly to remind the audience that they were watching theatre. In other words, Dürrenmatt's play was permeated by fictional signals which indicated that the world represented was to appear in the mode of our 'as-if' construction. The moment the director eliminated these signals, and hence the 'as-if' construction, he shifted the emphasis of presentation to that of a specific reality which the theatre-goer could verify in his own empirical world.

Such a production, by striving to *denote* reality, could only fail to fulfil its *figurative* role which, however vital for its author, was left hollow. Increasing an illusion of reality through an exclusive foregrounding of the denotative function, it was bound to raise the question of what such a representation was meant to achieve. For if we are confronted with something we already know for ourselves, the representation – unless it offers some especially refined technique – will strike us as redundant. If, however, redundancy itself were a mode of representation, then the figurative function would make its presence felt, since the redundancy would not be present for its own sake but would represent something else. This indeed is a mode used nowadays by documentary fiction, though it was clearly not the mode intended by Dürrenmatt.

It is evident from Dürrenmatt's remarks that the attempt to translate fiction back into reality involves the undoing of the 'as-if' dimension. The represented world ceases to be a basis for that which is to be conceived. If that leads to the destruction of the world represented, then second thoughts begin to arise as to whether representation can really be squared with mimesis. At the same time, the world represented cannot take on its determinate form or its truth of its own accord, but – owing to its being bracketed – must find these through its relatedness to something else. Strehler's 'blunder' vividly illustrates the duality of the represented world, which in an accurate production would only have retained enough of its denotative function to provide a basis for its figurative one (i.e. to enable the world to be experienced *as if* it were real). Denotation, then, has to be deprived of its original function if the world designated is only to be taken *as if* it were real, and through this change it fulfils the purpose foreshadowed by its figurative use. If the denotative function is reversed by making it fade into the figurative one, the dual nature of the represented world moves into focus: it is concrete enough to be perceived as a world, and simultaneously figures as an analogue exemplifying, through a concrete specimen, what the world is like. Thus an individual world merges into the general, and the general may then become a particular experience. We must now examine how this experience is brought about.

As the world of the text is to be taken only *as if* it were real, it cannot be present for its own sake. It becomes a part of a comparison which – according to the 'as-if' construction – has to be related to something 'impossible' or 'unreal' (i.e. in either case to something other than itself). To be viewed as … appears to be the purpose of the relationship to be established, and this implies creating a position from which the represented world becomes observable.

For it is not a characteristic of the world that it should possess the quality of its own observability. Thus the 'as-if' fiction uses the represented world to stimulate affective reactions in the reader. Attitudes will be produced through which the represented world will be gone beyond, while at the same time the 'impossible' or 'unreal' will take on a particular gestalt. As the represented world is not a world, but the reader imagines it as if it were one, clearly his reactions must be shaped and guided by that representation. Thus the 'as-if' fiction triggers acts of ideation in the recipient, making him conceive what the world of the text stands for or what it is meant to bring about. This activity eludes qualification as either subjective or objective, for the stimulated conceivability is patterned by the world represented, the surpassing of which will move it into perspective for the recipient. In this very process of ideation, again boundaries are overstepped: the world of the text is given life, and thus contact is established with a hitherto non-existent world. From the vantage-point of this hitherto non-existent world, the reader, in turn, may gain a new view of the world incorporated in the text. This two-way relationship spotlights both the practical use of the represented world as an analogue, and the significance of the experience it conditions.

Now let us briefly summarize what the fictionalizing act of the 'as-if' is able to accomplish. Self-disclosure of fictionality puts the world represented in brackets, thereby indicating the presence of a purpose which turns out to be observability of the world represented. Observability requires a stance, the necessity of which causes attitudes to be adopted by the recipient, who is made to react to what he is given to observe. Thus the purpose of the self-disclosing fiction comes to light.

Furthermore, if the world represented is not meant to denote a given world and hence is turned into an analogue, it may serve two different purposes at once. The reaction provoked by it could be directed towards conceiving what it is meant to 'figure forth.'[34] The analogue, however, could simultaneously direct the reaction to the empirical world from which the textual world has been drawn – allowing this very world to be perceived from a vantage-point which has never been part of it. In this case the reverse side of things will come into view. The very duality of the analogue will never exclude either of the two possibilities; in fact they appear to interpenetrate, making conceivable what would otherwise remain hidden.

At this point it is worth noting a substantial difference between the fictional and the symbolic. The 'as-if' construction brackets the reality represented in the text, thus indicating a hidden purpose. This purpose becomes manifest in proportion to the use the fiction is meant to have. The symbol, on the other hand, is not to be defined in terms of pragmatics. What it has to represent is a totality posited prior to symbolization and now to be rendered visible and identifiable. The symbol stands for a reality, whereas the 'as-if' serves to call forth reactions to that which it has bracketed. The 'as-if,' then, *leads* to a reality, whereas the symbol purports to *be* one. This is why, even in different historical situations, fiction can continue to be effective, which is certainly not always true of symbols.

The fictional 'as-if' stimulates attitudes to be adopted by the reader towards the world bracketed in the text, thus making him react to what he is given to imagine. Now the question arises whether these ideational activities released by the textual world have repercussions on the reader himself. In other words, does the 'as-if' not only cause an overstepping of the bracketed world, but also instigate the reader to extend beyond his habitual dispositions?

To help us answer this question, let us consider the concrete example of an actor playing the role of Hamlet. He cannot identify himself totally with Hamlet, not least because even he does not know precisely who Hamlet might be. Thus he must always remain partly himself, which means that his body, his feelings, and his mind function as an analogue, enabling him to represent that which he is not; this duality makes it possible for him to offer a particular embodiment of that which Hamlet might be. In order to produce the determinate form of an unreal character, the actor must fade out of his own reality.[35] Similarly with each of us as readers: to imagine what has been stimulated by the 'as-if' entails placing our faculties at the disposal of an unreality and bestowing on it a semblance of reality in proportion to a reducing of our *own* reality.

If the fictional 'as-if' is able to cause such a turnabout, then, structurally at least, this process endows our reaction to the textual world with the quality of an event. This event arises out of a crossing of boundaries and can no longer be equated with given frameworks, the surpassing of which qualifies the fictionalizing act. Our consequent journey to new and unverifiable meanings is what translates the imaginary into an experience – an experience which is shaped by the degree of determinacy given to the imaginary by the fictional 'as-if.' The event, as we experience it, is open-ended, giving rise to a tension that demands to be resolved, but resolution can only take place if that which has manifested itself in the event can be made to mean something. We know from gestalt psychology that the grouping activity involved in both mental and physical perception always tends towards closing off gestalts. Indeed it is only when a gestalt is closed that the object perceived or imagined can make its presence felt in our conscious minds. For this reason, we continually try new arrangements of data until we can pattern them in such a way that the tension is resolved and a degree of determinacy achieved by which the gestalt may be closed. In the same way, the fictional in the text sets and then transgresses boundaries in order to endow the imaginary with that degree of concreteness necessary for it to be effective; the effect is the result of the reader's need to close the event and to master the experience of the imaginary.

At this juncture it is worth considering one of the important findings of psycholinguistics – namely, the fact that all linguistic utterances are accompanied by the 'expectation of meaningfulness.'[36] For every utterance arouses the feeling that it must have a specific meaning, although at the same time it should be remembered that whoever wants to understand language must understand more than just language itself.[37] It is therefore only natural that the experience of the imaginary should set off in the reader the urge to impose meaning, so that he may bring the experience back to the level of what is familiar; this, however, runs contrary to the character of the experience itself, in so far as it can only become an experience by overstepping the borders of what is familiar. But even if the reader is aware of this fact, his knowledge will not prevent him from sounding out this event as to its possible meaningfulness. This drive is both natural and unavoidable. The expectancy of meaningfulness and the activities resulting from it have their origin in the tension brought about by the open-ended event indicating the presence of the imaginary, and so any meaning imposed must be in the nature of a pragmatization of the imaginary. Consequently meaning is not inscribed in the text as a solid be-all and end-all, but is rather an inevitable operation of transmutation triggered and sustained by the necessity to cope with the experience of the imaginary.

Should we, however, be inclined to consider meaning as the generating matrix of the text, the suspicion will mount that we interpolate our need for semantic closure as the basis of the text. Psychologically such an interpolation is thoroughly understandable, for it not only relieves the tension of the open-ended event but also meets our expectations of meaningfulness accompanying utterance. However, it also suppresses the vital fact that if we are to understand language, we must understand more than language, and this understanding is not confined to our tacit knowledge; it also applies to the ways and means by which we extend ourselves beyond what we are.

By moving these semantic operations into perspective, we are not trying to say that they have to be dispensed with. On the contrary, they are important in so far as they reveal the inescapable necessity of pragmatizing the imaginary; they embody the whole transmuting process by which we can assimilate an experience that arises out of our stepping beyond ourselves. If the fictional 'as-if' is considered to be a medium for moulding the appearance of the imaginary, the semantic operations conducted by the recipient translate this appearance into an understanding of what has happened. Thus the imaginary is both shaped and transmuted in these two interlocking phases; it turns out to be the constitutive basis of the text. If instead we were to interpolate meaning as the text's source, which we are so prone to do, we would definitely eclipse the very dimension out of which meaning arises.

The existence of this dimension is already abundantly clear from the history of interpretation, which shows how the same text can be understood in many different ways, according to the prevailing codes which have been brought to bear on the text. If the generative multiplicity of meaning – though enclosed within the literary horizon of the text – is not due to the inadequacies of thousands of Sisyphuses trundling in vain towards the hidden meaning, then polysemia sets limits on semantics itself. Furthermore it adumbrates a dimension accessible to experience without ever being pinned down, let alone exhausted by a semantic definition. Semantics can no longer be conceived as the principal referent when the constitutive matrix of the text comes under consideration. It is precisely for this reason that the same text can make 'sense' in a variety of historical situations, and as the sense itself is capable of many variations, it follows that any one meaning is merely a limited, pragmatic construction, not an exhaustive and objective datum. Instead of seeking to pin down a single meaning, we should be better advised to recognize the multiplicity of possible interpretations as a sign of the multiple availability of the imaginary.

V

All the acts of fictionalizing that we have distinguished within the fictional text have in common the fact that they are acts of boundary-crossing. Selection transgresses the limits of extratextual systems as well as the boundaries of the text itself by pointing to the referential fields which link the text to that which is beyond the page. Combination transgresses the semantic enclosures established in the text, ranging from the deconstruction of lexical meanings to the build-up of the principal event by making the hero infringe strictly enforced borderlines. Through the 'as-if' construction, fiction discloses its own fictionality, thus transgressing the represented world set up by the acts of selection and combination; it brackets this world and thereby indicates that it is to be used for an as yet undiscovered purpose. The self-disclosure has a twofold significance: firstly, it shows that the fiction can be known as a fiction; secondly, it shows that the represented world is only to be conceived as if it *were* a world in order that it should be seen to represent something other than itself. The text brings about one more boundary-crossing within the reader's experience: it stimulates attitudes towards an unreal world, the unfolding of which leads to the temporary displacement of the reader's own reality.

All these acts are interdependent, and in the main one can only distinguish between them by means of their functions. Being acts of boundary-crossing is their common feature, which, however, lends itself to remarkable diversification according to the operational intent of each of the acts. Thus multiple boundary-crossing becomes the function of the fictional text. The interrelationship of the fictionalizing act marks different stages of a continual, however distinctly graded, process of transformation, each one fading out the reality of whatever has preceded it or whatever is its referent: in selection it is the structure and validity of extratextual systems; in combination it is the existing relation between semantic enclosures; in self-disclosure it is the reader's habitual attitudes towards the represented world of the fictional 'as-if,' and ultimately it is the reader's own experience of himself and the world in view of the reaction stimulated by the textual event he finds himself confronted with. This interlocking sequence turns out to be a process of negating given realities. The consecutive acts undercut what they have invoked by their transgressing existing boundaries. In this respect the imaginary assumes its determinacy by way of the realities that the different acts negate. The fictional, then, cannot be separated from the real to which it refers and which it transgresses, and it is through both the determinacy of the fictional and its reference to existing realities that the imaginary can become an experience. Thus the fictionalizing acts mediate the dialectics between the real and the imaginary in the fictional text. In continually reordering realities given or posited, they reformulate them by overstepping them. Whatever has been outstripped can now be viewed from a stance beyond itself and turns out to be graspable. As the acts of fictionalizing are geared to each other and have a clearly punctuated sequence, their differing types of boundary-crossing ensure comprehension of a transformed world that issues forth from them.

The acts of fictionalizing to be discerned in the fictional text can be clearly distinguished by the different gestalt each of them brings about: selection results in intentionality; combination results in relatedness; self-disclosure leads to what we have called bracketing. In all cases they might be described by the phrase already quoted from Goodman: 'fact from fiction.'[38] They are, as we have seen, neither inherent in that which they refer to, nor identical to the imaginary. They are the non-given in relation to the given, and they are the determinate in relation to the imaginary. The fictional, then, might be called a 'transitional object,'[39] always hovering between the real and the imaginary, linking the two together. As such it exists, for it houses all the processes of interchange, and yet in another sense, it does not exist as a discrete entity, for it consists of nothing but these transformational processes.

Just like the meaning, the fictional element of fiction cannot be the basic constituent of the text. Meaning is primarily the semantic operation that takes place between the given text, as a fictional gestalt of the imaginary, and the reader: hence it is a pragmatization of the imaginary. The fictional, in turn, is a negating act which brings about a transformation of the realities incorporated in or posited by the text by overstepping them: hence it is a medium for the imaginary. While the imaginary attains its concreteness and its effectiveness by way of the fictional, its appearance will be conditioned by language. To be pressured into a linguistic structure, the imaginary inscribes itself into this structure by making it open-ended. This openness applies to all the gestalts we have mentioned, from intentionality through relatedness to bracketing.

There is no verbalization of the reason why certain choices have been made from extratextual realities through which intentionality manifests itself. There is no verbalization of the relatedness of semantic enclosures, let alone of the revolutionary event of their transgression, and there is no verbalization of the purpose underlying the bracketing of worlds and our natural attitudes towards them. Thus the cardinal points of the text defy verbalization, and indeed it is only through these open structures within the linguistic patterning of the text that the imaginary can manifest its presence. And from this fact we can deduce one last achievement of the fictional: as a negating act it brings about the presence of the imaginary by transgressing language itself. In outstripping that which conditions it, the imaginary reveals itself as the generative matrix of the text.

NOTES

1 The important role fiction has played in epistemology, most clearly represented in its various stages and turning-points by Bacon, Locke, Hume, Bentham, and

Vaihinger, calls for a separate investigation altogether, the execution of which promises insights into the function of fiction, which is quite different from that of the literary text and hence has to be reserved for a more comprehensive study.

2 For our present purpose, the 'real' should be understood as referring to the empirical world, which is a 'given' for the literary text and generally provides the text's multiple fields of reference. These may be thought systems, social systems, and world pictures as well as other texts with their own specific organization or interpretation of reality. 'Reality,' then, is the variety of discourses relevant to the author's approach to the world through the text.

3 By 'fictional' here is meant an intentional *act*, which has all the qualities pertaining to an event and thus relieves the definition of fiction from the burden of making the customary ontological statements regarding what fiction is. The time-honoured definition of fiction as an unreality, lies, and deceit usually serves as a contrast to something else (so-called reality), and this tends to obscure rather than illuminate the special quality of the fictional.

4 I have introduced the term 'imaginary' as a comparatively neutral concept that has as yet not been permeated by traditional associations. Terms such as imagination or fantasy would be unsuitable, as they carry far too many known associations and are frequently defined as human faculties comparable to and distinguishable from other faculties. The term fantasy, for example, meant something quite different in German Idealism from what it meant in psychoanalysis, and in the latter field Freud and Lacan had quite different notions of it. As far as the literary text is concerned, the imaginary is not to be viewed as a human faculty; our concern is with its modes of manifestation and operation, so that the word is indicative of a program rather than a definition. We must find out how the imaginary functions, approaching it by way of describable effects, and this we shall attempt to do by examining the connection between the fictional and the imaginary.

5 Edmund Husserl, *Phantasie, Bildbewusstsein, Erinnerung*, Gesammelte Werke XXIII, ed. Eduard Marbach, The Hague 1980, p. 535.

6 To designate the three parts of the literary text by notions which are converted adjectives bears witness to the fact that they are only components of the text, none of which could be equated with the text itself. It is their interrelation out of which the text arises.

7 See Nelson Goodman, *Ways of Worldmaking*, Indianapolis 1978, pp. 10–17 and 101f.

8 Frequently the ambivalence contained in the notion of 'author's intention' is glossed over. Intention as a biographical fact of the author is more often than not equated with intentionality in the phenomenological sense of the word as an act directed towards an intentional object. Whenever this distinction is allowed to collapse, confusion ensues.

9 T.S. Eliot, *Collected Poems 1909–1935*, London 1954, pp. 13f.

10 See Juri M. Lotman, *Die Struktur literarischer Texte*, German trans. Rolf-Dietrich Keil, Munich 1972, pp. 342ff.

11 Francis Bacon, *The Works* IV, ed. James Spedding et al., London 1860, pp. 315 and 292.

12 John Locke, *An Essay Concerning Human Understanding*, II, 30, London 1971, p. 316.

13 See Goodman, *Ways of Worldmaking*, p. 102.

14 Jonathan Culler, *Structuralist Poetics: Structuralism, Linguistics, and the Study of Literature*, Ithaca 1975, p. 261.

15 Ibid.

16 Lotman, *Die Struktur*, p. 334.

17 See Karlheinz Stierle, 'Die Identität des Gedichts. Hölderlin als Paradigma,' in *Identität* (Poetik und Hermeneutik VIII), ed. Odo Marquard and Karlheinz Stierle, München 1979, pp. 505–52 as well as my response, titled 'Figurationen des lyrischen Subjekts,' ibid., pp. 746–9, in which I try to elaborate on Stierle's thesis.

18 Johannes Anderegg, *Literaturwissenschaftliche Stiltheorie* (Kleine Vandenhoeck-Reihe 1429), Göttingen 1977, p. 93. The concept of relating is equally central to Anderegg's theory of style.

19 Goodman, *Ways of Worldmaking*, p. 93.

20 Ibid., pp. 29–33 and 102–7.

21 Jeremy Bentham, *Theory of Fictions*, ed. C.K. Ogden, London 1959, p. 15.

22 Ibid., p. 114.

23 Ibid., p. 29.

24 See Rainer Warning, 'Der inszenierte Diskurs. Bemerkungen zur pragmatischen Relation der Fiktion,' in *Funktionen des Fiktiven* (Poetik und Hermeneutik X), ed. Dieter Henrich and Wolfgang Iser, München 1982, pp. 183–206.

25 See, among others, Arnold Gehlen, *Urmensch und Spätkultur. Philosophische Ergebnisse und Aussagen*, Frankfurt 1975, pp. 205–16.

26 See Bacon, pp. 53–64.

27 See Hans Vaihinger, *Die Philosophie des Als-Ob*, Leipzig 1922, pp. 429–51.

28 Henry Fielding, *The History of Tom Jones*, XVI, 5, London 1957, pp. 307–11.

29 See Edmund Spenser, *The Shepherd's Calendar and Other Poems*, London 1960, pp. 6f., and the respective glosses to the eclogues, in which acts of fictionalizing are indicated, as the shepherds either 'feign' something, or implicitly stand for something which they are not. See esp. pp. 15, 16, 37, 49, 54, 55, 56, 63 and 70.

30 Vaihinger, *Die Philosophie des Als-Ob*, p. 585.

31 Ibid., pp. 585f.

32 Ibid., p. 591.

33 Ibid., p. 589.

34 This is the second time I have used this phrase. Though I am making it serve my purposes, I am aware that it has a distinguished history in literary criticism since Sidney's use of it.

35 See Jean-Paul Sartre, *Das Imaginäre. Phänomenologische Psychologie der Einbildungskraft*, German trans. Hans Schöneberg, Hamburg 1971, p. 296, from which I have taken the example of the actor. Sartre ends this part of his discourse with the statement: 'The role does not assume its reality in the actor, but the actor loses his reality in the role.'

36 See Hans Hörmann, *Meinen und Verstehen. Grundzüge einer psychologischen Semantik*, Frankfurt 1976, pp. 187, 192–6, 198, 207, 241, 253, 403f., 410f., and 500.

37 See Ibid., p. 210.

38 See Goodman, *Ways of Worldmaking*, pp. 102ff.

39 D.W. Winnicott, *Playing and Reality*, London 1971, pp. 1–25, develops a psychoanalytical view of the 'transitional object' which becomes of prime importance when the child is being weaned away from the mother and has to build bridges to its perceptual environment. Then 'transitional objects' have to be 'figured forth.' 'From birth, therefore, the human being is concerned with the problem of the relationship between what is objectively perceived and what is subjectively conceived of, and in the solution of this problem there is no help for the human being who has not been started off well enough by the mother. *The intermediate area to which I am referring is the area that is allowed to the infant between primary creativity and objective perception based on reality-testing.* The transitional phenomena represent the early stages of the use of illusion, without which there is no meaning for the human being in the idea of a relationship with an object that is perceived by others as external to that being ... The transitional object and the transitional phenomena start each human being off with what will always be important for them, i.e. a neutral area of experience which will not be challenged. *Of the transitional object it can be said that it is a matter of agreement between us and the baby that we will never ask the question: 'Did you conceive of this or was it presented to you from without?' The important point is that no decision on this point is expected. The question is not to be formulated* ... This intermediate area of experience, unchallenged in respect of its belonging to inner or external (shared) reality, constitutes the greater part of the infant's experience, and throughout life is retained in the intense experiencing that belongs to the arts and to religion and to imaginative living, and to creative scientific work' (pp. 11–14; my italics).

PART FIVE

IDEOLOGICAL PERSPECTIVES

FÉLIX MARTÍNEZ BONATI

The Stability of Literary Meaning

These reflections arise from perplexities that I share with many about several aspects of contemporary critical theory and critical praxis. Exciting new developments seem to inevitably produce some confusion. A characteristic sign both of the new directions and the pertinent confusions is the displacement of the expression *literary work* by the expression *literary text*. I think that there are good reasons to keep both terms in a determined relationship to each other, and that the extension of *text* to cover both its former ground and that of *work* is unfortunate from the point of view of conceptual precision.

I will define *text* as a particular set of signs that we recognize as such, and *work* as the product and the experience of the appropriate decoding of the text. The meaning of the text is the work. This meaning is successfully realized when the pertinent codes have been brought to operate upon the set of signs – all the pertinent codes and only the pertinent codes. The most basic of these codes is the natural language used in the text; more precisely: its pertinent historic phase. If the text is approached with wrong keys, it will make no sense, or little, or make sense only partially. We do not need to know 'what the author had in mind' in order to properly understand the text, i.e. reproduce the work. We only need to know what are the (many) codes involved, what are the games being played. This is a task for the intuitive powers of the reader and for the analytic reflection of the critic.

The basic hermeneutic operation is the production of the work from the text, and its most elementary aspect is the production of discourse from script. This operation, *reading*, in the proper sense of the word, does not produce an additional text; it merely follows the given text with the appropriate repertoire of responses, thus reproducing the work.

My considerations in this paper are mostly limited to this basic operation of reading. Most forms of criticism are not basic operations upon the text but rather secondary operations upon the work. (Deconstruction, for example, is never a primary operation upon the text. What is deconstructed is the construction of the work that is produced following the traditional forms of reading the text.)

When we read a literary text, most of us, amateurs of literature, will unreflectingly intend to get the meaning whose presumed existence has made the work in question a desirable object of our attention. We want to read it *well* in order not to miss what in it is supposed to be valuable and significant. We thus assume many things as given: that the copy we have is the right text; that everything in the text and nothing outside it is relevant for our purpose as reading amateurs; that all the elements of the text are interrelated and are designed to determine a meaningful experience; that such a differentiated entity cannot have more than one, certainly very complex, function or meaning. These and other presuppositions and norms define the traditional art of literary reading. The game of reading literature is constitutively determined by the effort to obtain, to repeat for us, *the* meaning and *the* significance which were available to the original public – a principle already explicitly stated by Alexander Pope in *An Essay on Criticism*. We readers thus assume that the meaning of a text can be repeated across time and in different circumstances.

When you sit down to write the text of a lecture (an example of literature *sensu lato*), you are moved by personal motivations but you also adopt the institutional will of all lectures. They are all deliberate human efforts of a kind. You will be addressing a certain type of public, defined by a common intellectual background and a common thematic interest. A part of the complex intentional structure of your act of writing is standard and traditional, and it may be that you are not explicitly aware of it while you are writing. In your terminology and allusions you will presuppose knowledge that is current to your kind of public, and only that – not, for example, unpublished information. Your subject will be one of presumable pertinence for all members of the public in question, your tone will abide by a certain decorum, and so on.

Thus, in order to construct your meaning, your statement, you will be repressing, and asking your readers or listeners to repress, not only an infinity of possible chains of signifiers, but also many possible meanings of the words you are using – meanings that happen to be irrelevant for your purpose. Style and tone, eminently, are instruments of repression of unwanted associations.

The gesture of writing for a public involves even more basically the assumption of a common intersubjective ground that, in principle, is accessible to anybody willing and able to assimilate the corresponding learning. You install your discourse from the beginning in a sphere of universality, separate from circumstantial privacy and private knowledge. The institutional objectivity of writing for a public becomes thus evident when we reflect upon this act. Now, is this an illusion? Are we not imprisoned in our own discourses, interpretations, subjectivities? Is there in fact communication at all, a common world beyond the chains of signs that pass across consciousness?

My main point is that the institution of literature would not have survived or even emerged if its principles of the universality and objectivity of meaning were illusory. My argument proceeds from the fact of literature and its constitution, a constitution designed for transcircumstantial significance, for the universal possibility of the reproduction of sense. I will try to show that the institutional form of literature is only conceivable as part of the construction of a perdurable common world of humanity, the utopian moments of this enterprise notwithstanding.

Praising great literary works as immortal is certainly an old, and now most unfashionable, commonplace of critical discourse. But we should remember that such a judgment seems to have been supported, until the eighteenth century at least, by apparently overwhelming evidence. Epic, dramatic, and lyric poetry written two thousand and more years before appeared to the educated reader as superlatively alive and powerful. This was still the view of Matthew Arnold as well as of, paradoxically, Karl Marx. A radical turnabout of the sense of the past and of literary experience has taken place since and has produced the opposite hyperboles. J.-P. Sartre remarked in his *Qu'est-ce que la littérature?*, of 1948, that novels should be consumed immediately after production, because their significance is circumstantial and perishable – as the best taste of bananas, he said, has to be caught by eating them ripe from the tree. Today, even Sartre's remark ought to sound naïve to many, since it presupposes the existence of one proper and original, albeit local and short-lived, significance for the novelistic text.

Was it only a naïve illusion to think that literary works may resist the course of time and maintain not just their identity and textual meaning, in a strict sense, but also their significance and value far beyond the epoch of their emergence?

Several assumptions are implied – as I said – in this traditional view. First, that a valid literary text has one and only one satisfactory meaning. Second, that it emerges possessing the virtue of a univocal and unique significance. Third, that being and significance of a literary work can be experienced by readers not belonging to the time and circumstances of its creation. In other words, the literary work would have, if not the timeless being of a Platonic idea, at least a stable identity and an enduring power within a continuous cultural tradition.

These traditional beliefs have been questioned many times. The historicity and cultural variety of human life, and particularly the mutability and the plurality of languages, constitute strong arguments against the premises of standard literary education. We probably agree that a literary work lives only in the recreative imagination of readers who reconstruct it following the text, the pertinent generic keys and literary codes, and the linguistically and otherwise codified experience of life. Since these codes, especially natural languages, are variable, not merely in their signifiers but also in their notional units, the reader's reconstruction, it seems we must conclude, will substantially differ according to historical and cultural variations. And thus, each literary work will change with the age and the customs. Unless ... unless it is a fact that readers can adopt, transitorily, other life-worlds and other semantic systems. If it is at all possible to assume an alien code of meanings, how and to what extent is this possible?

I will maintain in this essay that readers can imaginatively operate alien codes of life and language, and that this operation is what basically constitutes reading – the very demanding discipline of reading. Considering as the full meaning of a text that reading which comprises and unites all its elements, I will also assume that a literary text has one and only one full meaning, and that its significance and value are a function of that meaning and are not limitless variable attributes. I postulate that the being and the power of a work exist, as possibilities, from the moment of its inscription, and that they endure as possibilities as long as its codes are operable. (When I speak of the perduration of the literary work, I am using a shorthand for the persistence of the possibility of its reproduction.) I will discuss first and in the main how the imaginative acquisition and operation of an alien code and an alien life-world system can be thought of as possible and factual.

The acquisition of an alien code is possible in two ways: first, by living the life of the users, and second, by learning the equivalences between the alien code and one's own. Since we cannot live the life of past times, and only very limitedly contemporary ways of life different from our own, understanding literature presupposes the help of special kinds of 'bilingual' dictionaries, like the equivalences carried in footnotes by annotated editions of the classics. A dictionary is based on the assumption that one meaning or concept (one semantic unit) can be expressed by two or more word-signs or signifiers, or combinations thereof. Ultimately, the lexicological enterprise suggests the independence of each meaning from its several possible signifiers. If so, the accessibility and perdurability of literary texts would be warranted by the stability or the recuperability of meanings and concepts, regardless of the changes or varieties of the signifiers. In a rather crude version, this is Roman Ingarden's thesis, which holds that the objectivity and perdurability of literary works rest on the immutable being of ideal concepts (besides resting on the material inscription).

This Platonic view of Ingarden's, no matter how worthy of being rethought, will not seem convincing to most of us. The meanings of words – in the sense we are considering – are the notions we hold of the things designated by the words. Notions such as *triangle* or *justice* may be thought of as ideal concepts or immutable entities, but what about car insurance, Victorian morals, land-grant universities, and the like? Can these notions be analytically reduced to unhistorical ideal concepts?

I do not know whether or not they have been already clearly formulated, but it seems to me that these are the capital questions of hermeneutics: are all historical notions reducible to a set of non-historical concepts? If so, can we fully understand an alien experience through its abstract description? Is knowledge 'by acquaintance' (Bertrand Russell) analysable and thus exhaustible in conceptual terms, and, consequently, entirely translatable into knowledge 'by description'?

At the beginning of the *Quixote*, Cervantes presupposes that his reader is wholly familiar with the kind of 'hidalgo' his hero represents. The protagonist is 'one of those gentlemen who …' the narrator says. Nowadays, nobody is familiar with that long vanished life-form of Spanish provincial low-nobility, and only a few might know living relics of that historical species. At first, Cervantes briefly characterizes that social kind. The terms of his 'analysis' of this life-form are also mostly historical notions: 'one of those gentlemen who are wont to keep a lance in the rack, an old buckler, a skinny horse, and a swift greyhound.' This description can be reduced for the reader of today – using the pertinent scholarly information – to *old-fashioned, unused weapons, unwarlike horse, good hunting dog*. These few notions, in turn, speak to us; so much so that we begin to know what kind of hidalgo Alonso Quijano was. Now, 'weapons,' 'old fashioned,' 'unused,' 'unwarlike,' 'horse,' 'hunting,' 'dog' may not be timeless concepts, but they are at least common to various centuries of our culture, and, in some cases, like 'weapons,' they would be universals of human life. Let us also remark that the historicity or the ethno-relativity of these notions can be reduced further. 'Horse' and 'dog' can be translated as 'domesticated animals of such and such attributes,' 'hunting' (in the pertinent historical context) as 'a mixture of killing animals for food and pleasurable exercise,' etc.

Will these translations convey the *feeling* of that life, the historical notion in the unreflected familiarity it had for the men of that age? We may doubt it. At least, we expect that the construction, in the mind of the reader, of a felt notion of that typical routine existence would take a longer description. Well, what

Cervantes undertakes, in the following paragraphs of the first chapter, is precisely a more detailed continuation of the description of his hero's ordinary way of life. Although the description of the typical soon begins, in the same chapter, to be displaced by the characterization of what is extraordinary and unique about this hidalgo, there are still a good number of typical traits – such as dress, meals, and daily occupations – to make familiar the supposedly already familiar kind of life. This seems, on first reflection, strange. Is Cervantes being uneconomically redundant, conveying several times the same familiar notion to his readers? Or is he writing for readers who, after all, were possibly not familiar with the supposedly familiar circumstantial notions of his time? Is he perhaps writing also for posterity?

The fact is that, after reading the first chapter of the *Quixote*, we do not feel any need to know more about that subclass of the 'hidalgos' in order to optimally continue our reading. We feel the ironic, even satiric, and at the same time melancholic-friendly Cervantine attitude towards this stylish, impoverished, and somewhat marginal social type. We are inside the novel. We understand its world.

Nonetheless (and this points to the empirical difficulties encountered by the literary function of analytical reduction of historical notions), the descriptions of meals and dresses I just referred to are full of the most circumstantial concepts, and many of their words are either unknown today to the native speaker of Spanish, or they have now a very different connotation. Only the work of philological-historical erudition has made it possible to reduce those concepts to non-historical or, at least, long-term historical ones. Therefore, in this as in other passages, one can have the impression that Cervantes is predominantly activating, through more or less subtle redundancy, circumstantial notions of his contemporaries. But he can also be understood to be making available here a certain feeling of life to anybody. The elements he chose for objectifying that complex and non-universal notion of a life style end up being less than universal features of human environment. But they *are* close to being that – as their philological recuperation has proven. The implied reader of the *Quixote* is ambiguous. Sometimes, he is a common, quick-minded contemporary, sometimes a reader of the perennial creations of the classics. Is this duplicity of appeal not constitutive of literature?

It is true, then, that some of the terms of Cervantes' analysis of the hidalgo's way of living are relatively short-lived terms relating to customs, dress, and cooking, and that sometimes only felicitous erudite findings make them understandable. They also have to be, in their turn, analysed, until the hermeneut arrives at natural species like hen's eggs and porcine fat, and elementary culinary techniques such as frying or boiling. However, the reconstruction of such meanings is in principle possible, not only because the terms of Cervantes' analysis were widely known to his contemporaries (and consequently likely to be documented elsewhere), but more importantly because they are close to units of non-historical or transhistorical elements, such as natural species and almost universal technical procedures. Cervantes' analysis of that style of living also includes circumstantial value-indices: food and fabrics of rather inexpensive sort. They have socio-historical connotations which are reducible to quasi-universal notions of economy.

Indeed, even writing exclusively designed for one's contemporaries (let us say, the readers of one or two decades) has to assume that only the most general experiences are really shared by all of them. Thus, reaching the unknown other who is our contemporary is not essentially different from appealing to the reader of another age. Literature, being by definition an address to those who share only our *public* circumstances, is constitutively devoted to the analytic reduction of complex experiences of a subjective, regional, or temporary exclusivity into elements of less fragile nature, perdurable units of human knowledge. Only through these elements can the complex experience be objectified and reconstructed. Literature does on a large scale what a sentence does for the minimal units of communication.

If there is a way to know the literary works of the past (as well as those of our alien contemporaries – and indeed every contemporary is an alien) in their original being and significance, it has to pass through the part of our conceptual repertoire that consists of non-historical, universal notions of human life. More radically expressed, imaginative experience of alien lives has to be based upon the common stock of all human life.

The existence of such transhistorical and translinguistic concepts and experiences has been often enough denied or accepted only for narrowly limited parts of our notions. Ortega's thesis that each generation has its own life-world, incommunicable to other generations, is one well-known relativist conception of the historicity of human life. Linguistic relativism, on the other hand, is a recurring view since W. von Humboldt. A transcendental-idealist bent is noticeable in relativist theories of language such as Weisgerber's, Whorf's, and Saussure's, to name a few. Many seem today to assume that natural languages organize according to their own system the structure of the life-world of a community. Structuralist or semiotic transcendentalism wants to understand all orders of experience as linguistically grounded. And since a natural language is seen as a historical succession of autonomous systems, concepts, as part of the synchronic sign-system, seem to be imposed upon the world by a diachronic fate, and to be untransferable from one synchrony to the other. Under these axioms how then could the same notion be found in different systems, if each signified is determined by its 'internal dependences,' that is by its structural relations to all other signifieds of the same system, and since such relations would necessarily be different in different systems?

These structuralist premises lead not only to the assertion of the impossibility of strict equivalences of terms from different synchronies, but also to the rejection of a pre-linguistic order of experience and, consequently, to the denial of the hypothesis of a transcultural life-world of human experience. No common ground of understanding seems thus to unite men of different linguistic communities, or of different phases of the same natural language. Therefore, following this relativist argument, one may say, as Hans-Georg Gadamer does, coming from another line of transcendental idealism, that understanding a work from an alien historical horizon is always understanding *otherwise*; or even that it is always misunderstanding, since it would be necessarily a thought different from the original. Or one can pretend to give up the question of understanding, by denying original and intentional meaning. The scepticism of so-called post-structuralism seems to me to be a conceivable consequence of structuralist postulates.

What exactly is the part played by temporal and socio-spatial circumstantiality in the standard meaning of words? As Karl Vossler long ago emphatically remarked, no two words of a language or of different languages have strictly the same meaning: their context of usage will not be the same (the classes of persons using them, the situations of typical use); the associations they evoke (rarity, vulgarity, technicality, sacrality, locality, etc.) will differ, and the thing they denote will have a different value in the corresponding life-worlds, so that the stylistic auras of the words will always be distinguishable, even if their referential core is identical. If the stylistic connotations of its words are relevant in the constitution of the literary work, and if these connotations are untransferable from one language system to another, the integrity of the work should not persist beyond the limits of its time and idiom. Lyric poetry's indocility to translation has been often explained by recourse to this type of semantic differences, as well as to the aesthetic functionality of phonological matter. (However, the problem of translating lyric poetry and that of recovering the meaning of a lyric text are two different problems. The impossibility of the first enterprise does not imply the impossibility of the second one.)

A variety of things thus make up the fragile stylistic aura of a word. A dictionary may indicate roughly these associated values, but it will clarify only the abstract referential meaning. As Dryden remarked in *An Essay of Dramatic*

Poesy, texts of another age appear 'flat' because of our unknowing pertinent connotations. I do not wish to deny for a moment that we may encounter here unsurmountable limitations to the will for universality and perdurability of literary products. My intention is to explore how literature as a traditional institution meets the dispersion and erosion of its substance, and to what extent an anti-relativist stance can be saved.

If an author desires his work to perdure unchanged, or if it is the will institutionalized in literary tradition that works defy time as stable entities, the creation of the work will not rely substantially on those stylistic connotations of everyday life which are not only temporary but also spatially and socially limited. Since Naturalism, certainly, the linguistic realm of regionalisms and social jargons has been included in literature. The belatedness and the transitoriness or marginality of this opening is significant, as is the fact that the admission of prose into high literature was generally resisted for a time, and the equal status of the novel as a genre was refused by the poetics of Classicism until this tradition broke down at the end of the eighteenth century. It can be conjectured that a reason behind these restrictive discriminations is that prose and the novel are forms that more easily admit the contingency of minor detail and the concrete historical circumstantiality of life.

That the writer will only presuppose public, current knowledge in the reader is confirmed by exception when he alludes to his private circumstances, since this is a form of *publicizing* them, forcing the reader to learn them and the critic to annotate the casual facts and make them into lexical items of poetic vocabulary. But no considerable work will *rest* upon names and presuppositions not shared by the educated community. In our time, the social fact of the existence of a large group of professional interpreters and commentators may induce authors to play with recondite allusions and parodies. Still, the rules of this game exclude texts which do not belong to some canon or another.

Another observation belonging to this series is that works using dialect do not necessarily rest upon it. Usually, characters speak there a vernacular, while the narrator displays the standard language of the corresponding culture. And the same kind of motivation that makes the writer prefer the standard national linguistic norm to his native dialect (that is to render his work accessible to a larger number of his contemporaries) determines his choice of a 'literary' vocabulary inside the standard language. But here the specific motivation goes beyond reaching his contemporaries to reaching those who will come after: the resistance of literary language to the attrition of time is stronger than that of standard everyday discourse.

'Literary words' are more stable in their stylistic connotations than ordinary words because the circumstances of their use (which are literary works, that is iterable texts resting on inscription or memory) are more stable than the comparable situations in everyday life. The greater stability is here more than a matter of degree: singular, concrete situations of our life, by definition, happen only once, while singular, concrete situations which are only imagined *can* be imagined identically again. Fictionality opens the possibility of the repetition of concrete situations. (But, certainly, only the possibility, since the identity of the imagined cannot be secured without guiding marks that are permanent, that is, materially lasting icons and durable concepts.)

On the basis of inscription and transhistorical notions, the imaginary world of literature emerges containing its own imaginary linguistic praxis. These repeatedly imaginable fictive discourses enact perdurably the stylistic connotations of their words. An 'affective' aura accrues to the word in imaginary no less than in everyday usage. The corpus of classic texts constitutes an iterable linguistic praxis; and the so-called intertextuality of literature thus appears to be, at least in part, a recourse for overcoming chronic change and localism in the connotations of the vocabulary. The whole of the literary canon is the context of each of its works and of each of their words. It is therefore enough, in principle, that a good number of their words be referentially understood for it to be possible to open up the codes and life-worlds of others. And the key-words are those stable elements of the conceptual system which denote universal features of life.

The successful attainment of the goal of a stable cultured vocabulary in a literary epoch may approach the point of systematic classification of words according to their stylistic properties – as in the Roman distinction of *gravis*, *medius*, and *facilis* styles, and the so-called Virgilian wheel. The literary canon thus holds the language stable while the spoken language of the community continues to change. Eventually, the links between the two systems will become irretrievable without professional learning. The literary language can then be declared 'dead,' while indeed it will be revivable as long as the texts and the dictionary survive. And consequently those literary works will remain potentially identical at least to the extent that their linguistic elements are determinant; the stylistic moments will be conserved by the imaginary praxis of the canonical discourses, and the conceptual meanings will be reconstructed from transhistorical units. (The paradoxical fact that 'dead' or 'aged' languages can be the most secure fundament for the durable life of poems is well expressed by Hobbes in his 'Answer to Davenant's Preface to *Gondibert*.'

Structuralism has originated or reinforced the view that all in the meanings of all words is short-term historical and relative to the pertinent linguistic system. In its wake, some critics think that the recovery of word-meanings of another age is utopian, and that we should accept and free of repressions the operation of reading texts and inject *our* epochal notions (the only ones we supposedly can have) into their words. Since we cannot do otherwise, they seem to say in a Lutherian gesture, let us do it *fortiter*. According to this view, the text, as soon as it is inscribed, begins to drift away from the circumstances that produced it. The material signs may remain unchanged, but nothing else does, and thus the meaning that will be attached to the writing will lack a firm ground, will be each time different – controlled only, if at all, by historical fate.

If the loss of original semantic substance were the necessary and irreversible fate of literary works, philological hermeneutics would make no difference in reading an old text. Yet we know that it does make a difference. Further, if any transsystematic understanding were impossible, old literary works would long ago have lost any power they had, and translated novels would be full of casual and dysfunctional inconsistencies. We know this is not so, and we know that dictionaries are possible and make sense, even if we may not know exactly how much they mislead. The view I am criticizing seems to take for granted that all our notions are ours only, and none of them, and nothing in them, are the same as those held by people of other ages and cultures. Word-meanings are supposed to be simply a part of language, and consequently a part of a historical and autonomous system of internal dependences that will last for a time and then be displaced as a whole by another system. Hence, it appears necessary that unless we are inside the pertinent system, the notions will remain alien to us. But then, how would we know that they are really notions different from our own?

One could venture the thesis that understanding the life-world of a person we know is essentially more difficult than understanding the life-world of another culture, since the first effort has to go beyond institutionalized intersubjective codes. However, some degree of understanding is in both cases a fact, and being a fact, it has to be possible. How is it possible despite the undeniable variety of codes and life-worlds? Well, I have been suggesting that the possibility rests on the existence of a universal part of our experience. Lasting (natural and long-term historical) as well as short-term historical features define the human condition. Both universal and idiomatic notions are found in our conceptual heritage. There are local and also transitory customs, and generalized ones. There are words peculiar to a season, to a small group, to a region. And there are concepts such as water, fire, air, death. The vocabulary of a natural language is not a set of homogenous and equally lasting notions, not a synchronic system, but rather a conglomerate of systems of very different degrees of generality and temporal stability.

The old commonplaces that I am trying to reaffirm hold that literature survives because it appeals to the deeper and unchanging nature of man. But what features could we reasonably think of as constitutive of that 'deeper and unchanging nature of man'? We can assume that we share with all men that ever lived the condition of having or being a body (and also the ambiguity of the condition that is expressed in this 'having or being a body'). We move erect upon the ground impelled by needs of nutrition, of safety from natural hostility, and of human company. We have to take care for our life, and we are driven by a force of self-assertion. The body imposes definite possibilities and impossibilities on our desires, spatially as well as temporally and energetically, and it sustains a rhythm of activity and rest that relates to the rhythms of the planetary motions. We are bound to sexuality and its forces, no matter what ways the given culture imposes or tolerates, what distinguishes our inclination as particular, or what individual fixation or sublimation emerges in each case from this universal human condition. We also share with all men who ever lived the fact that we will die, as they did, and that we know it, as they did. Water and earth, fire and air are the dominant elements of our environment. Pleasure and pain divide and basically define sensations and feelings. Association in groups of common will, hierarchical submission, leadership, and also rivalry, enmity, and strife determine our social complications. We tend to accept some formulated idea of the universe and mankind's destiny. We hold truths. And we assert norms of human conduct and values that decide on the estimation we grant to and are granted by our fellow men. So, there is always the possibility of heroism and of villainy, and even the one who challenges the values of his time and thereby promotes what the others regard as evil deeds is asserting values and a model of heroism. We have a variable realm of choices and freedom, and we perceive that, all in all, we are overpowered by the trends of history, the forces of nature, the coincidences of random chance. I should add that all human beings overrun in imagination the limits of reality, and experience the frustration of their unlimited drive for life, power, pleasure, and knowledge, and long for another life, that would be commensurate to their desires.

(Some of these assertions may sound like an echo of Merleau-Ponty, some of Empedocles. My suggestion is, precisely, to keep in mind the things meant, not the historicity of the wording, and to keep in mind also that these topics are not alien to the substance of literature.)

Permanent features of human life and environment are the ground of possibility for transhistorical concepts. Natural kinds, for example, of plants and animals are much more stable than cultural epochs. Therefore, it is for all men possible to build in reference to them universal concepts of non-historical content. Not a Platonic realm of ideas, but a durable order of reality supports the stability of elementary semantic units.

Now, literature prefers the part of our vocabulary that is closest to transhistorical units. Lyric poetry is especially revealing in this respect because it is the genre in which the stylistic aura and the connotations of words are most relevant; it therefore should be, historically and culturally, the most relative of discourses, constituted as it is by meaning-traits normally the least able to endure. That lyric poetry does endure is due to three properties of its vocabulary: first, that it is limited, specialized, and conservative (those 'poetic words'); second, that it is a selection of the most stable part of the general vocabulary: not historical concepts or cultural items, but the features of our natural environment are its most distinctive referents (it will be granted that expressions like 'air,' 'water,' 'fire,' 'earth,' and such are more likely to appear in lyric texts than 'Victorian morals,' 'land-grant universities,' or 'car insurance'); third, that the stylistic aura is kept constant and alive because it is generated and supported by a single permanent context of usage: the lyric canon itself.

It is true that the vocabulary of literary prose is not subjected to these conservative limitations. But the use of words in prose is mostly referential, and not significantly bound to expressive connotations. Hence, prose is more easily translatable and more reducible to conceptual analysis. Besides, the sheer number of words in a prose text, as opposed to the brief lyric poem, creates a rich internal context, often sufficient for the stylistic determination of its words.

So far, I have argued in favour of the view that the variety of languages and the diachrony of conceptual and life-world systems are not sufficient reasons to deny the possibility of a transhistorical identity and a stable significance of literary works. My view regarding referential meaning has been different from the Saussurean model of autonomous conceptual synchronies, as well as from Ingarden's assumption of a set of timeless ideal notions. I have postulated a translinguistic continuity of human condition as the basis of the possibility of panchronic concepts. These concepts, in turn, are elements for the analytic reduction of historical notions that constitutes an essential part of the hermeneutic enterprise. As for the stylistic values of words, I have indicated that the imaginary linguistic praxis of the literary canon, as a repeatable set of discourses founded upon panchronic concepts, makes possible the stabilization of expressive connotations. Thus, not only formal features bound to the graphemes of the poem but also its substance of thought may persist.

The aspects of the literary institution designed to secure the regional and temporal universality of the work are not limited to vocabulary. They relate also to the regulation of fantasy and feeling, that is to assuring that the reader will not only articulate the pertinent concepts but also imagine and respond affectively in the way needed for the effectiveness of the work.

Reading is, of course, not merely the intellectual exercise of actualizing notions and combining them into larger units of discourse. Conceptual meaning is automatically translated, in the mind of the reader, into images of persons, places, and events. Fantasy thus operates a reorganization and transmutation of the material of the work, and so much so that at the end of, say, a novel we remember human presences, actions, atmospheres, but hardly any sequence of words that is a part of the text. The exercise of fantasy is certainly directed and controlled by the conceptual sequences of linguistic discourse. But not entirely, since many blanks of the conceptual description have to be filled imaginatively: all those aspects of the objects in question that are not mentioned in the text. Contemporary criticism has revealed part of the complicated net of codes and generic expectations that regulate the reader's imagining activity. The best known, perhaps, of these structures are those pertaining to the controlled point of view of narrative discourse, and the related forms of aspectual continuity and consistency. But not only the mode of presentation reduces subjectivity in the response of the reader. Style generally is a force of imaginative consistency that works to exclude impertinent types of images. Casual, 'subjective' recreation of the work is opposed by these fundamental literary forms. Remembering Henry James's statements on modal consistency and formal perfection, one could think that such technical and stylistic imperatives are rather imposed by aesthetic principles. But is not beauty of form the quality that suggests, precisely, the victory over time and particularity?

A long tradition of criticism beginning with Aristotle's *Poetics* maintains that the ultimate value of a work of literary art is to induce a certain definite state of feeling or a determined ethical attitude. If this is so, the affective and ethical effect of the work upon the recipient has to be controlled. Literary creations are in fact marked by multiple structures that are able to direct subjective emotional reactions and evaluations. I will mention only a few of them: gross or subtle manicheism, the division of agents into lovable and hateful ones, idealization and negative stylization, authorial commentary, and strategies of identification of the reader with one of the fictional parties. This 'rhetoric,' as Wayne Booth called it, is active also in the case of irony and ambiguity, since then the sympathy of the reader is directed to the 'objective' or detached vision of the implied author.

If we look at literature and ask ourselves what means it has of establishing a perdurable and stable identity for its works, we might be surprised to realize how many literary structures, traditions, and formal peculiarities seem designed to fulfil this goal or at least seem to have some relevancy to it. The existence of canons of great literary works, poetic vocabularies, traditions of themes and of generic forms, imperatives of technical and stylistic consistency, and codes of rhetorical controls of response (to name a few features of literature we have touched on in this essay) are part of the institutionalized effort of literary creation to overcome the contingencies of time and circumstantiality. Literary texts do not seem to have been created to be left to unrestrained drift and substantial alteration in a succession of historic worlds. It is consistent with this that they are durably inscribed or composed in view of the possibilities of faithful memorization. Their signifiers as well as their constructs of meanings are made to last, to be repeated identically. In recent years, critics are often accused of the ideological repression of the potential plurality of meanings of any text. Ideological or not, such a repression is constitutive of literature, of the works themselves, and of meaning generally. Giving up original or proper meaning as a regulating principle of reading, we not only give up the search for and the experience of unity and identity of the work, but also the quest for style and, more generally, design, necessity (as opposed to randomness), functional teleology, expressivity, and atmosphere – and the integrity of the text itself, the monumentality of the inscription. If we do not direct ourselves to searching for the original meaning, why should we respect and not change the words the author put on the page – the *original* words? We are thus led to semiotic entropy.

Even if it is granted that a text can only have one and the same meaning, and that this meaning is in principle repeatable across the ages, it remains a question how much of these goals of universality and perduration really can be accomplished by the resources of literature and the complementary efforts of scholarly hermeneutics. But it seems that it would be a loss if we were not to submit our readings to the institutionalized will of literature. For it is by following that will that we can reach into other worlds of the mind. Great poems may not be immortal, but it depends on us whether they live for our generation, and so for each generation.

GEOFFREY WAITE

The Politics of 'The Question of Style': Nietzsche/Hö[l]derlin

Ich halte mich dies Mal nur bei der Frage des Stils auf. ...
Nietzsche

INTRODUCTION (VIA GRAMSCI)

Let me make clear some of my prejudices and anticipate part of my hypothesis.[1]
The underlying thrust of my argument will be directed decidedly against what
Fredric Jameson in *The Political Unconscious* has identified as a dominant
climate of current theory and criticism in the West, namely a certain
Nietzschean instance within post-structuralism, including a substantial sector
of latter-day Western Marxism. My own concern here, however, diverges from
Jameson's production of what he calls 'a new, properly Marxist hermeneutic' to
the extent that my ultimate worry is less with Nietzschean *qua* 'anti-
interpretive' tendencies in post-structuralist or deconstructive literary theory
and practice than with the debilitating and otherwise dangerous political
ideology these specific forms of 'Nietzsche-ism' globally conceal. I should also
alert the reader to my conviction that it is necessary to link up contemporary
Marxist readings of Nietzsche (and not only Nietzsche) with an older tradition
of response: the one begun by Mehring, Plekhanov, Lenin, Gramsci, and Lukács
and, while ignored in the West, continued elsewhere, including by current
Soviet critics. My divergence from this, in my view properly mainstream,
tendency is more a matter of tactics and methodology (and to this extent, style)
than of strategy or substance.

Nietzsche's way of posing what has been termed 'the question of style,'
according to a powerful consensus view in the West that appeals, explicitly or
implicitly, *to* Nietzsche, most radically shatters the notion of 'the identity of the
text,' that is the dual claim that a document or other cultural artefact had, or has,

determinate signification and that the task of interpretation, explication, or explanation can, or should, be to search for such signification. I shall here analyse the question of textual identity in the specific form of the question of style as broached in exemplary and seminal fashion by Nietzsche. Then I show how the major trend in the current Western reception of Nietzsche, namely post-structuralism, works precisely to obscure the full complexity of Nietzsche's formulation of this question, most notably and perniciously this formulation's historical, ideological, and political dimension and impact. Finally I argue, in an overtly partisan manner, that *both* ways of posing the question of identity and style, that of Nietzsche and that of the post-structuralist reading formation based on Nietzsche, must be challenged. The question of textual indeterminacy must never be conflated with that of ideological and political overdetermination. My hypothesis *vis-à-vis* the topic of this volume of essays is that the very question of the identity of the text (the issue of the specificity of the *literary* text is to my mind theoretically moot and politically irrelevant) already occludes access to what is, in the last instance, the more significant question, namely the ideological and political identifications of the question and the questioner. It should be needless to add that my attempt below to criticize, or rather activate, certain features of current attacks on received notions of textual identity should not warrant a return to older, essentialist versions of the identity of the text.[2]

Now, the graphic, perhaps graphematic, at least typographical part of my title, 'Nietzsche/Hö[l]derlin,' does allude to and, in a sense to be demarcated, participate in the semi-linguistic, semi-mathematical, semi-psychological *stylistic* preoccupations of post-structuralist or deconstructive writing, writing that in fact represents a powerful 'misreading' of Nietzsche's philosophemes and rhetoric. So we would be invited to 'defer or differ' (Derrida) the two nearly proper names by means of some 'chronological or metaleptical reversal' (de Man); to slash their 'imaginary' identity (Lacan) in order to reveal not two exemplary personalities but two exemplary 'effects of subjectivity,' two 'regions of intensity of the schiz' (Deleuze/Guattari); or, alternatively, 'to put one name on top of the other' (N.O. Brown and Derrida), to divide Friedrich into Friedrich with whatever remainder. ... Above all, we would broach, apparently, 'the question of style' (Derrida).

Whatever we may suppose Nietzsche 'really meant,' it is certain that the word 'Nietzsche' now signifies less some proper (or improper) name than a series of specific, historically determined discursive sites on which ideological struggles have been and continue to be waged. In the 1930s this site was occupied and contested by writers, academic philosophers, and the popular press: by Bataille and the surrealists in Paris; by Adorno and Horkheimer, also in Paris; by Jaspers, Heidegger, and Goebbels in Germany; by Löwith in Japan; and by Lukács in Moscow. Today, half a century later, at no less crucial a conjuncture, the combatants have new names and some of the places are different, yet the struggle for and of ideology behind the sign 'Nietzsche' goes on. Post-structuralism may be stridently ignorant of the history of the reception of this discurso-ideological site, but for that ignorance no less complicitous in its actualizations. I shall not pretend neutrality in this struggle.

There are significantly different theoretical and practical ways of broaching 'the question of style.' Antonio Gramsci put the matter in this perspective:

The problem is that of seeing things historically. That all those Nietzschean charlatans in verbal revolt against all that exists, against conventionality, etc., should have ended up by accepting it after all, and have thus made certain attitudes seem quite unserious, may well be the case, but it is not necessary to let oneself be guided in one's own judgments by charlatans. In opposition to fashionable titanism, to a taste for wishful thinking and abstraction, one must draw attention to a need for 'sobriety' in words and in external attitudes, precisely so that there should be more strength in one's character and concrete will. But this is a question of style, not 'theory' [Ma questa è quistione di stile, non 'teoretica'].[3]

In recent years, the reception of Nietzsche, at least at the level of academic taste, has tried to shift away from fashionable titanism, but without a corresponding sobriety of critical insight. Yet a kind of stylistic, if not philosophical, titanism still manipulates banal, unguarded allusions to 'Nietzschean *affirmation*'[4] and even the more sibylline, but, for all its compulsive irony, no less mythologizing claim that Nietzsche's project 'is the very model of philosophical rigor.'[5] Certainly the hegemony of Western civil society has increased in complexity since Gramsci wrote his remarks on the Italian Nietzscheans. Both the hegemony and the intellectualist contribution to it, on the one hand, and the kind of concrete will needed in the 'war of position' combating them, on the other, are more intricate than Gramsci could have imagined from his prison cell in the 1930s. A fully elaborated, immanent critique or external criticism of post-structuralism and deconstruction, and of what Gramsci would have justly called the charlatanry of their rather different, but for the current scene in criticism equally significant, 'misreadings' of the discurso-ideological site called 'Nietzsche,' lies beyond my competence and intention. Certainly it would be wrong-headed to hypostasize some essence called, say, 'deconstruction' and then attack it for the wrong reasons – a practice common enough today. The significant question pivots not on some entity called 'deconstruction,' however, but on certain critical energies, their potential for productive and progressive activation. Any critical project is itself valid only within the larger purview and stricter horizon of an enlightened, historically oriented, emancipatory theory and practice. So it is that my own remarks below will necessarily remain prefatory to the degree that they, too, address only 'the question of style,' let alone the question of what I will call the 'Nietzsche/Hö[l]derlin' nexus.

'PARATACTICAL STYLE' (VIA WAGNER, ROHDE, AND ADORNO)

At least one difficulty of reading Nietzsche has been perceived from the earliest stages of his reception on, both in public (notably in the once eruptive, now relatively dormant 'Struggle over Nietzsche's *Birth of Tragedy*' initiated by Wilamowitz-Möllendorff) and in private (in the still largely neglected correspondence written *to* Nietzsche). Take for instance Erwin Rohde's more or less spontaneous response to the second *Untimely Meditation*, 'The Use and Abuse of History.' On 24 March 1874, he wrote Nietzsche in Basel:

You *deduce* far too little. Rather you force your reader much more than is good and proper to find *bridges* between your thoughts, statements, and sentences. Of course, the gradual derivation of the 2nd from the 1st, the 3rd out of the 2nd, etc. *in infinitum* is often enough deadly boring. But the opposite mistake can, pushed to the extreme, make books about a subject that is difficult to begin with unspeakably troublesome [unsäglich beschwerlich], like, for instance, what happens to *Wagner* in nearly all his writing (except in the essay on directing and the one on the Jews).[6]

Rohde's complaints about the undialectical, paratactical leaps of Nietzsche's *logic* touch a *rhetorical* complex that has continued to confound subsequent readers. It is a question of *style* that Nietzsche's philologist friend touched on here in this passage and later on in his letter when he conceded that the demand for a more lucid, cruder, more 'deductive' mode of argumentation is at root paradoxical. The true subject matter (*res*) of the second *Untimely Meditation* is in fact 'unspeakably troublesome.' Not only was it so for Rohde, Nietzsche, and their 'dear public' – it should remain so for us today. Surely the uncanny lurks unrestrained in the demand to clarify, make explicit, and increase the persuasive efficacy (*verba*) of a text which, in two senses, *will* not be heard by its immediately intended readers, by what Nietzsche elsewhere calls 'the uncannily social uncertainty of our present.'[7] Nietzsche's 'unspeakably troublesome' message is *intended* by him to be disjunctive, indeed politically disruptive, if not immediately, then, *a fortiori*, posthumously. *And it was to be this in fact.*

Nietzsche's ultimate concern, as represented, say, in 'The Use and Abuse of History,' was expressly to 'push over the brink what has become an entirely decorative culture' and its coterminous social infrastructure.[8] The 'radicality' of Nietzsche's style and rhetoric, shared in common with what was 'a prevailing tendency' among many German intellectuals (both in imperial Germany and later under Nietzsche's more or less direct influence) 'to seek irrational solutions ... by *stylizing* the unresolved problems to be answered,'[9] is *irresponsibly* motivated. It is, politically speaking, at best anarchistic and at worst proto-fascist. At the very least, stylistically speaking, it is parapractical in the sense of para*tactical*, if we can add final diacritical stress to Theodor Adorno's term as originally applied to Hölderlin.[10]

Begun in 1873, in the period immediately following the Paris Commune, a text like 'The Use and Abuse of History' is constituted by an anti-liberal ideology of post-1848 defeatism. All its dazzling verbal revolt, all its sometimes justified polemic against positivism, aberrant historicism, and *Bildungsphilisterthum*, turns explicitly away from a materialist view of history and from any authentically liberating praxis, collective *or* individual. The bourgeois intelligentsia of imperial Germany was, admittedly, an exceedingly complex phenomenon; it is no longer effective politics to conflate, for instance, its refined-decadent element – like Nietzsche – with its overtly fascistic type.[11] It is even possible to acknowledge the potentially positive contribution of texts written in the 1870s like 'The Use and Abuse of History' to a critique, say, of the culture industry, to the extent that Nietzsche can be read to expose the inherent contradiction in this aspect of mass culture between a once historically progressive pedagogic intent and effect, on the one hand, and the instrumentalization of its later praxis, on the other.[12] The problem would remain, however, that Nietzsche's polemic was directed primarily not at 'deconstructing' what he called 'egoism,' or what now is tendentiously and abstractly called 'the theory of the subject,'[13] but at destroying or at least occluding one historically concrete form of 'egoism' – namely nascent proletarian class consciousness.[14] Hence the ultimate thrust of Nietzsche's seminal attack, both in terms of its intent and, not exclusively but overwhelmingly, its deferred effect, is against what 'The Use and Abuse of History' baldly calls 'the introduction of history *qua* animal and human history' among 'the dangerous ... masses of people and the working classes [Volksmassen und Arbeiterschichten]' whom Nietzsche has no intention of 'educating.'[15] Quite the contrary.

Nietzsche's immediate intertext is, in effect, notions entertained by writings of Wagner during 1848–50 – themselves derived in typically obscure, paratactical, and, for Rohde, Nietzsche, and the later Wagner himself, 'unspeakably troublesome' fashion from Ludwig Feuerbach and The Communist Manifesto – such as 'Art and Revolution' and 'The Art Work of the Future,' and posthumously published notebooks which served as the base of those two texts such as 'Artisthood of the Future: On the Principle of Communism' ('Künstlertum der Zukunft: Zum Prinzip des Kommunismus') of 1849.[16] There Wagner had stated in no uncertain terms that the only perfect satisfaction of egoism is reached by communism, by the sublation of egoism, with communism as egoism's 'redemption.'[17] More telling still, at the level of cultural intervention at which Wagner and later Nietzsche worked, is Wagner's insistent argument that only a 'great *revolution of mankind*' (the early Wagner conveniently blurs the distinction between artistic revolution and other kinds), unlike its individualized, 'egoistic' but authentic predecessor in Greece, will make *all* human beings the material for 'the art work of the future.'[18]

Such recommendations, especially when their extreme idealism is stood on its head, make potentially dangerous reading indeed. Nietzsche could never forget, or forgive, them. His relationship to Wagner, overdetermined to be sure by other, explicitly psychological and philosophical determinants, was deeply informed by this problematic relation between, to paraphrase Adorno, failed insurrection and nihilistic metaphysics.[19] And it is, in the last instance, only in this full context of political ideology that a writer like Hölderlin was to be linked in Nietzsche's way of thinking with increasing explicitless both to Wagner and to *Nietzsche*'s version of 'the question of style.' But we must approach this question carefully and through the dominant version of it today.

ACTIVATING DERRIDA'S 'QUESTION OF STYLE'

We must be alert to the implicitly political resonance of Rohde's remarks in his letter to Nietzsche on the paratactical style of 'The Use and Abuse of History,' but we must be further attentive to all readings, from whatever camp they come, that tend, however remotely, to make Nietzsche's political ideology invisible. As is perhaps well enough known, the comparison of Nietzsche to Wagner and to other Romantic/post Romantic writers, like notably Hölderlin, *qua* psychopathological, cultural, and stylistic phenomena haunts Nietzsche himself recurrently (with important shifts of emphasis and varying intensities of self-reflection) from even before the last, troubled sections of *The Birth of Tragedy*, the final *Untimely Meditation* on Wagner, and the parodic impulse of *Thus Spoke Zarathustra*, on down deep into Nietzsche's last attempts to analyse the 'decadence' of Wagner (and even of himself). Certainly at least superficial comparison of Nietzsche and Romanticism has preoccupied a large sector of the academic reception of Nietzsche from the turn of the century to the present time.[20] But what is less well known, and when it occurs the ignorance is invariably symptomatic, is that this relationship is also profoundly political in nature. Nietzsche's writing is, at an absolutely crucial level of generality, inscribed by a deeply involuted relation to whatever may have been positive in the political intent of early German Romanticism, including the intent of much of, say, Hölderlin's own work, namely to help establish the 'kingdom of heaven' in this world, *hic et nunc*.[21]

The alleged 'genius' of Nietzsche as diagnostician of *many* aspects of his specific cultural conjuncture is always already contaminated by the ever dangerous implications for concrete politics of *all* his proposed cures. Even more important for us today, subsequent modes of the reception of Nietzsche repeat such involution at the level of critical practice, and even collaboration with currently repressive ideology. Nietzsche's texts, *as well as* much of the reception of them, are precisely irresponsible in that they take no responsibility for whatever historical efficacy they might disseminate into however near or distant a future, for whatever society they might, to repeat Nietzsche's own phrase, 'push over the brink.' *Nihilism, in the last instance, is no trope.* Nor should it be reducible to a '*style*,' however intricately it be conceived.

Perhaps Rohde intuited something of such issues already in his response to 'The Use and Abuse of History' – albeit in more familiar, because humanistic and moral, forms. Be that as it may, Nietzsche avoided responding to his friend's concerns. And so have subsequent readers. Confronted (consciously or not) by such a problematic, and wishing (for whatever reason) to avoid presumably 'philistine' recommendations that Nietzsche either deduce his arguments more precisely (Rohde's suggestion) or, say, assign more stable 'illocutionary force indicators' to his utterances,[22] the temptation has asserted itself among recent writers in the West to consider common-sense or empirical approaches to the challenge of Nietzsche's style somehow too thematic, too pretextual, or too pretropic. For are not all such approaches already always interdicted, themselves already bypassed by the thrust, the parry, the point, the goad, the spur, the *question* of his style and its 'property'? The summary response to Rohde would be that *there are no 'bridges'* and that any 'traditional,' 'philological,' 'hermeneutic' search for a 'true sense' is precisely disqualified.

And so even the ostensibly most notorious question about Nietzsche – his misogynism – is deflected, redirected, and deconstructed in the form of the nexus truth/art/woman. This form of the question of style is said by Jacques Derrida to

suspend the decidable opposition of the true and the non-true, instaurate the regime of the *epoché* in the form of quotation marks around every system of philosophical decidability, disqualify the hermeneutic project which postulated a true sense of the text, and free reading from the horizon of the meaning or truth of Being and from the values of production of the product or from the presence of the present. Whereupon that which is unchained is the question of style, *qua* the question of writing [la question du style comme question de l'écriture], the question posed by the spurring operation being more powerful than any content, any thesis, and any meaning.[23]

Now, such (*mirabile dictu*) Left-Husserlian, Left-Heideggarian deconstruction – at least more rigorous and internally consistent than its Anglo-American variant[24] – is itself inscribed by its own all-too-easy conflations. So, for instance, the Marxian category of production is lumped together with a Heideggarian critique of presence, with a resultant levelling out, not to say erasure, of specificity between distinct historical periods, social formations, and conceptual models, whereby late-nineteenth-century scientific analysis of surplus value in developing capitalism (Marx) is fused with quasi-mystical, neo-Luddite alienation during disintegrating imperialism (Heidegger). Derrida's supposedly 'radical' displacement of all referentiality, whereby historically determined, empirical style is vaporized into the metaphysical category of *écriture*, leads to a concomitant abandonment of any possibility to account for, or even identify, *historical* shifts in reception or analyse *ideological* difference. His 180-degree distortion of what he calls 'hermeneutics' is, in light of the theory or practice of contemporary hermeneutics, a facile misprision. And all such conflations are coeval with a valorization of 'play' that is passing vague, unreflected in spite of its hyperbolic self-consciousness, and certainly idealist at root. Derrida's strained, playful reading/writing explicitly conceives itself to be 'liberating' but is so in fact only at the level of voluntaristic interpolation and intellectualist delectation.

But let us suppose that such (ultimately, I think, valid) criticism of Derrida's project is wide open to the charge of resentful name-calling. Let us further suppose that Derrida's way of reading might be productively activated for our own ideological-critical purposes. The question asked by Derrida's writing can be then forced, however unwillingly, to address the question of the politics of Nietzsche's style, indeed the politics of the question of style and textual identity *per se*. And it can do so more precisely and radically than any other secondary text available to us. In what follows, I assume *ex hypothesi* that it does and see what happens. Certainly all of Nietzsche's readers should somehow confront the question of just how seriously they take Nietzsche's placement of 'quotation marks' around 'all' signifieds, indeed 'all' *referents*.

As is well known, Derrida isolates, frames, takes seriously, and plays with that phrase set in quotation marks in Nietzsche's notebook for fall 1881: '"Ich habe meinen Regenschirm vergessen,"' '"J'ai oublié mon parapluie,"' '"I've forgotten my umbrella."'[25] What exactly *is* this remark? What might it *signify?* More immediately, what are we going to *do* with it? Not a few readers would choose to ignore the phrase; but they would be hard pressed to defend this ignorance methodologically or theoretically. Indeed, it would not be too difficult to construct an argument that much of the issue of 'the identity of the text' is here at stake. If one does *not* ignore the phrase, what is apparently opened up is a question of far-reaching consequences. Derrida's partial but nonetheless scandalous conclusion (what the Greeks would have called *skandalon*) – if one can speak of a 'conclusion' in a text that is trying so self-consciously to prepare and perform every[26] term of this 'snippet' – is this:

> However far one might push a conscientious interpretation, one cannot deny the hypothesis that the totality of Nietzsche's text is perhaps, in some monstrous way, of the type: 'I have forgotten my umbrella.'
>
> Which is to say that there is no longer a 'totality to Nietzsche's text,' not even a fragmentary and aphoristic one.[27]

If Derrida, or rather the kind of Heideggarian tradition he represents, is right (or rather on the right spoor and/or *Holzweg*), then it would make no sense whatsoever to continue talking about, say, 'the identity of the text,' or 'Hölderlin's influence on Nietzsche,' or even 'Nietzsche's political ideology.' But let us now take another 'snippet,' another 'erratic exergue,' from Nietzsche's marginal (arguably *most* marginal) stylistic production, this time involving the seminal 'Romantic' poet Hölderlin. Then let us show where Nietzsche's version of the question of identity and style really leads.

THE UNTIMELY HÖ[L]DERLIN

Because of his recurrent headaches and faltering eyesight (both, as we know now, the result of a syphilitic infection), Nietzsche relied on the assistance of friends to correct the galley proofs of the second *Untimely Meditation*, 'The Use and Abuse of History.' On April Fool's Day 1874 (about a week after Rohde's initial reaction to what we have called the para*tactical* style of that text), Nietzsche was thanking Carl Gersdorff for proofreading the manuscript, but noted that his friend had overlooked something:

Thanks for the typos. But the most important one you missed: Höderlin for Hölderlin. But it looks beautiful, doesn't it? But not a soul [literally: not a pig] will understand it. My writings should be so obscure and incomprehensible!

[Dank für die Druckfehler: aber der wichtigste fehlt, Höderlin für Hölderlin. Aber nicht wahr, es sieht wunderschön aus? Aber es versteht kein Schwein. Meine Schriften sollen so dunkel und unverständlich sein!][28]

What looks 'so beautiful' in the uncorrected text? Certainly the published passage itself is an important one, since it can be read as a virtual summation of the central thesis of 'The Use and Abuse of History,' marking as it does a break between the older, allegedly 'dangerous' way of conceiving the past and some new (no less dangerous) mode. Presumably the misprint 'Höderlin' would mean that a 'little testicler' had become distressed about history while reading Greek philosophy. ('Höderlin' would be a kind of diminutive agent: *die Hode* = testicle; *Hoder* = testicler, etc.) But what is Nietzsche really implying to Gersdorff, what is it that no one, not a soul (not even a pig) would understand, or even attempt to understand? It seems to signify a parapraxis, a private joke about private parts, to which only Gersdorff is privy. Whatever the meaning of this joke at the expense of textual identity, Nietzsche would have all his writings – as Derrida would say, 'in their totality' – be as obscure and even incomprehensible as the (perhaps) Derridian pun: Hö[l]derlin. But I do not assume that Nietzsche knew its full significance.

Now, I am aware that fiddling around with puns, whether they be traceable to a printer's error (*lectio facilior* or *difficilior?*) or whatever, does not in itself nearly constitute philosophical deconstruction of the identity of the text. In fact, appearances to the contrary, for all Derrida's self-conscious punning, his own strategy of deconstruction more typically intends to avoid such insidiously empirical games. He will emphasize in a relatively early text that in his project a crucial concept like, say, 'originary trace' '*cannot be described by any concept of metaphysics whatsoever.*' And since it is *a fortiori* anterior to the distinction between regions of sensibility, to sound as to light, is there any sense in establishing a "natural" hierarchy between the acoustical imprint, say, and the visual (graphic) imprint? The graphic image is not seen; the acoustical image is not audible. The difference [*différence*] between the full unities of the voice remains unheard. Invisible also is the difference in the body of the inscription.'[29] But the rest is silence. And we are right to be wary of any Heideggarian conflation of empiricism with metaphysics.

Yet this Hölderlin with the absent, elliptic 'l' – with his/its phallic 'l,' once erected between the (private) parts of the arch (albeit 'seminal') Romantic testicler, now appropriately castrated by some anonymous printer's slip – is *undeniably* the figure inhabiting Nietzsche's unpublished literary remains. For here, much later (in the mid to late 1880s), the poet himself is still 'framed' by Nietzsche in genitally scurrilous ways.

Hö[l]derlin was certainly *untimely* for Nietzsche. By 1885–6, the time of the completion of *Thus Spoke Zarathustra* and two and a half years before Nietzsche's breakdown in Turin, his perception of the man he had once called the 'favourite poet [Lieblingsdichter]' of his youth *apparently* underwent a swift and indeed violent re-evaluation.[30]

Already by late summer 1884 he wrote notes to himself like the following:

German poets, namely when they are Swabian, e.g. Uhland decked out [herausgeputzt] with the sensibility of a noble maiden [Burgfräulein], or Freilingrath as — Or Hölderlin – – – [31]

The text is partially illegible, as the dashes indicate, but the (male chauvinistic) intent to degrade Hölderlin in such company is clear enough. A late letter to Georg Brandes in 1888 makes evident that Nietzsche never 'forgave' David Friedrich Strauss for having been a 'Stiftler' at Tübingen.[32] Milder diatribes against the 'Theologists of Tübingen' (Nietzsche has in mind Strauss, Schelling, Hegel, and certainly Hölderlin, too) appear in *Beyond Good and Evil* and in the unpublished notebooks (such as the one cited at length above) used for that book. They typically appear in the context of Nietzsche's struggle to formulate the crucial problem of cultural, historical, and even explicitly political 'order of rank [Rangordnung].'[33]

This kind of attack reaches a climax in published form a few years later in *The Antichrist*:

Among Germans one understands immediately when I say that philosophy is contaminated by the blood of theologists. The Protestant minister and Protestantism itself are the *peccatum originale* of German philosophy. Definition of Protestantism: the half finished paralysis of Christianity – *and* of reason ... One only need pronounce the word Tübinger Stift' to comprehend *what* German philosophy is – an *insidious* theology ... The Swabians are the best liars in Germany, they lie innocently. ...[34]

Other, unpublished notes leave no doubt that Hölderlin, in effect, belongs back in the Tübinger Stift and make clear what the reasons Nietzsche had are. Hölderlin and Leopardi (arguably the two greatest philologist poets before Nietzsche) are '*effeminate* males,' 'onanists,' 'impotents.'[35] Clearly and remarkably, Nietzsche reverts with increased violence to precisely those modes of judgment about Hölderlin and, for that matter, Leopardi[36] that had been common currency through the entire nineteenth century, namely to F.T. Vischer, August Koberstein, and all the rest. It is the bitterness, the scurrility, of Nietzsche's outburst which initially stands out in this axiological shift. It is reasonable to assume that by attacking Hölderlin (and all other Romantics) with such patently *ad hominen*, indeed *ad personem*, arguments (it is rather difficult to construct a more *ad hominem* argument than the 'accusation' of onanism, as Nietzsche knew all too well), he must, given his apparent early identification with Hölderlin, indeed his professed love for him, now be attacking himself or at least some moment in his own subconscious.[37] As is by now equally well known, Nietzsche's manipulation of historical periodization forces terms such as 'Romanticism,' 'metaphysics,' 'ultra-Platonism,' 'feminism,' 'false Idealism,' 'Christianity,' 'theology,' 'Protestantism,' 'idols,' 'socialism,' etc. into more or less the same witches' cauldron.[38] And of course Nietzsche repeatedly acknowledged that he too was, or had been, a 'Romantic *sang pur*,' his distinction being presumably his recognition of the fact and the fact's inextricable complicity with the question of style. 'I fear we shall never be rid of God because we still believe in grammar'[39] is perhaps the most cited and succinct formulation of this theme.

Nietzsche's most hyperbolic offensive against, say, Christianity is now (from the mid-1880s on) typically aimed at its '*radical castration* of passion [an der Wurzel].' As Hölderlin was castrated by the Tübinger Stift, as what he really needed was 'a wench from time to time,' so is his madness 'fair enough [billig].'[40] It is as part of this (later powerfully deferred) complex (involving his own fears about impotence, homosexuality, and masturbation) that, already in 1874, Nietzsche had been so intrigued by the typographical mistake 'Höderlin' in the second *Untimely Meditation*. The phallic 'l' was to remain 'under erasure' for Nietzsche from then on, as it had presumably been already earlier. The question of the Tübinger Stift, understood as stylus (*der Stift*) and as 'charitable' institution and pedagogic seminary (*die Stift*) was to be *one* necessary, constitutive part of Nietzsche's version of the question of style. But it is not a *sufficient* component.

The transformation of 'my favourite from high school days' (as Nietzsche had called Hölderlin) into the 'seminal little testicler,' castrated by Christianity and modernist historicism into justified madness, constitutes one of the many subterranean narratives with which the reader of Nietzsche, his or her wits honed perhaps by reading Derrida, will not be unfamiliar. Yet one need be no Derridian, surely, to recall the by now commonplace features of Nietzsche's complicated and uncanny relation to the (Romantic) tradition of philosophy and culture from which he struggled with varying degrees of success to free himself.

Nietzsche, to repeat, had early on intimated that in attacking and in praising a seminal source for him like *Wagner*, he had spoken to some extent always of himself.[41] What I call 'the Hö[l]derlin complex' seems to relate to a dual question: what was the effect on Nietzsche's thinking and writing of the charges made by Wagner against him of excessive masturbation, and/or sexual inversion, and/or impotency? And what was the effect of the occasional but increasing, and (given his apparent ignorance of his syphilis) not unreasonable fears that his various somatic disorders (notably vomiting, vertigo, headaches, and of course faulty vision) were indications that he might be going insane? We must take note of the fact that the chiffre or sign 'Hölderlin' is powerfully linked by Nietzsche throughout his life to the, for most readers more familiar, sign 'Wagner.' The specific repercussion of this linkage involves, but also sublates, the question of psychosexual pathology, since, as we have seen, 'Wagner' meant for Nietzsche, along with everything else, the problem of transforming art and the philosophical defence of art into some form of practical (paratactical) politics, although most assuredly *not* the kind of politics the Dresden Wagner had desired.

An outline of the extant evidence makes plausible the *Wagner-Hölderlin* nexus in Nietzsche's mind.[42] Nietzsche had begun reading (and then, as I've shown elsewhere, plagiarizing) Hölderlin in 1861 – at almost exactly the time he first encountered the name Wagner. (Wagner was the same age as Nietzsche's own deceased natural father and was to become, via some difficult transference, that father's cultural or spiritual replacement.) Nietzsche celebrated Wagner's birthday in May 1873 by having Gersdorff read aloud the so-called 'Scheltrede' against the Germans from Hölderlin's *Hyperion*. (At Christmas that year Cosima and Richard Wagner read aloud from *Hyperion* too ... and were most unpleasantly reminded of Nietzsche's labile personality.) In the following April (1874), Nietzsche had found the typo 'Höderlin' in the manuscript of the second *Untimely Meditation* and in May, one week after Wagner's next birthday, Gersdorff (also an intimate of the Wagners) wrote Nietzsche that Cosima had just remarked on 'the piece of Hölderlin's nature' in Nietzsche's own personality. This was no compliment. During the course of that same year Nietzsche purchased a copy of a new edition of Hölderlin's selected works and read the poet more intensively than he had done before or would do again. The poet was cited or alluded to in three of the four *Untimely Meditations* (all except 'Wagner in Bayreuth'), including a hidden reference to the ode *Socrates and Alcibiades* when Nietzsche was describing his own relationship to his teachers, notably his (and Wagner's) philosophical master, Schopenhauer. The next year (1875) Nietzsche cited at length from Hölderlin's 'patriotic' ode *Gesang des Deutschen* at the end of his highly complicated and even ambivalent birthday wishes to Wagner in May. By January of the following year (1876), Malwida von Meysenbug (who had given the Wagners their copy of Hölderlin's works) was talking to Nietzsche in a letter (and perhaps verbally) about the 'dangerous influence' on a mutual friend (and student of Nietzsche's) that Schopenhauer, Leopardi, and Hölderlin himself were exerting. Also during this year Nietzsche reread Malwida von Meysenbug's memoirs, containing significant references to the mad Hölderlin; and this was the year Nietzsche cited Hölderlin for the last time in his own published work. This last published reference occurred in the aphorism eulogizing pederastic relationships in ancient Greece, 'A Society for Men,' in *Human, All-too-Human* (published 1878) where Nietzsche quoted his favourite line from Hölderlin's *Empedokles* ('Denn liebend giebt der Sterbliche vom Besten') – a line he had also used at least twice in letters to intimate friends. During and following the periods of serious illness that eventually led to his resignation from the University of Basel, Nietzsche's friends and relatives were continually reminded (both to his face and behind his back) of Hölderlin's fate. (This connection was reinforced by Nietzsche's encounter with Hölderlin in that part of his collateral reading where the poet was mentioned.) These people included nearly all the important figures in Nietzsche's private life, some of whom were further linked to the Wagner Circle: Gersdorff, Meysenbug, and Richard and Cosima Wagner themselves, as well as Elisabeth, Rohde, Overbeck, and Gast. Then, during the composition of *Thus Spoke Zarathustra* – a crucial component of which was its parodic treatment of Wagner and his works – Nietzsche also lifted without attribution significant chunks from Hölderlin's *Hyperion* and *Empedokles*, including *Zarathustra*'s enigmatic subtitle: 'A Book for Everyone and No One.' And then, as we've seen, in the unredeemable solitude from the mid 1880s on, Nietzsche turned drastically against Hölderlin, as he had against Wagner, using *exactly* those genitally scatological charges against Hölderlin that he thought Wagner had levelled once against him.

But where does such a nexus lead us? What does it ultimately have to do with 'the question of style'? I wish to argue now that only to the extent that the Nietzsche/Hö[l]derlin nexus can lead to questions of Nietzsche's political ideology, and of the specific effects of that ideology historically and today, should this nexus be 'deconstructed.'

NIETZSCHE'S POLITICS OF STYLE

In a notebook used by Nietzsche in the mid 1880s, there occurs a reference to Hölderlin that I shall activate in a productive way, forcing it for my purposes here to take on exemplary status in Nietzsche's writing and in the reception of it. It is the only relatively positive reference to Hölderlin made by Nietzsche during the last sane period of his life. It occurs on one of three apparently heterogeneous pages in notebook w 1/1, the extreme importance of which for Nietzsche is announced by the notebook's title page: 'The Eternal Recurrence: A Prophecy. By Friedrich Nietzsche.' Three pages in the first third of the manuscript are of special interest to us. The first page contains the first important mention of Hölderlin's name by Nietzsche since *Human, All-too-Human* (1876–8) and stands just on the threshold of his violent turn away from him in subsequent notebooks. Nietzsche had just completed part 3 of *Thus Spoke Zarathustra* (in at least one sense the 'final' part of that text). Here Nietzsche, even now in the mid 1880s, still pays homage to Hölderlin's *style*, although he is only on the verge of consciously acknowledging to himself that he has long since abandoned Hölderlin the man. How aesthetically pleasing, and beneficial, Nietzsche writes, was the metric structure, the prosodic style of Platen and Hölderlin – but, alas, 'too strict' for us moderns. Thus Nietzsche reverts to a familiar nineteenth-century conception of Hölderlin as (mere) master of the ode form. (Comparisons of Hölderlin to Platen, a notorious homosexual, had been common currency.) This *stylistic* mastery, or rather the strategic and rhetorical *usefulness* of that style, must be rejected for some other, yet to be defined, purpose. The first reflection concludes thus:

The play with the most different metres and occasionally the unmetrical is right for us: the freedom that we have already gained in music from R. W[agner]. we should take for our prose! In the final analysis it is the only one that speaks powerfully to our heart! – Thanks to Luther![43]

The second page develops this pragmatic argument. The language of Luther and the poetic form of the Bible (both de-Christianized) are to be the basis for what Nietzsche (this 'good European') now calls 'the new German poetry.' This is claimed as uniquely his discovery. What he will later term the 'great style' cannot be helped even by Wagner. Perhaps some sort of compromise *vis-à-vis* Hölderlin is implied in this project for the 'new' and 'German' discursive practice that Nietzsche calls 'fictive.' But its strategic function is *not* aesthetic. On the contrary.

A declaration of war of the *higher humans* against the masses is necessary! Everywhere mediocrity is joining forces to become master! Everything that makes soft and gentle, or brings the *Volk* or the 'effeminate' to the forefront – all this works on behalf of *suffrage universel*, i.e. the rule of *lower* people. But we shall practise active repression [Repressalien] and drive out this entire mess [diese ganze Wirthschaft] (which began in Europe with Christianity) and brings it to trial [vor's Gericht].

Such pages are disturbed and shall not be simply willed, or rationalized, or *stylized* out of existence.

Nietzsche's notion of style or strategy is not that of the inflated, resentful martial imagery of our currently fashionable criticism.[44] Something emerges here in the unpublished notebooks of the 1880s that is already at least implicitly in force in Nietzsche's intent from the last section of *The Birth of Tragedy* onward, something that he largely laboured to conceal in his published writing (at least in its explicit, radical formulation), and something that was to be, in effect, Nietzsche's compensation for the lack of a Bayreuth to actualize his own thought in the political arena of imperial Germany. It was, however, the true legacy of Nietzsche's writing and thinking. Hölderlin's role in this new problematic had undergone a complicated two-stage transformation. First,

Hölderlin became Hö[l]derlin: Hölderlin had to be attacked in exactly the terms that Wagner had used to attack Nietzsche. Only then could Hölderlin *and* Wagner be finally merged with a much greater political project intended to rival and surpass Wagner's own. Although never realized, even by the Nazis, this project germinates on in all interpretations that are blind to its existence.

To Nietzsche's style was delivered over the task of initiating war, a real war: the higher 'centurions' (Nietzsche shares this term with Machiavelli) versus the masses and everything else 'effeminate,' 'impotent,' and 'castrated' like Hölderlin. Or 'decadent' like Wagner. The three notebook pages from w 1/1 are hardly heterogenous. They are exemplary symptoms of Nietzsche's much analysed and seldom understood project of linking 'great style' and 'great politics' – and of thereby effecting a transition from diagnosis to proposed cure of the culture and society he would rather *destroy* than *deconstruct*. For not only will Nietzsche require of this 'style' that it assume and/or undermine epistemological authority (de Man's problematic), not only will it assume and/or undermine all modes of metaphysical nostalgia, gravity, and textual identity (Derrida's problematic), it will have an explicitly reactive political mission.

Nietzsche is asking a different, far more dangerous and historically portentous 'question of style' than that presented by deconstruction. And he makes the question explicit, indeed he wanted to publish it, for those who can read it.

This time I'll focus only on the question of *style* [Ich halte mich dies Mal nur bei der Frage des *Stils* auf]. What is the sign of every *literary décadence*? That life no longer resides in the whole. The word becomes sovereign and leaps from the sentence, the sentence takes over and obscures the meaning of the page, the page is vitalized only at the expense of the whole – the whole is no longer a whole.[45]

Up to this point in the text: a description of de-construction *qua* musical (melocentric) and philosophical '*dé-cadence.*' Perhaps even, if you prefer, from a kind of philosophically totalitarian perspective, he gives us a criticism of what will become the deconstructive style. But even this is not the whole of Nietzsche's version of 'the question of style.' The text continues:

But that is the parable for every style of *décadence*: each time anarchy of atoms, disgregation of will, 'freedom of the individual,' to employ moral terms, – all this expanded into a political theory: '*equal* rights for all.' Life, *equal* vitality, the vibration and exuberance of life forced back into its pettiest manifestations, and all the rest *poor* in life. Everywhere paralysis, hardship, torpidity, *or* enmity and chaos: each one ever more obvious the higher one goes in the forms of organization. The whole no longer lives at all: it is composite, calculated, artificial, an artefact. –

When Nietzsche asks the question of style it is to attack *explicitly*, from the point of view of cultural elitism (this is his much-vaunted 'perspectivism'), a historically specific form of political 'anarchy': namely, nineteenth-century social democracy. Such 'artistocratic radicalism,' as the shamefaced Social Democrat Georg Brandes intuited from the first, is the actual condition of intelligibility of Nietzsche's 'radical' critique of Wilhelminian hegemony.[46] Post-structuralism and deconstruction have now replicated Nietzsche's political ideology by *at least implicitly* affirming political anarchy (defined as aestheticized politics, that is partial if not hopelessly naïve and passive politics), by representing a false, disarmed, depoliticized version of Nietzsche's question of style, by occluding its original, irrational, anti-democratic intent.

Nietzsche's 'Wagner,' the immediate referent in the passages cited above from 'The Case of Wagner,' remained, in the last instance, the Wagner of 1848. Behind all the manifest critique of Wagner's *stylistic* decadence lurks the latent 'revolutionary idealist,' 'the utopian socialist,' 'the improver of mankind,' and, note this well, 'the Parisian.'[47] This is the 'stylist' against whom, already back in 1874, Rohde had warned Nietzsche by comparing Nietzsche's paratactical style with Wagner's own. Today, paradoxically, the entire deconstructive operation of criticism, appealing to Nietzsche, is performed in exactly that 'decadent' style Nietzsche attacked in, say, 'The Case of Wagner.'

But the point is more complex still. Both kinds of what Gramsci sarcastically termed 'verbal revolt' – Nietzsche's *and* that of the powerful 'misreading' by deconstruction – end up inevitably, as Gramsci also predicted, by (at best) accepting 'conventionality' in reality after all. And (at worst) they both irresponsibly and voluntaristically intervene to destroy not merely what they cannot deconstruct, but also any possibility for real social revolution.

For all its considerable insight into intellectual and cultural decadence, perhaps just because its frame of reference remained locked at the level of cultural criticism, Nietzsche's political position was powerfully deluded, as are 'Nietzschean' ones of today.[48] When Nietzsche correctly notes, for example, that 'It is of deep significance that Wagner's ascent is coeval with the ascent of the "Reich,"'[49] the abject helplessness, indeed (one should not mince words here) the proto-fascistic nature, of his proposed remedies should never be passed over in silence. This is especially the case since, as Nietzsche in the next sentence 'predicted,' the nineteenth century was poised on the brink of 'the classical age of war.' This was a self-fulfilling prophecy if there ever was one. It was an age of war which Nietzsche, with the full thrust of the rhetorical technique that he had honed and rehearsed in his workbooks, did more to initiate than to prevent. All the 'parentheses for asses' and the belated, posthumously published propaganda in 'Ecce Homo' on behalf of German 'Liberalism' (Friedrich III) were indeed '*dim* resistance'[50] in the full light of his sustained irrationalism and elitism. Such rearguard actions brighten at most our image of Nietzsche's personality, making him appear somewhat healthier, his strength of will somewhat more concrete and sober. 'But let us take leave of Herr Nietzsche: what does it matter to us that Herr Nietzsche became healthy again!'[51]

Nietzsche's at best heterogenous political ideology (which, one should not forget, he exposes as well as flounders in) cannot be deconstructed with the same alacrity as, say, is misogyny, if indeed *that* can be deconstructed.[52] Deconstruction and post-structuralism seem always to pull up short and, by their symptomatic silences, ultimately collaborate with dominant ideology, its sources, influences, and reception. Determined perhaps by their own genealogies in formalism and structuralism,[53] they have always ended up by celebrating the break-up of the identity of Nietzsche's text as 'open *and* undecipherable'[54] or, alternatively, as criticism's most exemplary 'aporia.'[55] To read Nietzsche from a *fully essentialist* viewpoint,[56] that is to take him literally, *wörtlich*, only in terms of his style, whether by displacing political ideology by misogyny (the latter is for Nietzsche, as many of the passages we have seen show, a subcategory of the former) or by repressing the persuasive aspect of rhetoric, is to risk again and again the incalculably dangerous consequences of irrationalism. It is to be adrift all too comfortably and irresponsibly, whether playfully or ironically, with what Walter Benjamin, referring to Nietzsche, termed 'brilliant intuition ... in the abyss of aestheticism.'[57] This is to sacrifice for peace of mind the exemplary complexity and negative historical power of the question of style as posed by Nietzsche. The discurso-ideological site 'Nietzsche' *is* this question.

THE UMBRELLA OF TEXTUAL IDENTITY AND STYLE

Current ways of broaching the question of textual identity and style do not of course *intend* to answer any politically relevant question by asking what Nietzsche may have meant when he wrote, in quotation marks, ' "I've forgotten my umbrella." ' And hence any 'deconstruction' of what I've called the 'Nietzsche/Hö[l]derlin' nexus (the nexus of the question of textual identity, undecidability, and marginality, among other things) must take leave of such modes of questioning, even as it has participated in them. Derrida's neo-Heideggerian and really quite genial metaphysical enterprise has been to supplement and transcend the *empiricism* of what Nietzsche might have meant by his 'marginal' texts with what Derrida calls the *philosophical* 'question of style *qua* question of *écriture*.' In so doing, Derrida would open up the question of the status, the identity of Nietzsche's texts, indeed of texts *tout court*, including, necessarily, Derrida's own. I now claim, however, that this entire post-structuralist mode of handling the issue of textual identity serves as a kind of umbrella, protecting itself from more exigent and serious matters of political ideology and, ultimately, effective politics.

At the beginning of *Eperons*, Derrida's text questions whether we shall ever know the referent of another exergue, one snipped this time from a letter from Nietzsche to Malwida von Meysenbug concerning a 'little bundle' Nietzsche had sent her: 'Mein Bündelchen für Sie.'[58] Deconstruction's cloyingly coy parenthetical question ('Saura-t-on jamais ce qui fut ainsi eux nommé?') is *merely* rhetorical here, as it is everywhere when deconstruction is confronted by the problem of the referent, and moves to foreclose the problem of addressing it.

Elisabeth Förster Nietzsche and Peter Gast have little positive to tell almost anyone, but they could illuminate for Derrida, who has no patience even with Colli and Montinari, at least this one reference. The 'little bundle' – still in the Nietzsche Archive in Weimar – was made up of a photograph of Basel with a view of the Münster and the bridge over the Rhine, a copy of Rohde's anti-Wilamowitz-Möllendorff pamphlet 'Afterphilologie,' and Nietzsche's lectures 'The Future of Our Institutions of Learning.'[59]

Now, as Adorno and Marcuse might have further informed Derrida (deconstruction, at least, can learn from critical theory), the case of the forgotten umbrella may be no more difficult to crack by empirical research, at least at one level of grimy reality. On a trip together to the Upper Engadine, a sort of pilgrimage to Sils Maria, Adorno and Marcuse were told by an old man in the village who remembered Nietzsche about the red umbrella used by the philosopher to shield his aching, syphilitic eyes from the Apollonian, Alpine sun. It was an umbrella that Nietzsche could ill afford ever, however 'absent-mindedly' (the entire phrase about the umbrella may be overdetermined by this additional parabolic connotation), to forget. It was filled by the village children, the interlocutor of Adorno and Marcuse among them, with pebbles that rained down on Nietzsche's unprotected head whenever he would swing it open.[60] This umbrella, to be sure, constitutes a mere *signifié*, not to say empirical referent or even material object. But it is just such things that resist, and logically and ontologically precede, the object of deconstruction (all that 'materialism' of the signifier). This, in any event, would have been *Nietzsche's* conclusion when he whipped open the umbrella. There was then, and is now, nothing 'liberating' about what happened next.

Nevertheless *the quotation marks* around the umbrella in the exergue from Nietzsche's unpublished notebooks do remain. And remaining, too, is the full political dimension of the question of textual identity and style. For we still confront the far more significant *guillemets* placed by Friedrich Wilhelm Nietzsche around many of the key words of Wilhelminian Germany. The fact that Nietzsche's challenge to these terms cannot be reduced entirely to his specific historical conjuncture is amplified repeatedly in the form of his continuing reception and in the fact of his positive relevance to thinkers today. Yet if some of Nietzsche's analyses of these terms remain valid, it will always be in *inverse proportion* to what constitutes the criminal insanity of all his proposed solutions and cures. Nietzsche's mode of posing 'the question of style' can be shown to be at work even (or especially) in exceedingly oblique and marginal points of entry into his texts: such as his reading of typographical errors ('Hö[l]derlin') and apparently passing references to stylistic problems (Hölderlin's 'too strict' ode form) or Wagner's 'decadence.' The problematic of this complex differential calculus remains particularly in force whenever critics occlude access to the ideological and political dimension of Nietzsche's writing and its reception, whenever they, like Nietzsche, idealistically attempt to elevate historically specific conditions into general conditions of human existence, let alone 'style.'

'Nietzsche' provides an exemplary illustration of the proposition that 'Democratization necessarily entails aesthetic loss,' wherein each of the three main terms of the proposition requires diacritical stress. Democratization is *therefore* negative. Aesthetic loss is to be lamented more than *any* other. And, finally, for Nietzsche and for any consistent 'Nietzschean' position, this entailment is not merely a necessary but *the sufficient condition* for posing any really significant question. This historically important and, I think, vile and dangerous position is one of the strongest possible formulations of what is meant by the term 'aestheticism.' But particularly pernicious was *the attempt to practise politics on this basis*, an attempt made by Wagner *and, in his own way, by Nietzsche*. When in 1888 Brandes asked Nietzsche about his paroxyms (Jost Hermand's term is apposite) against democracy and socialism, Nietzsche evaded the issue – just as much earlier, near the beginning of his public career, he had refused to address Rohde's remarks about his 'Wagnerian' and 'para*tactical*' style. The question of this style and its politics must always be supplemented with the more significant question of the politics of such reading formations: Nietzsche's, no less than that of others who would avoid such matters, say, by worrying the question of the identity of the (literary) text.[61] Make no mistake: the most marginal point of entry into Nietzsche, as into *all* texts, leads to politics. No umbrella can protect you.

TOWARDS A CONCLUSION (VIA LUKÁCS)

For those of us who read Nietzsche, and read his readers, primarily within the discursive order of our pedagogic institutions – institutions, as Gramsci knew, that serve as 'non-coercive coercion' for hegemony, transnational capital, and surplus value – 'Nietzsche's question of style' remains particularly exigent to us as teachers and students. For this reason I agree with Georg Lukács:

When anything bad is being discussed, I always come back to Nietzsche. Nietzsche, for example, made out that proletarian class consciousness was nothing more than the resentment of slaves. And this ideology, as I know only too well from my youth, prevented many decent intellectuals of that time from joining up with the workers' movement, for their consciousness could not tolerate any resentment or support of resentment in an upstanding moral person. We therefore have the task of breaking through these kinds of inhibition.[62]

My argument here has been directed at such 'decent intellectuals' today. Perhaps broaching the question of textual identity and style is now the necessary condition for such a 'breakthrough.' If, however, as the sheer complexity of modern hegemony suggests, this is indeed the case, then Nietzsche's way of posing the question, as the history of its reception in Western post-structuralism will doubtless continue to reveal, cannot provide the sufficient condition for formulating or for answering it. 'This time,' Nietzsche had written, 'I'll focus only on the question of style.' Let there be no other time for him or for his followers.

NOTES

1 An earlier, shorter, and differently focused version of this essay appeared under the title 'Nietzsche and Deconstruction' in the Bulletin of the Midwest Modern Language Association, 16:1 (Spring 1983), 70–86.

2 For representative contemporary attacks on 'essentialism' in English studies, the largest discipline in the Anglo-American liberal arts, see: Re-reading English, ed. Peter Widdowson, London 1982, and Terry Eagleton, Literary Theory: An Introduction, Minneapolis 1983, esp. 'The Rise of English,' pp. 17–53. What needs to be raised in Marxist critiques of these attacks is the issue of empirio-critical relativism. See further the recently published essays by Raymond Williams, Writing in Society, London no date, esp. 'Cambridge English, Past and Present,' 'Crisis in English Studies,' and 'Beyond Cambridge English,' pp. 177–226. In my essay, I am attacking a variant form of essentialism, namely that of deconstruction itself; see my note 56 below.

3 Antonio Gramsci, Selections from the Prison Notebooks, ed. and trans. Quintin Hoare and Geoffrey Nowell Smith, New York 1971, p. 369. Cf. Gramsci, Quaderni del carcere, ed. Valentino Gerratana, Turin 1975, II, 1266–7.

4 Jacques Derrida, L'écriture et la différence, Paris 1967, p. 427.

5 Paul de Man, *Allegories of Reading: Figural Language in Rousseau, Nietzsche, Rilke, and Proust*, New Haven 1979, p. 118.

6 Letter from Rohde to Nietzsche, 24 March 1874; Friedrich Nietzsche, *Kritische Gesamtausgabe, Briefwechsel*, eds. Giorgio Colli and Mazzino Montinari, Berlin 1978, II/4, 421.

7 Nietzsche, 'Wagner in Bayreuth' 10; Nietzsche, *Kritische Gesamtausgabe, Werke*, eds. Giorgio Colli and Mazzino Montinari, Berlin 1967-, IV/1, 76. Hereafter cited as KGW with appropriate volume and page numbers. When quoting from this edition I use the system of reference established by its editors.

8 Nietzsche, 'Vom Nutzen und Nachtheil der Historie für das Leben' 10: KGW, III/1, 330.

9 Such is the position taken by Georg Lukács generally in his later work on Nietzsche, notably in *Die Zerstörung der Vernunft* (1953). This paraphrase of that position comes, however, from Leo Kofler in his interview with Lukács in *Conversations with Lukács*, ed. Theo Pinkus, trans. anonymously, London 1967, p. 49; my emphasis.

10 See Theodor Adorno, 'Parataxis: Zur späten Lyrik Hölderlins,' in Adorno, *Gesammelte Schriften*, ed. Rolf Tiedemann, Frankfurt am Main 1974, II, 463.

11 For an apposite and succinct location of Nietzsche in this ideological and historical problematic, see Sebastiano Timpanaro, *The Freudian Slip: Psychoanalysis and Textual Criticism*, trans. Kate Soper, London 1976, pp. 185–6.

12 For a lucid discussion of Nietzsche in the context of cultural politics in Prussia that bears directly on my discussion here, see Peter Uwe Hohendahl, 'Reform als Utopie: Die preussische Bildungspolitik, 1809–1817,' in *Utopieforschung: Interdisziplinäre Studien zur neuzeitlichen Utopie*, ed. Wilhelm Vosskamp, Stuttgart 1983, III, 250–72, esp. pp. 265–7.

13 For representative, allegedly 'materialist' rumination on this ubiquitous theme of Anglo-French post-structuralism, see Rosalind Coward and John Ellis, *Language and Materialism: Developments in the Semiology and the Theory of the Subject*, London 1977. All the major apologies for deconstruction have assimilated Nietzsche uncritically into this general position. See, for instance, Christopher Norris, *Deconstruction: Theory and Practice*, London 1982, esp. pp. 58–89 and Norris, *The Deconstructive Turn: Essays in the Rhetoric of Philosophy*, London 1983, esp. pp. 91–3 and 98–106. Two further expositions of deconstructive criticism claim a centrality, even a paternity, of Nietzsche with regard to deconstruction. See: Jonathan Culler, *On Deconstruction: Theory and Criticism after Structuralism*, Ithaca 1983, esp. p. 88; and Vincent B. Leitch, *Deconstructive Criticism: An Advanced Introduction*, New York 1983, esp. p. 252. Norris, Culler, Leitch, and others in this tendency (one can include Richard Rorty, as well), all view Nietzsche only through the woefully uncritical ideological optic provided by Derrida and de Man.

14 This is quite explicit in Nietzsche's work throughout. See, for the time period under discussion here, Nietzsche, 'Vom Nutzen und Nachtheil der Historie für das Leben' 9; KGW, III/1, 317–18.

15 Nietzsche, 'Vom Nutzen und Nachtheil der Historie für das Leben' 9; KGW, III/1, 318. For unambiguous remarks on Nietzsche's view of history and its influence on modernist literary theory in the West, see Robert Weimann, *Structure and Society in Literary History: Studies in the History and Theory of Historical Criticism*, Charlottesville 1976, pp. 117–22.

16 See 'Die Kunst und die Revlution' and 'Das Kunstwerk der Zukunft,' both in Richard Wagner, *Gesammelte Schriften und Dichtungen*, Leipzig 1872, III, 9–50 and 51–210. The notebook referred to was probably not seen by Nietzsche, since Wagner had turned away from his past political proclivities by the time Nietzsche met him and since it did not appear in print until later; see Richard Wagner, *Entwürfe, Gedanken, Fragmente*, Leipzig 1885, esp. pp. 11–33. For Wagner's own explanation of the word 'communism' – which he did not retract or abandon even in the 1870s – see his 'Einleitung zum dritten und vierten Bande,' *Gesammelte Schriften und Dichtungen*, III, 5–6. The entire text of 'Die Kunst und die Revolution' reads like a direct response to, not to say parody of, *The Communist Manifesto*. In this regard, it is very instructive to compare Marx's and Engel's discussion of Goethe's notion of comparative or world literature (*Weltliteratur*) as symptomatic of the cosmopolitan, expansionistic character of production and consumption (see 'Manifesto of the Communist Party,' Karl Marx and Frederick Engels, *Collected Works*, VI: *1845–1848*, New York 1976, p. 488) with Nietzsche's remarks in *The Birth of Tragedy* on the necessity for having a slave class in Alexandrian (read: modern) culture and on the vain consolations of *Weltliteratur* in that culture. See Nietzsche, *Die Geburt der Tragödie* 18; KGW, II/1, 115–16.

17 Wagner, 'Die Kunst und die Revolution,' *Gesammelte Schriften*, III, 36–7.

18 Wagner, 'Die Kunst und die Revolution,' *Gesammelte Schriften*, III, 49 and, in the same volume, 'Das Kunstwerk der Zukunft,' 158–9. Also: *Entwürfe*, pp. 32–3.

19 See Adorno, *In Search of Wagner*, trans. Rodney Livingstone, London 1981, p. 14.

20 Cf. Karl Joël's solid thematic studies: 'Nietzsche und die Romantik,' *Neue deutsche Rundschau*, 14 (1903), 458–501 and *Nietzsche und die Romantik* [1905], 2nd ed., Jena 1923. There has emerged an entire sub-industry on the topic 'Nietzsche and Romanticism' since Joel's work. For a representative modern approach, see Ernst Behler, 'Die Kunst der Reflexion: Das frühromantische Denken im Hinblick auf Nietzsche,' in *Untersuchungen zur Literatur als Geschichte: Festschrift für Benno von Wiese*, ed. Vincent J. Günther, et al., Berlin 1973, pp. 219–47.

21 See Walter Benjamin, *Der Begriff der Kunstkritik in der deutschen Romantik* [1919], ed. Hermann Schweppenhäuser, Frankfurt am Main 1973, pp. 8–9.

22 The massively unproductive exchange between John Searle and Derrida on the pages

of *Glyph* should not lead us to overlook this potentially interesting possibility of analysing Nietzsche's rhetoric.

23 Jacques Derrida, 'La question du style,' in *Nietzsche aujourd'hui?*, Paris 1973, II, 270. This essay has subsequently appeared in expanded form as a monograph with the title *Eperons: Les styles de Nietzsche* and is available in a dual language edition, *Spurs: Nietzsche's Styles*, trans. Barbara Harlow, Chicago 1979. Here the passage may be found on p. 106. When citing this text, I shall give references to both versions; the translation, however, will be my own.

24 For a *philosophically* exacting distinction of Derrida's mode of deconstruction from that practised by North American *literary* critics, see Rodolphe Gasché, 'Deconstruction as Criticism,' *Glyph*, 6 (1979), 177–215. This essay, which has been welcomed by many critics in England and North America (some of whom don't seem to realize that Gasché is attempting to attack their own imprecision), is seriously marred by its wholly uncritical embrace of Derrida. This is ultimately nothing more than *ipse dixit* exposition of the master.

25 The fragment (written during the composition of *The Gay Science*) about the umbrella may be located in Nietzsche, 'Nachgelassene Fragmente, Herbst, 1881' 12[62]; KGW, V/2, 485. Derrida's discussion is in *Eperons*, pp. 122–42; 'La question du style,' 280–7.

26 Unlike proper Derridians, I have little confidence that Derrida is aware of all the crucial etymological threads in the German language that he is trying to spin. While absolute control of language is certainly not Derrida's pretension (after all, 'die Sprache spricht'), it would seem nevertheless important, just in terms of his own argument and procedure, if not for the sake of philological accuracy, to account for the fact that the German word *Weib* (as the philologist Nietzsche was quite aware) derives from ancient forms meaning 'veiled' or 'veil.' Contrast, for instance, Nietzsche's really quite straightforward (albeit silly and lamentable) fascination with woman as a veil covering truth with Derrida's own more strained effort to play with various associations provided by the French word(s) *viole*.

27 Derrida, *Eperons*, pp. 132–3; 'La question du style,' 284–5. Interestingly, the general thesis here about the heterogeneity of Nietzsche's 'text' shares important features with much earlier 'existentialist' readings of Nietzsche (most notably that of Karl Jaspers). Nor perhaps are their respective political ideologies ultimately that different.

28 Nietzsche to Carl Gersdorff, 1 April 1874; *Kritische Gesamtausgabe, Briefwechsel*, II/3, 215. There is a rhyme at the end of the German text that seems to underscore its sense of enigma or riddle.

29 Jacques Derrida, *De la grammatologie*, Paris 1967, p. 95.

30 Some of what follows is based on a forthcoming book, *Nietzsche/Hölderlin: A Critical Revision* (Bonn), in which I trace Hölderlin's impact on Nietzsche and show

that his earliest reception of the poet, usually thought to be represented by the so-called *Schulpfortabrief*, was in fact marked by plagiarism and self-deception.

31 Nietzsche, 'Nachgelassene Fragmente, Sommer-Herbst 1884' 26 [307]; KGW, VII/2, 230.

32 Nietzsche to Brandes, 7 March 1888; *Gesammelte Briefe*, ed. Peter Gast and Elisabeth Förster Nietzsche, Berlin and Leipzig 1905, III, 290. In a letter to Gast a year earlier, Nietzsche had expressed delight that he was in the process of shocking the Stift and its supporters; see Nietzsche to Gast, 7 March 1887; Nietzsche, *Gesammelte Briefe*, IV, 283–4.

33 Nietzsche, *Jenseits von Gut und Böse* 11; KGW, VI/2, 19. See further, on the problem of '*Rangordnung*'; 'Nachgelassene Fragmente, Sommer-Herbst 1884' 26 [7–9], 26 [258], and 26 [297]; KGW, VII/2, 150, 215–16, and 227.

34 Nietzsche, *Der Antichrist* 10; KGW, VI/3, 174.

35 Nietzsche, 'Nachgelassene Fragmente, Sommer-Herbst 1884' 26 [405]; KGW, VII/2, 255.

36 On Leopardi see the seminal account given by Sebastiano Timpanaro, 'The Pessimistic Materialism of Giacomo Leopardi,' *New Left Review*, 116 (July–August 1979), 29–52.

37 Nietzsche thought (only partially correctly) that Wagner had accused him of all sorts of 'deviations' including excessive masturbation, impotency, homosexuality, and perhaps even of having a tiny penis. I discuss this problem at length in part 2 of my forthcoming book *Nietzsche/Hölderlin*.

38 This kind of generous terminological conflation in Nietzsche has been discussed by E. Kunne-Ibsch, *Die Stellung Nietzsches in der modernen Literaturwissenschaft*, Tübingen 1972. Her notion of what constitutes 'modern literary criticism,' however, is already out of date.

39 Nietzsche, 'Götzen-Dämmerung,' 'Die "Vernunft" in der Philosophie' 5; KGW, VI/3, 72.

40 See, again, the unpublished notes cited above in note 35 and also the note in Nietzsche, 'Nachgelassene Fragmente, April-Juni 1885' 34 [95]; KGW, VII/3, 171.

41 See, for instance, Nietzsche's retrospective claims to this effect in 'Ecce Homo,' 'Die Unzeitgemässen' 31; KGW, VI/3, 317. But this notion is entertained often in his late writing, especially with regard to Wagner.

42 Again, the following evidence is marshalled and analysed in my book.

43 Nietzsche, 'Nachgelassene Fragmente, Frühjahr 1884' 25 [172–4]; KGW, VII/2, 55–6. The following three quotations from Nietzsche also are taken from here.

44 For a critical description of this phenomenon see Edward Said, 'Reflections on Recent American "Left" Criticism,' *Boundary* 2, 8 (Fall 1979), 11–30.

45 Nietzsche, 'Der Fall Wagner' 7; KGW, VI/3, 21. The following quotation from Nietzsche also is taken from here.

46 See Georg Brandes, *Friedrich Nietzsche*, trans. A. G. Chater, New York 1909. In their joint correspondence Nietzsche typically 'overhears' or rather 'overreads' all of Brandes's specific comments on the 'social question' or the 'workers question.' Brandes often refers to these issues in those parts of his book where he analyses Nietzsche's philosophy, but refuses to push this analysis through to a criticism of the political implications of that philosophy. Hence he is 'shamefaced.'

47 See Nietzsche, 'Der Fall Wagner' 4–6 and 9; KGW, VI/3, 13–20 and 26–9.

48 Whether this summary judgment obtains equally in the East as well as the West is a good, and certainly topical, question. Nietzsche had a substantial impact on pre-revolutionary Russia, and even to some extent there after 1917. But an important recent turn in the reception of Nietzsche has been signalled by the way discussion of Nietzsche is being used today in nascent communist countries to breach residues of Stalininst restrictions on intellectual discourse. See Ernst Behler's report, 'Nietzsche in der marxistischen Kritik Osteuropas,' *Nietzsche-Studien*, 10–11 (1981–2), 80–96. I do not agree, however, with Behler's own ideological position, such as it emerges between the lines of his presentation, nor do I welcome the all too prevalent attitude in the West today that the motivation behind any and all interest in Nietzsche in the East should be embraced uncritically. These remarks apply as well to recent interest in Nietzsche's early impact on 'socialist' movements in Europe. See for instance, Behler, 'Zur frühen sozialistischen Rezeption Nietzsches in Deutschland' and V. Vivarelli, 'Das Nietzsche-Bild in der Presse der deutschen Sozialdemokratie um die Jahrhundertwende,' both in *Nietzsche-Studien*, 13 (1984), 503–20 and 521–69, respectively. Further: R. Hinton Thomas, *Nietzsche in German Politics and Society, 1890–1918*, Manchester 1983. What we need to know from all such studies is, first, how Nietzsche was actually read by that working class which groups like the SPD claimed to represent, only to betray and, second, what the impact was of 'Nietzschean' political ideology on that portentous sell-out, then *and* now. On these issues see my essay cited in note 61 below.

49 Nietzsche, 'Der Fall Wagner' 11; KGW, VI/3, 33.

50 This phrase, uttered in reference to resistance to Wagner's mass appeal, is Nietzsche's; see Nietzsche, 'Der Fall Wagner,' 'Nachschrift'; KGW, VI/3, 35. I discuss at length the historical context of German politics in 1888, and its bearing on Nietzsche's remarks in 'Ecce Homo' in favour of the 'liberal' Emperor Friedrich III, in my essay 'Nietzsche and Deconstruction' (see esp. pp. 84–5) and in part 3 of my book.

51 Nietzsche, *Die Fröhliche Wissenschaft*, 'Vorrede zur zweiten Ausgabe' 2; KGW, V/2, 15.

52 With regard to the question of Nietzsche's misogyny, the *effect* of Derrida's reading (it is not Derrida's intent to deal with this question exclusively or even directly) is to show that there are at least three modalities at work in Nietzsche's position

with regard to women. Woman is: (a) condemned as representative of lying; (b) condemned as representative of the continuing need for Truth; and (c) acclaimed as representative of the affirmative, dissimulating, artistic, and even Dionysian power of life itself. It is Nietzsche's 'reading' and 'writing' of woman in this triadic modality, indeed dialectic, that leads, according to Derrida's analysis and methodology, to the philosophical question of style *per se*. Now, the question of whether or not Derrida himself thereby hypostatizes 'woman' into an abstract category – and one that is at least as superficial, a-historical, and chauvinistic as any pre-Derridian interpretation of Nietzsche's misogyny ever was – is important. On the crucial importance for the women's movement of shifting away from 'generalized philosophical formulations about women ... to specific historical comments' (and, further, on the concrete ways in which the victories of that movement are exemplary indices of general social advance and liberation), see Juliet Mitchell, *Woman's Estate*, New York 1971, p. 78 *et passim*. In the context provided by Mitchell's book, it is impossible to see how either Nietzsche or Derrida's reading of Nietzsche can contribute in any substantive way to the women's movement. See further the excellent study by Marlene Dixon, *The Future of Women*, San Francisco 1983.

53 This point has been argued with regard to the relationship between deconstruction and formalism in literary criticism by Frank Lentricchia, *After the New Criticism*, Chicago 1980. For a more authoritative *philosophical* and *ideological* criticism of both structuralism and post-structuralism in their Platonist and empirio-critical variants, see Sebastiano Timpanaro, *On Materialism*, trans. Lawrence Garner, London 1975, esp. pp. 135–219.

54 Derrida, *Eperons*, p. 136; 'La question du style,' p. 286.

55 De Man, *Allegories of Reading*, p. 131.

56 Here I use the term 'essentialism' differently from common usage in contemporary literary theory, where it is the target of post-structuralist attacks on the notion of the identity of the literary text. For that literary critical usage see the books cited in note 2 above and the discussion of the 'essentialist fallacy' in Tony Bennett, *Formalism and Marxism*, London 1979. Essentialism, however, in the important scientific sense proposed by Karl Popper, *remains* a constitutive feature of post-structuralist deconstruction, namely *an attitude of mind that attributes excessive significance to words and their meanings*. See Karl Popper, *Unended Quest: An Intellectual Biography*, Glasgow 1976, pp. 17–31. It should be unnecessary to add that I do not agree with Popper's oft-repeated attribution of essentialism, in its variant form that he terms 'historicism,' to Marxist gnosiology and historiography.

57 See Benjamin's apt remarks on *The Birth of Tragedy* in his *Ursprung des deutschen Trauerspiels*, ed. Rolf Tiedemann, Frankfurt am Main 1955, pp. 82–5.

58 See Derrida, *Eperons*, p. 34; 'La question du style,' p. 235.

59 See the editorial note of Peter Gast and Elisabeth Förster Nietzsche in Nietzsche,

Gesammelte Briefe, III/2, 416. Also the last paragraph of Nietzsche's letter to Meysenbug, 7 November 1872. This is probably the edition of the letters Derrida himself consulted.

60 See the account by Adorno of the trip, 'Aus Sils Maria,' in Adorno, *Gesammelte Schriften*, X/1, 326–9.

61 I've attempted to address the issue of Nietzsche's own mode of reading and of the ways he in turn was read by the working classes in imperial Germany in my essay 'The Politics of Reading Formations: The Case of Nietzsche in Imperial Germany, 1870–1919,' *New German Critique*, 29 (Spring/Summer 1983), 185–209.

62 *Conversations with Lukács*, p. 90.

ROBERT WEIMANN

Textual Identity and Relationship: A Metacritical Excursion into History

To find oneself at the end of a series of theoretical statements on the identity of the literary text involves an awesome burden (doubly awesome if it is one in which repetition kindles expectation) but at the same time it provides me with an opportunity to stand back for a moment and view the extraordinary diversity of the responses that we have had in these essays. What strikes me more than anything is the way that this diversity in the approaches to the identity of the literary text appears to be entangled with the problem of defining the identity of identity, that is, the identity of that other text which provides this book with its title, namely, the Identity of the Literary Text. As a matter of fact some of the responses to this title text seem to be consistently divided as to whether, for instance, the identity in question was to be established empirically, as that of *one* literary text, or generically, as that of the literary text as a particular *kind* or *genre* of discourse. Obviously, this collection of essays attempts to provide answers not just to one problem but to quite different problem texts whose respective identities are defined, I suggest, not simply in terms of the semantic units of the title of this book but rather in terms of varying systems of referentiality and self-referentiality by which the contributors (of which I am one) relate to our problem through both their sense of the world and the sense of their position (or should I say: the sense of identity of their own selves) in this world.

But I do not wish to abuse the privilege of being able to glance back at these essays by indulging in the *post festum* observation that it can be as difficult to read a theoretical text as it is to define the identity of a literary one (as if I were at all exempt from this very difficulty myself). Rather, what this metacritical opening does suggest is that the problematic involved in the definition of our title text seems *paradigmatic* of some of the difficulties in defining our object proper, the literary text. To realize what in the course of this collection of essays has happened to the identity of the title text is one way of defining the nature of the methodological problem vis-à-vis the general question raised in this book. Let me, in looking back at this problem, attempt to suggest two or three conclusions.

First, the text of the title of this book (like, presumably, any other text) appears to achieve whatever identity it has not in any a priori fashion but, as it were, progressively as over the course of so many essays it has been responded to by a variety of writers. If, therefore, the identity of the title text has come to be affected (and distracted) by all these varying responses, then any definition of that identity would vary according to the point in the sequence when it was undertaken. In other words, such a definition would not produce any immutable text itself, but would have to take into account that the identity of the title text constitutes itself historically in reference to the text and the subtext of whichever response it receives. (The concept of 'subtext' is being used here in the sense that Fredric Jameson has defined the text as 'the rewriting or restructuration of a prior historical or ideological *subtext*, it being always understood that that "subtext" is not immediately present as such, not some common-sense external reality, nor even the conventional narratives of history manuals, but rather must itself always be (re)constructed after the fact.'[1]

However, if this first conclusion would tend to subject the identity of our title text to a process of distraction and modification, this reflects only part of the situation and energy which this title text and its respondents have helped to bring about. For, obviously and simultaneously, there is an opposite tendency at work which has to do with the fact that the title text itself has a subtext, and it prefigures some social and intellectual activity. The title text is not just an *object* of response; it has itself the character of a responding *subject*: it is situated in the world, it is enmeshed in time and place and circumstance but, at the same time, it is constitutive of the reality of our here and now. It is through this activity, which the text embodies but also helps to prefigure, that a number of restraints are placed on the modification and distraction of its identity. That is why the spectrum of response to the title text is, for all its diversity, limited. It is the structured prefigurement[2] in the text itself which constitutes a countervailing energy that, in drawing forth a certain limited spectrum of response, directly enters into the process of communication and clarification.

If, therefore, this second conclusion must be seen to contradict or at least modify the first, the reason is that – my third point – the energies of response to, and the energies of production in, the title text are mediated as well as sustained by a communicative situation which is relatively independent of the fact whether or not the identity of the literary text or even that of the title text can be conclusively established. Or should I go a step further and say that the communicative process itself profits from mediating tensions? And that the mediation is between on the one hand the contracting energies prefigured in the question itself and on the other those distracting energies exploding in the forcefulness of the answers provided? To take this step is to suggest that these two sides of the dialogic process – the contracting and the distracting of textual identity – should *not* be viewed as mutually exclusive. On the contrary, what the integrating and the disintegrating forces have in common is not only that – in any textual communication – they are simultaneously at work, affecting the identity of a text in the very act of their operation. What is even more important is that their joint presence turns the status of textual identity into a locus of tension, which tension, it seems to me, is a function of the involvement of the text in contradictory situations and relationships.

As long as our title text may so be used as a paradigm, let me submit the proposition that the best way to approach the identity of any text is in terms of its contradictory relationships. When I say 'relationships,' I do not of course wish to restrict this concept to the personal and purely empirical ways by which writers and readers *relate* their text either to some individual experience and correction or to those social schemata of norms and choices that they happen to subscribe to. To understand the identity of a text as a function of its involvement in contradictory situations is to look for the point of intersection where the variegated energies and restraints of all the in-forming relationships are made to clash and, as far as that is possible, interact with one another.

I

If, so far, I have used the title text of this collection of essays as a paradigm to suggest the degree to which the establishing of its identity is related to the functional situation, the historical time and place in which it is produced, communicated, and responded to, this paradigm (now that it has come to be viewed as involved in our own discourse as an actual event) can be seen, and astonishingly so, to open out of itself into a situation which is indistinguishable from the reality of the present state of literary theory and criticism itself. In other words, the paradigm turns out to be indistinguishable from that situation in reality within which and against which we ourselves have begun to formulate, discuss, and respond to a theoretical text which is part of and reflects upon criticism as a social and cultural institution. Relating to an institutional situation, which is also one of consciousness, this title text appears designed to function by helping to comprehend and, perhaps, affect the production and reception of other literary and theoretical texts. At its most basic level, it responds to certain needs and seeks to stimulate certain functions in the present state of literary theory and criticism, at least in North America and a few countries in Western Europe. It would not be helpful to ignore or dismiss as external this larger situation (which after all exists at the same level as the text and indeed our responses to it). On the contrary, some of the merits and attractions of the proposed wording, the 'Identity of the Literary Text,' result from the way this text can be used to intervene in a given historical situation. Again, this is a situation of conflicting relationships which the text itself helps to constitute but which, in its own turn, is constitutive of the identity of that text itself.

To illustrate this let me recall a remark by Jonathan Culler, who noted that only a few years ago the phrase the 'identity of the literary text' would normally have been associated with the editorial endeavours of textual criticism and bibliography. Or to consult my own experience and tradition, which is that of Lukács, Brecht, and more recent German and East European Marxist literary theory, I would find that the problem of the identity of the literary text has not presented itself with anything like the same urgency. There, the most immediate response to this phrase would likely be to suggest another type of signification according to which a concern for the identity of the literary text could be read as an emphasis on the specificity and, hence, the cultural function of literature as a unique and, indeed, indispensable source of sensibility and consciousness. Now although the present formulation of the title text might so be read as to leave room for the cultural function of literature as a vessel of civilized value, yet *such* identification of literary identity surely would provide too unspecified a point of departure to be useful as a description of the more strictly academic quality of the functional situation as it exists in North America today. As long as this particular context, with both its limited social resonance and its spirit of intense theoretical inquiry, allows for the kind of dialogue in this book, it may come as a shock to realize that this problem, which appears so pressing here in North America, can in other parts of the world, say in Asia, Africa, or Latin America, appear in an altogether different light. To be aware of this may serve as a useful reminder that the very formulation of the problem of the identity of the literary text must be read as a response to a situation in reality in which traditional notions and uses of the literary text have themselves become problematic both as objects of critical communication and as vehicles of cultural and educational endeavour.

I am saying this with a good deal of diffidence, if only because my respect for this debate and its participants is not in the least impaired by a critical perspective which, in a deeper sense than I have been able to explain so far, is also a historical one. Speaking as I do under the burden of both the need to look closely at what is to me in several ways distant and the privilege of being able critically to 'distance' what I am now so close to, I would like to confine myself to suggesting a number of historical-critical aspects of the subtext of this whole debate. In doing this my assumption is that these aspects may help to define both the genetic and the functional constellation through which alone the identity of the Identity of the Literary Text can be established.

First, the crisis of the concept of the literary work. As long as, say, in the heyday of the New Criticism the literary work as an autonomous object of interpretation was readily taken for granted, no one bothered seriously to define its identity except through the close reading of the text as a self-referential verbal structure. The notion of identity, had it been raised at all, would presumably have been defined in terms of a unifying wholeness, a reconciliation of opposite or discordant qualities. Nor was there any felt need for authenticating this type of holistic identity which seemed to be the more strictly definable by ruling out the various fallacies, intentional, affective, referential, by which the legitimation of the work of art was feared to be threatened in its self-enclosed existence. But today such a legitimation of the work (or the 'poem') as an autonomous entity and self-evident object of literary theory and history seems no longer possible. The 'work' appears ill-equipped these days to provide theoretical criteria of textual identity and already appears, in the world of Roland Barthes, as 'a traditional notion that has long been and still is thought of in what might be called Newtonian fashion.'[3] This is not the place to inquire into the history of this remarkable revaluation of the 'work' as a theoretical concept. But there is a connection, I suggest, between the decline of the approach to the poem as a self-contained organic whole and the crisis, culminating in the late 1960s, of the traditional definition of the cultural function of the humanities, and especially the study of literature. Once the post-Romantic concern for tension and unity in irony or paradox came to face the discontinuous order of the contemporary state of verbal discourse and social rebellion, it could no longer vindicate the identity of the self-contained work in reference to Coleridge's unifying imagination; nor could it sustain itself through further modernist supplements to the poetics of Romanticism and the idealist tradition in aesthetics and philosophy. Since the New Criticism itself had with considerable success displaced the earlier aims and standards of historical philology, there resulted a further break-up of the academic consensus and a growing sense of discontinuity in the critical tradition, which even now provides a significant background not only to the crisis of the concept of the work as a self-authenticating unit of literary study but also to the need for asking the question about the identity of the literary text.

Second, the formalist criterion of poeticity challenged. The formalist emphasis on the work as the self-contained unity of literary discourse has in the past presupposed a connection between the assumption that literature is linguistically autonomous and the notion that it is formally and functionally distinct from other kinds of verbal utterances. As a matter of fact the dualism and, even, opposition between poetic language and nonpoetic language constituted the most comprehensively important area of agreement between Russian formalism, Anglo-American New Criticism, and the dominating current in structuralist poetics. But with the decline of the formalist approach to the literary text, most of the recently prominent patterns of defining its identity in terms of 'poeticity' (as a verbal mode of deviation from traditional codes and standard usage) have quite collapsed. This became almost dramatically obvious when Stanley Fish (whose work is such an unfailing barometer of most of the recent directions in the critical climate) dismissed Michael Riffaterre's distinction between 'everyday language' and 'verbal art' as 'distressingly familiar deviationist talk.'[4] On the basis of post-Saussurean linguistics the poetic/nonpoetic language opposition now appeared as, in the words of Roger Fowler, 'one of the greatest sources of confusion and error in poetic aesthetics,'[5] especially since 'even the most cursory glance at the day-to-day behavior of a speech community can tell us that neither the formal nor the functional distinctiveness that the Formalists attributed to literature has any factual basis.'[6] There, it was the speech-act theory of language with its emphasis on the performative aspect of any utterance (its illocutionary and perlocutionary dimensions) which made it possible to recapture the similarities between literary discourse and other verbal activities. But once the linguistic foundations of the formalist concept of *literaturnost* were seen to crumble, the most crucial source of the postulated identity of the poetic text was no longer available. As the most widely held verbal criteria for differentiating literature from other orders of discourse turned out to be empirically unfounded, the whole liberal conception of the specific uses of poetic language as a cultural mode of knowledge and value was affected. If the new apologists for poetry had promoted literary identity in defence against an ascendent scientism and industrialism this social program of 'cultural apology'[7] was itself entering into a state of crisis, which above all was a crisis of its own cultural identity and social function.

Third, *fictivity, the problem of tradition, and the rejection of the canon.* As the Romantic sources of modern poetic thought declined and the formalist definition of the linguistic criteria of poeticity fell into disrepute, the crisis in the identity of the literary object was aggravated by far-reaching doubts about the adequacy of the traditional canon of literary study. These doubts revealed themselves on a superficial level in the weakening of the demand for having to master a specific body or canon of books as an educational prerequisite. Behind these doubts there was, among other things, the rise, in the 1960s, of a powerful new prose, documentary and autobiographical, which in its turn helped to refute the modern assumption that only the fictive utterances in a language could be identified as literature. Moreover, once it was recognized that, as Mary Louise Pratt noted, 'fictive or mimetically organized utterances can occur in almost any realm of extra-literary discourse,'[8] the criterion of fictivity as a mark of the identity of the literary text had to be surrendered on the theoretical level as well. At the same time, the previously unquestioned concept of tradition as a conservative idea of historical 'order' (T. S. Eliot) gave way to what Harold Bloom has called 'the anxiety of influence,' with its related need for 'fighting the battle of the Ancients and Moderns all over again in an historical chaos where nothing is definitely absolute.'[9] The revision and diffusion of the literary canon, its own loss of identity, is of course too complex an international phenomenon to be done justice to here. Suffice it to quote the egalitarian repudiation of the standards of 'high culture' and what Leslie Fiedler has scornfully called 'the finicky canons of the genteel tradition' – 'finicky' presumably in the light of 'the final intrusion of pop into the citadels of high art.'[10] But there are many more factors involved, such as the post-modernist exhaustion or parody of many of the traditional literary forms and genres in America; the anti-humanist orientation of an influential trend in French structuralism and post-structuralism (from Althusser and the *Tel Quel* group to Michel Foucault), the increasingly effective reception of Nietzsche as the earliest and still one of the most radical critics of the classical humanist tradition in Europe; the crisis of the traditional German *Literaturbegriff*, the more broadly cultural uses of *Rezeptionsästhetik*, and the new interest in *Trivialliteratur* and the culture of the mass media. These and a host of more or less related trends have weakened the status of the traditionally accepted canon and, even more important, they have further upset those literary institutions and social contracts between writers and their public which, by specifying the proper use of a particular cultural artefact, have in the past secured the viability of literary genres. If genre criticism can today be described as 'thoroughly discredited by modern literary theory and practice,' part of the reason is of course that 'with the elimination of an institutionalized social status for the cultural producer and the opening of the work of art itself to commodification, the older generic specifications are transformed into a brand-name system against which any authentic artistic expression must necessarily struggle.'[11] The plight of the canon, the crisis of poeticity, and the problematic of most of 'the older generic specifications' have as a matter of course profoundly affected theoretical definitions of the literary object, and they have helped to bring about a situation where, as Mario Valdés has recently suggested, 'it is no longer profitable to designate certain texts as literary and others as nonliterary and to base a logic of classifications on such a premise.'[12] It seems obvious that a functional situation so described must in the eyes of many undermine the traditional frame of reference within which – in respect to genre, tradition, and the literary canon – the identity of the literary text can be established and validated.

~ *Fourth, the crisis in the presence of the author.* Once the traditional notion of the literary work as a self-contained entity was relegated to the old-fashioned mechanical world of Newtonian physics, and once, in this connection, the Classical-Romantic tradition was challenged on several levels, the most distinctive factor of Romantic literary identity, the expression of personality, could not continue to provide a perspective on a renewed identification of the nature of the literary text. The criterion of personality as an identifying agency within either the literary work or the literary text collapsed finally and irrevocably when the signifying activity of the subject was seen to lose its autonomy and stability in that vast field of signification within which, according to Lacan, the unconscious is the discourse of the Other. But if it is only by repression or by dependence on the Other that a signifying subject can spell out the personal pronoun, then the use of the word 'I' can be no more than 'a stand-in for the "true" subject that cannot represent itself in that deceptively stable verbal index.'[13] Now even though modern psychological criticism continues to define the function of literature as 'to symbolize and finally to replicate ourselves,'[14] this does not involve a reinauguration of the author as an authenticating instance of textual identity. What critics like Norman Holland are concerned with above all is to argue that critics and *readers* perceive and experience texts in terms of their own identities: according to Holland's formula, 'unity is to text as identity is to self,' which amounts to saying that, in contrast to 'unity' and 'identity,' both 'text' and 'self' are to be considered as variables. As against that, the post-structuralist position, neatly articulated in Derrida's saying that 'writing is an orphan,' has of course the advantage of a radical consistency. If, in the words of Michel Foucault, there is no author, but only an author-function, then indeed Samuel Beckett's question ('What difference does it make who is speaking?')[15] can be taken to seal not only the issue of individual literary authorship but also yet another of the criteria that might have served as an authenticating agent of identity in the text itself.

Fifth, the critic's task and the critique of interpretation. At the time when the relationship between text and author had already come to be viewed as impersonal, T. S. Eliot in his essay 'The Function of Criticism' felt 'fairly certain that "interpretation" … is only legitimate when it is not interpretation at all.' But by reacting against 'a vicious taste for reading about works of art instead of reading the works themselves,' his aim was to reassert an authentic function of the critic as against that 'most pretentious critical journalism' which would 'supply opinion instead of educating taste.'[16] Thus, mid-twentieth-century English-speaking critics like F.R. Leavis and Cleanth Brooks still found themselves in a position to relate to the work of literature in terms of some modified pattern of interpretative critical activity and audience expectation. It was only when, in more recent days, these patterns came to be questioned that the critic's previously accredited presence vis-à-vis the literary object began to show signs of strain and self-consciousness. What is involved in the modern critic's lack of credibility is a crisis of legitimation which reflects more than the loss of authenticity in the critic's voice as a sensitive vehicle of a literary *communis opinio*. Whereas that loss of authenticity was perceived as early as in Eliot's critique of critical impressionism, much more radical and far-reaching doubts about the literary critic's presence are being articulated today through the challenges to both the practical cultural function and the epistemological status of interpretation. As an illustration, it must suffice here to refer briefly to that broad spectrum of criticism to which the traditional theory and practice of interpretation is exposed, from critics like Susan Sontag, to various phenomenological theorists, and most of the dominant representatives of post-structuralism, from Louis Althusser to Roland Barthes. If we follow Wolfgang Iser, who presents one of the most cogent arguments against interpretation, the charge is that interpretation constrains the text through 'the continuing application of a norm ... which seeks to restore the universal claims which art has in fact abandoned.' Hence, interpretation by 'its claims to universal validity' has 'the effect today of seeming to degrade the work as the reflection of prevailing values,' and it is through the awareness of this problematic that an interpreter must realize that he 'can no longer claim to teach the reader the meaning of the text.'[17] In other words, just as the author has forfeited any authenticating function of identity within his own text, so the critic surrenders his 'claim to teach,' that is his authority as a cultural mediator of identity, which is to say his critical function to identify the meaning of the text in reference to any generally valid criterion of value, knowledge, and truth. What remains after the critic is considered to have lost his capacity not just for cultural education but for establishing validity through interpretation is a literary text whose identity can no longer be established through or within a process of mediation: it cannot be defined *through* the critical mediation between literature and its audience, and it cannot be obtained *within* the hermeneutic contradiction whose resolution would involve comprehension (*Verstehen*) as well as exegesis or interpretation (*Auslegung*).

Sixth, the liberal idea of education and the concept of textuality. If, as Geoffrey Hartman notes in his essay 'Literary Criticism and Its Discontents,' critics have become 'defensive about their function' and their 'sense of a structured vocation seems to have weakened, if not entirely collapsed' the reason is not of course that, somehow, in the 1970s and early 1980s there is less talent and personal dedication available than, say, in the 1930s, 1940s, and 1950s. What we are facing is a changing situation in society and the university, the crisis of a social and educational ideology, at which Hartman points when he says: 'We are passing through a revaluation of the liberal ideal that education – and especially education in the arts – might prepare the individual for a life free of both instinctual and political constraints.'[18] In Western Europe this 'revaluation' has assumed varying forms and expressions, but some comparable challenges to the liberal ideal of education may well be traced in the early rise of the *Nouvelle Critique*, its fierce assault upon the *Critique Universitaire*, as well as in some aspects of the triumph of *Rezeptionsästhetik* in Federal Germany. What these developments have in common is the attempt to react to the declining functions and the crumbling foundations of the liberal ideal of education by absolving the discipline of literary criticism from its compromising ties with those premises and assumptions on which the humanist tradition in criticism and philology rested. If, as Geoffrey Hartman notes, today 'the word "dehumanization" seems more appropriate than "humanism" to the condition of criticism,'[19] one reason is that some of the basic values in the literature of the past have ceased to be either enriching or liberating for the cultural uses of criticism in the present. It is in a situation like this that a dominant trend in post-structural criticism is turning back on itself and is more than anything else engaged in considering the status of its own discourse. In other words, the scene is set for textuality as, in Derrida's view, a 'tissue de greffes,' a fabric of grafts, whose structure, since it is one of supplementarity and deferment, is marked by the absence of identity as a meaningful category. If indeed the text has energy, that energy itself destroys unity in an interminable self-deconstructing movement. Instead of identity, which presupposes presence and profile, 'there is no present text in general, and there is not even a past present text. … The text is not thinkable in an originary or modified form of presence.'[20] But if the text is produced by the perpetual reproduction of the 'always already' of another text then it achieves an autonomy which is the reversal and extinction of identity: the self-deconstructing logic of the supplement must necessarily reduce the practice of writing and reading as projecting a social and communicative relationship to a textualized shadow of its own discursive self.

This is not the place to review the problematic of textuality nor can these brief notes adequately answer the question on what grounds and to what extent from within the premises of textuality the identity of the literary text has not just become an impossible predication, but has been supplanted by categories of dissemination and desedimentation that are relativistic as well as dynamic, strategic as well as methodological.[21] But the point that, I think, can safely be made is that the general drift of post-structuralist criticism is towards the decomposition of traditional modes of literary identity and that this direction seems to confirm the logic of that cultural situation which a powerful strand in Anglo-American criticism (I am thinking particularly of the so-called Yale school) has for some time helped theoretically to formulate. Small wonder, then, that the impact on American criticism of Derrida or, for that matter, the post-structuralist Roland Barthes has become literally overwhelming, even though, on the surface, their influence seems to go against the very grain of what used to be the most vital elements in the North American tradition. Take, as perhaps the most articulate expression of this position, Roland Barthes's essay 'From Work to Text.' According to Barthes, 'the *Text is experienced only in an activity, a production* ... the Text cannot stop, at the end of a library shelf, for example; the constitutive movement of the Text is a traversal [traversée]: it can cut across a work, several works.' But once the Text 'does not come to a stop with (good) literature,' its potential identity has become quite incongruous not only with any particular work, any one book, or, for that matter, a shelf or a whole library of books, but with any literary genre, drama, narrative, poem, story, act, scene, verse, point of view, etc. Says Barthes' 'What constitutes the Text is, on the contrary (or precisely), its subversive force with regard to old classifications.'[22] But if the force of textuality is such that it subverts all those categories and units which mediate literary and extra-literary activities, writing and reading, fiction and criticism, then it is difficult to conceive how it can even heuristically be made to allow of any predication of identity. Textuality, in short, cancels out those conditions of identity which, theoretically and culturally, obtain through the richness of the mediating relationship in which the text can be produced, received, and circulated.

II

This brief and incomplete survey of the theoretical impasse of literary identity in contemporary criticism and theory calls for a reconsideration not only of the function of identity in literature but of the concept of the literary text itself. To reflect a historical situation is not to subscribe to its dominating assumptions. The most radical response to the problem of the identity of the literary text is to question and, if possible, to rewrite and restructure the conceptualization of the literary text itself.

As a first step in this direction it seems helpful, I suggest, to realize that there is no generally accepted definition of the text as a mode and concept of literary inscription. As far as I can see there are at least four or five differing versions of 'text.' To begin with, Roland Barthes's concept of the 'Text' (spelt with a capital T) cannot, I submit, be identical with the present critical use of the English lexical unit 'text,' such as the one in the title of this book. Whereas Barthes's and Derrida's usage denotes a 'text' which 'cannot stop, at the end of a library shelf,' since what it involves is the textualization of all discursive practice, the more empirical Anglo-American concept (as a second version) appears to allow for written discourse as language-event or linguistic usage as structuring the text itself. If that is so, then this definition has to be distinguished from yet another, third structuralist concept according to which 'text' defines itself within those linguistic systems where, instead of discourse as language-event, the sign (phonological or lexical) is the basic unit of language. Whereas the second version of 'text' as the inscription of discourse would have a temporal dimension involving subject and some form of reference, the structuralist concept would suspend the text from its temporal and referential dimensions and would formally enclose it as a self-sufficient system of signs. This structuralist system of signs can but need not be supplemented by a semiological approach to the 'text' which extends the term to any nonlinguistic code or even social activity with a communicative dimension. As against these three or four differing uses of the concept, there is finally yet another version of 'text' which, being derived from the historical tradition of philology, represents an unacknowledged but (in our context) consistently important challenge. For a recent articulation of this position, let me draw attention to Jerome J. McGann's article 'The Text, the Poem, and the Problem of Historical Method,' where the author (without distinguishing the varying approaches) refers to 'the contemporary fashion of calling literary works "texts"' as a deplorable and, indeed, 'vulgar usage' which 'confuses the fundamental difference between a poem's *text* – which is one thing – and a poem – which is quite another.'[23] McGann refers to Byron, Emily Dickinson, and especially Blake's *Jerusalem*, whose 'text' clearly does not comprehend any one particular concrete reality but at best 'a heuristic idea' so that it is possible for him to show 'how different texts, in the bibliographical sense, embody different poems (in the aesthetic sense) despite the fact that both are linguisticaly identical.' Thus, the conclusion seems to present itself that, paradoxically, this current use of 'text' suggests that poems and works of fiction possess their integrity *as poems and works of fiction* totally aside from the actual events and physical materials describable in their bibliographies. In this usage 'we are dealing with "texts" which transcend their concrete and actual textualities.'[24]

I have juxtaposed these differing versions of 'text' not because I think the linguistic and the bibliographical must necessarily be mutually exclusive but because, on the contrary, most of the current conceptualizations of 'text' seem insufficiently to take account of the full diversity of relationships and points of reference through which alone, I hold, identity in regard to the literary text can be established as a rich category. Once the concept of the literary text abstracts from the physical event and the poetic appeal of its existence and is taken to be equivalent to and coextensive with nothing but its linguistic structure, the all-important question is of course which linguistic norms and principles are presupposed as structuring the text? There is a difference whether the literary text is taken to enclose a system of signs or even a movement of discourse, or whether discourse itself, through its conception as event or speech act, is seen to open the text to a whole world of related activities. Whereas in the former case it seems difficult to obtain any concept of identity which points beyond the intrinsic criteria of a purely formal system or structure, in the latter case the criteria of literary identity will tend to involve the identifying subject and the social nature of its activity much more deeply.

At this point, my metacritical concern with the identification of our title text may have ceased to furnish us with a satisfying paradigm, but if it can still contribute anything it is the suggestion that the linguistic constitution of this inscription (which now serves for the title of this book) begins to provide guidance to its own theoretical and cultural identity only when and as soon as the inscription of linguistic data is viewed as an opening to discursive practice, including the 'dialogue' between the formulation of the problem and that of its responses.

But even such opening to discursive practice has its limitations and at a certain stage ceases to furnish an adequately comprehensive mode of integrating (and disintegrating) identity for either the writer or the reader of the text in question. For in the process of writing and in the act of reading the criteria of identity and integrity cannot be consistently developed on the basis of the linguistic unit of discourse, which is the sentence, nor on the basis of some structural parts of the literary utterance, such as paragraph, scene, or chapter, nor – bibliographically speaking – in reference to single sheets or pages. The production or reception of such fragmentary inscriptions of discourse must needs preclude the realization of fully sustained patterns of identity and integrity, and not only because the whole of all the sentences, scenes, and pages is so much larger than the sum of its parts. What seems even more important is the fact that the writing and the reading of the text itself involve dimensions of temporality and referentiality which are not subject to fragmentation. Writing and reading *involve* these dimensions; they do not *confront* an external world of time, and space, and reference, but absorb them as structuring constituents of their own activities. In other words, temporality and referentiality are so drawn into the whole process of writing and reading that, in each case, their realization presupposes standards of integrity and criteria of identity which transcend the sentence, scene, and page as textual units.

In emphasizing some element of wholeness as a condition on which identity can be predicated, I definitely do not plead for any holistic organicism, but for the most practically and theoretically effective unit within which, in literature, the actual contracting and distracting of identity can take place. There is of course not the slightest doubt that the sentence, the scene, the page can be immensely significant both in the production and the perception of textual identity; even so, identity is ultimately based on more than a sequence of sentences, a succession of scenes, a compilation of pages. But if, as Paul Ricoeur has said, 'A text is a whole, a totality. ... It is a cumulative, holistic process,'[25] the question must be asked: how can the text as *accumulation* and *process* be conceptually reconciled to its presumed conditions of wholeness and totality? In other words, can the accumulation of verbal data and the temporal quality of reading be considered as finite entities? The answer is that they cannot, except within those contractual and institutionalized patterns of social function by which the production and consumption of cultural artefacts are mediated in terms of social expectations, literary conventions (including genre), and aesthetic practice and theory. Within these patterns there do exist temporal and spatial limitations to the process by which identity is best achieved and maintained, where the forces of integration and disintegration can best operate on a locus of maximum tension and interaction.

Therefore, even though the assumptions of integrity underlying the literary work have been theoretically challenged, the question must yet be faced: does there exist a communicative unit to mediate writing and reading which, in terms of its temporal, referential, and physical-bibliographical dimensions, is more practically effective than the literary work itself? To ask this question is of course not to reduce the criteria of identity to the level of the poem, drama, or novel, and it is certainly not to argue in favour of a return to the Romantic conception of the work of art as an organic whole. But if the category of literary identity is to point beyond the intrinsic criteria of a purely formal system of verbal organization, the institutionalized, contractual, and communicative conditions upon which the most stable units of identity can be obtained must seriously be reconsidered as an element of social and cultural practice. Among the most stable and effective units there is not just the verse, the stanza, the scene, the chapter, but eventually the literary work itself. Rather than reducing the problem of identity to the problematic of the work itself, let me suggest that in terms of its total structuring relationships, pragmatic, semantic, and syntactic, the literary text as an inscription of discourse has, as one of its most powerful correlatives of identity, the literary work itself.

This of course is deliberately to challenge both the theoretical repudiation of the poem or work of fiction as a literary entity and its reduction to a series of textual strategies and linguistic operations. The importance of these have in the recent past been abundantly demonstrated and, again, their contribution to our knowledge about the nature of the literary text as a system of signs or an inscription of discourse can hardly be overestimated. However, since I cannot uncritically follow the trajectory of Roland Barthes's argument in 'From Work to Text,' let me raise the question if, at the same time, there is not in the writing and reading of literature a complementary movement from text to work?

As a first response to this question let me suggest that the customary distinctions between 'text' and 'work' seem altogether unsatisfying. Whereas the historical-philological tradition tended to limit the concept of the 'text' to the bibliographical data of the physical history of the original inscription of the work as some unquestioned entity, the post-structuralist differentiations between text and work remain vague as well as contradictory. They are vague when, for instance, Roland Barthes, after suggesting that 'The Text must not be thought of as a defined object. It would be useless to attempt a material separation ... of works and texts,'[26] proceeds to say, 'While the work is held in the hand, the text is held in language: it exists only as discourse.' But by blurring the distinctions between *book* and 'work' ('the work can be seen in bookstores, in card catalogues, and on course lists') as well as the difference between the various levels of discursive practice (oral and inscribed), the proposed differentiation appears to use a system of rather black and white categories: 'The work is ordinarily an object of consumption. ... The Text (if only because of its frequent "unreadability") decants the work from its consumption and gathers it up as play, task, production, and activity.'[27] But the metaphoric structure of such critical operation (*décanter* as, originally, 'transvaser un liquide qui a fait un dépôt') does not *clarify* the distinction between 'text' and 'work.' For it may well be asked, is not a work of poetry, or a drama (and, even more so, the recital of a poem or a dramatic work in performance) inseparable from that cultural function which involves 'play, task, production, and activity' ('pratique')? Indeed, it would not be difficult to argue that the space for and the volume of play, production, and activity would in these cases be larger than within the 'text' as purified from *sédimentation* qua consumption. Eventually, it is the self-isolating nature of such textualizing discourse itself which would inhibit any idea that the identity of the literary object cannot be achieved through the *décantage* of a pure text from its fettering relationships. The trouble with such attempts at differentiating 'text' and 'work' stems from the assumption (which appears unhelpful theoretically as it is culturally) 'that to write a literary work, or to write about one, is a specialized function with no simple equivalent or cause in everyday human experience.'[28]

Once it is recognized that the identity of the literary text is only partially obtained through its study as a system of signs or as an inscription of the verbal strategies of discourse, identity will broadly have to be defined as a function of the involvement of the text in historical situations and communicative relationships. Thus, if the methodological trajectory from work to text involves the textualization of all discursive practice, the trajectory from text to work involves the actualization of the inscribed discourse and its subtext. If the identity of the literary text is to be found anywhere, it will have to be contracted (and would simultaneously be distracted) at the intersection of these two different operations. The intersection is the point in history where the linguistic study of the inscribed systems of signs and discourse and the critical understanding of their actualized significance for a moment engage in a reciprocal relationship. This is the moment of whatever identity can be achieved when the inscribed acts of discourse confront and are affected by another dialogic level of discursive practice which is that of the actualizing action of the reader or critic. Whereas the two activities, the textual and the actualizing ones, never are the same, together they correlate the text to the work and the work to the text. In doing that they *enclose* literary identity in terms of the text and they *open* the text towards whatever identifying units of communication and reproduction are most effective – the scene, the chapter, the literary work itself.

In proposing these distinctions, with all the areas of unity and tension which they, in each particular historical situation, would allow, I do not claim to have presented an exhaustive account of the conditions on which and the means by which the identity of the literary text can be established. Even so, the proposed pattern of activities and relationships is perhaps comprehensive enough to suggest criteria of identity which, by correlating text and work, need not exclude or oppose those different claims upon identity that the bibliographical corpus of the autograph and printed letters on sheets and pages can be held to make. The confusion between a poem's text and the poem itself may not be abrogated by simply relinquishing the concept of the literary text as the inscription of discourse or by once again supplanting it, as Jerome McGann would have it, by a historical-philological redefinition of the text. But even when the concept of the text has irretrievably, I think, acquired these differing connotations, the difference between the varying criteria of identity does not preclude areas of concurrence. For example, it would be possible to have the linguistic and the bibliographical definitions of the literary object result in versions of identity where the verbal, the material, and the poetic dimensions of the literary text can at least for a moment be seen together. Textual strategies are encased in bibliographically concrete vessels of transmission and reception whose physical quality and quantity (and their circulation as a social mode of distribution) do affect the identity of the literary text in the range and direction of its cultural and intellectual appeal and response. What is more, there are interactive links between the circulation and the valorization, between the attribution and the appropriation of inscribed discourses, and in each particular situation in history these links can constitute highly effective and powerful relationships. The linguistic structure of signs and the cultural uses of discourse are deeply involved in these; for sign and discourse *inform* these relationships just as much as these relationships help to *prefigure* the structuring potential of verbal systems and functions. Thus, the bibliography and the circulation of a text do not constitute any external reality, any outside frame which can be detached from the status and identity of signs and discourses. Even before these (conflicting) conditions of the varying modes of verbal, poetic, and bibliographical identity come together, the conditions of the existence of each precedes, distractingly and contractingly, the identifying potential of the others. In that sense, the totality of these conditions and aspects of a literary text would comprise all those distracting and contracting forces which mar and make the identity of its poetic, linguistic, and bibliographical dimensions in history.

But to point to such areas of connection and contradiction between the linguistic, the bibliographical, and the poetic dimensions of the literary object can at best provide a heuristic idea of those wider constellations within which the dialectic of identity and relationship can be further explored. It is along these lines that 'identity' in literary texts can be viewed as a theoretical as well as a cultural problematic, and the question that then can finally be asked is that of the larger function of identity which, ultimately, must be answered on the grounds of its desirability or otherwise in literature and beyond.[29]

NOTES

1 Fredric Jameson, *The Political Unconscious: Narrative as a Socially Symbolic Act*, Ithaca 1981, p. 81.

2 This is the English equivalent (coined by Wolfgang Iser in *The Act of Reading: A Theory of Aesthetic Response*, Baltimore 1978, pp. 36, 107) of what Manfred Naumann and Dieter Schlenstedt have described as 'Rezeptionsvorgabe,' in *Gesellschaft-Literatur -Lesen: Literaturrezeption in theoretischer Sicht*, Berlin and Weimar 1973, p. 35, passim.

3 Roland Barthes, 'From Work to Text,' in *Textual Strategies: Perspectives in Post-Structuralist Criticism*, ed. Josué V. Harari, Ithaca 1980, p. 74.

4 Stanley Fish, 'Literature in the Reader: Affective Stylistics,' *New Literary History*, 2 (1970), 155.

5 Roger Fowler, *The Language of Literature: Some Linguistic Contributions to Criticism*, New York 1971, p. ix.

6 Mary Louise Pratt, *Toward a Speech Act Theory of Literary Discourse*, Blooming-ton 1977, p. 6. The 'performatory' or (as he later came to call it) 'performative' dimension of language was of course first developed by J. L. Austin, *How to Do Things with Words*, Cambridge, Mass. 1962, pp. 6–8 passim.

7 Cf. John Fekete, *The Critical Twilight: Explorations in the Ideology of Anglo-American Literary Theory from Eliot to McLuhan*, London 1977, p. 47. This pro-vides a historical dimension which revealingly complements Murray Krieger's *The New Apologists for Poetry*, Minneapolis 1956, and related studies.

8 Pratt, *Toward a Speech Act Theory*, p. 92.

9 Geoffrey Hartman, 'Literary Criticism and Its Discontents,' *Critical Inquiry*, 3 (1976), 211. See my critique of some of the dominant concepts of 'tradition' in *Structure and Society in Literary History*, Charlottesville, Va. 1976.

10 Leslie Fiedler, *Cross the Border – Close the Gap*, New York 1972, pp. 64, 78. Gerald Graff (who quotes Fiedler) has explored the unresolved problematic in the egalitarian rejection of 'high culture'; cf. *Literature against Itself: Literary Ideas in Modern Society*, Chicago 1979, p. 82.

11 Mario J. Valdés, 'Heuristic Models of Inquiry,' *New Literary History*, 12 (1981), 253.

12 Jameson, *The Political Unconscious*, pp. 105, 107.

13 Terry Eagleton, 'Text, Ideology, Realism,' in *Literature and Society*, ed. Edward W. Said in *Selected Papers from the English Institute, 1978*, Baltimore 1980, pp. 149–73; see p. 156. In arguing that 'ideology is, so to speak, the "Unconscious" of the text,' Eagleton draws attention to 'the fact that what the work speaks of is never quite what it says; we are examining, as critics, the ways it never quite says what it speaks of. Submitted to the dominion of the Other, the text can never quite be identical with itself: like Lacan's subject, it is continually "fading" in the play of signifiers it attempts to "suture"' (pp. 160f.).

14 Norman Holland, 'Unity Identity Text Self,' *PMLA*, 90 (1975), 816.

15 Cit. Michel Foucault, 'What Is an Author?' in *Textual Strategies*, ed. Harari, p. 160.

16 T. S. Eliot, 'The Function of Criticism,' in *Selected Essays 1917–1932*, London 1932, p. 29.

17 Iser, *The Act of Reading*, pp. 12f., 19.

18 Hartman, 'Literary Criticism,' pp. 206f.

19 Ibid., p. 205.

20 Jacques Derrida, 'Freud and the Scene of Writing,' trans. Jeffrey Mehlman, *Yale French Studies*, 48 (1972), 92. Derrida goes on to note that 'The unconscious text is already woven of pure traces, differences in which meaning and force are united; a text nowhere present, consisting of archives which are always already transcrip-tions. Originary prints. Everything begins with reproduction. Always already:

repositories of a meaning which was never present, whose signified presence is always reconstituted by deferment, *nachträglich*, belatedly, *supplementarily*: for *nachträglich* also means supplementary.'

21 Cf. Fredric Jameson, 'The Ideology of the Text,' *Salmagundi*, nos. 31–2 (Fall 1975/Winter 1976), pp. 205f., where he notes that the textualization of data may extend 'the interpretative situation to the totality of social life itself.'

22 Barthes, 'From Work to Text,' p. 75.

23 Jerome J. McGann, 'The Text, the Poem, and the Problem of Historical Method,' *New Literary History*, 12 (1981), 277.

24 Ibid., p. 274.

25 Cf. Paul Ricoeur, 'The Model of the Text: Meaningful Action Considered as a Text,' *New Literary History*, 5 (1973), 92–6. Taking Emile Benvéniste's distinction between language and discourse ('sign' and 'sentence') as his point of departure, Ricoeur (p. 111) concedes the legitimacy of the structuralist model ('the very constitution of the text as text and of the system of texts as literature justifies this conversion of the literary things into a closed system of sign, analogous to the kind of closed system which ... de Saussure called "la langue"'). But in developing a methodology of text-interpretation as a paradigm for interpretation in general in the field of the social sciences, he defines the 'text as 'more than a linear succession of sentences. It is a cumulative, holistic process. ... A text is a quasi-individual ...' (p. 107). Thus, even within Ricoeur's own discourse the unresolved antinomies between structuralism and hermeneutics constitute yet another level of incongruity between current uses of 'text.'

26 See Roland Barthes, 'De l'œuvre au texte,' *Revue d'Esthétique*, 3 (1971), 226, where his original phrase (for 'or defined object') is 'un objet computable.'

27 Ibid., p. 230. Here the author is more cautious than his (otherwise excellent) translator: 'Le Texte. ... décante l'œuvre (si elle le permet) de sa consommation – et la recueille comme jeu, travail, production, pratique.'

28 Edward W. Said, 'Roads Taken and Not Taken in Contemporary Criticism,' *Contemporary Literature*, 17 (1976), 332.

29 In this direction, the social and cultural uses of the contraction and distraction of literary 'identity' have scarcely begun to be explored. On the one hand, identity presupposes distinctions, and distinctions are the most basic prerequisite for a meaningful pursuit of knowledge, especially at a time of its unprecedented expansion on an interdisciplinary level. Nor would one wish to limit the therapeutic uses of identity, as allowing 'a limitation of the cancerous and dangerous proliferation of significations within a world where one is thrifty not only with one's resources and riches, but also with one's discourses and their significations' (Foucault, 'What Is an Author,' p. 159). If any value in the *contracting* of identity is to be asserted as against such dangers of intellectual imprecision and waste (or the absence of discur-

sive 'thrift') this value is functional in the sense that it serves the effectivity of discourse and the requirements of knowledge and its communication. On the other hand, there is certainly value in the *distraction* of identity when the literary texts themselves constitute loci of social and aesthetic tension. By precluding any unity between *Darstellung* and *Bedentung*, between what is said and what is meant, such distraction would be valuable in that it functions as a structuring correlative to those contradictory situations and relationships in which the writing and the reading of literary texts help to ascertain what is our own (meaning) and what is not. This points to *Aneignung*, with its dialectic of appropriation and objectification (or alienation) which I have developed in the introduction to *Realismus in der Renaissance: Aneignung der Welt in der erzählenden Prosa*, Berlin and Weimar 1978.

CONCLUSION

MARIO J. VALDÉS

Conclusion: Concepts of Fixed and Variable Identity

The main concern of this book is the identity of literary texts through time, with respect first to the text as writing, then to the underlying issue of meaning, and eventually to questions of reference. These issues link up at various points with other aspects of identity, such as the unity of a text, the unity of an author's work, and the unity of genre. One of my concerns in bringing the various viewpoints of this volume together has been to understand how our identity concept operates when we write literary criticism, and in this response I also try to address why it is that this concept is so central to our thinking and whether we can justify seeing literature in terms of such a concept. I shall not presume to speak for or against any of the contributors to this volume, but I will restrict myself to eliciting the basic issues which run through their contributions.

CRITERIA FOR IDENTITY

In recent years a number of writers have attempted to analyse our concept of literary identity in terms of the interrelations between various and successive readings of a text.[1] This kind of analysis implies that there is a conceptual connection between textual identity and the various readers' concretizations of a text which might be established by a record of a succession of readings. These conditions make up what I call the consensus criteria of textual identity. These criteria of identity have typically been regarded as essentially comprising two kinds of elements: continuity and coverage. Thus if the continuity factor encompasses the successive readings by each reader and the coverage factor accounts for the various individual readers, the combination of both factors will yield the consensus of identity. In spite of the obvious appeal of this common-sense approach to our problem, I will argue that consensus identity is an arbitrary construct much like the notion of 'average man.'

We must re-examine the argument and ask two fundamental questions. First, can we describe the persistence of a text as dependent on the occurrence of a succession of formal features that stand in some distinctive unity-making relationship? For example, do the opening lines of Don Quixote and the ensuing succession of lines which have not changed since a critical edition was established constitute the persistence of the text? Second, how can we account in observational terms for the way in which these formal features provide us with persistence of the entity we call Don Quixote? Our usual answer to the first question is clearly affirmative, but we hesitate before the second question, which demands more than an affirmative or negative answer and elicits an explanatory response. Furthermore, we may even go so far as to say that the answer to the first question is always affirmative irrespective of whether we can successfully answer the second question. Our idea of the persistence of a text is basically a theoretical extension of our notion of the empirical persistence of ordinary objects around us. What we mean, in common-sense ordinary usage, when we speak about a literary text such as Don Quixote, is more or less that the established sequential order of written (printed) words is the basic evidence of the entity we have designated by this title. There is no doubt whatsoever about this fact.

But the pressing objection to letting the issue rest at this point is contained in the second question I posed. How can we account in empirical terms for the way in which the persistence of the established sequence gives us a *meaningful* unit under the cover of the title? For we are not content to say that the entity Don Quixote is a fixed sequence of words; we press on to include the purported meaning of the full sequence, and this is where we enter the main task of my commentary.

There is an unwarranted assumption in ordinary usage that the persistence of the sequence also carries a persistence of an established meaning of the words. It is in this light that the issue of identity is a real problem and not an intellectual game. Let us, however, suppose for the sake of argument that a description of a text that was not tied to an established persistence of words would be less coherent than a description in terms of the sequence. If this is so, it would appear to follow logically that there is a theoretical advantage in describing at least the basis for identity in terms of the established sequence. But on closer examination this argument fails to give us any linkage between formal and meaningful identity, and it is for this reason that it seems to me to be a reductionist distortion. There is not and cannot be any intrinsic unity through time in the sense of a unity that cannot be adequately redescribed in different terms. Nor can there be any relationships that are intrinsically unity-making, in the sense of a relationship that cannot be coherently separated from its unity-making role in our search for identity. Hence the persistence of any conceivable text can be taken as a mere succession of sounds or marks, if we choose to look at it that way.[2]

The issue is not whether we can or cannot choose to stop our inquiry with a formal description. The real issue is that our use of identity in critical discourse implies a meaningful whole, and this is a concept not covered by the mere persistence of words in sequence.

A text considered solely from its formal aspects cannot have any meaning and therefore can be described ahistorically as a fixed sequence. But a text with implied meaning is always immersed in the historical reality of the world of action. The specific intelligibility of writing is rooted in the preunderstanding of language as social action. Thus writing as communication is always historical. The writer, the medium of language, the reader, the social group which provides the means for writing, all are historical phenomena. I would therefore insist that we must constantly be reminded that symbolic mediation must be understood as social mediation.[3] If we are to understand a written page we must first situate the page within the body of the writing, then place the writing within a particular practice of writing – newspapers, lectures, poems, etc. – and then in the experience of social interaction by rapid succession we try to locate our page within the whole network of conventions of writing, of beliefs and commitments to these beliefs, of institutions and the whole configuration of the historical make-up of culture as we understand it. My point is a simple one and I do not want to belabour it: the second criterion for the identification of the text is its historicity. If a text were to be deprived of its history it would also be deprived of meaning. For example, when we read that the fanatical clergy burned thousands of manuscripts because they were written in a language they could not read and were presumed to have been the work of the devil, we are concerned with texts which did have the formal criteria but lack the second condition of historicity of production.

The third criterion of identity is the continuing potentiality of being read. A text of course does not achieve meaning within its own formal boundaries, but only when it passes the threshold of potentiality into the experience of a reader. The most fundamental presupposition of a literary text is that it is a mode of communication. On a written page, someone has written something with a meaningful content about something for somebody else to read and therefore realize. The formal structure of a text therefore carries with it the fundamental supposition that what is written was written about something intended for someone other than the writer.[4] Thus the basic requirement of the text is a writer, a referent, and an addressee. The writer's use of language has been considered through the formal characteristics of the text. The historicity of writer and the linguistic medium has been considered through our second criterion. We now turn to that of the addressee; in our case, the reader. The expectation of recognition and therefore communication is a component of the writer's meaning as Wolfgang Iser and others have so clearly shown.[5] Thus we can speak of the implied reader as part of the very process of meaning. Such is the first part of my argument that the identity of a text is directly tied to the potentiality for completion of meaning as reading matter. But what is meant by reading matter and how does the text's potentiality as reading affect its identity? The semantic autonomy of the text means that author's intention and the meaning of the text no longer coincide. What the text means to its readers now matters more than what the author meant when he wrote it. If the relation of text and reader is now recognized as carrying the burden of assigning meaning, we must also hasten to add that the relation of text and reader grows out of the ability to utilize the formal patterns we have described as our first criterion and it is also dependent on the historical encounter we have outlined as the second criterion of identity.

Nothing can be more naïve than to attempt to link meaning to an abstract atemporal figure of reader.[6] Also let us be quick to point out that just as there is an intentional fallacy which posits author's meaning as an absolute given, there is also the fallacy of an absolute text which raised its head with New Criticism in North America. This is the fallacy of attempting to consider the text as an authorless entity. If the intentional fallacy is blind to the semantic autonomy of the text, the isolated-text fallacy is also blind, blind to the essential historicity of the text. The text was written by someone, about something, for someone to read. It is impossible to cancel out the historicity of a text without reducing it to a physical phenomenon such as waves in the ocean, for even rocks have a geologic history. Our question is identity, but as it is now clear the question of identity is fully tied to interpretation by the reader.

Let us construe this final criterion of identity as fully as possible. In spoken discourse the dialogic situation provides the full realm of identity but a written text is addressed to unknown readers and potentially to countless readers in the future who have the capacity to read. This universalization of the audience can lead to only one conclusion and that is that identity can never be completely fixed; it will change because it is the response of the present and the future and each makes, and will continue to make, the text important or unimportant. This potentiality for multiple readings is the dialectical counterpart of the semantic autonomy of the text. It therefore follows quite markedly that the appropriation of the text is a struggle that generates the whole dynamics of interpretation and concludes with a temporary sense of identity.

My argument is that identity is an expression of understanding which depends on the interaction of three independently generated factors: (a) the established formal sequence of written words; (b) the history of this sequence which includes aspects of production, value, and function as well as assigned categories of classification; and (c) the reading experience as potential concretization. This argument is based on suppositions of a phenomenological approach to the philosophy of language.

Of course, these views on identity of the text can be challenged, as indeed they are by a number of essays in this volume. The challenge can be generated from a variety of premises. One of these disputes my implied sense of text; another disputes that there is a valid distinction to be made for discourse as a literary text, and still others that identity is in any way separable from self-identity of the reader. To summarize, I have proposed three closely related criteria for textual identity: the persistence of an established sequence of words, the historical context in which this sequence is situated, and the potentiality for concretization as a reader's experience. These three criteria can be regarded as providing competing accounts of textual identity, but I think of them as complementary and together constituting the essential conditions for identity. If any one of the three is missing the identity of the text in question is lacking. For example, if the sequence is altered the necessary condition of persistence in time is denied. Secondly, if the text does not have a historical context it is an unknown text since it has not left any record. Thirdly, if the text cannot be read, it may have existed but may have been lost leaving only some historical traces.

The point which emerges from my argument is that there is the most intimate connection between my concept of the identity of a specific text and my definition of a text as a spatio-temporal and qualitatively construed sequence of words with the continuous potentiality of being read. It is implicit in this identity concept that the presence of the succession of words satisfying the three conditions constitutes at least a *prima facie* basis and perhaps even a conclusive basis for making a judgment of identity.

COUNTER-ARGUMENTS

I now wish to expand my proposition that the three criteria of identity come together in an act of appropriation which bestows identity to the text. The aim is not and can never be one of finality or truth, but rather one of participation in the humanistic tradition of commentary. This affirmation will immediately bring upon me the charge of relativism from those who see the task of criticism as a quest for truth. My response is that the purpose of humanistic inquiry must be above all to avoid self-deception and to enhance dialogue.[7] To my mind, the highest form of self-deception is to believe that we can know the truth about ourselves by knowing a set of objective facts.

I maintain that the idea of fixed identity for a literary text is contrary to the spirit of humanistic inquiry, for if we convert the text from something discursive, something incompletely attained by continual adjustments of ideas (a process I have called appropriation) – if we do this – we turn the text into a solely physical object. Let us make no mistake about it, this hypothesis can be an escape from the responsibility for our choice among competing ideas. The urge to find the absolute is the urge to eliminate our freedom for the comfort of the mental conformist. Thus the charge of relativist can be an escape from freedom. The charge is not false; it is mistaken, because the aim of the enterprise has not been understood. The identity we are proposing is not a project to get rid of the burden of thought, but quite the contrary, to join in the project of humanistic commentary. Those of us who have delved into the writings of Unamuno are all too familiar with the claim that the thinker who sees inquiry as self-enrichment is unconcerned for his fellow man, but I argue that the opposite is the case.[8] Since literature is above all a redescription of reality, the search for fixed identity would necessarily reduce all possible descriptions to one and in the end deny humanistic inquiry.

How is it that the counter-argument is misdirected? Is identity the resulting designation of the subject-object relationship or is it an arbitrary assignation? In the first case the identity of a text would be designated by those properties which can be recognized by the subject as the particular characteristics of a specific piece of writing. In the second case identity is designated by the maker of the text who can be either the author or the reader. If the debate were to be limited to these two positions I think we would be caught in a stand-off as old as philosophy between dualistic and monistic philosophy. It is my contention that both positions lack the fundamental ground of history. The rejection of both the dualist and the monist position does not abrogate the designation of identity, but only of a *fixed identity*. My argument is that neither the reader nor the text stands alone. Both are caught up in a historical context of process and change; thus all recognition and all attribution of qualities must be temporary.

I would be remiss in not pointing out that there is in this volume a minority opinion of some importance which holds to the necessity of a fixed identity for the literary text. The basic tenet expressed with distinction by Martínez Bonati[9] is the following: there is a basic stability in works of literature which serves to give a text its identity. Let me be clear why it is that I disagree with this thesis. Although the fictional character of Don Quijote, for example, has a number of features which link him to a specific socio-economic class of sixteenth-century Spain, it is not the possible verification of these indicators which give Don Quijote his identity, but rather his unique departure from the norm. My argument is that the text *Don Quixote* is grounded in a historical context because it has formal persistence but it is incomplete without its reader. It is the historical connection of the story in both the author's production of the text and the reader that makes the reading experience possible. When this connection is traced it may well turn out that what appears to be folly can be taken as idealism and vice versa. But my basic point is that the historical connections must not only be made with reference to the text and its historicity, but also with regard to the reader in his.

The basic disagreement with the thesis of fixed identity is that the character of Don Quijote cannot be treated as a possible-but-not-actual individual. He is neither possible nor actual. He is much more and much less, for Don Quijote has the potentiality of continuous description of shared characteristics of humanity. My response therefore is twofold. On the one hand, it is not warranted to assign a certain truth-value to the linguistic formula in words which the individual reader has not yet realized. On the other hand, there is a remarkable tradition of countless readers who have shared in the pursuit of the redescription of the world through the text and it is in this tradition that we will find the identity of *Don Quixote*. As the philosopher Richard Rorty states, hermeneutics is the philosophy of edification not of the epistemological quest for truth.

The position taken by deconstructionist critics is at the other extreme of the fixed-identity thesis; this argument holds that identity is only a temporary by-product of the supplementation process.[10] This vigorous contemporary view of identity is attractive in several respects: first, because it recognizes the basic role of the reader in the process of understanding a text and, secondly, because it probes deeply into the plurivocal nature of language. The fundamental difficulty I find with this position is that in rejecting the significance of the historicity of production for purposes of interpretation they also reject the historicity of the re-producing situation of the reader. My queries to this position are several and they take me into sketching what I consider to be the parallel but separate relationships of author-text and text-reader. Some basic statements on what I understand by the term *text* are in order before undertaking the task of sketching the bifurcated status of author and reader.

For purposes of clarity I would like to limit the field of inquiry: a text for our purposes is any written discourse, i.e. a symbolic organization within a linguistic system, and a literary text is written discourse which participates in a tradition of humanistic commentary. The written nature of the text is fundamental, for it effectively removes the writer from the act of realization of the text. The writer is absent from the act of reading. The relationship of writer-text is parallel but quite clearly removed from the relationship of text-reader. Five effects are immediately discernible when we pass from oral utterance to written discourse: writing fixes discourse and makes it accessible across time and space; writing also gives discourse a historical dimension and relates it to a universe of other written texts (this being the cultural phenomenon we call literature); writing makes detailed analysis possible; writing allows the receptor of the discourse to be radically distanced from the event of writing (the writer's reader becomes part of an unknown, general, and possibly alien group); the context of dialogue is replaced by a referential redescription of reality which I shall call the textual world.

Let me recapitulate my argument: a work of literature is a text of varying length, but it has an established sequence and its form is a closed totality. A work of literature is codified discourse which permits it to participate in the tradition of texts we call literature. As a work of literature a text is capable of being distinguished as a unique assemblage with its own dimensions. In other words, a literary text is an artefact which has been produced by a writer's labour as a specific work which stands alongside a vast number of others in a tradition.

The most important factor of our consideration of a text as a work of literature is the acknowledgment that it is the result of labour, that it has been produced. This concept is the basis for the *formal* stratum of the text. Since the artefact is a composition, it follows that there are discernible patterns of organization and there is an implicit structure. The philosophical foundation for all formal analysis of written discourse rests on the idea of composition. Formal inquiry of a text by its very methodological approach objectifies the discourse of a literary work and constructs a structural model; but the point I am making here is that this stratum of the text is only possible when the text is considered as a product of human labour.

There is a second aspect of the text as work which I must stress before going on to the other issues of texts, and that is that a work is not only a product of labour but also an artefact which must be removed from the control of its producer in order to be realized. In other words, the text as work is essentially separated from its author and is inserted into the reading process at an alienating distance from its reader; a distance which is never completely overcome but which is reduced through the process that I term appropriation following Ricoeur and Weimann. The characteristics of a text are that it is written discourse with a discernible unit totality, that is a composition, a product of a writer's labour which is available only through an immersion in the text-reader relationship and that the author-text relationship is the event of composition.

Following Gadamer, I hold to the idea that what a text signifies does not coincide with what the author meant.[11] From the moment the text is completed and given to the reader, textual meaning and authorial intentions have separate and often far removed destinies. Thus a third and also basic characteristic of a literary text is that it transcends its author's psychological and sociological conditions of production. In the words of Umberto Eco, it opens to an unlimited series of readings each of which will have a specific historicity of particular psychological and sociological dimensions. In other words, the loss of original context, which is only partial and often mitigated by historical scholarship, gives way to the necessary creation of a new context which belongs to the reader-text relationship.

The position which I follow eschews both the direction of Romantic hermeneutics, which sought to grasp the genius of the author as exemplified by his texts, and the contemporary paths of structuralism, which would restrict criticism to reconstructing the structure of the work, and post-structuralist deconstruction, which would reduce it to the status of an event with a trace left behind. The aim is to examine the reader-text relationship and thus approach the redescribed world of the text. If we take the formal structure of the text as the *sense* of the text then *reference* is the implicit task of redescription. Thus with Ricoeur let us ask what happens to discourse when we consider it in its essential constitution of human work. Since the author-reader relation cannot exist as in a dialogical situation because of the bifurcation we have described as two separate and parallel relationships, that of author-text and that of reader-text, we must examine each relationship separate from its counterpart. The reader-text relationship at first sight appears to be self-referential with no discernible tie to the world of human action. This is a false assumption, for all literary discourse achieves meaning only by reinsertion into a historical context which is that of the reader and is certainly anchored in reality. Husserl's concept of *life-world*[12] and Heidegger's *being-in-the-world*[13] adequately describe the essence of the new context of the work. The unique referential dimension of the literary text is best explained by what Ricoeur has called the split-reference of literary discourse – by which he means the interplay between the self-referential aspect of poetic language and the necessary ground in the world of human action.[14] A literary text offers its readers a purported state of affairs; this is a proposed world which can be realized only through the intervention of the reader. The redescription of reality which ensues as the essential outcome of reading is thus the exclusive property neither of the text nor of the reader but is rather the unique creation of the dynamic relationship between the two.

The final characteristic of the text is that there is a discernible mode of *taking-in* the proposed world of the text by the reader. The reader as commentator has the opportunity of discovering his mode of appropriation of the text. It is not a question of imposing upon the text our finite capacity of understanding but of exposing ourselves to the text and receiving from the encounter an enriched self. Consequently the critique of ideology which is exemplified by Jameson has a specific role in bringing about an understanding of the process of appropriation with which the reader realizes the text.

I have suggested three criteria for the identity of a literary text: continuity in time of a sequence of words (form); a historical context of production; and the possibility of realization of a text through reading. I have also engaged in some discussion with some of the basic positions taken on the nature of the text. It remains to be considered to what extent identity of the text has an independent status from the historical context of either writer or reader or both. We can argue that to the extent that the unity of a text can be said to depend on formal characteristics (which can be described analytically) the unity of the text depends on the empirical fact of the writing, but, as I pointed out at the outset of this discussion, writing itself is meaningless if it is separated from the whole of human activity. Ultimately the identity of the text depends on how the text relates to our human interests and purposes. I do not wish to imply that I am in agreement with the thesis that a text is not fully objective matter, but only that it is much more than that without denying its empirical facticity. In my tripartite description of identity I have tried to do justice to this richer notion of the text.

IDENTITY AND LITERARY CRITICISM

Of what significance is a particular concept of identity with regard to literary criticism? I believe that it is of the greatest importance because it is usually the fundamental presupposition on which a particular system or approach of literary criticism rests for the critics who pursue that particular route. I make this judgment because I am convinced that there cannot be a general theory of literary criticism, and therefore each approach consciously or unconsciously maps out the terrain of its undertaking on the basis of what its practitioners understand the literary text to be. I would like to defend the statement that there cannot be a general theory of literary criticism. If the sole purpose of a theory is to explain, something must be explained, and this means that there must be an already existing problem or issue that calls for explanation.[15] This statement leads me to go further and argue that a theory's scope cannot be determined by its subject-matter, that is by whatever the theory is about. The scope of the theory, if its function is to explain a pre-existent issue, is determined by its purpose and by its clarification of the problems to which it offers a solution. Further, the survival of a theory, its continued use and development, is determined by its correlation to practice.

A theory of literary criticism, if it is to be a theory at all, can only be a theory about certain features which have been selected as being the ones that matter. Thus by definition a theory of literary criticism is a specific logical argument which purports to explain the problems of dealing with a specific concept of identity of the literary text; it is not a plan to explain what literary criticism is. The purpose may be, for example, to provide the necessary rules for the solution of a certain class of problems which obtain because the text has been determined as the object of hermeneutic interpretation, or in another case when the text has been bifurcated into discourse and story and rules of operation are needed for the semiotic analysis of discourse. The names of the various theories of literary criticism are a capsule of identity since they allude to the basic issues, and these are the specific relationships which have been given a major focus as they occur in the phenomenon called the literary text. This is precisely the point at issue here. It is in the presupposition of the identity of the text that we will be able to find the essential source and direction of any approach to literary criticism. For example, a structuralist theory of criticism describes specific formal relationships as they are perceived to occur in the linguistic organization of a text. Another theory of criticism may be designed to provide the operational rules needed to examine texts as a reflection of social patterns (Lukács, *Ästhetik*, part I, sec. 3). Still another example would be a theory of criticism whose stipulated purpose is to provide the ground rules for establishing links between the author's insight and the text (Jung, *The Spirit in Man, Art and Literature*, New York 1966, p. 93). In these examples, taken at random, the theory of literary criticism can provide a solution to specific problems arising out of the work done with literary texts which have been selected as being of interest, and, more importantly, which have been given a specific status of identity. In short, my claim is that the concept of identity is the benchmark of theories of literary criticism.

I would now like to turn to the last of the questions I posed at the outset of this response. To what extent can we justify approaching literature in terms of a specific concept of identity now that we have ruled out the possibility of a general theory of literary criticism? Literary study, as I understand it, is a pluralistic encounter of individual minds. Thus we have only the choice of engaging other minds or practising advanced self-delusion and convincing ourselves that a select number of other minds see the world through our biases. I make reference to encountering other minds and this phrase has many connotations which I endorse, but it has one which must be mitigated, for I believe that an encounter need not be synonymous with a clash; an encounter can be and often is an experience of mutual enrichment. When someone asks about a specific theory of literary criticism, the very asking of the question reveals a highly developed set of commitments. Thus, if an extended discussion were to ensue on the relative validity of the theoretical proposition or propositions, the exchange would only be possible in the context of a specific problem even if that problem has not yet been clearly articulated. My argument is twofold: if there is no antecedent there can be no theoretical argument, and if the identity of the text does not emerge in the process of discussion there is scant possibility of an understanding being reached between the discussants.

It is because I have dismissed claims to a general theory as a reduction of reality to conform with the particular interests of the individual that we now face the root question which can be asked of all relativistic argument. What can we hope to achieve through the shared experience we have been sketching as the encounter of identity-concepts? The aim of the encounter must be to formulate a framework within which alternative theories can be compared and in terms of which their features, aspects of their scope, their comprehensiveness of inquiry and adequacy of application can be ascertained.

We now come to the key question in the minds of most students of literature: the possibility of elaborating procedures or methods of criticism in a context I have characterized as the encounter of identity concepts. If what I have presented before is acceptable, how can we proceed so as to ensure that these observations on identity are in fact an overview of the issue and do not constitute one more theory among others? Unavoidably, there have been crucial points in my argument at which directions have been taken by me which are at least in part predetermined by my particular way of identifying the literary text. My response has two parts. First, eclecticism is not a true option, for it is no choice at all to accept diverse tenets of theories irrespective of their argument; thus, pluralism should not be taken as another name for eclecticism. Secondly, a theoretical discussion, whatever the starting point, must be able to address the issues with a degree of concomitant adequacy to the implicit or explicit identity concept used.

Let us take the case of a historicist theory of literary criticism. In probing into the outlines of the theory the objective of the inquiry must be to lay bare the basic premise which any historical theory would have to hold. This inquiry, therefore, would accept the argument that a historical reconstruction of the author-text relationship is a viable option to pursue, but we must also underscore that the historically reconstituted text is a particular identity concept of the literary text, and cannot be accepted as a given fact. A historical reconstruction can be aimed at and pursued with diligence, but its very premise is far more speculative than most rival theories. I would therefore turn the historical issue around. In place of arguing that the historical event of composition is the paradigm for the reconstruction of the text's meaning, I propose that the event of production, together with the formal organization, is the precondition for the reader's realization which is always new.

It is my hope that these essays will prove to be an enriching experiment in critical pluralism, but that judgment is now in the hands of our readers.

NOTES

1 The most notable writer to pursue this route is Stanley Fish, whose articles have been at the forefront of theoretical discussions for more than a decade. Cf. 'How to Recognize a Poem When You See One,' in *Is There a Text in This Class?*, Cambridge, Mass. 1980, pp. 322–37.

2 I have profited greatly from my study of Eli Hirsch's excellent book *The Concept of Identity*, Oxford 1982. I am especially indebted to chapter 8, 'A Sense of Unity.' Cf. 'My argument against the empiricist position consisted in maintaining that there is nothing about the world which could have taught us to adopt our ordinary criteria of unity, had we started out without these criteria' (p. 262).

3 I would like to acknowledge the work of Alfred Schütz as the basis of much of my thinking on communication and the social group. *Der sinnhafte Aufbau der sozialen Welt* was first published in Vienna by J. Springer-Verlag in 1932 and has been translated into English by George Walsh, *The Phenomenology of the Social World*, Evanston 1967; see especially 'The Meaning-Context of Communication,' pp. 129–32.

4 Cf. Paul Ricoeur: 'What do we understand by the referential relation or referential function? In addressing himself to another speaker, the subject of discourse says something about something; that about which he speaks is the referent of his discourse. ... All discourse is, to some extent, thereby reconnected to the world. For if we did not speak of the world, of what should we speak? ... As we shall see, the text is not without reference; the task of reading, *qua* interpretation, will be precisely to fulfill the reference.' Cited from 'What Is a Text,' in *Hermeneutics and the Human Sciences*, Cambridge 1981, pp. 147–8.

5 See Wolfgang Iser, *The Act of Reading*, Baltimore 1978. Iser writes on p. 28: 'there are three types of "contemporary" reader – the one real and historical, drawn from existing documents, and the other two hypothetical: the first constructed from social and historical knowledge of the time, and the second extrapolated from the reader's role laid down in the text.'

6 One of the great ironic twists of contemporary theory is that the concept of a super reader or fixed norm of reading is little more than an objectification of the critic's own reading experience. On this issue see Iser, *The Act of Reading*, and Hans Robert Jauss, 'Theses on the Transition from the Aesthetics of Literary Works to a Theory of Aesthetic Experience,' in *Interpretation of Narrative*, ed. M.J. Valdés and O.J. Miller, Toronto 1978, pp. 137–47; see especially p. 143: 'Whoever reduces the role of the implied reader to the behaviour of an explicit reader, whoever writes exclusively in the language of a specific stratum, can only produce cookbooks, catechisms, party speeches, travel brochures, and similar documents.'

7 Richard Rorty in his recent book, *Philosophy and the Mirror of Nature*, Princeton

1979, p. 361, sums up the argument: 'objectivity should be seen as conformity to the norms of justification (for assertions and for actions) we find about us. Such conformity becomes dubious and self-deceptive only when seen as something more than this – namely, as a way of obtaining access to something which grounds current practices of justification in something else. Such a ground is thought to need no justification, because it has become so clearly and distinctly perceived as to count as a philosophical foundation. This is self-deceptive not simply because of the general absurdity of ultimate justifications reposing upon the unjustifiable, but because of the more concrete absurdity of thinking that the vocabulary used by present science, morality or whatever has some privileged attachment to reality which makes it *more* than just a further set of descriptions.'

8 See my introduction to *An Unamuno Source Book*, Toronto 1973, p. xxi, note 15.

9 For a fuller understanding of Martínez Bonati's thought, see his recent *Fictive Discourse and the Structures of Literature*, Ithaca 1981, and his essay 'Hermeneutic Criticism and the Description of Form,' in *Interpretation of Narrative*, pp. 78–99.

10 The deconstruction position is of course derived from Jacques Derrida's theory of polysemy in which he maintains that the semantic operation we call deconstruction is a continuous mode of play with the text by the reader, and its major aim is to destroy the illusory notion of a fixed textual meaning. Every meaning which is presumed to stand by the commentator is shown to be no more than a play between simulation and dissimulation. The true nature of every text therefore is to be in a state of flux as long as it is engaged by the reader and is reduced to a mere trace when the engagement is over because the text has no determinate essence. Derrida apparently endorses the following passage he cites from Rousseau's *Emile*: 'The dreams of a bad night are given to us as philosophy. You will say I too am a dreamer; I admit it, but I do what others fail to do, I give my dreams as dreams, and leave the reader to discover whether there is anything in them which may prove useful to those who are awake.' See *Of Grammatology*, Baltimore 1976, p. 316.

11 The author of a text is thus a historical fact and has significance within an effective history of composition for the text in question. This position stated briefly here is derived from Hans Georg Gadamer's major study *Wahrheit und Methode*, Tübingen 1960. The English translation, *Truth and Method*, by Garrett Barden and John Cumining, taken from the second German edition of 1965, was published in 1975. I cite a key passage from p. 266: 'The naiveté of so called historicism consists in the fact that it does not undertake this reflection, and in trusting to its own methodological approach forgets its own historicality. ... True historical thinking must take account of its own historicality. Only then will it not chase after the phantom of an historical object which is the object of progressive research, but rather will learn to see in the object the counterpart of itself and hence understand both.'

12 Cf. Edmund Husserl, *Erfahrung und Urteil: Untersuchungen zur Genealogie der Logik*, Hamburg 1948; repr. 1974. English translation: *Experience and Judgment: Investigations in a Genealogy of Logic*, trans. J.S. Churchill and K. Ameriks, Evanston 1973. I cite from p. 41 of the English translation: 'All predicative self-evidence must be ultimately grounded on the self-evidence of experience. ... The retrogression to the world of experience is a retrogression to the *life-world*, i.e., to the world in which we are always already living and which furnishes the ground for all cognitive performance and all scientific determination.'

13 Being-in-the-world (In-der-Welt-sein), as I understand it, means the *capacity* which human beings have a priori to have relationships both with things and with other human beings. I cite from *Sein und Zeit* (1926), English translation: *Being and Time*, New York 1962, p. 119: 'In understanding a context of relations such as we have mentioned, Dasein has assigned itself to an *in-order-to*, and it has done so in terms of a potentiality-for-Being for the sake of which it itself is one which it may have seized upon either explicitly or tacitly, and which may be either authentic or inauthentic.' This statement was Heidegger's response to the question he had just asked: 'And what is that wherein *Dasein* as Being-in-the-World understands itself pre-ontologically?'

14 Cf. Paul Ricoeur, *The Rule of Metaphor*, Toronto 1978, pp. 297–300.

15 I am greatly indebted to my colleague F.E. Sparshott for his clarity in arguing these issues. His book *The Concept of Criticism*, Oxford 1967, is one of the finest training manuals for anyone seeking to work out a theoretical argument on the nature of criticism.

References

ADORNO, Theodor W. *Prismen: Kulturkritik und Gesellschaft.* Berlin 1955
- *Ohne Leitbild: parva aesthetica.* Frankfurt 1967
- 'Parataxis.' *Gesammelte Schriften.* Ed. Rolf Tiedemann. Frankfurt 1974
- *In Search of Wagner.* Trans. Rodney Livingston. London 1981
ALLISON, David B. 'Destruction/Deconstruction in the Text of Nietzsche.' *Boundary 2*, 8 (Fall 1979), 197–222
AMOSSY, Ruth, and Elisheva Rosen. 'Du titre au poème: une expérience surréaliste.' *Revue des sciences humaines*, 44 (October–December 1978), 153–71
- *Les Discours du cliché.* Paris 1982
ANDEREGG, Johannes. *Literaturwissenchaftliche Stiltheorie.* Göttingen 1977
APOLLINAIRE, Guillaume. *Oeuvres Poétiques.* Ed. M. Adéma and H. Décaudin. Paris 1965
- *Calligrammes: Poems of Peace and War.* Trans. A.H. Greet. Los Angeles 1980
ARISTOTLE. *The Organon. The Categories. On Interpretation.* Ed. Harold P. Cooke. London 1938
AUSTIN, J.L. *How to Do Things with Words.* Ed. J.O. Urmson. Cambridge, Mass. 1962
BABILAS, Wolfgang. *Tradition und Interpretation.* München 1961
BACON, Francis. *The Works.* Ed. J. Spedding et al. London 1960
BAILEY, J.O. *The Poetry of Thomas Hardy: A Handbook and Commentary.* Chapel Hill, North Carolina 1970
BAKHTIN, Mikhail. 'Problema teksta-Opyt filosofskogo analiza.' *Voprosy literatury*, 10 (1976)
- *Esthetika slovesnogo tvorchestva.* Moscow 1979
BARTHES, Roland. *S/Z.* Paris 1970
- 'An Introduction to the Structural Analysis of Narrative.' Trans. Lionel Duisit. *New Literary History*, 6 (Winter 1975), 237–72
- 'From Work to Text.' *Textual Strategies: Perspectives in Post-Structuralist Criticism.* Ed. J.V. Harari. London 1980

BEHLER, Ernst. 'Die Kunst des Reflexion: Das frühromantische Denken in Hinblick auf Nietzsche.' *Untersuchungen zur Literatur als Geschichte: Festschrift für Benno von Wiese*. Ed. Vincent J. Günther et al. Berlin 1973, 219–47
– 'Nietzsche in der marxistischen Kritik Osteuropas.' *Nietzsche-Studien*, 10/11 (1981/2), 80–96
BENJAMIN, Walter. *Ursprung des deutschen Trauerspiele*. Ed. Rolf Tiedemann. Frankfurt 1955
– *Des Begriff der Kunstkritik in der deutschen Romantik*. Frankfurt 1973
BENNETT, Tony. *Formalism and Marxism*. London 1979
BENTHAM, Jeremy. *Theory of Fictions*. Ed. C.K. Ogden. London 1959
BERTAUX, Pierre. *Hölderlin und die französische Revolution*. Frankfurt 1969
BINDER, Hartmut, ed. *Kafka-Handbuch*. 2 vols. Stuttgart 1979
BLANCHOT, Maurice. 'L'absence du livre.' *L'Entretien infini*. Paris 1969
BOOTH, Wayne C. '"Preserving the Exemplar": or, How Not to Dig Our Own Graves.' *Critical Inquiry*, 3 (Spring 1977), 407–23
BORGES, Jorge Luis. 'Pierre Ménard, Author of the Quixote.' *Labyrinths, Selected Stories and Other Writings*. Trans. J.E. Irby. New York 1964
BRANDES, Georg. *Friedrich Nietzsche*. Trans. A.G. Chater. New York 1909
BRETON, André. *Clair de terre*. Paris 1966
BRONTË, Emily. *Wuthering Heights*. Ed. David Daiches. Harmondsworth 1965
BROOKS, Cleanth. *The Well-Wrought Urn*. New York 1947
BROOKS, Peter. 'Freud's Masterplot: Questions of Narrative.' *Yale French Studies*, 56 (1977)
BROWN, Norman O. *Closing Time*. New York 1973
BULST, W. 'Bedenken eines Philologen.' *Medium Aevum Vivum, Festschrift für W. Bulst*. Ed. H.R. Jauss and D. Schaller. Heidelberg 1960
BURKE, Kenneth. '"Kubla Khan," Post-Surrealist Poem.' *Language as Symbolic Action: Essays on Life, Literature, and Method*. Los Angeles 1968, 201–22
BUTOR, Michel. *Répertoire: Etudes et Conférences 1948–59*. Paris 1960
CHASE, Cynthia. 'The Decomposition of the Elephants: Double-Reading *Daniel Deronda*.' *PMLA*, 93:2 (March 1978), 215–27
CHATEAUBRIAND, François-Auguste-René. *Les martyrs, œuvres romanesques et voyages*. Paris 1969
COHN, Robert G. *The Poetry of Rimbaud*. Princeton 1973
COMPAGNON, Antoine. *La Seconde main ou le travail de la citation*. Paris 1979
COWARD, Rosalind, and John Ellis. *Language and Materialism: Developments in Semiology and the Theory of the Subject*. London 1977
CULLER, Jonathan. *Structuralist Poetics: Structuralism, Linguistics and the Study of Literature*. London 1975
– 'Presupposition and Intertextuality.' *Modern Language Notes*, 91 (December 1976), 1380–96

- 'Derrida.' *Structuralism and Since: From Levi-Strauss to Derrida.* Ed. John Sturrock. Oxford 1979, 154–80
- *The Pursuit of Signs: Semiotics, Literature, Deconstruction.* Ithaca 1981
- *On Deconstruction: Theory and Criticism after Structuralism.* Ithaca 1983
DÄLLENBACH, Lucien. *Le Récit Spéculaire.* Paris 1977
DELEUZE, Gilles, and Félix Guattari. *Capitalisme et schizophrénie, 1: L'anti-Oedipe.* Paris 1972
DE MAN, Paul. *Allegories of Reading: Figural Language in Rousseau, Nietzsche, Rilke and Proust.* New Haven 1979
DERRIDA, Jacques. *De la grammatologie.* Paris 1967
- *L'écriture et la différence.* Paris 1967
- 'Freud and the Scene of Writing.' Trans. Jeffrey Mehlman. *Yale French Studies,* 48 (1972)
- *Positions.* Paris 1972
- *Glas.* Paris 1974
- 'White Mythology: Metaphor in the Text of Philosophy.' Trans. F.C.T. Moore. *New Literary History,* 6 (Autumn 1974), 5–74
- *Of Grammatology.* Trans. Gayatri Spivak. Baltimore 1976
- 'Coming into One's Own.' *Psychoanalysis and the Question of the Text.* Ed. E.G. Hartman. Baltimore 1978
- *Eperons: Les Styles de Nietzsche.* Paris 1978
- 'Living on: Border Lines.' Trans. James Hulbert. *Deconstruction and Criticism.* Ed. Harold Bloom et al. New York 1979
- *Spurs: Nietzsche's Styles.* Trans. Barbara Harlow. Chicago 1979
- *Dissemination.* Trans. Barbara Johnston. Chicago 1981
- 'Télépathie.' *Furor,* 2 (1981), 5–41
DIXON, Marlene. *The Future of Women.* San Francisco 1983
DOLEŽEL, Lubomír. 'Extensional and Intensional Narrative Worlds.' *Formal Semantics and Literary Theory.* Ed. John Woods and Thomas G. Pavel. Special issue of *Poetics* (1979), 193–211
- 'Truth and Authenticity in Narrative.' *Poetics Today,* 1 (Spring 1980), 7–25
- 'A Short Note on a Long Subject: Literary Style.' *Voz'mi na radost'. To Honour Jeanne van der Eng-Liedmeier.* Amsterdam 1980, 1–7
DUCROT, Oswald. *Dire et ne pas dire: principes de sématique linguistique.* Paris 1972
EAGLETON, Terry. *Myths of Power: a Marxist Study of the Brontës.* London 1975
- 'Text, Ideology, Realism.' *Literature and Society.* Ed. Edward W. Said. Baltimore 1980, 149–73
- *Literary Theory: An Introduction.* Minneapolis 1983
ECO, Umberto. 'Two Problems in Textual Interpretation.' *Poetics Today,* 2 (Autumn 1980), 145–61
EDWARDS, Paul, ed. *An Encyclopedia of Philosophy.* New York 1967

ELIOT, T.S. 'The Function of Criticism.' *Selected Essays 1917–1932*. London 1932, 23–34

– *After Strange Gods: A Primer of Modern Heresy*. London 1933

– *Collected Poems 1909–1935*. London 1954

FAIRLEY, Irene R. 'Experimental Approaches to Language in Literatures: Reader Responses to Poems.' *Style*, 13 (1979), 335–64

FEKETE, John. *The Critical Twilight: Explorations in the Ideology of Anglo-American Literary Theory from Eliot to McLuhan*. London 1977

FELMAN, Shoshana. 'Turning the Screw of Interpretation.' *Yale French Studies*, 55/56 (1977)

FIELDING, Henry. *The History of Tom Jones*. London 1957

FISCHER, Hugo. *Nietzsche Apostata: oder Die Philosophie des Argernisses*. Erfurt 1931

FISH, Stanley. 'Literature and the Reader: Affective Stylistics.' *New Literary History*, 2 (Autumn 1970), 123–62

– *Is There a Text in This Class? The Authority of Interpretive Communities*. Cambridge, Mass. 1980

FOUCAULT, Michel. *L'ordre du discours*. Paris 1971

– *Les Mots et les choses*. Trans. as *The Order of Things*. New York 1973

– 'What Is an Author?' *Textual Strategies: Perspectives in Post-Structuralist Criticism*. Ed. J.V. Harari. London 1980

FOWLER, Roger. *The Language of Literature: Some Linguistic Contributions to Criticism*. New York 1971

FRANK, Manfred. *Das individuelle Allgemeine-Textstrukturierung und Interpretation nach Schleiermacher*. Frankfurt 1977

FRANKENBERG, Ronald. 'Styles of Marxism; Styles of Criticism. *Wuthering Heights*: A Case Study.' *The Sociology of Literatures*. Ed. Diana Laurenson. Keele 1978, 109–44

FRYE, Northrop. *Anatomy of Criticism*. Princeton 1957; repr. New York 1966

– *A Study of English Romanticism*. New York 1968

GADAMER, Hans Georg. *Wahrheit und Methode*. Tübingen 1960

GARNER, Richard. 'Presupposition in Philosophy and Linguistics.' *Studies in Linguistic Semantics*. Ed. Charles J. Fillmore and D. Terence Langendoen. New York 1971, 22–42

GASCHÉ, Rodolphe. 'Deconstruction as Criticism.' *Glyph*, 6 (1979), 177–215

GEHLEN, Arnold. *Urmensch und Spätkultur. Philosophische Ergebnisse und Aussagen*. Frankfurt 1975

GERRATANA, Valentino. 'Heidegger and Marx.' *New Left Review*, 106 (November–December 1977), 51–8

GOLDMAN, Lucien. *Lukács et Heidegger*. Paris 1973

GOODMAN, Nelson. *Ways of Worldmaking*. Indianapolis 1978

GRAFF, Gerald. *Literature against Itself: Literary Ideas in Modern Society*. Chicago 1979

GRAMSCI, Antonio. *Selections from the Prison Notebooks*. Ed. and trans. Quintin Hoare and Geoffrey Nowell Smith. New York 1971

GRICE, Paul H. 'Logic and Conversation.' *Speech Acts (Syntax and Semantics 3)*. Ed. P. Cole and J.L. Morgan. New York 1975, 41–58

GRIVEL, Charles. *Production de l'intérêt romanesque*. Paris 1973

GRÜNDER, Karlfried, ed. *Der Streit um Nietzsches 'Geburt der Tragödie': die Schriften von E. Röhde, R. Wagner, U.V. Wilamowitz-Möllendorff.* Hildesheim 1969

HAMLIN, Cyrus. 'The Temporality of Selfhood: Metaphor and Romantic Poetry.' *New Literary History*, 6 (Autumn 1974), 169–93

– 'The Hermeneutics of Form: Reading the Romantic Ode.' *Boundary 2*, 7:3 (Spring 1979), 1–30

– 'I.A. Richards (1893–1979): Grand Master of Interpretations.' *University of Toronto Quarterly*, 49:3 (Spring 1980), 189–204

– 'The Conscience of Narrative: Toward a Hermeneutics of Transcendence.' *New Literary History*, 13 (Winter 1982), 205–30

HARDY, Thomas. *The Complete Poems*. New Wessex Edition. Ed. James Gibson. London 1976

HARTMAN, Geoffrey. 'Literary Criticism and Its Discontents.' *Critical Inquiry*, 3 (Winter 1976), 203–20

– 'Psychoanalysis: The French Connection.' *Psychoanalysis and the Question of the Text*. Ed. G. Hartman. Baltimore 1978, 86–113

HARVEY, William J. *Character and the Novel*. London 1965

HEGEL, G.W.F. *Wisenschaft der Logik*, II. Die philosophische Bibliothek, vol. 57. Ed. Georg Lasson. Hamburg 1966

HEIDEGGER, Martin. 'Der Ursprung des Kunstwerks.' *Holzwege*. 3rd ed. Frankfurt 1957

– 'Der Satz der Identität.' *Identität und Differenz*. Pfullingen 1957, 13–34

– *Being and Time*. New York 1962

HEINTZ, John. 'Reference and Inference in Fiction.' *Formal Semantics and Literary Theory*. Ed. John Woods and Thomas G. Pavel. *Poetics* (1979), 85–99

HENRICH, Dieter. 'Hegels' Logik der Reflexion. Neue Fassung.' *Die Wissenschaft der Logik und die Logik der Reflexion. Hegel-Studien, Beihefte*, vol. 18. Bonn 1978, 204–324

– '"Identität" – Begriffe Probleme, Grenzen.' *Identität*. Ed. Odo Marquard and Karlheinz Stierle. *Poetik und Hermeneutik*, 8. München 1979, 133–86

HIRSCH, E.D. *Validity in Interpretation*. New Haven 1967

– *The Aims of Interpretation*. Chicago 1976

HIRSCH, Eli. *The Concept of Identity*. Oxford 1982

HOHENDAHL, Peter Uwe. 'Reform als Utopie: Die preussische Bildungspolitik, 1809–1817.' *Utopieforschung: Interdisziplinäre Studien zur neuzeitlichen Utopie*. Ed. Wilhelm Voss Kamp. Stuttgart 1983. III, 250–72, esp. 265–7

HOLLAND, Norman. 'Unity Identity Text Self,' *PMLA*, 90 (1975)

HOMANS, Margaret. 'Repression and Sublimation of Nature in *Wuthering Heights.*' *PMLA*, 93:1 (January 1978), 9–19

HORKHEIMER, Max. 'Bemerkungen zu Jaspers' "Nietzsche."' *Zeitschrift für Sozialforschung*, 6 (1937), 407–14

HÖRMANN, Hans. *Meinen und Verstehen. Grunszuge einer psychologischen Semantik.* Frankfurt 1976

HOUSTON, John P. *The Design of Rimbaud's Poetry.* New Haven 1963

HUSSERL, Edmund. *Experience and Judgement: Investigations in a Genealogy of Logic.* Trans. J.S. Churchill and K. Ameriks. Evanston 1973

– *Phantasie Bildbewusstsein, Erinnerung* (Gesammelte Werke XXIII). Ed. Eduard Marbach. The Hague 1980

HUTCHENS, Eleanor N. 'The Novel as Chronomorph.' *Novel* (Spring 1972), 215–24

HUTCHEON, Linda. 'Ironie, et parodie: stratégie et structure.' *Poétique*, 36 (1978), 467–77

– 'Ironie, satire, parodie.' *Poétique*, 46 (1981), 140–55

ISER, Wolfgang. *The Act of Reading: A Theory of Aesthetic Response.* Baltimore 1978

JACOBS, Carol. '*Wuthering Heights*: At the Threshold of Interpretation.' *Boundary 2*, 7:3 (Spring 1979), 49–71

JAFFE, Adrian. *The Process of Kafka's Trial.* East Lansing, Michigan 1967

JAKOBSON, Roman. 'Closing Statement: Linguistics and Poetics.' *Style in Language.* Ed. T. Sebeok. Cambridge, Mass. 1960

– 'Linguistics and Poetics.' *Style and Language.* Cambridge, Mass. 1960

JAMES, Henry. *The Art of the Novel: Critical Prefaces by Henry James.* New York 1953

JAMESON, Fredric. 'The Ideology of the Text.' *Salmagundi*, 31–2 (Fall 1975/Winter 1976)

– *The Political Unconscious: Narrative as a Socially Symbolic Act.* Ithaca 1981

JASPERS, Karl. *Nietzsche: Einführung in das Verständnis seines Philosophierens.* 3rd ed. Berlin 1950

JAUSS, Hans Robert. 'Theses on the Transition from the Aesthetics of Literary Works to a Theory of Aesthetic Experience.' *Interpretation of Narrative.* Ed. M.J. Valdés and O.J. Miller. Toronto 1978, 137–47

JEAN, Raymond. *Lectures du Désir.* Paris 1977

JENNY, Laurent. 'La Stratégie de la forme.' *Poétique*, 27 (1976), 257–81

JOËL, Karl. 'Nietzsche und die Romantik.' *Neue Deutsche Rundschau*, 14 (1903), 458–501

– *Nietzsche und die Romantik.* Jena 1923

JOHNSON, Barbara. *The Critical Difference.* Baltimore 1981

JUHL, Peter D. *Interpretation: An Essay in the Philosophy of Literary Criticism.* Princeton, N.J. 1980

JUNG, Carl G. *The Spirit in Man, Art and Literature*. New York 1966

KEENAN, Edward L. 'Two Kinds of Presupposition in Natural Language.' *Studies in Linguistic Semantics*. Ed. Charles J. Fillmore and D. Terence Langendoen. New York 1971, 45–52

KERMODE, Frank. *The Classic*. New York 1975

KRIEGER, Murray. *The New Apologists for Poetry*. Minneapolis 1956

KRISTEVA, Julia. *Théorie d'ensemble*. Paris 1968, 80–93

– *Semiotikè: recherches pour une sémanalyse*. Paris 1969

– *Révolution du langage poétique*. Paris 1974

– *Pouvoirs de l'horreur: Essai sur l'abjection*. Paris 1980

KUNNE-IBSCH, Elrud. *Die Stellung Nietzsches in der Entwicklung der modernen Literaturwissenschaft*. Assen 1972

LACAN, Jacques. 'L'instance de la lettre dans l'inconscient.' *Ecrits* I, Paris 1966

– *Les Quatre Concepts fondamentaux de la psychanalyse*. Paris 1973

LAGARDE, André, and Laurent Michard. *XXᵉ siècle*. Paris 1968

LAUSBERG, Heinrich. *Handbuch der literarischen Rhetorik*. München 1960

LEITCH, Vincent B. *Deconstructive Criticism: An Advanced Introduction*. New York 1983

LENTRICCHIA, Frank. *After the New Criticism*. Chicago 1980

LEVENSTEIN, Adolf, ed. *Friedrich Nietzsche im Urteil der Arbeiterklasse*. Leipzig 1914

LEVIN, Samuel R. 'The Status of Nondeviant Expressions in Poetry.' *The Semantics of Metaphor*. Baltimore 1977

LOCKE, John. *An Essay Concerning Human Understanding*. London 1971

LOTMAN, Juri M. *The Structure of the Artistic Text*. Trans. Gail Lenhoff and Roland Vroon. Ann Arbor 1977

LUKÁCS, Georg. *Die Zerstorung der Vernunft*. Berlin 1953

– *Conversations with Lukács*. Ed. Theo Pinkus. London 1967

LYONS, John. *Semantics*. 2 vols. Cambridge 1977

MACHEREY, Pierre. *A Theory of Literary Production*. Trans. Geoffrey Wall. London 1978

MACPHERSON, Crawford B. *The Political Theory of Possessive Individualism: Hobbes to Locke*. Oxford 1962

MARGOLIS, Joseph. *Art and Philosophy*. Brighton, Sussex 1980

MARX, Karl, and Friedrich Engels. *Collected Works*. New York 1976

MC GANN, Jerome J. 'The Text, the Poem and the Problem of Historical Method.' *New Literary History*, 12 (1981), 269–88

MILLER, J. Hillis. 'The Stone and the Shell: Wordsworth's Dream of the Arab.' *Moments Premiers*. Paris 1973, 125–47

– 'The Critic as Host.' *Deconstruction and Criticism*. Ed. Harold Bloom et al. New York 1979

– *Fiction and Repetition*. Cambridge, Mass. 1982

- 'The Metaphorical Plot.' *Metaphor: Problems and Perspectives.* Ed. David S. Miall. Sussex 1982
MITCHELL, Juliet. *Woman's Estate.* New York 1971
MOLIÈRE (Jean-Baptiste Poquelin). *Oeuvres Complètes I.* Ed. M. Rat. Paris 1959, *Les Fâcheux*, II, 2
MUKAŘOVSKY, Jan. *The World and Verbal Art.* Trans. John Burbank and Peter Steiner. New Haven 1977
MUSSELWHITE, David. '*Wuthering Heights*: The Unacceptable Text.' *Literature, Society and the Sociology of Literature.* Ed. Frances Barker. Proceedings of the Conference held at the University of Essex. July 1976, 154–60
NAUMANN, Manfred, and Dieter Schlenstedt, eds. *Gesellschaft-Literatur-Lesen: Literaturrezeption in theoretischer sicht.* Berlin 1973
NESSELROTH, Peter W. 'Lautréamont's Plagiarisms, or, the Poetization of Prose Texts.' *Pretext/Text/Context.* Ed. R.L. Mitchell. Columbus 1980, 185–95
NIETZSCHE, Friedrich. *Kritische Gesamtausgabe, Werke.* Ed. Giorgio Colli and Mazzino Montinari. Berlin 1967
- *Kritische Gesamtausgabe Briefwechsel.* Ed. Giorgio Colli and Mazzino Montinari. Berlin 1978
- *Kritische Studienausgabe.* Ed. Giorgio Colli and Mazzino Montinari. Berlin 1980
NORRIS, Christopher. *Deconstruction: Theory and Practice.* London 1982
- *The Deconstructive Turn: Essays in the Rhetoric of Philosophy.* London 1983
OHMANN, Richard. 'Speech Acts and the Definition of Literature.' *Philosophy and Rhetoric,* 4 (Winter 1971), 1–19
PARKER, Patricia. 'Anagogic Metaphor: Breaking Down the Wall of Partition.' *Centre and Labyrinth: Essays in Honour of Northrop Frye.* Ed. Eleanor Cook et al. Toronto 1983
PARSONS, Terence. *Nonexistent Objects.* New Haven 1980
PAVEL, Thomas G. '"Possible Worlds" in Literary Semantics.' *Journal of Aesthetics and Art Criticism,* 34:2 (1976), 165–76
PLATO. *Republic.* Loeb Classical Library. Trans. Paul Shorex. Cambridge, Mass. 1970
POLITZER, Heinrich. *Franz Kafka, der Künstler.* Frankfurt 1965
PONGE, Francis. *Le Parti-pris des choses.* Reprinted in *Tome Premier.* Paris 1965
- *Entretiens de Francis Ponge avec Philippe Sollers.* Paris 1970
- *The Voice of Things.* Ed. and trans. Beth Archer. New York 1972
POPPER, Karl. *Unended Quest: An Intellectual Autobiography.* Glasgow 1976
PRATT, Mary Louise. *Toward a Speech Act Theory of Literary Discourse.* Bloomington 1977
PROUST, Marcel. *A la Recherche du temps perdu.* Paris 1954
RAJEC, Elisabeth M. *Namen und ihre Bedeutungen im Werke Franz Kafkas.* Frankfurt 1977

321 References

RENAUD, Philippe. *Lecture d'Apollinaire*. Lausanne 1969
RICARDOU, Jean. *Nouveaux problèmes du roman*. Paris 1978
RICHARDS, Ivor Armstrong. 'Toward a Theory of Comprehending.' *Speculative Instruments*. London 1955, 17–38
– 'The Future of Poetry.' *So Much Nearer: Essays Toward a World English*. New York 1968, 150–82
– 'Factors and Functions in Linguistics.' *Poetries: Their Media and Ends*. The Hague 1974, 1–16
RICOEUR, Paul. *Freud and Philosophy: An Essay in Interpretation*. Trans. Denis Savage. New Haven 1970
– 'The Model of the Text: Meaningful Action Considered as a Text.' *New Literary History*, 5 (Autumn 1973), 91–117
– *The Rule of Metaphor*. Toronto 1978
– 'What Is a Text?' *Hermeneutics and the Human Sciences*. Ed. and trans. John B. Thompson. Cambridge 1981
RIFFATERRE, Michael. *Semiotics of Poetry*. Bloomington 1978
– *La Production du texte*. Paris 1979
– 'Sémiotique intertextuelle: l'interprétant.' *Revue d'Esthétique*, no. 1–2 (1979), 128–50
– 'Syllepsis.' *Critical Inquiry*, 6 (Summer 1980), 625–38
– 'La Trace de l'intertexte.' *La Pensée*, no. 215 (October 1980), 4–18
– 'L'intertexte inconnu.' *Littérature*, 41 (1981), 4–7
– 'Interpretation and Undecidability.' *New Literary History*, 12 (Winter 1981), 227–42
RIMBAUD, Arthur. *Oeuvres Complètes*. Ed. Antoine Adam. Paris 1972
RORTY, Richard. *Philosophy and the Mirror of Nature*. Princeton 1980
RYAN, Marie-Laure C. 'The Modal Structure of Narrative Universes.' Unpublished ms.
SAID, Edward. 'Roads Taken and Not Taken in Contemporary Criticism.' *Contemporary Literature*, 17 (Summer 1976), 327–77
– 'Reflections on Recent American "Left" Criticism.' *Boundary 2*, 8 (Fall 1979), 11–30
SARTRE, Jean-Paul. *Qu'est-ce que la littérature?* Paris 1948
– *Das Imaginäre, Phänomenologische Psychologie der Einbildungskraft*. Trans. Hans Schöneberg. Hamburg 1971
SCALIGER, Julius. *Poetices libri septem*. Lyons 1948, 185
SCHILLER, Friedrich von. *Theoretische Schriften*, v. Ed. Fricke and Güpfert. München 1959
SCHORER, Mark. 'Fiction and the Matrix of Analogy.' *Kenyon Review*, 2 (Autumn 1948), 539–60
SCHÜTZ, Alfred. *The Phenomenology of the Social World*. Trans. George Walsch. Evanston 1967
SEARLE, John. *Speech Acts: An Essay in the Philosophy of Language*. London 1969

- 'The Logical Status of Fictional Discourse.' *New Literary History*, 6 (Winter 1975), 319–32
SILK, M.S., and J.P. Stern. *Nietzsche on Tragedy*. Cambridge 1981
SOLLERS, Philippe. *Entretiens de Francis Ponge avec Philippe Sollers*. Paris 1970
SPARSHOTT, Francis E. *The Concept of Criticism*. Oxford 1967
SPENSER, Edmund. *The Shepherd's Calendar and Other Poems*. London 1960
STEVENS, Wallace. 'The Idea of Order at Key West.' *The Collected Poems*. New York 1954
STIERLE, Karlheinz. 'Die Identität des Gedichts – Hölderlin als Paradigma.' *Identität*. Ed. O. Marquard and K. Stierle (Poetik und Hermeneutik VIII). München 1979, 505–52
- 'Sprechsituation, Kontext und Sprachhandlung.' *Handlungstheorieninterdisziplinär*. Ed. Hans Lenk. München 1980
STRAUSS, Leo. *Thoughts on Machiavelli*. London 1958
SULEIMAN, Susan, and Inge Crosman, eds. *The Reader in the Text: Essays on Audience and Interpretation*. Princeton, New Jersey 1980
SYPHER, Wylie. *Loss of the Self in Modern Literature and Art*. New York 1962
TATAR, Maria M. 'The Houses of Fiction: Toward a Definition of the Uncanny.' *Comparative Literature*, 33 (Spring 1981), 167–82
THOMAS, R. Hinton. *Nietzsche in German Politics and Society 1890–1918*. Manchester 1983
TIMPANARO, Sebastiano. *On Materialism*. Trans. Lawrence Garner. London 1975
- *The Freudian Slip: Psychoanalysis and Textual Criticism*. Trans. Kate Soper. London 1976
- 'The Pessimistic Materialism of Giacomo Leopardi.' *New Left Review*, 116 (July–August 1979), 29–52
TOBIN, Patricia Drechsel. *Time and the Novel*. Princeton 1978
TODOROV, Tzvetan. 'Poétique.' *Qu'est-ce que le structuralisme?* Ed. F. Wahl. Paris 1968, 97–166
- *Symbolisme et interprétation*. Paris 1978
TOLIVER, Harold. *Animate Illusions*. Lincoln, Nebraska 1974
TOMPKINS, Jane P., ed. *Reader-Response Criticism from Formalism to Post-Structuralism*. Baltimore 1980
VAIHINGER, Hans. *Die Philosophie des Als-Ob*. Leipzig 1922
VALDÉS, Mario. *An Unamuno Source Book*. Toronto 1973
- and O.J. Miller. *Interpretation of Narrative*. Toronto 1978
- 'The Scope of Ricoeur's Hermeneutical Reflection on Literature.' *Proceedings of the IXth Congress of the International Comparative Literature Association*. Ed. Zoran Konstantinovic, H.R. Jauss, and M. Naumann. Vol. 2: Literary Communication and Reception, Innsbruck 1980, 95–9

323 References

- 'Heuristic Models of Inquiry.' *New Literary History*, 12 (Winter 1981), 253–367
- *Shadows in the Cave: A Phenomenological Approach to Literary Criticism Based on Hispanic Texts*. Toronto 1982
VULTUR, Smaranda. 'Situer l'intertextualité.' *Cahiers roumains d'études littéraires*, 3 (1981), 32–6
WAGNER, Richard. *Gesammelte Schriften und Dichtungen*. Leipzig 1872
- *Entwurfe, Gedanken, Fragmente*. Leipzig 1885
WAITE, Geoffrey. 'The Politics of Reading Formations: The Case of Nietzsche in Imperial Germany 1870–1919.' *New German Critique*, 29 (Spring/Summer 1983), 185–209
- *Nietzsche / Hölderlin: A Critical Revision*. Bonn, forthcoming
WARNING, Rainer. 'Der inszenierte Diskurs. Bemerkungen zur pragmatischen Relation der Fiktion.' *Funktionen des Fiktiven* (Poetik und Hermeneutik x). Ed. Dieter Henrich and Wolfgang Iser. München 1983, 183–206
WATT, Ian. *The Rise of the Novel*. Harmondsworth 1963
WEBER, Samuel. 'The Struggle for Control.' Unpublished ms., Université de Strasbourg
WEIMANN, Robert. *Structure and Society in Literary History: Studies in the History and Theory of Historical Criticism*. Charlottesville 1977
- *Realismus in der Renaissance: Aneigung der Welt in der erzahlenden Prosa*. Berlin 1978
WEINRICH, Harald, ed. *Positionen der Negativitat. Poetik und Hermeneutik, 6*. München 1975
WIDDOWSON, Peter. *Re-reading English*. London 1982
WILLIAMS, Raymond. *Writing in Society*. London (no date)
WIMSATT, William K., Jr. 'When Is Variation Elegant?' *The Verbal Icon: Studies in the Meaning of Poetry*. New York 1960
WINNICOTT, D.W. *Playing and Reality*. London 1971
WOOD, Donald C. 'An Introduction to Derrida.' *Radical Philosophy*, 21 (Spring 1979), 18–28
WOODS, John Hayden. *The Logic of Fiction: A Philosophical Sounding of Deviant Logic*. Paris 1974
WOODS, John, and Thomas G. Pavel, eds. *Formal Semantics and Literary Theory*. Special issue of *Poetics*, 8:1–2 (April 1979)
WORRINGER, Wilhelm. *Abstraktion und Einfuhlung*. München 1918

Index of Authors Cited